KT-494-410

# Category Management in Purchasing

*For Elaine, Emily and Hugh*

# Category Management in Purchasing

A strategic approach to maximize business profitability

Jonathan O'Brien

KoganPage

LONDON  PHILADELPHIA  NEW DELHI

First published in Great Britain and the United States in 2009 by Kogan Page Limited
Third edition 2015

2nd Floor, 45 Gee Street
London
EC1V 3RS
United Kingdom

1518 Walnut Street, Suite 1100
Philadelphia PA 19102
USA

4737/23 Ansari Road
Daryaganj
New Delhi 110002
India

© Jonathan O'Brien, 2009, 2012, 2015

The right of Jonathan O'Brien to be identified as the author of this work has been asserted by him in accordance with the Copyright, Designs and Patents Act 1988.

ISBN     978 0 7494 7230 6
E-ISBN   978 0 7494 7231 3

**British Library Cataloguing-in-Publication Data**

A CIP record for this book is available from the British Library.

**Library of Congress Cataloging-in-Publication Data**

O'Brien, Jonathan, 1967- author.
    Category management in purchasing : a strategic approach to maximize business profitability / Jonathan O'Brien. – Third edition.
    pages cm
    ISBN 978-0-7494-7230-6 (hardback) – ISBN 978-0-7494-7231-3 (ebk)   1. Purchasing.
2. Industrial procurement.   3. Business logistics.   I. Title.
    HF5437.O26 2015
    658.7'2–dc23
                                                                2015031275

Typeset by Graphicraft Limited, Hong Kong
Print production managed by Jellyfish
Printed and bound by CPI Group (UK) Ltd, Croydon, CR0 4YY

# CONTENTS

## 10    Guaranteeing success – now and for the future    409

# LIST OF FIGURES

# LIST OF TABLES

# FOREWORD

**D**eployed effectively, category management delivers many benefits to the organization through optimizing the value that can be derived from the supply chain. It gives a clear structured framework that can be applied across the organization's purchasing requirements. Category management provides an approach to procurement which gives an organization-wide view of procurement spend and ensures the buy-in of key stakeholders to the sourcing strategy, ensuring that not only is the strategy agreed but that it is implemented and the benefits are delivered to the organization.

*Category Management in Purchasing* fills a need in the literature available on this topic and provides the reader with a thorough insight into the principles and application of category management.

*Ken James*
*Former CEO of the Chartered Institute of Purchasing & Supply*

# PREFACE

In writing and researching this book I was horrified to find a distinct absence of titles around purchasing category management. I found vast numbers of titles around sales and marketing, all suggesting a common theme of 'getting the edge on your customers'. In contrast I found only a handful of good books on strategic purchasing that aimed to help the purchasing community stand up to this onslaught, and most of those were written 20 or 30 years ago, with only superficial updates to justify the reprint and new cover, but with little that adequately reflects the modern purchasing environment. This book aims to well and truly fill that large hole.

To avoid confusion I will use the terms 'purchasing' and 'category management' throughout this book, as both appear to be widely accepted. It seems there is no single accepted global name for the thing we do. Is it 'buying' or 'purchasing' or 'procurement' or 'sourcing' or 'supply chain management', or is it 'strategic purchasing', 'strategic procurement' or 'strategic sourcing'?

Some organizations don't use the word 'purchasing', as they feel it is not strategic enough. Many don't use 'procurement', as junior or non-office staff often don't understand the term. Some insist that 'procurement' is transactional while 'purchasing' covers the more strategic activities. Others insist the reverse. To avoid all of this confusion some prefer to call it 'sourcing'. The names or labels that people are most comfortable with are the product of country, local, individual and organizational history and culture, as well as being the language favoured by the regional publications in this field.

The same is true for category management. Organizations sometimes feel the need to distinguish category management from its marketing equivalent or wish to personalize their use of the approach. Some common names include 'strategic sourcing process', 'purchasing category management', 'purchasing improvement process', 'the Acme Company strategic sourcing process' or 'sourcing group management' and so on.

# ACKNOWLEDGEMENTS

**B**eing asked to write a third edition for any business book is recognition that the text has made a difference in some way. Six years since *Category Management in Purchasing* was first published I continue to receive e-mails from all over the world telling me how much this book has helped people to understand and apply category management. So my first thank you is to everyone who has so far bought this book in one of its various forms and languages, and who have enabled a third edition to become possible.

Since this title was first published, I have written two further titles. These three combined conclude my ambition to create a suite of books that provide purchasing practitioners with the tools and techniques they need to be highly effective and make significant contributions in the organizations they work for.

When I first set out to write this book, it became a journey that was longer and harder than I could have imagined, but which was hugely rewarding. Taking a familiar topic and turning it into a precise set of words makes you question everything you thought you knew, and research the topic thoroughly so as to be sure of accuracy. Attempting to make a business book even slightly interesting was the second challenge, and here I drew on all the experiences of working in purchasing and working with category management. Since the original publication the world has plummeted into and out of one of the worst economic downturns ever seen, and so writing the third edition afforded the opportunity to update the book to show how category management is even more relevant in uncertain times and to redefine how it is deployed as the world around us changes.

Thank you to all the practitioners I have worked with over the years that collectively have shaped the concept of category management. Some of you may recognize examples in this book and so I thank you for helping my understanding, which in turn has helped me write this book. I cannot claim any credit for inventing category management. It is out there in many different forms; all I have done is collect what I believe are the best of the best elements and combined them in a cohesive and practical way to help others adopt what is a proven concept.

I need to thank many people for their contributions to this book. Thanks to Andy McMinn at the NHS for sharing some of his many great procurement successes in applying category management. Thanks to Steven Robinson at City of Cardiff Council and Scott Parfitt at Knowledge Transfer Partnership and University of South Wales Procurement Best Practice Academy for sharing their success story of implementing category management at Cardiff Council. Thanks to Joe Meier from GlaxoSmithKline for the kind permission to use GSK as a case study of excellence in the original edition, which is still included in this third edition, and to Jim Keiller for making the necessary connections here. Thanks to Henrik Balslev of Scanmarket for help on the e-auction section. Thanks to Dave Smith for some early input on the first few chapters of the original publication and continued input for this edition. Thanks to Joanna Hunt for insights into supply value chain mapping and for sharing a photo of mapping in action. Thanks to Alex Watson-Gandy for the help with the retail category management section. Thanks to Philip Usherwood for helping some early thinking for the first edition. Thanks to Iain Anderson for help researching the learning model mix for category management. Thanks to the various commissioning editors at Kogan Page for patiently waiting for the completed typescript; I can't imagine how many times you hear the words 'It's nearly there.' Thanks too to all those I have worked with who have contributed to reading, re-reading, proofreading and critiquing sections – a process that taught me how to use a semi-colon properly; no, really it did!

The biggest thank you is to my family, who once again have put up with a husband and father being welded to a laptop a bit too often.

Finally, thank you to you for buying this book. If you've bothered to read this section you are probably serious about working through the rest of the book and so I hope it helps you with what you are trying to achieve.

Where I have included an established model or concept I have made every effort to properly research, reference and duly credit all work of others; however, I apologize in advance for any omissions. Other models and concepts in this book are new and original work; many are groundbreaking.

# ABOUT THE AUTHOR

**Jonathan O'Brien** is the CEO of the international purchasing consultancy and training provider Positive Purchasing Ltd (**www.positivepurchasing.com**), and has over 25 years' experience working in purchasing. He has worked all over the world to help global organizations increase their purchasing capability through training, education and working directly with practitioners and executive teams to drive in the adoption of Category Management, Supplier Relationship Management, Negotiation, and other strategic purchasing methodologies.

Jonathan is an electronics engineer who ended up in purchasing. His career in engineering soon moved into supplier quality assurance, and it was the hundreds of supplier audits undertaken involving detailed examination of business practice and process that provided a sound understanding of how organizations work, and thus began the process of working with companies to help them improve. A move to senior buying role in a large utility company shifted his focus to the commercial aspects of purchasing and this career path in culminated in a global category director role for an airline business. Jonathan moved to an internal consultant role and helped lead a series of major organizational change programmes. A subsequent move into mainstream consultancy, initially with a large global strategic purchasing consultancy and later with his own business, provided Jonathan the opportunity to work with some of the biggest and best-known companies in the world to help improve purchasing capability, and he gained a rich experience along the way.

Jonathan holds an MBA from Plymouth University Business School, a diploma in marketing and an HNC in electronics, is a Member of the Chartered Institute of Purchasing (MCIPS), an NLP Master Practitioner and a former registered Lead Assessor of quality management systems.

Jonathan and his team at Positive Purchasing Ltd have developed and created the *5i® Category Management* process, the *Orchestra of SRM®* including the *5A™ Strategic Collaborative Relationship* process, and the *Red Sheet®* negotiation tool that has become the way many individuals and corporations approach negotiation.

Jonathan is an award-winning author and this is his fifth book across three highly popular titles, available worldwide in different languages. He is also an accomplished broadcaster and artist and lives with his family in Plymouth, UK.

You can e-mail Jonathan at **jonathan@jonathanobrien.co.uk**

# Introduction

## Using this book

This is a book about 'category management' – a strategic approach to maximize value, benefit and profit to the organization through structured procurement intervention and business-wide involvement and participation.

This is a practical book for those who want to get on and make purchasing category management a reality and realize the dramatic value and benefits that are possible when it is well executed. It is a book about value and how to secure the best possible value from the supply chain through planned and structured purchasing intervention. It is also a book about changing the game, about doing something fundamentally different and achieving breakthrough improvements.

This book is not like so many books that simply explore academic or theoretical concepts and leave it to the reader to interpret and apply these in practical terms. This book represents the culmination of years of experience of practising category management for real and delivering real dramatic benefits to global organizations. It represents a current best-practice view of purchasing category management and not only provides the necessary framework and toolkit but explains in a clear sequence how to use them. In this, the third edition of this book, a suite of new templates has been provided in the Appendix to help practitioners make category management a reality.

The book is designed to provide insight and a reference point for executives and stakeholders who want to use or understand the approach within their organizations, as well as for practitioners who want to learn how to use category management on a day-to-day basis.

As we will discover through this book category management is much more than a process; it is a philosophy, and when embraced holds the potential to deliver a dramatic benefits to the organization. It is also a prime enabler to help build stakeholder value and brand equity by creating competitive advantage or differentiation.

I have been practising category management and working with organizations to deploy it for more than 25 years now, and whilst the approach is 'the way to buy' in some sectors, for many it feels like it is only just beginning to be embraced, understood or gain traction. Many companies claim to practise category management, few truly do. If purchasing intervention is little more than an approach based around tendering and contracting for repeat requirements 'by category' then this is not category management; it is tendering and contracting under a different name. Here benefits will be limited to small incremental improvements only. True category management changes the game, but achieving this demands a quality deployment, and requires the entire organization to embrace, live and breathe the philosophy.

As we move through this book I will explain what category management is and we will explore in detail the process behind it, providing deep explanation of each of the core tools. I have also included a range of templates and support tools to help practitioners. But before we get to that we will explore the core principles and enablers behind a quality category management deployment, and what is needed for an organization to embrace and embed the philosophy.

# A strategic purchasing trilogy

This was originally my first book and is now in its third edition. Since the original version I have written two further books on key strategic purchasing methodologies. These three books have been written as a collection, each designed to enhance, complement and integrate with the frameworks and approaches of category management, Supplier Relationship Management (SRM) and negotiation planning. Indeed many of the tools you will find in these pages can also be found applied slightly differently within SRM and negotiation approaches. These three separate methodologies are in fact the core strategic approaches necessary for modern, best-practice strategic procurement and to be effective need to work in concert with each other. Therefore this book has been written so as to be used together with *Supplier Relationship Management* and *Negotiation for Purchasing Professionals* (both published by Kogan Page). Where a tool has already been expanded in one of these other works it is not repeated again in this book but referenced at a high level. It is recommended all three publications are used together to provide the complete strategic purchasing approach

## 15 pathway questions

This book is organized so as to explore all aspects of category management in the most logical way possible. It seeks to provide answers and practical steps for 15 key or 'pathway' questions. If you can answer all of these questions with confidence then you're in great shape. However for many organizations these are difficult questions that represent the gap between aspiration and reality. They also help reveal the pathway to move towards making effective category management a reality. This book will help to not only form answers to these questions but will help to develop real actions that enable the firm to progress and realize great value from a quality category management deployment.

**Category management pathway questions**

1  How can purchasing intervention make a strategic and significant contribution to my business?

2  What is category management and how can it add benefit?

3  What are the right categories to work on?

4  How can I identify and prioritize potential opportunity for each category so I can direct my resources accordingly?

5  What is required in order to successfully adopt and implement category management?

6  How do I engage the wider organization within a category-based approach?

7  For any given category, how do I identify what the organization needs to buy?

8  For each and any category, what is my current position?

9  How can I identify the optimum, and ideally breakthrough, future sourcing strategy for a category?

10  How do I ensure all our future sourcing strategies are based upon a robust understanding of all market and external drivers and factors?

11  How can I effectively implement new sourcing strategies so they become a reality and we realize the benefits?

**12** Once improvements are implemented, how do I continue to drive them?

**13** How should I manage those suppliers who are important to my business?

**14** How does the company need to structure and organize itself to deploy category management effectively?

**15** Is category management an approach that will still be relevant in the future?

# Introducing category management

This chapter aims to provide an introduction to category management, why it is highly relevant for leading companies all over the world and the significant value it can bring to organizations. It explains how this value can be realized in different economic and market conditions and how the approach can help respond positively to a variety of different business needs and drivers.

Pathway questions addressed in this chapter:

1 How can purchasing intervention make a strategic and significant contribution to my business?

2 What is category management and how can it add benefit?

## Category management explained

Category management is a strategic approach that focuses on the vast majority of an organization's spend on goods and services with third-party suppliers. It is a process-based approach and incorporates many familiar aspects of business improvement processes and change management. It is not an approach that is confined to purchasing but typically requires the active participation of and engagement with stakeholders, functions and individuals across the business to make it successful. Organizations therefore have to make an investment in time and commitment in order to deploy category management; however, the return on this investment is potentially very large.

Category management is defined as:

> The practice of segmenting the main areas of organizational spend on bought-in goods and services into discrete groups of products and services according to the function of those goods or services and, most importantly, to mirror how individual marketplaces are organized. Using this category segmentation, organizations work cross-functionally on individual categories, examining the entire category spend, how the organization uses the products or services within the category, the marketplace and individual suppliers.

This extensive review process is structured to actively challenge what has gone before, and seek out and implement breakthrough opportunities that will generate significant value for the organization. Value might take the form of leveraging dramatic reductions in purchase price but it could equally be about reducing the whole-life cost or total cost of ownership, mitigating price increases in a rising market, reducing supply chain risk, improving effectiveness and efficiency or securing increased collaboration and innovation from the supply chain to help build our brand equity.

# Category examples

There are fundamentally two types of category:

- direct categories: raw materials, components or services that are directly incorporated into, or help produce, the final product; and
- indirect categories: products and services that are non-product-related or enable the company to function overall.

Organizations deploying category management will often organize the programme of work and cross-functional teams around direct and indirect categories in order to identify potential linkages and opportunities between categories. For example, an indirect category team working on the indirect category of car fleet would ideally be the same team or close to the team that is working on another indirect category of insurance (the cost of fleet insurance being linked to the selection and specification of vehicles).

A typical but not exhaustive list of direct and indirect categories is shown in Table 1.1.

The precise list and the categorization of direct and indirect will vary from organization to organization, according to what it does. For example, the category 'print' is often an indirect category, containing general printed matter used by marketing and not part of producing finished goods. However, in a publishing business print would be a direct category.

**TABLE 1.1**    Examples of direct and indirect categories

| Direct categories (typically) | Indirect categories (typically) |
| --- | --- |
| Packaging | Utilities |
| Castings | Legal services |
| Plastic mouldings | HR services |
| Bulk chemicals | Fleet |
| Fabrics | Facilities management |
| Tomatoes | Consultancy |
| Polythene bags | Contract labour |
| Bottles | Insurance |
| Yarns | Marketing, design and agency |
| MRO (Maintenance, repair and operations) parts | Logistics |
| | IT |
| Fasteners | Telecoms (land, mobile, video, web) |
| Chicken breasts | Capital equipment |
| Machined products | Civil engineering |
| Hip and knee joints | Reprographics |
| Steel rope | Waste management |
| Sheet metal | Travel |
| Printed circuit boards | Buildings and grounds maintenance |
| Process filters | Stationery |
| Sub-assemblies | Print |
| Social care | Catering |
| Motors | Security and guarding |
| Soft drinks | Cleaning |
| Control and automation | Pest control |
| Tyres | Software |
| Paint cables | Production machinery |
| Rubber | Networks |
| Airport landing slots | Healthcare |
| Wound care | New building fit-out |
| Electronic components | |
| Cans | |
| Sugar | |
| Syringes | |

# How it all started

Category management first appeared in purchasing in the late 1980s. There does not appear to be a single pioneer of category management, but rather the approach grew up across a relatively small number of progressive companies working at the forefront of strategic purchasing. It was in response to the need to counter the growing power of suppliers born out of globalization and of suppliers getting smarter and finding new ways to secure and retain their routes to market. It was also in response to a growing realization that organizations could gain advantage if purchasing could play a more strategic role. These early pioneers began to develop similar strategic approaches that combined tools and techniques from purchasing, economics, quality management and organizational change theory. Over the years different practitioners and consultants have refined the approach based upon what has been proven to work. Today you will find category management presented in various forms, each having subtle variations in structure and content, but the underlying principles remain the same.

If you run an internet search for 'category management', you could be forgiven for being confused by what you see. Search results are most likely to have a marketing or retail theme. If you talk to marketing professionals or retailers, they will most probably understand the term 'category management' but they will be thinking of an approach very different from the one outlined in this book (although we will touch on it in the next chapter).

The term 'category management' originated in the world of sales and marketing in the early 1980s. The definition a marketer would recognize is 'a brand management approach to manage groups of products according to how the consumer uses the products'. This is different from the purchasing version of category management, and clearly the role of brand management in a business is not usually something undertaken by purchasing. Whilst the two approaches are quite separate for most, there is a clear similarity between this and category management in purchasing. In retail however they are less separate.

## *Marketing category management*

Big retailers learned that they could improve sales and profit if they could more efficiently administer all their different products and product classifications. The idea was to see a retail outlet not as an aggregation of products but as an amalgam of categories, with each one unique and based on what the consumer does with the product and how this is predicted to change over time. For example, instead of managing products at the level of Kellogg's Corn Flakes or Quaker Porridge Oats, marketing category management seeks to focus on the category of 'breakfast cereal', its various target customers, its place in the store and how best to merchandise, present and promote the category in order to maximize sales and profit. Whilst consumers will enjoy apparent brand choice, often a single manufacturer will be given a certain 'primacy of presence' across the category with the least possible unproductive competition between their individual brands. This of course comes at a price, with that manufacturer discounting heavily, running promotional offers and perhaps even supporting the retailer by helping to manage the category on behalf of the retailer. The net result is increased profit for the retailer.

## Purchasing category management

Throughout this book, this core principle of 'categories of products' remains the same – except here we are segmenting third-party spend, not finished goods, and it is not 'how the consumer uses the product' that drives the segmentation but the function of the products or services and the discrete marketplaces they originate from. As with much of purchasing best practice, many elements are the reverse of the marketing approach. Indeed, many of the strategic analysis tools contained within this book originate from marketing tools but have been adapted to work 'in reverse' to benefit the buyer.

# THE RELEVANCE OF CATEGORY MANAGEMENT TODAY

Kraljic (1983) stated that 'no company can allow purchasing to lag behind other departments in acknowledging and adjusting to worldwide environmental and economic changes'. He was saying that purchasing skills had been developed and established in an era of relative stability, but that as the pace of economic change was about to accelerate at global level, purchasing had to change too. That was more than 30 years ago and since then we have seen profound changes within our world, organizations, international business and how we live our lives. We have also experienced one of the greatest economic downturns since the Great Depression of the late 1930s. The role and expectations of the purchasing function have also changed considerably in this time and continue to change.

When I began my career in purchasing the role of the function as seen by the wider organization was to 'buy things'. Decisions regarding what to purchase and which supplier to use had usually already been taken by marketing, production or R&D, of course in consultation with the supplier. Purchasing would be called in toward the end to 'do the deal' and negotiate things like delivery charges and returns policies. If we could also get a bit more off the price, this was considered an excellent result. In contrast today's leading-edge businesses will position purchasing as a strategic function, often with board-level representation, and the function will have a clear remit to own and manage the commercial relationship with the supply base. Smart organizations do not allow technical functions to make purchasing or buying decisions alone, but rather encourage a culture of collaborative working to identify and implement the most effective sourcing approach.

Today purchasing functions are presented with opportunities to add significant value to the organization and its stakeholders like never before with category management being one of the important enablers needed in order to realize these opportunities. To understand what these opportunities are, and how they have come about, it is necessary to look at how technology, markets and our lives have evolved over the past 30 years or so and how these changes now point to the need for a new modern and more strategic approach to purchasing within organizations.

## Technology as an enabler

The internet, e-mail and e-commerce have revolutionized business on a global scale. This is old news and now the generation of social, mobile, analytics and cloud (SMAC) are continuing that journey. Purchasing transactions in large companies are almost entirely electronic, often with little or no intervention for regular or routine purchases. Using the same principles as eBay, but in reverse, purchasing teams can now run reverse auctions with suppliers bidding against each other in real time to win a specific piece of business, all conducted over the internet in quick time without either party ever meeting the other. Reverse auctions (or e-auctions) have made the process of running a tender much simpler and quicker and have created the ability to leverage price to the best point in the market.

Advances in technology have made the process of buying much more effective, but that's not all. Technology now allows teams around the world to work together and collaborate in a way that was thought impossible

20 years ago. Today we have mobile and desktop applications that allow us to network, message, get answers, connect, see and share with anyone, anywhere, whenever we choose. 'Virtual meetings' are commonplace, with most desktops equipped with some sort of meeting and messaging app and most global organizations using virtual conferencing suites as routine. Some of these are so sophisticated the meeting experience is almost as if the life-size people talking to you from the other half of the table are really in the same room as you and not halfway around the world. Crucially, though, workplace skills and culture have developed to embrace and use these tools. Running an effective telephone, video or web conference is now as much a part of a professional person's toolkit as hosting a face-to-face meeting.

For non-differentiated products the lowest price is now just a few clicks away and gaining insights into a marketplace or a supplier can be achieved almost entirely online with good research skills where once the business of providing specialist market knowledge was an industry all of its own. The global buying community now shares information and knowledge and in turn propagates best practice.

It is easy to forget how far we have come, but these advances in technology are important because they have enabled purchasing functions to become more effective, consume fewer resources for the day-to-day business of purchasing and instead direct our energy into working across geographical boundaries in those areas that will add the greatest value.

## The world is a smaller place

Purchasing functions now have greater access to larger marketplaces. The world has opened up and the global marketplace has long since been open for business. What previously were either holiday destinations or under-developed countries are now 'emerging markets' or credible players, capable of producing repeatable good-quality output and with a hunger for Western currency that means the producers will do whatever it takes. However the nations that supply the world are changing.

Countries like China and India offer the latest state-of-the-art, well-equipped factories with low-cost, motivated workforces, an absence of trade barriers and early stages of enforced regulation for safety and HR, so it is no surprise that many of the goods originate from these regions.

China equalled the United States in terms of manufacturing output (Markillie, 2103), but as China's workforce came to expect their pay to rise, the economy began to slow down some, with other developing countries waiting in the wings to take on the world's manufacturing at lower cost. India is pushing Japan aside to become one of the biggest purchasing nations on the planet. Other economies are on the global stage or at least about to enter it; Brazil and Russia were once well talked about but have stalled somewhat. Don't lose sight of emerging Asian and African countries such as Sri Lanka, Indonesia, Nigeria, Rwanda and Ivory Coast. Iran's economy shows great promise, as does Iraq's and Mongolia's, with its mining boom from the advent of copper production in the Gobi desert fuelling an 18 per cent growth in GDP in 2013, and economies such as Macau may take us by surprise.

You might think that the cost associated with moving goods and raw materials around the world would counteract the competitive advantage these countries can offer, but it doesn't. For example, it costs just £6 to ship a washing machine from China to Europe. Smaller items are proportionally cheaper according to size.

Our planet is now one with more people on it and many more on the way, living in more densely populated regions, who move around more and interact more. Global communication is just a tweet away and global commerce requires just a click or two. Suppliers, or at least some of their operations, can now operate from anywhere on the planet, wherever there is a willing, capable and organized workforce with sufficient infrastructure to make it viable. The suppliers of tomorrow may not reside in the countries they are in today and may not even exist in any single building or location but rather could be sprawled across the globe, connecting and interacting though technology. The world is no longer a collection of different groups of people isolated by geography and culture, but a giant network, connected in real time.

The development of these new economies presents purchasing functions with an incredible opportunity to secure great value at low price points providing they can work out how to source reliably from these regions. As new economies respond to the challenge of ever-changing customer preference, smart purchasing functions are beginning to take advantage of the increased leverage that results from new competitors entering the marketplace. However, this opportunity comes with responsibility and there is a note of caution here.

## You don't have to wear sandals to talk about 'sustainability'

'Sustainability' is a relatively new word in the business community. It now appears in all sorts of business discussions and at all levels and is a growing factor within decision making. We could also talk of Corporate Social Responsibility (CSR) or Corporate Responsibility (CR) and mean the same thing. Anyone talking about the need for 'sustainability' 20 or 30 years ago would stimulate little interest at executive level of most businesses. But things have changed and ensuring the actions of business are sustainable is no longer just the concern of a small group of sandal-wearing activists.

As purchasing functions source more globally, achieving sustainability within the supply chain becomes increasingly difficult. The rate of change of some global economies is so fast that textbooks may soon need to be rewritten as new, previously unseen, economic dynamics also emerge. Huge global organizations have begun to amass unprecedented levels of power over supply chains and whilst this creates leverage it also increases the likelihood of purchasing in a way that is unsustainable. Not only that, it is also exceptionally difficult to control what really happens at the plantation or garment factory many contractual steps up the supply chain.

Whether or not 'sustainability' matters to an organization today is determined by factors such as the overriding brand principles and values of the organization, the company's internal policy, customer and stakeholder expectations and need for brand protection. In the future the driving force here is likely to be legislation, with companies becoming obliged to be responsible beyond their immediate contractual relationship with suppliers.

What happens many contractual steps removed up a supply chain can no longer be ignored when engaging the immediate supplier. Today most consumers now expect companies to be socially responsible (Penn Schoen Berland, 2010) and some even manage to factor this into their buying decisions, although there remains a significant gap between good intention and action (Pelsmacker *et al*, 2005). While this gap will most likely close, there seems to be a growing expectation on the companies we buy from, that they have their entire house in order. Perhaps sustainable, fair trade, responsible, ethical can no longer be a unique differentiator that attracts premium pricing, but a basic feature for everything a company does. Perhaps the person who picks the coffee beans is as much part of the product as the experience of the outlet itself. If our societies didn't hold this expectation then there wouldn't be so many investigative journalists trying to find cracks in the reputation of big corporates for what lies in their supply chains and organizations wouldn't be so worried in case something unexpected gets uncovered. It seems customers and consumers are also now paying more attention to stories of how household names operate and are ready to question any suggestion that things are not in good shape.

Here the opportunity for purchasing is first to understand what happens within the supply chain and to drive the right interventions so as to align what happens upstream with organizational objectives. This in turn can help claim competitive advantage, protect and even enhance a brand with the right approaches. Achieving this can in fact be incredibly difficult, and sustainability initiatives rarely succeed as stand-alone projects, but if they become an integral part of how the purchasing function is operating and moving forward, then sustainability can become a reality. The primary opportunity for purchasing here is therefore to respond to the organization's sustainability aspirations and make them part of how the organization buys.

# Our love affair with brands, bargains and something just for me!

Our lives have changed considerably over the past 30 years. Today in many First World countries our everyday lives are now built around products and services from the global marketplace, with our buying choices driven by our love of brands and the simple fact that as consumers we love a bargain. Today we are more aware of the brand or specification we want and the best place to get it at the best price. Walmart has built its entire business empire on this phenomenon and has managed to lower prices constantly through economies of scale and by finding new efficiencies in the supply chain. In fact, Walmart was credited with changing the global economic weather and keeping the US inflation rate down through repeatedly enticing consumers back for 'just one more bargain'. When the US economy started to take a downturn in 2008, Walmart's profits increased even further as cash-strapped customers who had previously shopped elsewhere switched to Walmart to keep their shopping bills down.

Shopping online is now mainstream, allowing new, low-overhead sellers to outperform big established names and offer the same product for less; that is unless the manufacturer is restricting routes to market in order to reduce competition and preserve price points. Try comparing prices for genuine brand-name perfumes from different retailers around the world and you'll find there's not a lot of difference. This has little to do with market dynamics or the cost of making a bottle of perfume (which is a relatively small percentage of the selling price) but is part of a well-executed pricing strategy for a unique product people want to buy; and that brings me to the value of brands.

Despite our love of cheap, we will still pay more for a product we believe is exceptional, that is unique and differentiated or shows we can afford a premium brand. The intangible benefits we get from wearing the right trainers or driving a certain car makes us part of the right group of people or projects the outward signs of success that make us feel good. But that is not the end of the story. What we want as consumers is changing and there is a new kid on the block that could prove even more desirable than a brand. Now the ability to create something personalized and unique for every customer is opening up a new differentiation opportunity enabled through module production and using new technologies such as 3D printing.

Where there is no differentiation, 'Better, faster, cheaper' still stands and although we expect 'cheap' we don't need it. As consumers become more affluent with more choice than ever before we seem to know where to find the best price but yet consumers are prepared to pay for something branded and something unique. Perhaps 'better, faster and just for you right now' seems to better describe the consumer appetite. The implications of this are enormous, and they now shape the world of global business; the challenge for companies to compete and succeed becomes ever more difficult but crucial in order to survive.

It is here that purchasing is presented with the greatest opportunities of all, which if realized can bring huge value to the organization. The first opportunity for purchasing here is to help the organization compete effectively in this ever-more competitive landscape. If 'cheaper' is part of what is needed to do this, then purchasing must find ways of reducing the cost of producing the goods or providing the service, including driving down the cost of raw materials, production (or service provision) and the route to market.

However if the organization needs to compete through differentiation, either through brand or uniqueness then the second opportunity is for purchasing to help create the differentiators that bring competitive advantage and enhance brand value by connecting supply chain possibilities with consumer needs and desires, including those the consumer doesn't realize yet.

Supply chains represent potential 'goldmines of innovation' – specialist companies who understand their respective marketplaces and are working on the 'next great idea'. If you can connect what your suppliers are working on with what you believe your customers need and could want, then you have unlocked the potential to greatly enhance your brand. The secret to unlocking this is first in knowing what your suppliers are working on (and not just the obvious ones) and second in having the right relationship with these suppliers so they bring innovation to you first and not to your competitors or where it is possible to work together to create something significant. It is here where the opportunity for purchasing is so great. Keep your purchasing function supplier-facing and you'll have a function that buys things. Have purchasing work across the entire 'end-to-end' value chain, collaborating with customer-facing functions and you begin to connect supply chain possibilities with end-customer needs and desires.

**CASE STUDY** How the supply chain put honeycomb in IKEA's table

IKEA's 'Lack' coffee table has been one of its most successful products ever with more than 10 million sold worldwide each year. Its thick square legs and the 50 millimetre-thick veneered tabletop design were an instant success but the winning factor here was its affordability. IKEA offered the table at a price point to suit any budget, yet its appearance was so solid it was perceived as great value for money. The secret behind this is simply due to IKEA connecting customer needs, desires and preferences with supply chain possibilities. These possibilities, however, didn't come from any of IKEA's table manufacturers. In fact, the production and shipping costs associated with manufacturing a 50 millimetre-thick tabletop using traditional veneered fibreboard or chipboard techniques would prevent IKEA achieving their desired price point. Instead the innovation came from a door supplier by using the same technology of creating a thick substrate by laminating a thin paper honeycombed inner between two thin laminated sheets. The result is an incredibly strong and thick but lightweight tabletop that could be manufactured and shipped in high volumes cost effectively, and one that IKEA's customer base loved.

## IT'S ALL ABOUT VALUE

All of the opportunities described above mean purchasing functions have the potential to be a primary value generator for any organization. Category management is a key enabler here and if well executed with a visible and effective level of purchasing intervention across a business, category management has the potential to deliver dramatic results. Furthermore, it is possible to respond directly to the drivers of the organization and the sector it operates within as well as the prevailing macro-economic or any specific market conditions. In some organizations achieving lower prices for bought-in goods and services may be all that is required. If the goal is 'better, faster, cheaper and just for you', category management has a proven track record here. There remains a mindset in some organizations and amongst some purchasing professionals that the sole focus of efforts with suppliers should be to reduce price. This is an admirable pursuit, but much more is possible through a good level of purchasing intervention. The reality, however, is that in many businesses there is a disconnect between what the organization is trying to achieve and the day-to-day activities of purchasing teams, further exacerbated by an ignorance of the huge potential that can be realized.

Good modern strategic purchasing supported by category management requires a shift in our focus and one that allows us to pursue multiple sources of value that will benefit our organization and our end customers in line with wider organizational goals. For some organizations the best possible value improvement may not be a price reduction but could be to secure innovation from the supply chain that will enhance the value proposition to the end customer and improve the brand. Value is also linked to the sector we are in, with different industries typically having differing priorities. For example, historically in the oil and gas industry, reducing the cost of third-party spend was important, but bringing a new pipeline on line faster or ensuring security of supply was even more important, as when the oil flows so too do the dollars at levels beyond our imagination. Yet as oil prices began to fall the priorities shifted to cost reduction.

## Securing the value the organization needs

The value an organization most needs at any one time will change according to what is happening around us. At the turn of the century as developed economies were growing fast, the primary outcome sought by companies in many sectors using category management was to reduce the cost of bought-in goods and services. By 2008, as world economies started to take a downturn fuelled by inflation and rising oil and food costs, this had shifted to mitigating price increases and maintaining assurance of supply as the survival of many companies was threatened. By 2012 as the world was trying to pull out of the slump, category management was also being used to ensure the relationship with key suppliers was sustainable, using pricing structures that could protect against volatility in raw material costs. In 2015 organizations were recognizing the potential of category management as an enabler to new business growth through a range of different types of value from the supply base. It seems also that suddenly the importance of supply chain innovation was being realized and firms were re-galvanizing cross-functional teams to help achieve this. By then category management was also now being firmly embraced in the public sector.

Category management can therefore deliver dramatic value improvement in terms of reduced price but can also deliver reduced cost and risk, increased innovation, brand value, greater effectiveness and a stronger competitive position. It can make a clear contribution to the bottom line or EBITDA (earnings before interest, taxation, depreciation and amortization) and can also make a solid contribution to shareholder equity. Informed shareholders increasingly want to understand the approach to purchasing within the companies in which they invest, and for companies with stock exchange listing, purchasing is increasingly seen as possessing the capability to uplift, protect or recover the share price. Category management is not limited to the commercial sector. In the not-for-profit and public sectors category management can deliver dramatic improvements in performance and yield greater returns against allocated budget; it can help secure better patient outcomes in healthcare, secure more and better social care and public services, provide taxpayers with more for what they pay and can deal with years of poor purchasing where suppliers have gained advantage.

Despite the huge potential the supply base can offer here there are many organizations, including some who claim to be deploying category management, that still fail to realize the full value possible. To understand why we need to look at how organizations operate.

# Value and the virtual brick wall

Category management requires a 'value-based' approach. If we have this then it can help achieve key goals and objectives. However, unlocking value isn't just a case of the purchasing function pressing a magic button. In fact, if the initiative is confined to the purchasing function it will be unsuccessful. Instead category management must have the support and involvement of the entire organization with active collaboration across functions. The reason for this is simply because if you want to increase overall value to the organization you need to look at all the places where value is added. Porter (1985) describes the concept of the 'value chain' with products passing through an organizational business unit and each business function either directly or indirectly adding value in some way to create the final product (or service). This internal value chain is bounded by the inputs and outputs of the organization. However, expanding our perspective reveals a chain that extends all the way back to the start of the supply chain and also forward to the ultimate end customer. Growers, raw material suppliers, service providers who provide products or services to other suppliers, each adding some sort of value by processing, building, mixing, packaging, co-ordinating, shipping etc to create the products or services an organization buys. Then within the organization all the different functions add further value in some way to create a final product (or service) that then in turn provides some sort of value to the end customer, and perhaps even an end customer beyond that. Porter (1985) calls this end-to-end view the 'value system' and it is a concept that is well founded in economic theory.

The end-to-end value concept may seem obvious; the problem is that in many organizations we've lost sight of this value flow and we fail to recognize its importance. It is as if there were a barrier – a virtual brick wall – between suppliers and end customers (Figure 1.1). Marketing looks after the end customer and purchasing looks after the suppliers. Somewhere in the middle is a production or service process and an organizational hierarchy keeping the two firmly apart with any potential for new supply chain possibilities to enhance the customer experience being missed. By its nature, category

**FIGURE 1.1**  Value flow and the virtual brick wall

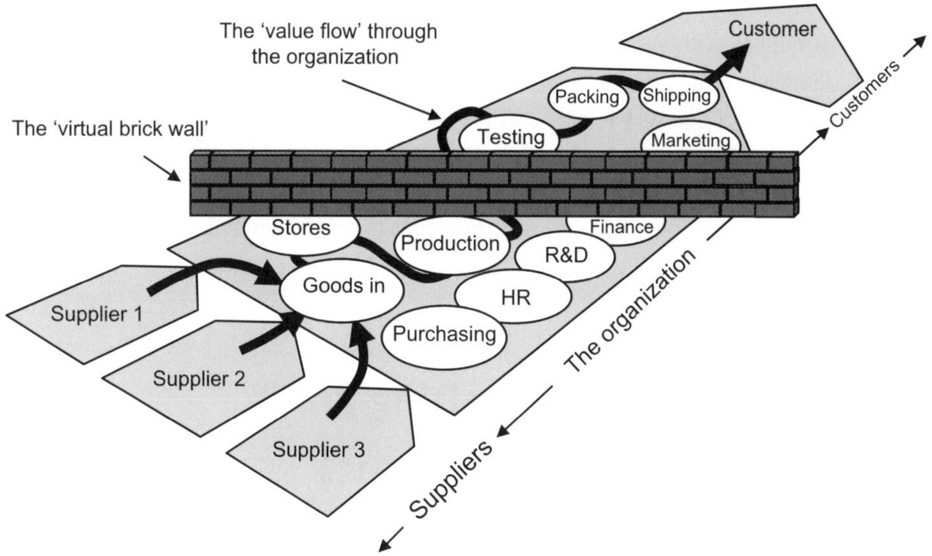

management overcomes this and encourages cross-functional working and collaboration throughout the business, getting people working together to achieve significant results. The potential available by connecting what customers want or might want with what your supply base is capable of should not be underestimated, but realizing this potential requires internal collaboration. If the only forum for a key supplier to share what they're working on is a review meeting with the buyer and the details go no further than the meeting minutes, the opportunity will be lost – or, worse, taken to your competitors.

**CASE STUDY**   How end-to-end value helped build Body Shop

Body Shop opened for business in the UK in 1976 and over the next 29 years Anita Roddick would devote her passion and energy to creating a brand that would support nearly 2,000 stores worldwide serving 77 million customers. Roddick's mission was to build a business based around the pursuit of social and environmental change and to offer products that complied with a strict ethical, environmental and social framework. Over the years this was further shaped by the growing needs and desires of its customers, creating a huge global business.

One of the key success factors for Body Shop was the way end-customer desires and market opportunities were connected with supply chain possibilities. The value to the end customer in buying a product that is guaranteed to be 'responsible' could only be achieved through careful alignment of sourcing strategies with stated brand values. Strategic suppliers to Body Shop dedicated themselves to helping build the brand and enjoyed long-term relationships but only after a rigorous selection process to ensure that they were organized around certain ethical, fair trade and green principles. In addition, suppliers had to demonstrate compliance with these principles through their supply chains and participate actively in a series of initiatives to develop communities in need.

# The value of maximizing profit

Category management can generate many forms of value for an organization but it is still its ability to maximize business profitability that gets attention in the boardroom so we will explore this some more.

In many organizations, external purchases or third-party spend account for the single biggest cost. Figure 1.2 shows a typical breakdown of where the money generated from sales goes, with third-party spend comprising just under half of it. Whilst this chart is typical for many manufacturing companies the breakdown would vary from business to business and industry to industry. For example, in the automotive sector, spend with suppliers accounts for a high proportion of turnover whilst professional services that are people-centric, such as consultancies, will typically have a much lower relative spend.

Taking a simplistic view, an organization seeking to maximize its profit can do this in two ways: it can increase the 'size of the pie' by increasing sales (Figure 1.3) or it can reduce the size of other segments, ie reduce costs.

Each of the segments in Figure 1.2 has typically received some sort of attention from organizations over recent years. Profit has received direct attention from sales and marketing functions tasked with finding ways to increase sales and therefore profit by growing market share, finding new markets or finding new products.

Organizations have also focused on improving profit by reducing costs and the cost of people has probably received the most attention in recent

**FIGURE 1.2** Where money from sales goes

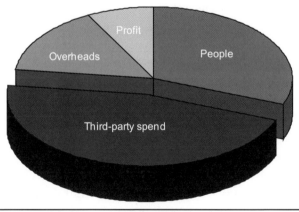

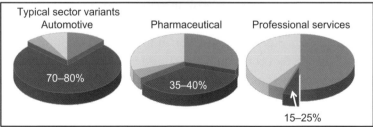

**FIGURE 1.3** Approaches to maximizing profit

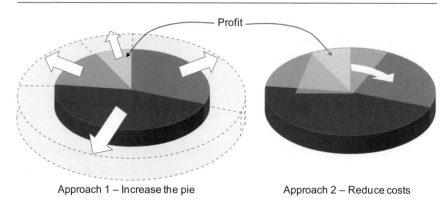

Approach 1 – Increase the pie          Approach 2 – Reduce costs

decades. Many of us will be familiar with restructuring and headcount reductions or where wholesale outsourcing of large areas of the business to 'low-cost labour' geographies has taken place. Overheads too have been tackled by a vast range of efficiency-improvement initiatives in all areas of business, including business process re-engineering, lean manufacturing or Six Sigma, increased use of IT, increased automation, relocation, downsizing and home working. However, with third-party spend typically being the largest expenditure area it is therefore the area that can present the biggest opportunity for organizations, yet in some sectors and some organizations it remains the area that receives the least attention.

Nevertheless, strategic initiatives that focus on reducing this cost can dramatically improve profit and this profit potential doesn't just come from price reduction but from the combined effect of all interventions that add value and help reduce the overall cost of third-party spend. It also requires a new strategic perspective to identify the opportunities that are 'game changing' and will deliver significant profit improvements. Furthermore, it is often much easier to increase an organization's profit by reducing costs than by increasing sales. For example, consider a manufacturing business making plumbing fittings. The company has a sales revenue of €1 million, of which €450,000 is spent on raw materials and bought-in goods and services. The company makes a profit of 10 per cent of turnover (€100,000). If it could achieve a 3 per cent reduction in the cost of bought-in goods and services (€13,500), the profit of the organization would increase to €113,500. This has the same effect as increasing overall sales by 13.5 per cent (turnover increased to €1.135 million, profit at 10 per cent is €113,500). For most organizations the sales effort and investment required to secure a 13.5 per cent increase in profit would be significant. Therefore if an organization can save just £1, €1 or $1 in the cost of bought-in goods and services, this can go straight to the bottom line as increased profit. This is a simplistic view and a variety of accounting and taxation factors could change this for some situations. However, the principle of third-party spend savings making a bottom-line contribution is robust.

Category management can therefore help organizations secure significant additional value from the supply chain by increasing profit by reducing the spend and cost of bought-in goods and services and also through increased sales resulting from securing supply chain innovation.

# DETERMINING CATEGORIES

Category management requires a segmentation of third-party spend into categories that can be worked on individually by a cross-functional team with the aim of identifying and implementing the optimum sourcing strategy for that category (see Figure 1.4). In order to determine categories, third-party spend needs to be segmented into discrete market-facing areas. This is not as straightforward as it might seem. Even when equipped with good spend analysis information, there are a number of factors that must be considered – in fact there are five vital considerations here, each of which will be explored in turn:

1 identifying spend;
2 directing resources only on addressable spend;
3 directing resources on the categories where there is a worthwhile opportunity;
4 identifying market boundaries so categories become market facing;
5 the most appropriate level to work at.

# 1 Identifying spend

A good analysis and breakdown of third-party spend are required to begin to identify categories. However, businesses often have little detailed understanding of what they spend. The company will have developed and grown over time. Mergers, acquisitions, multiple geographical locations and different decision-making processes mean big companies can end up with multiple legacy IT systems, often differing from country to country, with no or little communication or integration between them. Few large corporates have managed to reach the point where they have a single fully integrated information system that can provide the ideal information at a push of a button. Furthermore, even if spend analysis data is available, the breakdown may not be suitable; for example, a breakdown by supplier instead of by what the supplier is providing will make it difficult to identify categories, as will analysis derived from missing, incomplete or miscoded data at the original point of entry.

If good data is not available, then an alternative approach is required, and the marketplace is full of providers offering spend analysis services. Some have sophisticated systems that can be installed alongside company IT systems. These have clever software that can interface with multiple internal systems and will periodically extract, manipulate and analyse company finance and purchasing transactional data to provide good data when required. Other providers are adept at bringing in teams of people to analyse transaction history. Some combine both. Most can usually sort, cleanse and optimize the data to a high degree of accuracy to provide good insightful spend analysis data.

An alternative 'do-it-yourself' approach to spend analysis can often work too, and with time, effort and energy it is usually possible to gain something meaningful. Approaches that can work include some or all of the following:

- data extraction: using an IT systems/data expert to extract, manipulate and combine data from multiple systems to provide a view regarding spend and segmentation of spend;

- interrogation of purchase orders: reviewing historical purchase orders over a period of time, one by one, and recording and categorizing the spend for each to arrive at a final spend analysis snapshot;

- asking the suppliers: requesting a breakdown by category of spend from key suppliers for the past 12 or 18 months;

- liaising with stakeholders or budget holders to understand what they spend in key areas;

- analysing finished goods and volumes shipped, to derive raw materials and input volumes and thus calculate spend data;

- taking a view based on experience.

## 2  Directing resources to addressable spend

Not all the spend will be addressable. That is to say, there will be a percentage of spend where it is either impossible or very difficult to influence or change what is spent, short of not making the expenditure in the first place – and even this may not be possible. Examples of non-addressable spend might include:

- tax;
- rates or charges by governmental bodies;
- rent (although it may sometimes be addressable);
- regulatory or government-set licence fees.

In identifying non-addressable spend it is important to be clear about why an area of spend might be considered non-addressable, as an opportunity could easily be missed. With the right approach and incentives, governments can make tax concessions, rent can be lowered and so on. There will, however, always remain some areas that are truly non-addressable. These should be identified and ruled out early on – but only after the reasoning behind categorizing an area of spend as 'non-addressable' has been considered and challenged.

## 3  Directing resources where there is opportunity

When segmenting categories, the Pareto principle typically applies: 80 per cent of spend is usually with 20 per cent of suppliers, and 20 per cent of spend with 80 per cent of suppliers. It is the 80 per cent of spend that should form the primary focus for segmentation of third-party spend into categories. This requires the acceptance that it is impossible to address the entirety of third-party spend and there will always be a portion where it is uneconomic to expend effort working on small spend areas (termed 'rest of spend' in Figure 1.4). An approach to help here is given in Chapter 3.

**FIGURE 1.4**   Segmentation of third-party spend into categories

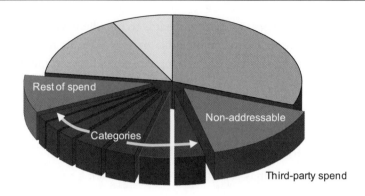

## 4 Identifying market boundaries so categories become market facing

In order to maximize the potential from category management, the segmentation of spend into categories that will be worked on must reflect their market-facing nature, ie they must mirror how the individual marketplaces are organized where the market boundaries lie. We are therefore seeking to develop a definition of each category based not only on spend or how we are organized, but also according to the boundaries of the market from which we are sourcing. Our thinking here, and how we view the market boundaries for each category, is crucial if category management is to open up dramatic opportunities. It is here where we are presented with our first significant game-changing opportunity with category management; narrow-minded thinking at this stage will dilute potential benefits later – the wider the market boundaries the more choice we have and the greater the opportunity.

Market boundaries take many forms and all markets are bound in one or more ways. Boundaries can be natural or artificial. For example, taxi firms exist the world over, but it is not a global market; it is a natural collection of small markets, each bound by practicality, licences to operate and ultimately the limited demand for long-haul taxi services. Factors that determine market boundaries are:

- Form – the type and nature of the market, eg a physical space, online etc.

- Size – how big the market is, usually measured in total volumes sold, people employed or how much is spent in the market. For example, the size of the US fast food market is estimated at $120 billion per annum.

- Scale – the geographical reach of the market.
- Location – where the market is based and what its boundaries are.
- Types of participants – for example, are they individuals or companies?
- Types of goods or services – what they are, the function they perform or the need they fulfil.
- Generic choice – the generic or proprietary nature of what is being sourced.
- Restrictions – any factors that limit a market or the freedom of trade such as government sanctions or regulations reducing the quality or quantity available.

In each case these factors introduce boundaries. If we set out to buy glass bottles we will only look for glass bottle suppliers, but what about plastic, or a completely different packaging solution? (We will return to this later.) A physical market is limited by the space available and where it is; for example, a traditional village square market could only ever be as big as the number of stalls that the space could accommodate. If we buy from a government-subsidized market then these subsidies will naturally prevent competition. Geographical reach depends upon economic practicalities and differences in regional need. For example, in the category 'fleet' (company cars and vans) the marketplaces appear global, and companies such as Toyota and Ford are global brands; so a 'single badge' sourcing strategy would seem possible. But regional differences in models, regulations and infrastructures introduce barriers. The big car brands may have a global presence but they are not typically organized in a way that can service global accounts, which are still very much regional with different products and support networks in each territory. Here, an apparent global market is, in fact, a collection of smaller natural markets and so categories would need to be qualified by including the boundaries within the name, eg 'US fleet category', 'European fleet category', etc.

In identifying the marketplace our category faces off against, it is crucial to challenge thinking, open boundaries and identify the widest potential market, and that may involve looking at alternatives to how we have sourced traditionally. Modern freight means emerging countries might also be able to offer what we need. Modern IT means the physicality of a marketplace is less relevant, as a specialist in India can work alongside us as if in the office next door. Determining the right marketplace is part of category management later in the process once equipped with good market data, but is also something that must happen now in order to define the category we will work on. We are therefore making an initial identification of category segmentation based upon the information available but recognizing that the scope and definition of a category might need to shift later.

It is not only the nature of markets that introduces boundaries but also our choices and how suppliers attempt to maximize their position. Cleary it is in the supplier's interest to seek to reduce our options so that we have, or are made to believe we have, little choice, thus increasing their power by reducing the apparent size of the market they occupy. Offerings that are branded or differentiated have some form of unique added value or are uniquely bundled do just this. If this drives our choices, then we are limiting the potential market we can source from. For example if we set out to buy 'an Apple iPad' rather than 'a tablet computer' then we have limited our potential marketplace by selecting a proprietary product. Figure 1.5 shows the effect of market boundaries on opportunity.

**FIGURE 1.5**    Effect of market boundaries on market opportunity

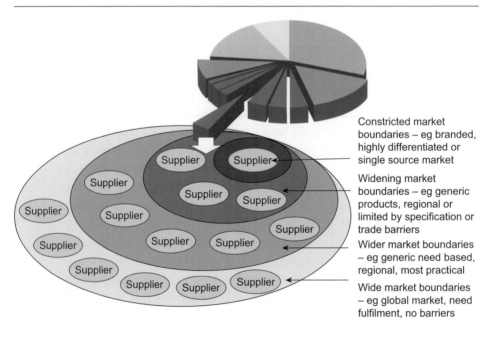

Constricted market boundaries – eg branded, highly differentiated or single source market

Widening market boundaries – eg generic products, regional or limited by specification or trade barriers

Wider market boundaries – eg generic need based, regional, most practical

Wide market boundaries – eg global market, need fulfilment, no barriers

# 5 Most appropriate level to work at

There is one final dimension to category segmentation and that is the fact that in order to be successful the categories we work on must be large enough to find opportunities and small enough to work on. It is worth dwelling on this part, as getting it right can dramatically influence the potential benefits possible, yet there may be a conflict here between what we might naturally choose to work on and the way the market is organized. For example, consider a global business with a significant spend on travel (Table 1.3 shows what the spend breakdown might be). The category of 'travel' frequently appears in lists of segmented categories that companies identify.

At a high level this is appropriate, but there is no marketplace for travel as such. Corporate travel agencies would be quick to suggest that they constitute a marketplace for travel in all its forms; however, the reality is that such agencies are not the market itself but are a well-organized means of connecting a client with multiple marketplaces. The actual marketplaces here are 'air travel', 'hotels', 'hire cars' and so on. 'Travel agency' is a marketplace but only for the process of matching a requirement with available travel options in different marketplaces, making the booking and providing support to the traveller. Failure to appreciate this could lead to the development of a sourcing strategy for travel as a package, perhaps with an outsourced arrangement with a single travel agency. This might initially appear to be a good approach but the price paid will depend on the deals the travel agency has negotiated with different carriers and hotel chains, many of which will be influenced by partner relationships and rebate arrangements that often remain hidden. With such significant spends on each of the travel components here, undoubtedly there are greater opportunities by working on each individually. Airlines will offer greater discount structures to high-spending customers on specific 'city pair' routes (for example, between office locations), so that they can maximize aircraft yield on those routes. Similarly, global or regional hotel chains rarely provide significant across-the-board discounts for all their locations but will agree preferential rates for specific hotel locations where there are significant bed nights for a particular customer, again perhaps reflecting office locations.

The optimum category segmentation here would therefore be to work on each of the market-facing travel components as categories but with 'travel' as the overarching area. One category manager might typically work on travel as a whole but be responsible for five or six subcategory projects within it. This overarching view is important, as it allows the category

**TABLE 1.2**   Breakdown of travel spend

| Area of spend | Global spend last year | Predicted global spend next year |
| --- | --- | --- |
| Air travel | $42m | $45m |
| Hotels | $17m | $21m |
| Travel agency | $4.1m | $4.3m |
| Hire cars | $4.1m | $4.2m |
| Rail travel | $2.8m | $2.7m |
| Taxis | $1.9m | $2.1m |

manager to identify and act on any synergies or issues between individual categories.

There may even be more synergies or opportunities further afield which should be considered; for example, if the same organization has a high spend on the category 'marketing events', involving the staging of large events attended by many customers or potential customers, there will be a significant travel requirement here also. Suggesting that the travel categories be expanded to include this additional marketing spend on marketing events is likely to create a tension, and marketing may feel under threat if their work with events providers is scrutinized. Furthermore, there will almost certainly be a backlash from the marketing suppliers, who will argue that it is better if they have the freedom to provide the entire event using their own arrangements with travel providers (often with hidden rebates!).

Structuring the segmentation of spend into categories is an exercise that usually only needs to be done once at the outset when an organization is about to deploy category management. Determining the right list of categories makes it possible to work on the entire organizational spend in each marketplace, which will then maximize the potential returns for each category. This process of segmentation may well introduce tensions with other functions who feel they are responsible for certain areas of spend and the associated sourcing decisions. Strong executive leadership is required here, otherwise the segmentation activity may fail to develop the optimum list or break down as a result of appeasing the concerns of other functions.

# Defining category segmentation

So in summary category segmentation is about identifying what the market-facing categories are, considering the widest possible market boundaries and seeking to match as much as possible of the aggregated spend of the entire organization against this market. However here we are also making a clear choice about how wide we want to go. There may be a good business reason not to attempt to widen market opportunity and to deliberately source from a very small or even single supplier market. In this case category management can help to verify this choice, but it might be more appropriate to switch to a Supplier Relationship Management (SRM) approach. We will cover this in Chapter 8 and it is expanded in full in my third book *Supplier Relationship Management*.

A useful test question to verify if category segmentation has been successful is therefore:

> Are we confident that the entirely of spend in a discrete area reflects a specific, identifiable marketplace with the widest possible or appropriate market boundaries to maximize our potential opportunity?

Once we are clear about category segmentation, wherever possible categories should be defined based upon their boundaries as this then defines the scope for individual category project, eg European fleet, Global telecoms, bottles (European), PCB assemblies (global) and so on.

# THE BENEFITS POSSIBLE

There are two questions I frequently get asked; first, what benefits will category management deliver; and second, can you guarantee a certain return on investment if we do it? Reasonable questions, and what might be expected of a CPO or CFO contemplating adopting such an approach. It seems there is a commonly held belief that there is some standard answer to these questions – a magic number, substantiated by experience that can help justify a business case for action. There is not and the answer to both questions is 'it depends'.

Category management is not something that can be simply be bought in, acquired or bolted on; just like so many other business initiatives, in fact, attempting to implement category management with such a mindset will most likely doom it to failure. The benefits of category management, whilst potentially dramatic and game changing, will only be realized with the right organizational approach and deployment. Category management is both a process and a philosophy. The process drives what happens but the philosophy is the way the organization embraces the approach, organizes and aligns itself for strategic procurement intervention using a category management framework, perhaps together with other strategic procurement initiatives. The philosophy cannot reside in the procurement function alone but must become significant business wide and demand the winning of hearts and minds beyond the bounds of the procurement team.

# Scale and nature of benefits possible

So if benefits can be game changing, to what order of magnitude? Category management can deliver many types of benefits. Look around and you'll find all sorts of claims. For hard savings alone the range is huge. I've been part of category teams that have achieved 10, 20, 30 or even 40 per cent savings. One project, addressing a category where a single supplier had enjoyed a comfortable position in a changing marketplace, delivered 98 per cent savings yet other projects have struggled to find just 1 or 2 per cent. The consultancy ADR (2011) suggest 10–30 per cent is possible, Future Purchasing (2014) place the figure at between 10 and 15 per cent, but crucially make a clear link between the return and degree of procurement maturity. This is supported by KPMG (2012) who state there is a direct link between cost savings and maturity in category management as well as strategic sourcing and SRM. The Hackett Group (Flores, 2011) suggest that the return on investment varies according to how 'effective and efficient' the organization is – the factors they define as primary attributes of world-class procurement. They suggest that organizations that are world class achieve nearly a 12× return for savings vs cost compared with a non-world class function that achieves on average 3.45×.

There is a direct correlation between the 'quality' of category management and the return on investment. I have worked with firms that are proud to tell me they have implemented category management; however, when the 'category management label' is peeled back it soon becomes apparent that they are doing little more than tendering and contracting under a category framework. They may even have a good process but are either box ticking or skipping over key steps. Such an approach will only ever yield small incremental benefits. In such cases the senior team seem to either be able to fool themselves into believing they are doing category management or they fail to truly understand how category management needs to be implemented.

Generally, if the category teams are not finding and realizing game-changing benefits, chances are they are not actually practising category management effectively.

So what is possible with quality category management? What is that magic savings number? Based upon what we have seen so far it might seem that we can simply pick a number here, but in fact the level of benefit and return on investment is, in fact, more predictable once we have identified a market-facing category, and depends upon:

1 Category opportunity – determined according to market difficulty, degree of 'added value' or scope for price flexibility and how mature or immature a category is (ie how much has it been worked on to date).

2 Quality of deployment – the effectiveness of category management including capability, process, available resources and governance.

3 Procurement maturity – the degree to which procurement has evolved in the organization and is effecting planned and systematic supply base interventions that make a strategic contribution to the business.

4 Organizational readiness – the degree of alignment, participation and buy-in of the wider organization to the cause of procurement, and the ability to drive change in the organization in support of implementing new sourcing strategies.

With these things in mind, it is possible to gauge with some confidence the likely outcomes of any category management project; it is also possible to identify that magic number and later I will outline an opportunity analysis approach that can help here!

The potential for hard savings will always secure the attention of the executive team and category management can in fact deliver a range of benefits both hard and soft. Post global downturn other benefits have become more relevant. Today, as marketplaces have changed and become more volatile, and security of supply has become a bigger issue, it is much more being seen as an enabler to provide assurance of supply, improve efficiency and effectiveness, and reduce supply chain risk with savings becoming a secondary consideration in some instances. As such the relationship between category management and SRM has strengthened, with organizations now recognizing that the benefits they seek require both approaches working alongside each other.

At a strategic level, category management can help create competitive advantage and find differentiators that can contribute directly to brand equity or stakeholder value. A key contributor to this is innovation – not solely that from a marketing or R&D team, but won from the supply base where we can find a rich treasure trove of future possibilities if only we figure out how to tease it out to our future benefit. Category management provides the means here and in doing so can demolish the 'virtual brick wall' I described earlier, enabling us to connect end-customer needs and desires with supply chain possibilities.

There are soft benefits too, which are both benefits and enablers in themselves. Category management requires some form of spend analysis, which in turns helps drive greater transparency of spend. Category management demands cross-functional working, which once established yields the great results that come when people get together, share and work towards a common goal. Similarly category management both demands and yields common language and ways of working together with knowledge sharing. Finally category management is a strategic approach and needs to be approached and positioned as such; however in turn, if it is well deployed it also drives more strategic sourcing within an organization. Table 1.3 summarizes the hard and soft benefits possible through category management.

There is much here we can do to directly influence and determine the potential benefits we can realize from the supply base and chances are they will be significant. It is possible to effect interventions to secure and sustain these benefits. Category management provides the framework to do just this but demands a quality deployment in order to do so – the rest of this book outlines how.

## Surely someone has already thought of this?

With such dramatic benefits possible from category management, why is it only now that this concept is beginning to be recognized as essential by many global organizations? The answer is that in many companies these benefits have remained hidden, with executive teams failing to see the opportunity. Indeed, there has often been a commonly held view that there was little remaining opportunity in the supply base – if there were, 'someone would have spotted it'. There are two main reasons for this view: one, this is how your suppliers want you to feel, and they do a remarkably good job of ensuring you do; and two, to unlock the hidden benefits of category management you need to do something fundamentally different across the entire organization.

**TABLE 1.3** Hard and soft benefits possible from category management

| Benefit type | What is typically possible | What is required in order to realize these benefits |
|---|---|---|
| **Hard, tangible benefits** | | |
| Cost reduction | 10–20 per cent reduction in the price of bought in goods and services | • Business must organize itself so as to implement category management effectively<br>• Low category maturity<br>• Non-difficult market<br>• Ability to drive organizational change<br>• Category is generic – low differentiation<br>• Category has 'added value' components |
| Improved value and effectiveness | • Improved efficiency<br>• Reduced waste<br>• Additional value (more bang for the buck)<br>• Sustainable results | • Cross-functional working<br>• Means to identify and pursue opportunities (eg Lean or Six Sigma approaches)<br>• Active supplier involvement |
| Innovation | • Improved value proposition to our customer using supply base innovation<br>• Process improvements<br>• Synergies from collaboration | • Reason for suppliers to share or work on innovation (mutual benefit)<br>• Shared understanding and sharing goals or needs<br>• Collaborative joint working with key suppliers |

**TABLE 1.3**  *continued*

| Benefit type | What is typically possible | What is required in order to realize these benefits |
| --- | --- | --- |
| Reduced supply chain risk | • Greater security of supply<br>• Reduced risk of brand damage (eg through poor practice upstream in the supply chain)<br>• Reduced risk of loss (eg of IP) through increased supplier and supply chain understanding | • Risk assessment<br>• Market and supplier understanding |
| Competitive advantage, differentiation and improved offering to customers | • Improved value proposition to our customer<br>• Increased profit margin<br>• Differentiation or offer or delivery mechanism | • Cross-functional working – connect 'sourcing' with 'satisfying'<br>• Reason for suppliers to contribute (mutual benefit)<br>• Collaborative joint working with key suppliers |
| **Soft benefits** | | |
| Total spend under management | • Greater transparency (especially relevant for public sector)<br>• Improved accuracy of spend breakdown<br>• Ability to prioritize resources<br>• Better framework agreements through improved market understanding (public sector) | • Robust spend analysis<br>• Robust category segmentation |

**TABLE 1.3**  *continued*

| Benefit type | What is typically possible | What is required in order to realize these benefits |
|---|---|---|
| Cross-functional working | • Augmentation of results (through sharing and interaction)<br>• Alignment to a common purpose<br>• Ground swell of effort to deliver results | • Organization-wide approach to category management and mandate to participate<br>• Executive buy-in<br>• Active promotion of initiative through the organization |
| Common language and ways of working | • Faster results<br>• Increased organizational capability | • Single process and toolkit accessible and utilized by all – common templates<br>• Common learning and development programme<br>• Language and process rigour expectations reinforced by senior team |
| Knowledge sharing | • Increased organizational capability<br>• Organizational learning | • Means to sharing key information (category strategies, market insights, success factors etc)<br>• Actively making time to share key learnings |
| Strategic sourcing | • Procurement as a strategic contributor to business success<br>• Customer value proposition shaped by supply chain possibilities | • Procurement embraced as a strategic function<br>• Procurement 'C' level/executive level representation |

Suppliers' salespeople are often competitive and driven individuals whose living, or at least the bonus they've come to expect, depends on them persuading you and your organization to buy and continue to buy, and to buy more. Suppliers are often better resourced, better funded and receive more training than the buyers they interface with, so the starting point is one where the supplier has a distinct advantage.

If the suppliers have been outwitting us, why hasn't anyone noticed? The reality here lies in why the potential benefits in the supply chain are hidden. For the supplier to continue to enjoy the advantage, they have to ensure buyers believe they hold all the power, even if that is not the case; so the supplier will work hard to maintain this illusion, offering concessions carefully to project a sense of 'best possible deal'. Suppliers also use clever tactics to maintain their position beyond their relationship with the buyer. It is war out there as far as the supplier is concerned, and their goal is to win. For the supplier it is all about seeing information as power, nurturing relationships through the rest of the business to gather information, dividing and conquering to disarm purchasing, questioning the buyer's technical team about the 'available budget', and so on.

Buyer–seller relationships which are equal or balanced are entirely possible and there are many good examples where this is the case. It is equally possible for a buyer to gain advantage and have leverage over certain suppliers. However, neither eventuality will happen unless there is solid purchasing intervention to counter efforts on the supplier's side. Category management provides a robust solution and, if well executed, can bring about a reversal of the balance of power in a buyer–seller relationship. However, this is only possible if the organization fully embraces category management, frees up the required resource and establishes cross-functional teams to work through the process towards implementing breakthrough sourcing strategies.

### Chapter 1 summary

Recap on the key points from this chapter:

1 Category management is a strategic approach that focuses on the vast majority of an organization's spend on goods and services with third-party suppliers.

2 It is the practice of segmenting the main areas of organizational spend on bought-in goods and services into discrete groups of products and services according their market-facing nature.

3 Great opportunity lies within the supply base, and as our world changes around this so too does the nature of this opportunity, and what is important to organizations. Category management is a proven approach to realize this opportunity.

4 Category management holds the potential to secure game-changing value including significant price reduction but also improved value and effectiveness, and reduced risk, but can also help build the value proposition to our end customer through supply base innovation or collaboration to create new differentiators or competitive advantage.

5 To unlock these benefits a 'quality' deployment of category management is essential.

6 Success also depends upon robust category segmentation – prioritizing the categories we will work on at the outset based upon addressable spend so a category faces out to the widest practical marketplace.

# The principles of category management

In this chapter we shall examine the essential foundations and overriding principles that are required in order to achieve success with category management.

Pathway questions addressed in this chapter:

**2** What is category management and how can it add benefit?

**5** What is required in order to successfully adopt and implement category management?

## THE THREE FOUNDATIONS OF CATEGORY MANAGEMENT

Category management is built on three solid foundations (see Figure 2.1), each a prerequisite to unlock the power of the process in delivering dramatic value improvement to the organization. These foundations are:

- a strategic approach to sourcing;
- strong market management;
- robust change management.

**FIGURE 2.1**  Foundations of category management

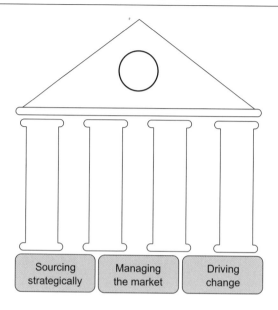

Sourcing strategically | Managing the market | Driving change

# Foundation 1: Sourcing strategically

There is plenty of debate in business about what 'strategy' is, and the terms 'strategy' or 'strategically' are often misused. Johnson and Scholes (1993) offer a definition of corporate strategy as: 'the direction and scope of an organization over the long term, ideally which matches its resources to its changing environment, and in particular its markets, customers or clients so as to meet stakeholder expectations'.

A strategy is therefore much more than a programme or plan, or a definition of future direction, although these would form key components.

Within purchasing, when we talk of strategy there are two areas where strategies are required; an overall strategy for the purchasing function, aligned with and responding to higher-level corporate strategy, and individual sourcing strategies for discrete areas of spend. Considering strategy in terms of purchasing, the following definitions reflect the views of Johnson and Scholes:

- *Strategy for the purchasing function.* This sets the direction and scope of the purchasing function over the long term. It must align with overall corporate objectives and stakeholder needs and expectations. Ideally it matches the function's resources and capability to these objectives as well as the changing environment, external markets and best-practice sourcing approaches.

- *Sourcing strategy*. This sets the direction and scope of a defined and discrete area of spend over the medium term, defining what and how the organization will buy. Ideally the sourcing strategy delivers the immediate and future needs and wants of the organization and its end customers, matched against current and potential future marketplaces. Individual sourcing strategies should also align with overall strategy and objectives. For example, if 'No child labour made our products' is part of an organization's policy and brand proposition, individual sourcing strategies must align with this and therefore shape the sourcing arrangements that are put in place.

It is this second area, the strategy for a discrete area of spend, that is shaped, defined and realized through category management; but this is not straightforward.

## The time-travelling helicopter

Imagine climbing into a time-travelling helicopter and being able to fly above the organization and look down on everything it does, the marketplaces from which it buys and the end customers it supplies. With such a vantage point you would easily be able to make informed decisions about how to manage your spend. You would see into your suppliers and how they operate as well as alternative supply markets and sourcing options, and you would see other suppliers, possibly in markets you hadn't previously considered. You would see how the goods or services work through the organization and how each function uses or processes them. You would also see what the end customer is doing with the products or services your organization supplies and how they get there. This should sound familiar because from this helicopter you would be looking down on the end-to-end value chain described earlier, except now this unique perspective means you could easily see how to make improvements because inefficiencies and opportunities would be obvious, as too would opportunities to connect end-customer needs or desires with innovation or capability you see in the supply market.

Because this helicopter can travel in time and show you what the future holds, you would have a very powerful tool to see what new things your customers might want and how your supply markets will change. Equipped with this insight you could identify the optimum sourcing strategy and how this must change over time as well as how best to implement this strategy.

In reality, with no time-travelling helicopter at our disposal, this bird's-eye, time-spanning perspective might seem like nothing more than a crazy idea, but it isn't. The purpose of category management is to attempt to build a similar view as best we can. Instead of a time-travelling helicopter this strategic insight must be built through cross-functional working, research and analysis of the market, suppliers and the organization, and working with marketing functions in understanding the current and future needs of end customers. Sourcing strategically is therefore a key foundation for category management with the entire process built around the tools and approaches that enable this.

## Making sourcing strategic

Sourcing strategically does not come from the traditional mindsets still held by many organizations, purchasing functions and individuals that believe the role of purchasing is little more than to buy things. Neither will it come from working through a process, applying tools or shouting more loudly at suppliers. Instead the way purchasing acts and is viewed across the organization must change and it must be seen by all as a key enabler of value to the organization whose involvement is essential. This must be reflected in the way purchasing is positioned within the wider organizational structure and the degree of executive representation and support. There is also a personal dimension here too – if we see ourselves as 'there to buy things', perhaps because that is how we have been conditioned to think, then that is just what we will do. However if we see ourselves as there 'to enable our sourcing approaches to make a strategic contribution to the business' we will begin to think and behave differently.

## Sourcing, satisfying and strategy

Category management, and indeed any sort of strategic purchasing intervention, is successful when it is embraced as an organization-wide philosophy. If it is to have any significant impact then it must be an integral component in the way the organization connects its *sourcing* with the way it *satisfies* its end customers and the overarching *strategy* of the firm (Figure 2.2), and in doing so work to take down the 'virtual brick wall' described in Chapter 1.

The traditional view of procurement is that the function looks after, and is the main interface with the external parties from which it sources.

Organizations need to source materials, goods, services or people in some way. It's hard to picture an organization that doesn't. Purchasing (and indeed

**FIGURE 2.2**   The 3S Model

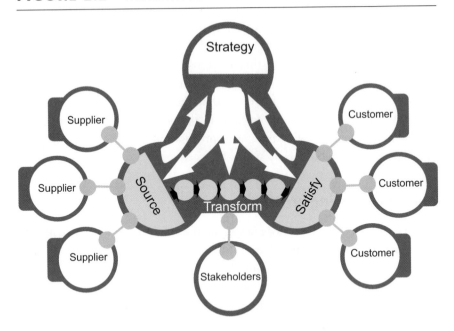

any dedicated supply chain management function) therefore has one of the organization's primary externally facing roles to *source* on behalf of the organization. At the other end, the other primary externally facing role is that of *satisfying* what customers need and might want; a role usually fulfilled by sales and marketing teams amongst others who interface with customers in some way or are part of the process of fulfilment. In between these two are all the different functions, departments, processes, handoffs and steps that transform what is sourced into something that satisfies the customer so they buy and keep buying. Ideally this transformation adds some value in some way as described by Porter's 'value chain' concept (Porter, 1985).

Whilst the internal value chain between *sourcing* and *satisfy* adds the value that the firm then exploits, similar value chains exist within each supplier back upstream in the supply chain extending back to the original growers, raw material suppliers or service providers. Each entity in the supply chain therefore adds value in some way by enhancing, combining, processing, building, mixing, packaging, coordinating, shipping and so on to create products or services that our customers buy.

Most purchasing functions will have some sort of goal to improve some aspect of *sourcing* effectiveness. This is good and in turn benefits our end customer but such goals are frequently inwardly focused. Instead if the purchasing intervention of a business can be driven more by how the entire business can better *satisfy* its end customers then this change in perspective can change our entire view of the value we need from the supply base in order to create the value customers want or need.

The value that *satisfies* the end customers is called the *value proposition* (Lanning, 1980), which is the reason they buy; because a need or want will be fulfilled in some way. It is a promise of value to be delivered together with a belief held by the customer that the value will be secured or experienced. The value proposition is the way a supplier defines what it will do and offer and how it organizes itself so as to provide value to the customer experience. *Satisfying* customers therefore requires companies to be clear about the value proposition that will resonate with customers and will therefore drive demand. This means the firm must get close to customers, develop a deep understanding of what they would value (especially the value they haven't realized they need or cannot articulate) and develop a differentiated offering. This is much more than any initiative from marketing function but requires a corporate strategy based around satisfying customers with the right value proposition and requires the entire organization to be structured, aligned and organized behind this so as to deliver competitive advantage. It also demands a means to capture the often untapped source of value and innovation available if can organization can figure out how to capture it – that which lies in the supply base.

Linking end-customer value with value we source, drives a change in mindset in the role of our supply base and the way we need to interact with it. If we view our suppliers as there only to fulfil orders, and assume they present no risk or opportunity then their role is purely tactical and the supply base has little or no bearing on the way the organization satisfies its customers beyond fulfilment of current need; sourcing is merely a responsive activity. Indeed this is the traditional model of purchasing, commonplace for many years. Yet organizations now need more from the supply base because customers want more from them. Add to this increased scarcity and security of supply issues and a supply base can no longer be managed tactically.

The idea that the supply base is host to new and future sources of value is not a new concept. Indeed organizations have in fact been taking ideas, concepts and innovations from willing suppliers for years, crucially though this has tended to be at an individual level rather than as part of an organized corporate approach. For example, individuals within an R&D, NPD or marketing function tasked with creating or developing new products engage with and develop relationships with the suppliers that have something to offer here. This is good, but the problem is suppliers gain power through relationships with designers and it is in the supplier's interests to develop these relationships; if they can get their product, service or technology incorporated at the design or concept stage, and especially if they can get it defined in a specification, then it almost guarantees a future revenue stream. Purchasing rarely gets invited to be part of such discussions, and by the time they do, the supplier is mandated leaving little opportunity to influence commercial terms. What is required is an approach that connects the value of category and supply chain possibilities with the value proposition that satisfies the customer and this means the convergence of *sourcing* and *satisfying* with organizational *strategy*.

*Strategy* is the direction we take (Johnson and Scholes, 1993). Corporate strategy is only effective if it can be implemented and therefore has to be translated so each part of the business can play its part in following the overall direction set. Traditionally this has, for most organizations, demanded a separate translation of strategy into actions for supplier facing functions (eg purchasing) and those who are customer facing (eg sales and marketing). This strategic cascade is – based upon how most text books present it and how many firms are organized – one directional; flowing down from the top of the organization. The problem with a 'top down only' strategic management approach means there is no real need for purchasing to engage with marketing as both take their direction from the top. Indeed functions can exist as silos with hand-offs between them. Cross-functional working can help but only if the organization is encouraging this throughout and of course this in itself requires top down remit. Furthermore success depends entirely upon getting the strategy absolutely right including determining all the factors that could cause it to fail and taking advantage of those that can help.

So how does *strategy* connect to *sourcing* and *satisfying*? Johnson and Scholes (1993) suggest that strategy must match its resources to its changing environment. The supply base represents an integral part of the firm's resources and so for any corporate strategy to be effective it needs to consider the role of the supply base to support how the organization will achieve its goals. Effective corporate strategies must therefore respond to and be determined by the external environment within both the supply base and customer base. Strategies are therefore two way; they inform and are informed by end-customer current and potential wants and needs together with what might be possible in the supply base. This is the fundamental concept that underpins and creates a purpose for category management as well as Supplier Relationship Management and any other strategic purchasing initiative.

**CASE STUDY**    Transitioning from tactical support to strategic enabling

In this case the company, let's call it WD Instruments, makes highly complex electronic test equipment for the IT and telecoms industry. WD identified that in order to remain competitive in the global market it needed to cut costs and better leverage the potential of its significant global spend. WD focused on its procurement function and began to review the biggest cost and risk areas with spend on printed circuit boards (PCBs) identified as a priority.

*The situation 10 years ago.* WD Instruments was organized around the products it supplied. The product teams reporting out of the R&D function assumed full responsibility for specification and supplier selection for key components and would develop and maintain relationships with the key suppliers they wanted to work with. Purchasing was regarded as a support function whose role was largely to conclude the commercial arrangements. Product teams had little need to work cross-functionally. PCBs were critical items, many using highly complex multilayer technology, and product teams would therefore work closely with their chosen supplier to optimize PCB design to the PCB manufacturing process. WD Instruments had a total of 15 different PCB suppliers, all in one country, of which around half maintained a close relationship with one or more product teams.

Purchasing ensured the contractual and commercial arrangements were defined in an agreement and would respond to a weekly planning schedule and ensure PCB orders were placed in good time. Purchasing would also attempt to defend any price increases and had carried out some benchmarking that suggested WD was paying too much for these products. Various ideas for reducing PCB spend had been proposed by the purchasing team, including aggregation of spend and sourcing from emerging markets, but these ideas gained little traction with product teams who were reluctant to move away from the existing arrangements.

*How things have changed since then.* WD has since positioned purchasing as a strategic function with executive-level representation. Purchasing now has clear targets aligned to overall business objectives and key purchasing initiatives receive boardroom airtime. A matrix-based organizational structure is now in place allowing strategic enabling functions including purchasing, HR and marketing to work across product teams. Transactional purchasing is now the responsibility of a separate team, allowing the core team to focus on more strategic purchasing projects and working more closely with product teams and key suppliers.

The intervention from purchasing is now welcomed (although it wasn't at first) and there are good relationships across the business. In direct response to a board-driven project, purchasing started to lead a series of cross-functional teams each focused on a key area of spend or risk. These projects delivered a series of step-change improvements in performance.

*A strategic approach for PCBs.* The PCB project was one of the first cross-functional projects led by purchasing. Together with representatives from production, planning and selected product/R&D functions, the team reviewed the spend, sourcing and usage for PCBs across the entire product range and how future business direction would impact on the future need for PCBs. Initially there was resistance to any sort of change here but with determination the team began to identify some interesting possibilities. As expected, the PCBs that were considered highly complex were the most expensive but these accounted for only about 20 per cent of the total PCB volume (equal to about 55 per cent of overall spend). The remaining 80 per cent of the PCBs were relatively simple and there was no shortage of potential suppliers, including the overseas sources offering more attractive pricing. This spend was therefore consolidated with just two suppliers, achieving a 32 per cent cost reduction. For the remaining specialist products, switching supplier was not straightforward in every case so the team focused on identifying two preferred suppliers (of which one had also been selected for the simple PCBs) who would provide all new products and who could begin to take over some of the high-demand specialist items.

The project delivered significant cost reduction and changed the relationship with the new preferred providers, making WD a 'priority customer' and creating a new degree of collaboration around design and planning as well as an ongoing structured approach to managing the relationship and driving improvements. The project marked a sea change in shifting from a business with purchasing as a tactical supporter to one with it as a strategic enabler.

## Barriers to sourcing strategically

There are a number of barriers to sourcing strategically:

- *Vertical silos.* Getting departments to talk to one another and work together on purchasing projects requires huge energy as well as clear and visible senior management encouragement and support.

- *Vertical incentives.* If vertical silos were not enough, if an organization motivates and incentives its people based upon functional success, there is little reason to support sourcing projects that focus on the flow of value horizontally through multiple functions. Strategic sourcing requires new 'organizational outcome' based motivation for those involved.

- *Crystal ball.* If only we could see the future! Planning effectively for the future may sound straightforward and logical, but of course there are many real barriers to its achievement. Understanding what the business needs today is hard enough, but predicting into the future seems impossible. Fluctuations in demand and changes in technology are often hard to predict.

- *Tug of war.* There are natural conflicts within an organization around purchasing, with different people wanting different things from the same purchase. Finance wants the best price, marketing wants the best quality, and operations wants the best performance.

- *Perceptions.* If purchasing is perceived as merely the function that buys things, it will struggle to break out and offer real challenge and insight to the wider business. I have sat in meetings where angry design people, on the receiving end of a challenge from purchasing people, have said, 'Surely purchasing's job is to place the orders. It's us who decide what we buy and who we buy it from.'

- *Lack of creativity.* How is creativity relevant to strategic sourcing? It is very relevant, because some of the best sourcing strategies have occurred as a result of someone saying, 'Why do we buy it that way?'

- *Making it happen.* It is great to develop groundbreaking sourcing strategies, but if you can't turn them into reality they are worthless. Driving change in organizations is a tough challenge.

These barriers are not impossible to break and category management is structured to overcome them but success requires the organization to fully embrace and embed the methodology.

# Foundation 2: Managing the market

The second foundation of category management changes our focus to look entirely outside the business. Here we are concerned with understanding the market, how the business relates to that market, the power structure in the market and sometimes even changing the market itself. If you understand the market you can then determine how best to manage it and what sort of interaction is needed.

Researching and understanding a market are often a complex task involving piecing together fragments of information, with a lot of time spent following up leads and dead ends, and facing lies and misinformation. Combine this with the often subtle perception that the buyer as customer holds the power, and there is almost an excuse for failing to understand the market. When you work for a large, perhaps transnational, organization, there is a temptation to believe that you have power in the market and when your spend is many millions, there is a temptation to believe that you have leverage. Furthermore, suppliers behaving deferentially or with subservience will reinforce the perception that you are in control. Often this is not the case, but without a solid understanding of the market and dynamics at play, it is both difficult to realize the true balance of power and impossible to know how the situation could be improved.

It seems a basic challenge but do you understand the market you're buying from and the markets you could buy from? Do you understand what is happening in these markets and what might happen? Much of the waste and many of the missed opportunities in sourcing come from simply not understanding the market and the impact of the sourcing decisions taken. For example, there may be many suppliers offering facilities management services, but if these services have been sourced as a complete package of managed services, perhaps together with specialist maintenance, security and cleaning, the number of potential suppliers in the market who provide the complete bundle is reduced. This can destroy your leverage.

## The barriers to managing the market

Managing the market may seem straightforward, but the reality is that many organizations miss great opportunities or lose their competitive edge by failing to manage the market as a result of one or more barriers. Once again category management helps overcome these by building up a precise understanding of the marketplace and using this as the basis for developing the optimum sourcing strategy and effective market management:

- *Knowledge is power.* Markets change rapidly, some more rapidly than others. New entrants, substitute products, developments in technology, consumer trends, global events and changes in demand all fuel changes in the marketplace. Failure to maintain a current and far-reaching understanding of a marketplace from which you are sourcing reduces the ability to manage that marketplace.

- *Setting boundaries.* Organizations often fail to see beyond the market they are currently sourcing from. Initiatives to reduce price or cost often focus only on looking in the current market. However, with some creative thinking there may be other marketplaces that could help fulfil the same need but in a different way. There may even be other marketplaces which, with some encouragement, could adapt to provide what you want, and this would then shift the dynamics in the marketplace.

- *The power base.* The balance of power within a supplier or indeed a marketplace depends on many things: how difficult that marketplace is (ie how difficult it is to switch suppliers), how many suppliers there are and the degree of competition. Where the balance of power seems to rest with the supplier, it is often assumed that this cannot be changed. However, by detailed analysis and understanding it is possible to consider what it would take to change this.

# Foundation 3: Driving change

Good strategic purchasing is more about change management than anything else. If you develop the finest sourcing strategy for an area of spend that will add great value to the organization, it is worthless unless you can implement the strategy effectively. This is something that purchasing can rarely do alone; it requires the support, cooperation and active participation of other parts of the organization.

The product development team may be absolutely confident that they alone should set specifications, and HR may be sure that they are the best people to control temporary labour, while the marketing department may believe that it alone should manage the appointment of design agencies. It's no wonder they don't want to take time to discuss the needs of the business, no surprise that they don't want to change the way things work, and you can predict that favoured suppliers will still get awarded business no matter what the arguments are.

A key feature that distinguishes a strategic purchasing function from one operating tactically is the ability to drive change. This means initiating and leading projects, working cross-functionally and managing the project through implementation with an energy and persistence that would shame a bull terrier. As a consequence, strategic purchasing teams require new skills additional to the usual purchasing competencies. Individuals need to be practitioners in project management, leading and facilitating teams and running internal communications that keep the wider organization informed and supportive.

Practitioners also need to have a good appreciation of the softer side of change dynamics. As humans we naturally resist change, whether we are aware of doing so or not. Organizations are littered with failed projects where a fundamentally good idea simply was not adopted because resistance to change could not be overcome. If I think of my own experience I can recall many initiatives launched within organizations I have worked in that have simply fizzled out. The reality is that getting people to move away from what they know and feel comfortable with requires huge effort and energy. Lewin (1958) suggests that it is not enough to define just the objective of change but that the will of the subject or individual to change must also be considered. He describes this as creating a 'felt need' within the people who are undergoing change.

The dynamics of organization change may seem like the role of the HR department, not purchasing. This may be true for organizational restructuring programmes; however, organizations undergo many types of change, all impacting and involving the individuals within them in some way, and being led by many different functions. For a strategically focused purchasing function sourcing strategies may involve changing the way people work, their role, how they interact with a supplier or use the goods or services or it may even impact specific individuals' jobs or even negate the need for the individual. The ability to effectively lead and drive organizational change is a necessity, and so the practitioners need to attend to the human side of change management.

The reality with any organizational change is that change involves pain and for that reason it is a natural human tendency to resist change. There is no way of avoiding it, but it can be minimized with hard work, involvement and communication, together with a strong awareness of how humans naturally respond to change and the emotional roller coaster that individuals experience during difficult changes.

**CASE STUDY**    The human response to difficult changes

A major utility company launched a project aimed at rationalizing the way technicians in vans made house calls to resolve customer problems. The ways of working in which house calls were made had been largely untouched for many years. For some employees this role had been their only job since leaving school 20 or 30 years before. However, business pressures meant things needed to change. It was no longer feasible to allow these staff to manage their work and appointments or be the direct contact point for the customer. The business was suffering as a result of low productivity and poor customer service – in some cases individuals would make only two house calls in one day.

A project to improve customer service was launched. This meant central call handling and appointment making, a system of allocating jobs and measuring performance and customer satisfaction. A natural consequence of the change was a reduction in headcount as the new team would be much more productive, with individuals making on average eight appointments per day, as opposed to just two.

The change team worked directly with the men and women who did these jobs before, during and after the change. They communicated what needed to happen and why, staff were involved in helping design the change, and the change team worked as sympathetically as possible to minimize the impact and reduce casualties by offering early retirement or redundancy deals. The change team witnessed the full emotional effect on these individuals; for some it was the first time they had experienced such a change. In the early phases people acted irrationally, with emotional outbursts of anger (mostly aimed at the change team as the 'bringer of change'), apathy, stress-related problems, and general unhappiness. Grown men broke down in tears in workshops. People shared stories of going home and shouting at their husbands or wives or partners without understanding why.

The project marched on and with much energy from the change team the new, smaller customer-facing team started adopting the new ways of working. Soon encouraging performance results began to galvanize the team with a new sense of purpose. The new team started to become enthusiastic about their role and the prospect of having finally fixed many of the 'old problems', ideas were abundant, and hope was everywhere. The difficult change was a success.

## Barriers to driving change

But resistance to change is not the only barrier to driving change. Beginning with it, barriers include:

- *Resistance to change.* This is the single most powerful reason why projects in organizations fail, be that through conscious, planned and organized activity amongst staff or reluctance and emotional outbursts due to subconscious resistance. Resistance is not always as obvious as this. It can come in many forms without the individuals concerned even realizing it. If you've ever been involved in implementing a change perhaps you've heard people say 'If it isn't broken, don't fix it,' or 'I heard that was tried before, and it failed.' These are often signs of resistance to change as too are apparent offers of help that are really seeking to deflect attention, for example: 'Let me help you; don't waste your time looking at this problem; the real problem is over there in that department' or 'I'm really keen on helping and I want this to succeed but right now I'm too busy. Can you come back next week?'

- *Lack of involvement.* This is the precursor to resistance. If people have not been involved or feel they have not had the chance to be involved, then they will naturally resent being required to change. Research shows that participation reduces resistance to change. In an organization it is not feasible for everyone to participate in designing every change, but with approaches using consultation to solicit views, information and representation from the involved parts of the business, a balanced approach to participation is possible.

- *Lack of executive support.* If the people involved in the change cannot see visible support from senior management for the project, then the project will lack teeth and be regarded as unimportant. There will also be no compelling reason for those outside the project team to engage in the project because, quite simply, no one is telling them they need to.

- *No felt need.* If people do not share a belief in the necessity for the change, there will be little to compel them to support it. This is more acute the harder the change. You may be implementing a new travel category strategy that involves a policy change that takes away perks that have been enjoyed for many years. But if staff believe the new policy is essential for the future survival of the business, they are more likely to comply, with minimal resistance.

- *Inadequate resources.* Implementing change will not happen by itself. It requires huge energy. Identifying the strategy or what one is going to do and how it will be done are relatively easy compared with the hard work needed to make the strategy a reality. Change projects must be adequately resourced, with staff having time to drive the organization through the change.

# THE FOUR PILLARS OF CATEGORY MANAGEMENT

By themselves, the foundations provide an excellent view of the challenges for deploying category management and begin to define the mindsets that the methodology is founded upon. The four pillars of category management build on these foundations to take advantage of the sure footing these provide. The pillars are rooted in practice and are based upon what has been found to be needed to drive insight and success within category management.

**FIGURE 2.3**    Four pillars of category management

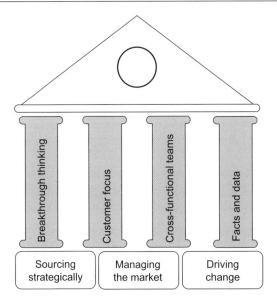

The four pillars are: breakthrough thinking, customer focus, use of cross-functional teams, and a facts-and-data approach (see Figure 2.3). The pillars are only possible once the foundations are in place.

## Pillar 1: Breakthrough thinking

There are big prizes out there. Very few organizations manage sourcing so well that there is no room for new big gains. Category management is about changing sourcing in a radical way or a way that gives radical improvements. Whether it is using competition to drive down prices, changing the internal processes, using suppliers to change the value of your products or simply eliminating needs, category management is about delivering far better value to the organization than traditional incremental improvement activities such as ad hoc negotiations can deliver.

A breakthrough is a step-change improvement in performance when compared with current performance. In purchasing, continuous improvement might typically represent a series of tactical negotiations with a supplier to try to keep prices as competitive as possible. 'Do nothing' would be as the name suggests, and it is important to note that in this case performance would decline over time as suppliers take advantage of the situation and competitors and peers overtake you.

The step change associated with a breakthrough would represent a fundamental change in the game and a move from current state to new state, often in a short period of time (although some breakthroughs can take years).

It is usual for a dip in performance before the change occurs as heavy resource is directed towards preparing for and making the change.

**CASE STUDY**    The breakthrough bottle

A brand-name soft drink company deploying category management set out to apply it to the largest spend areas including the category 'glass bottles' used for a particular branded product with the aim of achieving a reduction in bottle costs. The bottles were unique and made exclusively for this product. The shape and patterns within the glass were an extension of the brand itself.

Purchasing created a cross-functional project team including representation from marketing and production to ensure the right internal customer focus. Initially the project focused on understanding the marketplace for glass bottles and potential ways in which a new sourcing strategy could achieve greater leverage. However, with the cost of glass rising and fewer suppliers concentrating on glass, early research began to suggest that a significant reduction in price might not be possible. The purchasing category manager leading the team turned his attention to plastic bottles, a marketplace previously unexplored by this company. Research and evaluation of potential sources revealed that a suitable bottle could be made in plastic and the potential savings were so significant that this opportunity could no longer be ignored. This appeared to be a potential breakthrough opportunity.

The proposal to consider a plastic alternative was put to the cross-functional team and individuals liaised with their respective functions. The marketing department said 'No,' stating that the glass bottle and its design were fundamental to the brand attributes, essential to preserve brand recognition, and helped to project the brand as a quality product. The production department also said 'No.' It had previously run trials with plastic bottles and deemed them unusable, as they had no stability on the moving conveyor systems when empty and thus would frequently fall over, causing a line-stop-and-reset procedure.

Despite these outright rejections the purchasing category manager persisted. More facts and data around this supply opportunity were collected and used to develop a business case that suggested a multi-million-euro cost reduction with a move to plastic. The initial rejection by the cross-functional team members had not been made lightly; in fact, the matter had been discussed at length across the business. As a consequence, during a senior managers' meeting someone stood up and said, 'If the benefits from a move to plastic are so huge, why are we rejecting the option?' Consequently the team was tasked with broadening the scope to evaluate more fully the option of plastic bottles before recommending the future sourcing strategy.

Work by marketing with end-customer product evaluation panels revealed that over the medium to long term a switch to plastic would not detract from the customer's perception of the brand or the product. Furthermore, work with potential suppliers also revealed that the unique shape and features of the original bottle could be reproduced in plastic, so the product would appear the same on the supermarket shelf. Production ran some trials and concluded that with some modifications the production lines could run with plastic bottles. Following a tender and supplier selection process and a series of negotiations, a new plastic bottle supplier was given the contract to supply plastic bottles to replace the previous glass versions. Production was switched to plastic.

There was minimal internal resistance to the change. New, plastic-bottled versions of the same product appeared on supermarket shelves, with the same recognizable look as the old glass version. Consumers briefly noticed the change but didn't seem to care and there was no detriment to sales. In fact, as time went by, sales increased because the move to plastic opened up possibilities to introduce new larger-capacity bottles in plastic and sell more product. The organization made an annual multimillion-euro saving. All in all, the project was a success.

Breakthrough improvements don't just happen, and often lie hidden in blind spots such as 'We've always done it that way'. Breakthroughs need to be hunted down with determination and the will to challenge. Spotting break-throughs requires an open mind and immersion in every conceivable piece of knowledge about the category. And even when breakthroughs are spotted, the battle to overcome resistance to change will most likely begin and could stand in the way of realizing them.

# Pillar 2: Customer focus

A good barman remembers your name, he knows when to offer a refill, when to chat and when to leave you alone to your thoughts – not that I've spent that much time sitting in bars! Customer focus means understanding who your customers are and engaging with them to understand and respond to their needs and desires. In category management, customer focus is about the ongoing ability of purchasing to do this throughout the process.

Purchasing has many internal customers, and this pillar is about how we engage with these, but it is equally about how we contribute to *satisfying* our external customers. Customer focus in category management requires some sort of engagement or connection with all customers, whether directly or together with other functions, to understand their needs, desires, issues and concerns, and respond with a sourcing strategy that addresses these.

## *Engaging with internal customers*

Consider a purchasing department that negotiates a better price but this prize involves switching suppliers or changing specification. If this is done in isolation there will most likely be rebellion by the internal customers and users who have not been consulted. Resistance to change will reign supreme and users will find every reason to demonstrate that the change is not working. However, if the internal customers are actively involved in the process of change from the outset, they will own it; and thus any compromises or difficulties required to secure the results gained will be agreed and accepted by all.

If the category being worked on is 'temporary labour', then customer focus here would require us asking: Who uses it? Who are the people involved? Who controls it? Who pays for it? Understanding the needs of the business is a foundation for sourcing strategically, and the needs are expressed through your internal customers. A lower hourly rate for temporary labour is good, but if it doesn't comply with the regulatory requirements of human resources and involves more work for operations staff, the savings are soon lost.

It is important to note here that the category management approach is unlikely to meet every expressed desire of every internal customer. Different customers have different needs, and these often conflict, while some customers struggle to express their needs. There is no magic wand to create the perfect sourcing solution. The aim is to understand internal customers and involve ⁄

them in the sourcing process, challenging where appropriate and agreeing compromise to make sure requirements are balanced and that the solution works.

## Engaging with external customers

For external customers it is unusual and often inappropriate for purchasing departments to start talking directly with the end customer. Indeed, the marketing and sales functions that typically interface with the end customer would most likely have concerns about such an approach. External customer focus in category management is about working internally with the people who interface with the customer, typically sales and marketing, in order to understand that customer's needs and desires and build sourcing strategies based upon these.

There is one final point here. Customer focus extends beyond understanding and responding to internal and external customers' needs. As we have already seen, if you find a way to connect end-customer desires and aspirations with supply chain possibilities, then an extremely powerful connection is effected that can make a dramatic contribution to the business. Understanding the end-to-end value chain is therefore core to realizing customer focus.

As Cezar Ritz said: 'The customer is never wrong. They may be misguided, stubborn, ill-informed, rude and obstructive, but they are never wrong.'

# Pillar 3: Cross-functional teams that work

A large part of category management is centred on teamwork across the business, and there is a simple reason for this. If category management is only a purchasing initiative it will almost certainly fail. If one person from purchasing tries to drive change, the wider organization will probably have little appetite for it, especially for hard changes.

Cross-functional teams are therefore teams comprising representatives from the relevant functions across the organization, with a team leader who is probably the purchasing category manager. Experience in some organizations suggests that for category management to be successful it is necessary to avoid using language that might suggest purchasing is 'leading', as this can have a negative effect, especially if purchasing is still perceived as a tactical support function which has yet to prove itself in any other form.

The reality here is that purchasing must lead the category teams, as it is the function best placed to do so, assuming the individuals involved have the skills to do this. However, changing the language can defuse potential concerns; using words such as 'coordinator' or 'facilitator' can be less emotive.

In the breakthrough bottle example it was clear that the powerful breakthrough was only possible because it came from a team comprising representatives from the internal departments who had a major interest in the area of spend, ie bottles. Production was responsible for using the products on the shop floor and ensuring that production flowed successfully. Marketing was responsible for how the product looked and was perceived by the end customer. It was only by working with these two key departments that the breakthrough was possible, despite initial resistance to the change.

Typically, cross-functional teams will begin with little interest in the project purpose, they will fight with each other, do the wrong work badly and generally stir up problems. But as the team settles they will also be the people who begin to understand the power of the project and who begin to work together, who uncover the data which is needed, who have the best breakthrough ideas and, most importantly, who will support and drive the implementation. They will take the ideas back to their own and other departments and, after weeks or months of complaining about the time wasted on category management, will become evangelists for change. The category manager must therefore understand and be able to attend to the human side of team formation and development.

The size of the team is important. Too small, and the wider organization may not be fully represented or there may be insufficient resources to work through the process. Too large, and the team becomes unwieldy and unable to make good progress or take decisions. The ideal size of a category management cross-functional team is between three and eight people. If the project is so massive or covers such a wide category or geographical area that many people want to be involved, then the team should be structured as a lead team with sub-teams working on specific, defined activities.

It is also important that the team members who represent the wider business are carefully selected. Of course, the everyday pressures and resource limitations of any organization will present challenges, and participation in a category management team requires a good degree of commitment for the duration of the project. Success of category management depends on the ability of the organization to make the right resources available for the task. Cross-functional team members should ideally:

- have a sufficient understanding of the goods or services within the category and how they are used within the organization;
- be able to commit to spending sufficient time supporting the category management project;
- have the full support of their managers or senior teams;
- be capable of acting as ambassadors for the rest of their department, actively communicating between the category team and the wider business;
- be strong enough to challenge the function they are representing when they are convinced a breakthrough opportunity is worth progressing.

For example, a cross-functional team for a 'printed packaging' category might include representatives from R&D, shipping, production and marketing. It might be led by the purchasing category manager and supported by an external facilitator.

The commitment required by team members for category management projects is significant. For a large global or regional category project that lasts 12 months, team members working on the project could expect to need to commit, on average, around half a day a week to the project. This might typically comprise:

- participation in workshops during the early phases of the project – each one might be a day in duration;
- support to gather internal, market and supplier data and information;
- progression of quick-win opportunities;
- internal communications and stakeholder engagement;
- soliciting input from members' own functions to identify current and future needs and wants around the category of spend;
- work on actions between meetings.

With this level of commitment it is clear that organizations embarking on category management must secure the right cross-functional level of resource. This will undoubtedly mean that other activities need to be sacrificed to make room. Getting cross-functional team members to provide this sort of commitment requires active and visible support and endorsement from senior management across the business. It also requires individuals to have some sort of imperative and desire to get involved. It is my experience that people will often claim they are too busy and have no capacity for a project unless they want to do it or stand to gain in some way, eg financially or in terms of career progression, new opportunities etc. Then, somehow, people find the time.

If all this still sounds impossible, then consider your own viewpoint. If the organization views category management as just a purchasing-led initiative and just one of the many initiatives within the business, then resources required are unlikely to be made available. However, if the organization views category management as a primary company-wide initiative to add dramatic value across the business, actively involving the entire business, then support and resources are more likely to be provided. Organizations that fully embrace category management across the entire business and make it 'the way we buy' are the ones that tend to be successful. Those that are serious about it incorporate category management objectives in the personal objectives of individuals both within and outside purchasing, at all levels, and even link success to personal bonuses or rewards.

A direct consequence is that simply convincing senior management that category management is a good idea is not enough. Instead, the initiative needs to be robustly marketed and communicated across the business. Executive teams must understand the power of the process and embrace it, making it an organizational priority and directing resources accordingly.

The entire business must understand the concept at a basic level and the need to get involved, thus requiring effective internal marketing and communications.

Progress and success stories must be well communicated on a continuous basis so as to maintain the momentum and help create an internal desire to be associated with success when it comes.

Cross-functional category management teams require training and development. As a concept, category management may initially appear complex and difficult to understand. Furthermore, until you have actually done it for real, gathered the data, gained insights from the analysis tools, driven in hard changes etc, it is hard to appreciate the true power of the process. New cross-functional team members, who have not seen category management before but who have been instructed by managers to 'get involved', could be forgiven for wondering why they have to do this instead of all the important things waiting back at their desks. Training for the cross-functional team members in category management is therefore essential. A high-level introduction to the process combined with ongoing short bursts of training in specific tools or techniques as the team works through the process is usually enough.

The required competencies of the category manager (the individual leading the team) should not be underestimated. Typically this person will be from purchasing and clearly this individual needs to be a capable category management practitioner who has undergone intensive training and perhaps some initial coaching. However, the individual also needs the skills to lead a team. While they may also possess the softer skills from previous roles, my experience is that purchasing people frequently do not naturally have the right skill set for the task. This is largely because before category management the role of purchasing in many organizations did not require these skills in any abundance.

The required skill set additional to the core purchasing and category management ability includes:

- motivational skills and understanding of team dynamics;
- facilitation skills, both as leader of and participant in meetings;
- meeting process skills (eg facilitation techniques such as meta-planning, brown-paper planning, brainstorming etc);
- listening skills;
- meeting management skills;
- coaching skills;
- project management skills;
- action planning and prioritization skills;
- presentational skills.

Individuals can be taught these skills to a degree through training, and can learn the repertoire of tactics on which to begin to practise. But becoming proficient in these areas is simply a case of doing it, doing it again and doing it some more. In addition to training, ongoing coaching is essential so that category managers can practise, with some support mechanism, leading a category team for real.

Part of leading a cross-functional team is about understanding team dynamics. New teams, ie groups of people who have not worked together in a particular combination or way before, do not instantly become great teams. This only happens over time and with great effort, almost certainly with some pain involved. Bruce Tuckman (1965) describes this effect as the four phases of team development. He suggests that teams naturally go through four phases in sequence: 'forming', 'storming', 'norming' and 'performing'. This is a good model that describes what a team must go through to get to the point where it does great things. There is no shortcut here, but hard work, good communication and lots of support to both the team and individuals can help.

Finally, the composition of the cross-functional team may not stay the same throughout the life of the project. People may leave, conflicting requirements of the business may necessitate a change of a team member, or there may be a member who is not contributing or not fitting in and needs to be changed. Apart from these occasions it may be entirely appropriate to undergo a wholesale review of the team part-way through the project. At the outset the team will be focused on gathering information, analysing data, understanding the marketplace, looking for opportunities and determining the most appropriate sourcing strategy. The project requires team members who can make the best contribution in these areas. The later part of the project will be about implementing this strategy, driving change in the business, setting up new supply arrangements, measuring supplier performance and getting to a steady state where the strategy is implemented and the relationship with the suppliers moves into continuous improvement. It is entirely possible that the project will require new and different contributors for this stage, and these may be people who are best placed to turn a strategy and plan into reality, who are good at making change happen or who will ultimately own and manage the new supplier relationship.

# Pillar 4: Facts and data

Many people make decisions that are not fully rational. In organizations, decisions are made in many ways; for example, a committee might take a vote, the CEO might say what is to happen, or a decision may even be taken on the flip of a coin. In some cases decision making may be entirely based upon one individual's instinct regarding what needs to happen. There are many global corporations that have become successful as a result of one individual having the courage to take bold steps and make high-risk decisions based upon little more than a hunch.

In large organizations there is often little opportunity for entrepreneurial decision making based on instinct. Accountabilities to shareholders, risk of litigation, and fiduciary duties of directors mean that senior individuals taking decisions will be reluctant to act without some sort of assurance they are doing the right thing. This assurance is often gained through consultation with peers, following what others have done, or from facts and data.

Making a decision when armed with good facts and data is probably the most powerful way to take the risk out of the decision. Notable leaders are rarely quick to make decisions but hold back until the latest moment when the decision must be made. This allows them to accumulate the up-to-the-minute facts and data that will help ensure that the decision is correct. Similarly, within category management, facts and data help to de-risk decision making. Before signing off sourcing strategies that recommend new and previously untried sources of supply or changes to specification, senior managers and stakeholders would almost certainly want to understand the risk of things going wrong and the actions to mitigate those risks or provide contingency. If a production director agrees to a new source of supply to cut costs, and the supply fails, causing the production line to stop, the finger of blame will not be pointed at purchasing first but at the production director. In the example of the breakthrough bottle, the production department would only agree to the change once it had run thorough tests to ensure the new plastic bottle would work.

However, it doesn't stop there. Facts and data also help to make compelling cases for change. If a senior individual within an organization is blocking a change, perhaps because of covert factors such as what they stand to lose, historical relationships or simple reluctance to change, then facts and data can provide an unarguable basis to support the change. This was illustrated in the breakthrough bottle example, when the facts and data associated with the potential savings were so huge that they could not be ignored.

There is another reason why facts and data are important to organizations and category management. This is to do with the actual process of collecting facts and data. When consultants are brought into a business they are often unpopular and know little about the specific situation. Their first job is to collect plenty of data. The action of asking for the data and information helps to win people over and to understand different stakeholders' views. By bringing together different elements of data, the power of understanding and analysis is increased. Presenting ideas based on solid data becomes much easier and much more persuasive than presenting the same ideas based on hunches or intuition. The fact that the consultants have had the time and space to talk to people in the organization and involve them in the course of data collection means that those people feel involved and included, and so the process of minimizing future resistance to change has begun.

Facts and data play a vital role in three areas within category management:

- de-risking decision making;
- providing compelling business cases for change;
- providing a reason to engage with the business and key stakeholders and get them involved.

The collection of facts and data runs through the entire category management process. As we shall see in later chapters, the second stage of the process contains a section that is dedicated to the collection of facts and data associated with suppliers and the supply market, and with how internally goods or services are used and bought.

# CATEGORY MANAGEMENT IN THE PUBLIC SECTOR

Some people tell me that category management doesn't lend itself to public sector procurement. Those making these claims typically suggest 'things are different here', citing regulation or different/unique objectives as the reasons behind the claim. Yet others suggest category management works and can point to projects that have delivered significant benefit. The commonly held belief that category management doesn't translate to the public sector is in fact incorrect and one that is increasingly being dispelled by public sector organizations who are embracing category management as a key enabler to deliver cost efficiencies.

Category management and the underlying principles outlined in this chapter are just as relevant in the public sector as in a commercial organization; however, category management does need to be applied slightly differently or it will fail to deliver.

In a public sector organization the strategic imperatives are different. First there are different objectives – organizations are guided by such needs as being able to demonstrate value for taxpayers' money, transparency of spend or improving outcomes for the resident, patient, passenger etc. Second; procurement approaches are required to operate within a regulated framework that invokes strict rules around how contracts are awarded, designed to demonstrate transparency in all engagements with suppliers, to minimize corruption and to drive fairness to suppliers. Sometimes governmental legislation will demand positive discrimination towards suppliers in certain minority groups. In the United States a programme of 'Supplier Diversity' demands that a certain percentage of spend by public sector organizations is with minority suppliers. In the EU similar programmes can be found with government targets to place a certain amount of business with SMEs (Small to Medium-sized Enterprises) or minority-owned businesses. In the UK The Social Value Act (2012) requires that the public sector opens up more opportunities for social enterprises (not-for-profit organizations with primarily social aims) to win bids for delivery of public services and to consider how what is bought might improve the social, economic and environmental well-being of the area.

# EU procurement legislation

Different regulation exists the world over and each is an entire specialism of its own so further reading is recommended here. In Europe, legislation defines the requirements for procurement in public bodies. Directives and regulations collectively known as *EU Procurement Legislation* are founded upon the four pillars of European Union Law. These are: subsidiarity (the principle of needs and problems being dealt with at the most immediate or local country level, typically through local supporting, not subservient, bodies that are part of the whole); transparency; equal treatment; and pro-portionality (ensuring the correct balance of the different but related needs that must be satisfied). At the same time it seeks to ensure that the public sector is pursuing simplification, value for money, sustainability, innovation, efficiency, opportunities for SMEs, and growth whilst maintaining the single market and complying with World Trade Organization rules.

EU Procurement Legislation governs any governmental or public pur-chasing entity for expenditure above certain published thresholds. In this case the opportunity must be advertised in the *Official Journal of the European Union* (*OJEU*). Prospective suppliers can then register their interest and potentially be invited to participate in some form of competitive bidding exercise according to one of a number of set procedures.

# Adapting category management for the public sector

The various legislative obligations that shape how procurement exists and operates within the public sector drive a unique process and approach that seeks to preserve these principles. If category management is to drive worth-while results whilst maintaining compliance it needs to be deployed slightly differently. Merely 'bolting it on' to an existing bidding/tendering and con-tracting approach will do little and results will be suboptimal – it is just tendering and contracting within a category framework. Instead category management needs to be applied with rigour to work up breakthrough sourcing strategies that then inform and shape the tendering and contracting activity. In essence it means spending more time early on within a category management project to be certain about what we want to buy, to have a precise definition of what is required and to determine in advance how we are going to contract for it so at the point we approach the market we can clearly set out our requirements so all those interested can have equal opportunity. It also demands different approaches to supplier engagement and dialogue. For category management in the commercial sector it is often normal practice to engage with suppliers at any stage of the process to solicit information or ideas that might contribute to the formation of a sourcing strategy, prior to the market being formally approached. Whilst there is still provision for this in public sector, it must follow a strict procedure to manage this competitive dialogue and ensure fairness and transparency to all.

There are, in fact several key areas where our deployment of category management needs to be different when used in the public sector:

- *Requirements definition.* In the commercial sector the definition of requirements for what we will go to market to source might be shaped, formed and refined by engagement with internal customers as well as with suppliers to understand what might be possible. Suppliers might be engaged at any time in pursuit of this goal. However in the public sector we are less free to engage suppliers in this way. Instead we either need to develop our requirements and be absolutely clear and precise about what they are before we approach the market, or we must follow a strict 'competitive dialogue' process. Here any dialogue with suppliers must be fair and transparent to all, with no scope to favour a supplier, and this extends to discussions around capabilities or what might be possible. An engagement with one supplier must be replicated identically with all other suppliers under consideration, as if all were in their own swimming lanes progressing forward individually, but identically in terms of discussion and engagement.

- *Running a competitive bidding process.* In the commercial world a range of approaches can be found for running a competitive bidding process and selecting a supplier. In the public sector what happens here is guided by strict procedures set within the legislation.

- *Negotiation.* Hard 'dog-eat-dog' negotiations can be standard practice for many commercial companies. It may be 'fair game' for a competitive bidding process to be followed by additional negotiation until the most favourable outcome is secured; suppliers might even be played off against each other. There is little to prevent extreme negotiations with what is appropriate tending to be determined only by corporate policy or culture, the personal beliefs and ethics of the individual or the degree to which a future relationship is needed. Many negotiation approaches found in the commercial sector would fall foul of historical public sector procurement legislation as they are in conflict with the underpinning pillars of equal treatment, transparency and proportionality. However in 2014, changes in EU Procurement Legislation have moved some way forward with the introduction of new negotiated procedures.

- *Driving improvement and managing the supplier relationship.* In the commercial sector we might elect to manage the supplier in some way, perhaps to drive improvements ongoing or even to build a collaborative relationship with a supplier that is of strategic importance. Such improvements or relationships may build and be developed over time. In the public sector, things cannot easily change from that which was bid for. Therefore the concept of driving ongoing improvements or building a future supplier relationship is at odds with the legislative provision. Instead things need to be at arm's length and fair so if we need to drive improvement or want some sort of collaborative relationship the nature of this and the way it will work and be measured must be defined from the outset so all suppliers can bid to have a chance of being part of a defined way of engagement. It cannot build and become different from that defined when suppliers bid for the work.

Some of these may seem to be quite burdensome. Opponents here might argue that public sector legislation restricts best-practice procurement and drives suboptimal results – making it harder to create a competitive tension between suppliers. However, advocates for EU procurement legislation would counter that it has a much bigger agenda than the needs of an individual entity and seeks to balance good procurement with a wider social and country progression. In other words, it is a necessary part of the bigger picture.

It is in fact possible to balance both here and deliver highly effective procurement whilst complying with public procurement legislation. However, an advanced level of capability is required to be confident in ensuring compliance. It also means those leading public sector buying functions need to guide teams to think more about the most effective route through, how to make the legislation work for them, and working to prevent buyers from only following the safe route through. For example it is easy to default to using a contracting approach based upon running a tender or competitive bid process instead of maximizing the opportunity using the full range of compliant contracting approaches available.

# PURCHASING CATEGORY MANAGEMENT IN RETAIL

As we have already seen, category management originates from the world of retail, as a strategic approach to manage, increase sales and maximize profit. It can also help to reduce competition between brands that might be unfavourable to the retailer. Whilst the retailers' shelves might hold the full range of brands, providing clarity to the customer or guiding the customer to certain brands can maximize profit. But what about retailers who have adopted this 'customer-facing' category management, and who want to adopt category management in purchasing? Retailers need to be highly effective at purchasing in order to secure good margins and compete. Those who are good at this practise both forms of category management and the two are integrally connected and drive the entire business. If that sounds familiar then it is the retail world that has long since identified the need to connect *sourcing* with *satisfying,* informing and being driven by corporate *strategy.* The rest of us can learn some lessons here.

At the heart of purchasing category management in retail is an exceptionally strong end-customer focus. This is much more than simply understanding what the end customer might need or want, but rather positively informs, shapes and determines the purchasing category strategy together with a pro-active strategy to maximize sales and profit including:

- how the customer will be conditioned to buy (eg shelf positioning, promotions, layered rebates, point of sale);
- range management to present the customer with the optimum choice so as to maximize profit;
- how profit can be maximized.

Retail category management provides a means to structure these elements whilst putting the customer at its centre. Whilst marketing category management and purchasing category management are two separate approaches for many organizations, in retail they are inextricably joined up. In practice this means that when the sourcing strategy is determined there are some additional factors and considerations that need to shape the strategy which include:

- the customer-facing market landscape, segmentation, trends and competitors;
- customer needs and preferences, now and anticipated;
- options to maximize profit, price policy, range management, customer conditioning and promotion into the sourcing strategy;
- the possible selection of a 'supplier partner' as a category champion who will help maximize sales and profit across the entire customer-facing category in return for prime positioning;
- logistics and ways to optimize the supply chain;
- negotiation, supplier selection, contract planning and ongoing supplier management and measurement based upon ability to deliver end-customer-centric strategy.

### Chapter 2 summary

Recap on the key points from this chapter:

1 Category management is built upon the foundations of adopting a strategic (rather than tactical) approach to sourcing, understanding and managing the marketplace and the ability to drive organizational change.

2 There are four pillars within category management; approaches and principles that are rooted in practice based upon what has been found to work. The pillars are breakthrough thinking, customer focus (internal and external), cross-functional team working and using facts and data to develop robust sourcing strategies.

3 Category management is appropriate to, and can deliver significant benefits in both the commercial and public sectors. However, in the public sector regulation and different objectives mean category management deployment needs to be approached slightly differently to ensure compliance with relevant procurement legislation.

4 Purchasing category management applied in retail operates slightly differently to category management in other sectors as it opens up the opportunity to deploy a true end-to-end category management approach, with sourcing strategy shaped and determined by end-customer needs and preferences as well as how profit can be maximized.

# Laying the groundwork for success

This chapter explores what needs to happen prior to embarking on a category management programme within an organization including the process of identifying opportunities and prioritizing which categories to work on. We examine the time dimension associated with category management, and specifically the discrete phases or stages associated with the process. Finally we consider the different routes through the process.

Pathway questions addressed in this chapter:

**2** What is category management and how can it add benefit?

**3** What are the right categories to work on?

**4** How can I identify and prioritize potential opportunity for each category so I can direct my resources accordingly?

**5** What is required in order to successfully adopt and implement category management?

# BEFORE YOU START

## Creating the right conditions for category management

Effective category management requires a number of things to be in place before you can begin deploying the process. I have seen enthusiastic individuals experienced in category management join a company that has not yet embraced the concept, and start to attempt to use the approach on discrete areas of spend alone. The results are usually suboptimal as the buy-in from the organization has not been established, so cross-functional teams are not willing or permitted to spend time on the project and the potential benefits are not understood or believed.

Category management projects must therefore be part of a wider category management programme, properly set up, with full support from across the business, and with the following firmly in place:

- A complete category segmentation, mapping the categories the organization buys and that reflects the market-facing nature of what the organization spends.

- An opportunity analysis across all categories to identify the early, high-level view of those categories where effort will be worthwhile (covered next).

- A prioritized category programme plan, based on the opportunity analysis and providing a sequenced schedule of all the categories that are to be worked on based upon available resources.

- Some form of governance structure including reporting, communications and benefit tracking (we will explore governance more fully later).

- Agreement, buy-in and support from senior executive level down, with cross-functional resources available and instructed to get involved.

## Category segmentation and opportunity analysis

Category opportunity analysis is about identifying what market-facing categories to work on. It is important to direct precious resources at the right categories in order to achieve the required business outcomes, whether that is delivering savings or other value. It is usually important to demonstrate benefits early on.

Category opportunity analysis takes place before commencement of one or more category management project, in order to determine which categories or sub-categories hold the greatest potential or might deliver benefits easily. It is a tool typically used by a senior team ahead of kicking off category management within the organization and ahead of assigning people to work on specific categories. The output from category opportunity analysis enables the organization to create a programme plan, matched against available resources for each category project and the overall sequencing of projects in the near term. This cannot be a precise science, but rather a macro-level activity designed to help guide an organization to move forward and work on the categories that are likely to be the most impactful. Later, for individual category projects, opportunity analysis is repeated at a category-specific level with the aim of verifying the opportunity in a more informed way.

Category opportunity analysis is best accomplished in a workshop, ideally with good facilitation, and follows a five-step process culminating in the completion of the opportunity analysis matrix shown in Figure 3.1.

## Step 1: Category segmentation

In Chapter 2 we explored the determination of categories culminating in the production of a category map based upon the market-facing nature of individual categories. This forms the starting point for our opportunity analysis. Remember we will work, and apply category management, at the level of individual market-facing categories. However, it often makes sense for a category manager to be assigned a project at the umbrella category level. For example the umbrella category 'bulk chemicals' contains different market-facing categories; some share common suppliers, some don't. We therefore conduct this macro opportunity analysis at the umbrella category level, together with all other umbrella categories and taking a view on the individual market-facing categories that comprise each, with the aim of identifying which category projects the organization wants to prioritize. Later, as the agreed category projects get under way, each category manager would then repeat the opportunity analysis step, but this time focusing on the individual categories that comprise the overall umbrella category and prioritizing which ones to work on first and in what sequence the remainder should be handled.

**FIGURE 3.1** 'Pre-programme' category segmentation and opportunity analysis process

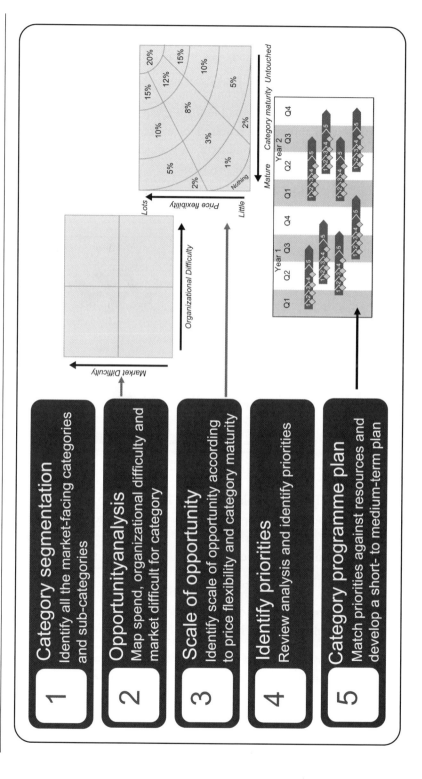

## Step 2: Opportunity analysis

Once we have mapped our categories, we can conduct a high-level opportunity analysis (OA) to identify which ones might be worth further investigation. In its most simple form opportunity analysis is about comparing the potential benefits that might be possible for a given category against the ease of implementation and what is required to realize this (Figure 3.2). This simple tool could be enough to conduct a very quick and dirty classification of categories so as to identify the priorities.

**FIGURE 3.2**   A basic opportunity analysis matrix

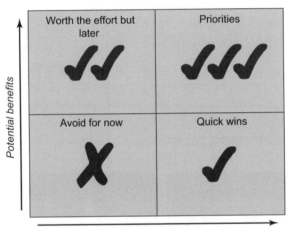

Potential benefits here would be savings in the form of a reduction in price and cost; however, it is important to also consider potential savings from efficiency gains, reduced risk or added value from the supply chain. Using the tool effectively may require separation of cost or price benefits from other added-value benefits. When doing an OA it is important to be clear about the type of benefits that are possible and the alignment of these benefits with overall organizational goals.

Ease of implementation, however, encompasses two dimensions:

**1** How easy it would be to effect the change within the organization. If the change can be rolled out quickly, with little or no resistance from the internal stakeholders or users, then it is an easy change. The reality here is that for complex changes that affect many people, there is a level of organizational difficulty that prevents change from happening easily, or at least without considerable effort.

**2** How easy the marketplace is. This is often referred to as market difficulty and is about the ease with which you can source something within the marketplace. The best test that can be applied is to consider how easy it is to switch suppliers. If you are buying basic stationery or office supplies, then if one supplier is not performing it is easy to switch to another; the marketplace offers many potential alternatives, each with comparable products and levels of service. But if you are buying government-accredited nuclear waste transportation services, then you are unlikely to find a very long list of such suppliers readily. The market here is difficult.

Having considered these two dimensions, it is possible to plot categories within the OA matrix and then determine how to proceed. There is little logic in beginning by spending effort on categories in the 'Avoid for now' quadrant (it is possible that these may be worth some effort, but perhaps later, once all the other benefits have been obtained and the organization has become used to category management).

An example of a completed OA for apparel categories is given in Figure 3.3. This clearly helps to identify visually where we should be putting our effort:

**FIGURE 3.3** Using the basic opportunity analysis for apparel categories

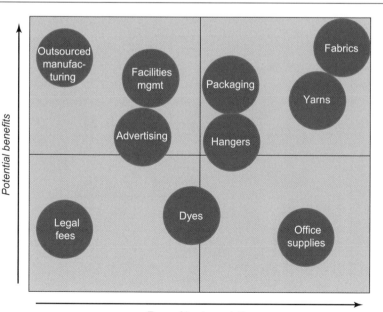

*Potential benefits*

*Ease of implementation*

fabrics, yarns, hangers and packaging represent the priorities for our immediate attention. In addition, there is a series of other projects that can follow
these, as well as a quick win. We would also put to one side for now a couple
of further categories.

A drawback with this use of the OA is that it is not possible to understand from the completed matrix what would prevent a category from being
'easy'. If we can understand what drives this difficulty for any given category
positioned on the far left of the matrix, we can consider if we can influence
it. If the market is difficult we might be able to change it if we have significant leverage or scale, but often the market difficulty is a given. If the
difficulty is coming from the organization, then it can be altered with the
right change programme and executive support. Furthermore, whilst we
might consider the potential savings possible to plot a given category on the
matrix, this OA does not show the spend for each category which prevents
us being able to easily explain the logic behind our assessment.

A more useful, yet more involved form of OA can be used here to gain a
further insight and provide a more compelling visual explanation; this is
shown in Figure 3.4. Here we separate out 'ease of implementation' factors

**FIGURE 3.4**    OA plotting market and organizational difficulty
together with spend

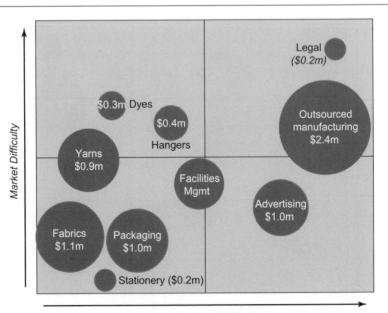

and instead plot organizational difficulty against market difficulty. Then we plot our categories onto the matrix, using different size bubbles so that the size of each bubble represents the relative size of the spend in that area. Note at this point we have not quantified the scale of benefits, and that is part of Step 3.

## Step 3: Scale of opportunity

Step 3 is about quantifying the scale and nature of category opportunity that is possible. This is an important step as most organizations will hold some sort of expectation that the projected return on investment of time and money in a significant category project can be identified and quantified.

We begin to quantify the scale of opportunity by considering the degree of savings in price that might be possible. So what is that magic number? What is the percentage of savings that category management can deliver? Of course it all depends. As we saw in Chapter 1, it depends primarily upon the quality of deployment of category management within the organization. Assuming that the organization has embraced all the components of good category management, the scale of price reduction benefits possible for an individual category depends upon two factors:

- *Price flexibility* – the scope to secure a price reduction. There is price flexibility if the category features lots of 'added value' elements, the market is not overly competitive (ie high margins) or there is little or no regulation.

- *Category maturity* – the degree to which this category has already been worked on and how recently. The more work that has been done, the more the potential opportunities are diminished. Here we need to consider the degree of understanding of the market, the process and supply chain that exists and how much purchasing thinking has been applied here.

By considering these two factors together for a given category it is possible to make an assessment of the potential savings benefits that are possible. This is given in Figure 3.5, which shows different savings percentages. This model allows us to identify the potential savings possible by considering if price flexibility and category maturity are low, medium or high. There is a health warning here, as determining the size of the potential benefits is not an exact science, but rather an assessment based upon experience. There is no reference point I can give for these potential savings percentages, and these are not based upon any empirical study. However, they are based

**FIGURE 3.5**    Identifying the scale of potential savings considering price flexibility and category maturity

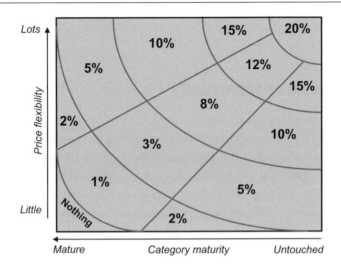

upon years of doing this and what seems to have been possible for category projects given the two variables. I have developed and used this model for many years and it just seems to be a pretty solid predictor of what might be possible.

There is one further dimension to the scale of opportunity and that is the identification of benefits other than price – the value opportunity. This is the scope for any additional value such as reduction in risk or increased efficiency, effectiveness, speed to market or access to innovation for this category. Whilst cost and savings drive most businesses, there are many situations where other forms of value are more or at least equally important. Therefore these should be identified. If they can be quantified in some way then this is great and that number can be summed with the predicted price saving to give a definitive benefits number. However, this is rarely possible and so instead the value opportunity should be a simple list of what value might be possible beyond price reductions.

## Step 4: Identify priorities

Within Step 4 we consolidate the opportunity and scale of benefit analysis. We can show the potential savings on our OA matrix by adding a 'savings segment' to indicate what might be possible for each category (Figure 3.6). This visual representation begins to become a very useful means to identify

**FIGURE 3.6**   Mapping the scale of opportunity for each category

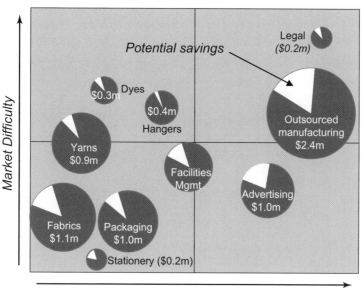

priorities and provides the basis for discussion around which categories to progress with. We can summarize each component of our opportunity analysis, including the value opportunity, using a table such as that shown in Figure 3.7 where we can also record the conclusion of discussions around priorities. This process is highly effective and clears the mist that surrounds knowing where to start, helping to provide a clear way ahead. When I've worked this with teams embarking on category management, typically in a half-day workshop, it has served to transform thinking, moving a team from a state of not quite knowing where to begin to being really clear about what to do next.

## Step 5: Category programme plan

Finally, once we have prioritized the categories we wish to work on, and matched these against our available resources, it is possible to develop a category programme plan for the categories we will work on and the sequencing of these. It is also possible to then link this plan to individual milestones within the process of such stage reviews and category workshops (covered in the next section). This is an important part of the arrangements

**FIGURE 3.7** Summary opportunity analysis matrix

| Category | Spend | Organizational difficulty | Market difficulty | Price flexibility | Category maturity | Savings % | Projected savings $ | Value opportunity | Priority |
|---|---|---|---|---|---|---|---|---|---|
| Fabrics | $1.1m | Low | Low | Medium | Low | 10% | $110k | Improve supply chain and reduce CSR risk | 3rd |
| Office supplies | $0.2m | Low | Low | High | Low | 20% | $40k | Simplify ordering process | |
| Packaging | $1.0m | Low-Med | Low | Low | Low | 5% | $50k | Standardize packaging | |
| Yarns | $0.9m | Low | Medium | Medium | Medium | 8% | $72k | Reduce CSR risk | 5th |
| Facilities management | $0.8m | Medium | Medium | High | Medium | 10% | $80k | Improve service levels and overall effectiveness | 4th |
| Hangers | $0.4m | Medium | Medium-High | Low | High | 1% | $40k | None identified | |
| Dyes | $0.3m | Low-Medium | Medium-High | Medium | Medium | 8% | $24k | Reduce CSR environmental | |
| Advertising | $1.0m | Medium-High | Low | High | Low | 20% | $200k | Reduce need to run a bid process each time | 2nd |
| Outsourced manufacturing | $2.4m | High | Medium-High | High | Low | 20% | $480k | Reduce risk and secure innovation | 1st |
| Legal | $0.2m | High | High | Medium | Low | 10% | $200k | Move towards standard frameworks | |

required for any organization seeking to manage a category management programme effectively. We will return to this later when we explore category management governance.

# THE 5i CATEGORY MANAGEMENT PROCESS

## A circular process

Category management is a process that involves completing many discrete activities in an overall sequence. Some steps of these activities are sequential and need to be completed before moving on, others happen in parallel, and some run throughout the entire process. Overall, category management has a start point and potentially an end point and is fundamentally a serial process. However, it is important to recognize that, as with most improvement initiatives, you never quite reach the nirvana that is true excellence, and there are always further opportunities to secure additional value from the supply chain.

The process should therefore be viewed as circular. When maturity is reached and improvements have been realized, there comes a point when it is appropriate to start the process again. This is because the rest of the world, markets and organizations are constantly changing around you while you are deploying category management. However, as the process is repeated on a single category a level of maturity tends to develop and there is a shift in the way the process is used. For example, relationships with suppliers may need to become more strategic and be managed more closely and the focus may shift away from category management to Supplier Relationship Management. The tools within category management therefore continue to be used but in different ways to achieve different outcomes.

There are five separate phases or stages of category management, and I'm going to call these the five I's. They are Initiation, Insight, Innovation, Implementation and Improvement (Figure 3.8).

There are many variations on this theme. Organizations and purchasing consultancies using category management have developed variants, each with different labels and numbers of stages. Some have three, some four, some even seven or eight, each accompanied by claims that it is 'the right approach'. The reality is that it really doesn't matter how many stages there

**FIGURE 3.8**    Five I's of category management

are or indeed what labels are used for each stage, provided the fundamental category management process is largely followed. Critical success factors here are:

- only one process should be in place within an organization;
- everyone should understand it and actively embrace it;
- the language of the process should be relevant to the organization;
- the process should broadly follow and reflect the fundamentals of category management, change management and best-practice business improvement.

This 5i methodology is well established and proven, and it has been adopted and is in mainstream use by big-name companies the world over.

## Moving through the five stages

Before we explore the tools and approaches within each stage in detail, it is necessary to explain how organizations need to move through the five stages. We have already seen that cross-functional working is one of the pillars of category management. The cross-functional team is the small group of appropriate representatives from across the business who have been tasked by their departments, with executive support, to work together on a category project. However, effective cross-functional working is more than simply getting a team together; rather, it requires a planned and structured approach for the team to engage in. The most effective and proven method of achieving this is to conduct a series of workshops at points throughout the process. These workshops act as focal points for all of the cross-functional team activity, each having a separate aim, each requiring the team to work through specific tools and process steps (see Table 3.1), and each identifying actions for team members to complete before the next workshop (see Figure 3.9).

**TABLE 3.1** Content and structure of cross-functional workshops

| Workshop | Typical areas covered |
| --- | --- |
| **Workshop 1**<br>Kick-off | • Executive sponsor kick-off and inspirational message.<br>• Defining category scope and boundaries.<br>• Gaining common understanding amongst team of the category, current issues and opportunities.<br>• Team formation, perhaps using a team-building activity.<br>• Team define how they will work together.<br>• Identifying the key stakeholders, who needs to be involved or who can help and agreeing actions for engaging them.<br>• Developing a plan for communication of the project to the wider business.<br>• Carrying out some early analysis and insight.<br>• Identifying the 'early view' of the business requirements for this category.<br>• Identifying potential sources of value (value levers review).<br>• Identifying and agreeing actions for any quick-win opportunities to secure early benefit.<br>• Planning the project, including future workshops and activities between them.<br>• Action planning for gathering data ready for second workshop. |
| **Workshop 2**<br>Situation analysis | • Review and sharing of supplier, market and organizational data.<br>• Strategic analysis of data using a variety of tools and techniques.<br>• Developing insights from analysis.<br>• Identifying any new sources of value (value levers review).<br>• Reviewing and updating the business requirements, communications plan and arrangements for stakeholder engagement.<br>• Reviewing progress towards achieving quick wins.<br>• Agreeing new data-gathering actions. |

**TABLE 3.1**    *continued*

| Workshop | Typical areas covered |
|---|---|
| **Workshop 3**<br>Options generation | • Reviewing new data, further strategic analysis and insight.<br>• Summarizing insights and work to date.<br>• Identifying any new sources of value (value levers review)<br>• Identification of the evaluation criteria that will be used to select the strategic sourcing option that represents the best way forward.<br>• Creative 'free-flow' generation of potential strategic sourcing options informed by the insights gained.<br>• Evaluation of the options against the evaluation criteria to select a single option and strategic way forward.<br>• Building the detail behind the chosen option.<br>• Conducting an analysis of risk and potential contingencies associated with a single option.<br>• Developing a high-level plan for implementation.<br>• Agree actions to complete the Source Plan and secure business sign-off.<br>• Review progress towards achieving quick wins.<br>• Reviewing and updating the business requirements, communications plan and arrangements for stakeholder engagement. |
| **Workshop 4**<br>Implementation planning | • Detailed implementation planning including resources required.<br>• Possible team change; new team formation including redefining how the team will work together.<br>• Review progress towards achieving quick wins.<br>• Reviewing and updating the communications plan and arrangements for informing stakeholders.<br>• Identifying potential sources of value (value levers review)<br>• Action planning for ongoing team support of implementation. |

**FIGURE 3.9**   Category management process with workshops

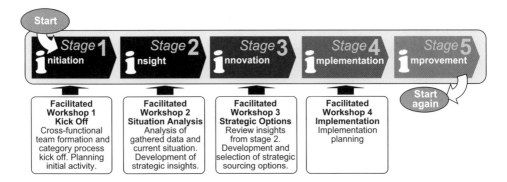

A minimum of four workshops, organized at key points in the process, is typically required. For the workshops to be successful, they should be:

- a day in duration, longer if needed;
- organized well in advance and made as mandatory as possible to maximize participation;
- fully facilitated, ideally by someone other than the category project leader, either using skilled internal support or an external facilitator;
- well structured, with agendas, action planning and output notes.

The cross-functional team members should be tasked with various actions between workshops (eg data collection, stakeholder engagement, etc). Completion of actions is given a high degree of focus, with strong project management and follow-up between meetings to ensure no scope for slippage.

The outputs of the cross-functional workshops form key building blocks for the final sourcing strategy document (called a source plan), with the build of the document beginning right at the outset of the process.

Inspiring the team to make this project a prime focus is an important factor to ensure success. Category managers leading teams therefore need to be equipped with the skills and capability required for team leadership as well as organizing activities to build the team and foster teamwork. They also need to be able to maximize the participation of the team in working through the process. This means the team must be engaged in working key tools and process steps, as opposed to the category manager simply presenting pre-prepared outputs for sign-off. However, category projects are often led by purchasing people who have worked up through the organization and hold senior purchasing roles, focusing on strategic commercial issues, but who have had little experience of leading a team. Here, early leadership training and coaching are essential.

## Reviewing progress

Regular review of category team progress is important to ensure the team is progressing at the required speed and with sufficient process rigour and challenge. Within the process there are four points when it is appropriate to conduct a stage review (see Figure 3.10).

Stage reviews are often used as 'gateways' that cannot be passed through until the work to date has been verified as acceptable. They would therefore typically form part of a bigger governance approach and we will examine such an approach in detail later.

**FIGURE 3.10** Category management process with stage reviews

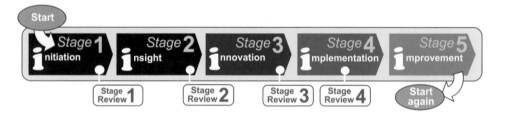

## Realizing the benefits

Projects within organizations often start with a great fanfare and much promise. However, over time things change, other projects come along, new priorities emerge and the competition for precious resources continues to be fierce. In such an environment, projects that take time to deliver results are always at risk of resources being pulled away, or even of cancellation. Maintaining a high profile for the project within the organization, and at executive level, is therefore essential.

Category management projects can take many months to deliver substantial results, so securing some early quick wins is essential in order to create project momentum and demonstrate the potential for a return on the investment in time and effort. The typical benefit profile for category

**FIGURE 3.11**    Category management process with benefit realization

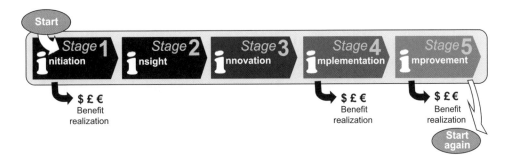

management is shown in Figure 3.11, with some early results then much bigger benefits being realized as the project reaches maturity. These benefits may take many forms and could be achieved from price or cost reductions or other forms of value improvement such as efficiency gains, reduced risk, delivering projects early or enhancing brand value.

It is essential that the benefit profile for category management projects is clearly understood and that there is a balance between pushing for early quick wins versus the more substantial long-term benefits. Many category management projects have failed simply because senior management keep demanding more and more immediate quick-win benefits from the category team and in doing so eliminate the team's capacity to find the bigger break-through benefits. It is also essential that there is a way to measure and agree benefits, ideally using an approach developed and agreed with the finance function. We will explore this in Chapter 9.

## The full process

So we have arrived at the point where we can present the full process, combining everything we have explored so far. The full category management process is as shown in Figure 3.12.

At first glance this may appear complex, but the diagram contains both high-level and supporting detail in each of the stages. Some of this detail around language, terminology and the mix of tools and approaches may also need to vary with the organization, to fit with its established practices. When category management is deployed, this process diagram serves as the anchor point for practitioners. Plastic-coated versions pinned up at people's desks and posters in the department help to move this from something of

**FIGURE 3.12** Full category management process

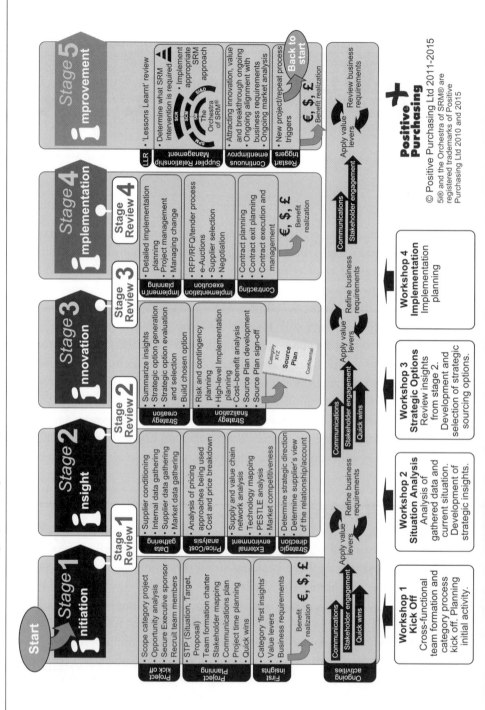

passing interest to the way the organization buys. Combine this with line managers taking every opportunity to check progress of individual category management projects and talking 'process language' as reinforcement, and the approach becomes embedded in the minds of the practitioners.

# APPLYING THE PROCESS

## Process duration

So how long does it take? Well, that depends upon many factors, including the category, its complexity, the market complexity, the number of people within the organization who need to be involved, the technological change within the category and how fast moving it is. It also depends on how fast you move, how much resource the organization puts into the project and how quickly it can withstand rapid change, especially if multiple company sites are involved.

There is one constant relationship. The initial stages require the most effort and energy but are accomplished in the quickest time, while implementation and beyond is typically a long, hard activity requiring a steady level of energy in order to make things happen and ensure they are embedded. Figure 3.13 provides some typical project durations for two extremes in terms of category project. The first three stages are taken together up to the point where the recommended sourcing strategy is identified. This is because the process up to the end of stage 3 is largely about team-based research, analysis, investigation and developing the future strategy. Beyond this point the project takes on a new shape during implementation, as it does again once implementation maturity has been reached.

**FIGURE 3.13** Project duration

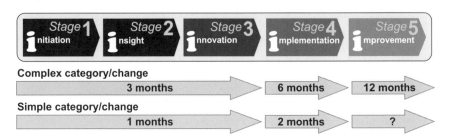

The duration for implementation depends upon the scale and complexity of the change required; it is also influenced by the speed at which you are able to roll out new arrangements. Think of large-scale changes you have experienced or witnessed where supply arrangements involving multiple people and sites have had to alter. It is rare for the change to be made over-night, and it will be fraught with risk and unforeseen problems that could jeopardize the business. Effective implementation therefore requires detailed planning and strong project management.

Beyond implementation our category becomes more 'steady state' as we enter the improvement stage. Here we are managing and monitoring the arrangements that have been put in place. This final stage lasts as long as the time it takes until it is appropriate or necessary to repeat the category management process; however, the amount of effort required here is typically low when compared to the preceding stages.

# Knowing what to leave out

I once asked a friend of mine who used to be a professional drummer what it was that makes the difference between a good drummer and an excellent drummer. His answer was, 'It's really simple; it's about knowing what to leave out.' It is the same for category management – getting good is simply about knowing what to leave out. Working through every single tool or process step shown in Figure 3.12 is a huge undertaking, but whilst some category management projects will demand this, others will not. Where the change is complex and sourced from a difficult market with many organiza-tional impacts demanding the involvement of multiple stakeholders, a full process approach is essential. But where the category is very simple, perhaps with only one or two key stakeholders who are already supportive, and the change is relatively easy, a faster-track route is acceptable. All that is required is knowing what to leave out and when it is appropriate to leave it out. That comes only from experience; however, throughout this book I will attempt to identify those tools and activities that are essential and should always be used if a category management project is to be successful.

Organizations deploying category management attempt to address this by determining the extent to which the process should be applied to individual categories in advance. Some companies introduce multiple routes through the category management process or indeed two or more category management process variants, each demanding different mandatory tools or steps to be worked. These might typically be:

- *Full process*. Virtually all tools and process steps are mandatory; some are optional, depending upon category – used for complex, multi-stakeholder categories.

- *Fast track*. Around half the tools and process steps are mandatory; the rest are optional – used for simple categories with small and supportive stakeholder base.

- *Just do it*. Simple process for very simple categories with few stakeholders and limited opportunity for breakthrough. Use just a handful of tools and process steps.

## Working through the process

Over the next five chapters we will work through the entire category management methodology step by step, expanding each step in turn. This will act as a guide or route map for any practitioner seeking to deploy category management. This is supplemented by the tools and templates provided in the Appendix. Each stage within category management contains a series of individual steps, and each falls into one of three types:

- *Tools* – Things you work or apply to gain an insight or outcome.

- *Activities* – An approach or step to work through in order to progress something or achieve a specific outcome.

- *Enablers* – Techniques or steps necessary to enable something else to happen or to lay groundwork for a later activity.

As we saw previously the degree to which each step must be completed depends upon the route through the process that is appropriate. For low-complexity/easy-change projects an experienced practitioner might make an informed decision to omit certain non-mandatory tools not relevant to the project. For other projects all steps might be relevant. Yet a number of the steps within category management remain essential or mandatory for every project, as without them the result could be suboptimal. As we move through the next five chapters I will explain and signpost each step according to its type and whether it is *essential* or *optional*.

## Chapter 3 summary

Recap on the key points from this chapter:

1 In order to deploy category management successfully there are a number of things that need to be in place or carried out prior to a programme commencing; categories need to be identified and from this a macro-level opportunity analysis needs to be completed in order to identify the priority categories to work on. These can then form the basis for a category programme plan, linked to available resources and a programme of organizational governance to help realize the plan.

2 The 5i category management process provides a robust framework for applying category management. It is a five-stage process comprising Initiation, Insight, Innovation, Implementation and Improvement.

3 Category management is a circular process; we never finish it but as a category project reaches maturity there comes a time, based upon changes in the market, suppliers, technology or our requirements, when it is appropriate to restart the process.

4 We move through the five stages of category management by working through the individual tools and steps. Not all are essential and knowing which ones we need to apply or leave out comes with experience.

5 Category management requires cross-functional working. 5i recommends four workshops at key stages involving all those who are involved in the project.

6 Key reviews of progress are essential throughout the process, ideally effected by wider governance arrangements to ensure process rigour and provide opportunity for challenge. There are four review points within 5i category management.

7 Benefits are realized within category management at different times through the process. The main benefits come from Stage 4 following a successful implementation. Further benefits might come from Stage 5 from ongoing improvement activities. However, it is also important to secure early benefits from quick wins during Stage 1 to demonstrate early success of the project.

# Stage 1: Initiation

This chapter explores the tools, techniques and process steps within the first or initiation stage. We examine how the category project is established and how the team is formed. We look at some of the early analysis that is conducted to gain some initial insight into the category and verify the opportunity. We explore how the wider business is engaged to secure buy-in and understand the business needs for the category. Finally we examine how the category project is planned.

Pathway questions addressed in this chapter:

**4** How can I identify and prioritize potential opportunity for each category so I can direct my resources accordingly?

**6** How do I engage the wider organization within a category-based approach?

**7** For any given category, how do I identify what the organization needs to buy?

**8** For each and any category, what is my current position?

## The initiation toolkit

Stage 1, initiation, is about kicking off the category management process and conducting the early project planning. There are a number of things that need to be established at the outset of the process. The most important of these is the cross-functional team, as it is now that the team is established and formed, and work is done to align thinking and agree a common purpose.

Initiation is also the first time we explore the category in question. It is our first opportunity to define the scope of the category and its boundaries and to establish some goals for the size of benefits we wish to attain. Initiation therefore seeks to achieve a number of key objectives:

- formation, alignment and motivation of the cross-functional team that will work on the category project;
- verification of the opportunity, along with gaining some early insight into and understanding of what is happening in the category;
- identification of how stakeholders will be engaged and how project progress and results delivery will be communicated to them and the wider business;
- formation of a precise statement of the business requirements;
- identification of potential sources of value;
- delivery of early benefits;
- planning of the project.

For initiation to be successful a series of early project activities or steps are required; these are given in the process diagram (see Figure 4.1).

# KICKING OFF THE CATEGORY MANAGEMENT PROCESS

Category management projects typically begin with a lone category manager or purchasing practitioner having been assigned a category to work on. Initially, this can feel quite daunting but it doesn't need to be and the first steps in the process are concerned with orientation as to what the category is and who is going to help work on it.

## Scoping the category project

This step is an *Enabler* and is *Essential*

Before the project begins to take shape, clarity as to what it is about is essential. If the boundaries of the category project are not absolutely clear,

**FIGURE 4.1**   Stage 1: Initiation

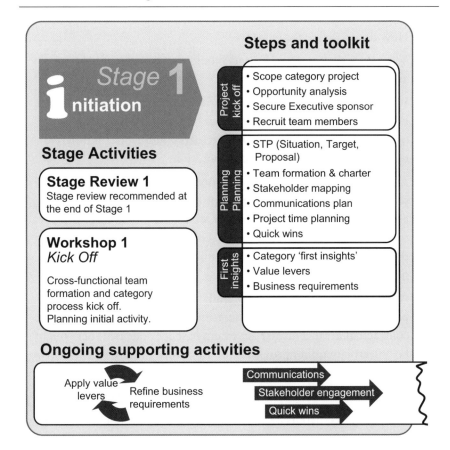

then an activity to gain alignment and an early definition of the scope of the category must be carried out by the cross-functional project team. This should be one of the first activities in the first kick-off workshop.

In a multi-project environment the scope would ideally be determined in advance of the project commencing by the senior leadership team responsible for category management organization-wide. It is possible that wider consultation with the business is required here. It is also possible that once the project begins, and following discussion by the team, the scope may need refinement or even redefinition and that is why this is the first activity identified within the process.

Defining the scope requires careful thought, and caution is required if breakthrough opportunities are not to be excluded at this early stage. Constrained thinking here will constrain the whole project, so effort should be put into making sure the scope is correct and precisely defined. Key questions to answer here are:

- How do we define the category?
- What does the category do, and should the scope be based around this?
- What are the geographical boundaries? Defining geographical boundaries must reflect how the marketplaces for the category are organized, but multiple category projects could work on different territories, with overarching collaboration.
- Are there any time-frame implications that would define the scope? For example, a tour operator may organize business around the annual bulk printing of all holiday brochures for the forthcoming season. The category scope may be to look to provide the sourcing strategy for a defined number of seasons or time periods.
- Are there any organizational boundaries that need to be imposed, perhaps where pre-existing arrangements prevent changing current contractual arrangements? An example scope statement here might be: 'Electricity utility provision for all European sites except the two German factories'. However, be careful not to exclude areas without good reason; you could be excluding a breakthrough!

The output required here is a simple statement or definition of the scope of the project. Using facilitation, the cross-functional team should explore their understanding of the scope, then develop and refine this to arrive at an agreed definition. If reaching an agreed definition is proving difficult, then the team should identify what is preventing alignment. Defining exceptions is often a good way to overcome difficulties. Some sample category scope definitions are:

- printed packaging: for all US operations;
- travel agency: global travel agency provision for all sites except Australia;
- bulk chemicals: bulk supply (ie loads over 1 tonne) to all UK sites of sodium hypochlorite, sodium bisulphate, ferric chloride and calcium nitrate.

It is possible that as the project progresses it becomes necessary to go back and revise the scope. If this is the case, then the work to date through the process will also need to be revisited and possibly reworked.

# Opportunity analysis revisited

This step is a *Tool* and is *Optional*

In the last chapter we explored the process of opportunity analysis, typically conducted at a macro level to define the overall category management pro- gramme and determine the prioritized category projects that will be worked on. Ideally this would be reasonably detailed, delivering multiple-category opportunity analysis using spend data, market knowledge and consultation with stakeholders. The initial OA might typically be carried out using external support, as a provider who has broad knowledge across many categories will be able to use this knowledge to gauge the scale of the potential benefits in each of the marketplaces. However this initial macro-level opportunity analysis will only ever be as good as the information and time available so may lack certainty.

Here we are now working on one of the categories identified as a priority and we now have the option to revisit this tool within our category project in order to verify the opportunity. Whilst this may appear to be duplicating activity, it can be an important step in order to be certain the category really does hold the potential identified and also what sort of intervention would be needed to get at it. It also provides the opportunity to conduct a more thorough analysis.

We use the same process and opportunity analysis tool outlined in Chapter 3, except instead of mapping categories, we typically operate one level down to map the sub-categories that exist within the main category or umbrella category assigned to us. This not only verifies the overall opportu- nity but helps us prioritize the sub-categories to work on. Start by mapping spend on each sub-category against market and organizational difficulty (as per Figure 3.4, and a template is provided in the Appendix). Identify the potential benefit by mapping each sub-category according to its price flexibility and sub-category maturity (as per Figure 3.5), then update the opportunity analysis with the potential benefits. Figure 4.2 gives an example of a completed opportunity analysis for a marketing category, showing each of the marketing sub-categories and the potential opportunity identified.

Finally review the outputs and prioritize action or identify next steps. The summary opportunity analysis prioritization matrix can help here (see the example back in Figure 3.7 and the template provided in the Appendix). Discussion and debate might be needed here in order to identify how the

**FIGURE 4.2** An example completed opportunity analysis with potential savings for all the marketing category showing all marketing sub-categories

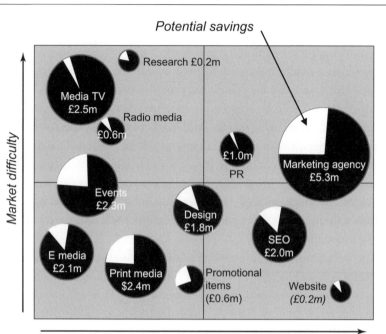

project should move forward. In this example tackling *marketing agency* would present the biggest benefit, but it is likely to be the hardest to realize so starting with this could mean our project will take a long time to secure benefit and might stall out. Instead tackling *print media, promotional items* and perhaps *events* will deliver lesser benefits but are easier to get at.

Opportunity analysis is not a once-only activity, but rather something we should revisit as we progress through the category management process, refining and updating our assessment of the potential benefits as we gather insights along the way. This helps to give confidence that our project continues to be worthwhile, or possibly to cut our losses and abandon the project if we discovered the opportunity was in fact not worth the effort. The opportunity analysis tool also informs our internal communications so we are able to describe with confidence what benefit our project will deliver.

# Securing the executive sponsor

This step is an *Enabler* and is *Optional*

Recruiting an executive sponsor is highly recommended and is crucial to ensure project success for difficult changes.

Appointing the sponsor is not straightforward. Ideally, the organization has prepared itself for the need for executive members to play sponsor roles to support category management projects. This preparation and understanding typically only arise after there is board-level commitment to an organization-wide category management programme. If this is not the case, then the need for the sponsor does not change, but the process of recruiting one and getting the required commitment takes longer.

The choice of sponsor is important. While this individual's role within the project is small in terms of time commitment, it is still important that the person is available when required at key points in the process. They must be senior enough and have the necessary gravitas to gain the support of the organization and convince peers. If you are unsure, then ask how the organization would respond if this individual were to say, 'I trust I can count on your support for this.' Would they be ignored or would people follow? The sponsor must also be willing to get involved.

When recruiting sponsors it should not be assumed that because they are senior they know what to do. The reality is that they may not have been asked to do such a thing before and will almost certainly not know what is required of them. The category leader should broker a meeting to formally request the sponsor's involvement. Depending on how such things are done within the organization, this may be set up directly or through the usual chain of command. The agenda for this meeting should include:

- a very brief introduction to category management and the cross-functional nature of the process (except where this is well understood already by the potential sponsor);
- the nature and anticipated scale of the opportunity;
- the role of the executive sponsor within category management and the commitment required;
- the request for the individual to become the sponsor;
- planning the actions ahead.

An executive sponsor needs to encourage the cross-functional team to engage in the project, by convincing peers to release people to join the team; they also need to inspire the organization to embrace the change that originates from the category team. Without this, team members may be pulled away mid-project. And if no one in authority stands up when the change is ready to be implemented and says, 'This is the way forward. I need your help to make this happen', there is little to compel people to change what they do. There are some very simple category management projects that can work without a sponsor, but in general an executive sponsor is a fundamental requirement if the category management project is to be a success.

During the project the executive sponsor has a defined role. It should be set out in the team charter (which we cover later in this chapter) and would typically include:

- being the figurehead and visible executive lead for the project;
- being responsible for securing the initial and ongoing provision of the cross-functional team members and any other resources;
- briefing and inspiring the team, ideally by attending the first kick-off workshop for 30 minutes at the start of the day;
- e-mailing cross-functional team members and their line managers to thank them for getting involved and requesting their continued commitment etc;
- communicating the project and its progress at executive level;
- ensuring that any high-level business requirements or issues that might impact the project are communicated to the team;
- signing off the sourcing strategy (most likely following consultation with key stakeholders);
- smoothing the way by being the ambassador for implementation, and securing the necessary support and resources required to convert the strategy and plan into action;
- removing any obstacles.

The commitment required here by the sponsor is minimal. However, the category project leader must work to make sure the sponsor continues to do their job despite all the other pressures faced by executive people. Regular short meetings between the sponsor and the project leader to report progress and agree specific actions required at executive level are therefore appropriate.

The idea of a category project leader – probably a middle-level individual within the organization – working directly with a senior executive may be unusual in some organizations. It may be stepping outside traditional hier-archical ways of working. Great! That means this project has the potential to make a difference. This way of working has been proven to be powerful. With the right approach, securing sponsorship should not be difficult. Fundamentally people love to be associated with a success story, and if an executive has the opportunity to put their name to something that will bring radical benefits, then they are going to be very keen to be seen as an active contributor.

# Recruiting team members

This step is an *Enabler* and is *Optional*

Category management projects are most successful when a cross-functional team comprising the right individuals from across the business form and work through the process to identify and implement a new sourcing strategy. Cross-functional working is one of the pillars of category management, so getting the right cross-functional team is vitally important for project success.

This shifts the project from a purchasing initiative to a company initiative demanding resources and solid commitment. This is possibly one of the earliest challenges in deploying category management, especially if the wider organization is not ready or prepared to release people to join such a team. I frequently encounter projects where the organization is unable or un-willing to resource teams to work on category management projects. If this cannot be changed we can only work within the boundaries set. Where a cross-functional team is not possible, a purchasing run initiative with a strong degree of stakeholder engagement can sometimes work, and can yield sufficient cross-functional working, but it is a compromise and could lessen the scope to deliver breakthrough results as those in the business will not be actively involved in driving a change. Basic cross-functional working might be enough for a simple, low-complexity category with minimal stake-holders, but anything more than this really needs some sort of team approach. Remember, category management is most successful when it is embraced as an organization-wide philosophy.

A team of between five and seven, perhaps occasionally extended by some additional members, is the ideal size. Any more and the group will find it hard to progress, any fewer and the depth of organizational input may be lacking.

**FIGURE 4.3**   Typical category management team composition

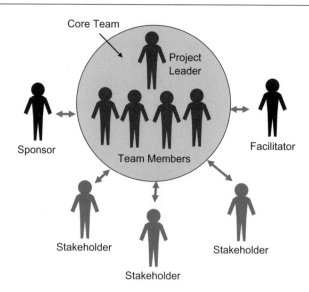

Success in recruiting team members is about ensuring:

- the right people;
- the right commitment;
- the right availability;
- the right executive support.

First, let's look at the right people. Figure 4.3 shows a typical team composition for a category management project and comprises the core team led by the project leader together with the executive sponsor, wider business stakeholders and possibly even an external facilitator to help maximize team effectiveness.

The core team make-up should reflect the needs of the category. Individuals throughout the business should be recruited on the basis of their knowledge of the category, interest in the areas that might be affected by any change, mix of skills, ability to champion change or their standing in the business. If the category is 'printed packaging', then the optimum team might comprise marketing, production, shipping and R&D, with purchasing leading. A category to look at 'temporary labour' might comprise HR representatives from different business units and from high users of temporary labour. The category 'wound care' might comprise clinicians, other medical staff and purchasing. A category looking at marketing design agencies might be just a combination of marketing and purchasing; and so on.

Constructing a team with 100 per cent representation across the business will almost certainly not be possible. So it must be recognized that even a team with a wide representation may have to address some gaps. This is achieved through team members assuming the responsibility for communicating to, and gaining the input, views and contribution of, parts of the business that are not represented. For example, if the scope of our temporary labour category spans the requirements of six business units, then if there are two HR team members from two of these business units, they must assume the role of engaging with the remaining four. If they do not, then the buy-in for the areas not directly represented on the team will not be secured.

The right commitment, availability and executive support of team members are essential. If representatives sign up to participate in the project but subsequently cannot make meetings or do not fulfil their actions, then their representation is worthless. At the outset, potential team members must clearly understand the level of commitment that is required of them and agree that they will provide it. Gaining this commitment is not only a case of contracting with the individuals, but requires the support and endorsement of their managers and ultimately the members of the executive team who are responsible for their areas of the business. This is the first job for our executive sponsor.

The team-member role demands a reasonable level of time commitment. Participating in category management projects is not usually a full-time job, but it will typically require a series of days of work. Activities that will demand the attention of team members throughout the project include:

- participation in the four cross-functional workshops;
- delivery of actions arising from each workshop;
- communications activity and engagement with stakeholders;
- collection of data and information;
- pursuing quick-win opportunities.

One final point here: it may be necessary to change team members midway through the process. The most obvious potential change point is before Stage 4 (implementation) begins, when it may be appropriate to swap some team members for those who are better placed to turn the strategy into reality. Equally if a team member simply isn't working and is hindering the project, there should be some sort of intervention to address the issue, and ultimately if this fails the team member would need to be replaced.

# PLANNING THE PROJECT

## The STP tool

This step is a *Tool* and is *Essential*

Situation, target, proposal (STP) is a wonderful tool and is essential for all category projects. This is the first time we use it, but it could equally be used in every stage. The STP can be used as a general purpose problem-solving tool, to get group alignment regarding an issue and on how to move forward. I even know someone who will do an STP on a blank piece of paper stuck on his fridge with his kids, to help them decide what to do about difficult problems at school.

STPs are completed by brainstorming the three words in the acronym in turn. Its greatest power comes when it is used within a group, with outputs captured on flip charts, as the process of brainstorming delivers alignment of thinking throughout the group.

Before you start it is important to define the problem or issue you are trying to understand or, where there is no particular issue, the scope of the STP. This is an important step as it frames people's thinking to make precise contributions. You may come across a variant of this tool called the *pSTP* for this reason. Once there is alignment of understanding of the scope, STP key headings can be explored.

'Situation' is straightforward. Brainstorm and list everything you know about the current situation, eg spend, who uses it, current issues, historical factors, quality problems, value we are getting, where the technology is heading and so on. At this stage detailed research is not necessary, but rather this list should be a pooling of the knowledge from team members. The list is typically long, so some post-brainstorm sorting is advisable to make the final STP list succinct.

'Target' is the heading that catches most people out. Consider the example of the situation being simply 'I'm hungry.' The natural response is to suggest, 'Go eat food' as the target. This is not a target, but a proposal. It illustrates the common mistake in using this tool. Most of the time when we define a problem or a current situation, we naturally jump to solutions. The intermediate step of asking, 'Where do we want to be?' is often ignored or done without conscious thought. So, for this simple example of 'I'm hungry,' a suitable target might be 'to feel satisfied', with the subsequent proposal

**FIGURE 4.4**   STP for printed packaging

| STP – Printed Packaging |
| --- |
| **Problem definition:** Printed packaging is purchased from many different suppliers |
| **Situation:**<br>• No co-ordination of purchasing<br>• Consolidation savings are being ignored<br>• Similar and even the same products are purchased from more than one supplier<br>• Quality problems widespread and difficult to trace<br>• Localized buying from favoured suppliers<br>• Specifications, terms and performance vary widely |
| **Targets:**<br>• 100 per cent of printed packaging sourced from one or two suppliers in 24 months<br>• Standardized specifications, T&Cs etc in use<br>• Suppliers' performance monitored and continuously improving |
| **Proposals:**<br>• Identify all printed packaging needs<br>• Measure total acquisition costs<br>• Develop standard policy, specs, procedure etc and implement<br>• Negotiate new contracts with one or two suppliers capable of delivering to all requirements<br>• Develop performance measurement/improvement process |

being 'Go eat food.' Thought should be given to ensuring that the target is well defined and is in direct response to the situation. Here the SMART rule (specific, measurable, actionable, realistic and time-bound) is appropriate for setting the target.

'Proposal' is where we list what we are going to do to achieve the target. If we are embarking on a category management project then clearly the next step is to work through the process. There is no need to list all the individual steps, so a simple statement such as 'Follow the category management process' will suffice. There may, however, be some specific, additional or alternative proposals that might be listed or the proposal might include immediate next steps, or indeed specific actions with owners and dates assigned. Figure 4.4 shows a typical STP. A template is also provided in the Appendix.

Other variants on STP exist. You can have an *STPP* which has an extra 'plan' added, an *STPBV* which has 'benefits' and 'value' added, and you can even have an *STPPBV*. In negotiation we use *STEP* to guide process with 'event plan and post event' replacing the original 'P' (See *Negotiation for Purchasing Professionals,* also published by Kogan Page). In the world of supplier management we use an *STPDR* process for managing supplier improvements and we will cover this in Chapter 8.

The variant you use is a matter of personal choice – but keep it simple. Whatever variant you choose, it is beneficial to ensure that there is a common language and that others in the business use the same format. A template for the STP is included in the appendix.

# Team formation and the team charter

This step is a *Tool* and is *Optional*

The first cross-functional workshop may well be the first time the team gets together to work on the category project. Team members will have been recruited from across the business, and they may even have a reasonable understanding of what is required of them, but they may not fully understand their role in the team. The team charter (sometimes referred to as a project charter) is not so much a tool but an output. It is a key record that summarizes a series of discussions around how the team will work together and function. You would be strongly advised to have a team charter where a team-based approach is being used.

The team charter seeks to answer a series of questions that are relevant at this early stage of the project. They are:

- What are the structure and composition of the team?
- Who is the project or team leader?
- What is the role of the project or team leader?
- Who is the sponsor and what is their role?
- What are the roles of the team members?
- What is the purpose of the project and are there any boundaries?
- Where do we want to be, what are our targets and are there any constraints?
- Are there any special roles that specified individuals have, eg communications, project management etc?

It is likely that the answers to many of these questions will be known by the time the team arrives at this key first team workshop, and that there will be a reasonable degree of understanding across the team. However, a team charter serves many purposes:

- to gain alignment of understanding of the project and respective roles through the entire team;

- to serve as a basis to discuss with the sponsor what is expected of them;
- as a basis to secure agreement for the remit the team has;
- to provide a definitive document that summarizes the project, its aims, its people and its target;
- to gain the commitment of the team to the project.

This last point is important. If individuals have engaged in the process of creating a charter that defines the project and the commitment each team member will give, it is difficult for them subsequently to move away from it; after all, a commitment has been made.

The team charter should only ever be worked up with a group; project leaders should avoid arriving at a meeting with a pre-completed version for discussion or sign-off, but rather each section should be worked up collaboratively around a flip chart or an onscreen projected version.

Figure 4.5 provides an example of a completed team charter and a template is provided in the Appendix.

Each section is relatively straightforward to complete:

- *Category name and boundaries.* These should have already been explored as part of the first step of Stage 1. Following discussion and agreement with the team, insert the definition of the scope here.

- *Category team purpose.* What are the purpose and aims of the project? The STP target previously completed will help to inform this.

- *Category team membership.* Here the team members should be listed. If there are core team members and occasional or part-time team members, then make this distinction.

- *Resources required.* Time commitment and other resources required to support the project.

- *Targets and constraints.* Again, targets can be taken from the STP, but completing this section also gives the team members the opportunity to explore and note any constraints that might hinder reaching the targets.

- *Team member responsibilities.* It is important to get this right and that there is an open and full discussion regarding what team members need to do to support the project. The discussion may be the first time that some team members gain a full appreciation of what is required of them. For example, a team member may have

**FIGURE 4.5** Team charter

## Team Charter – Printed Packaging Category Team

**Category name and boundaries**
Printed packaging
All printed packaging used in production worldwide, except Germany

**Category team purpose**
To develop and implement a strategic Category Management change to fulfil business requirements including cost reduction

**Category team membership:**
*Core:*
Purchasing  Production  Distribution
*Also involved:*
Sales, Commercial, New Product Development.

**Targets and constraints**
• To develop a draft strategy in 24 weeks
• To implement the strategy within 2 years
• To deliver cost reduction and value improvement in line with corporate targets (Currently €7.4m, to be agreed at strategy stage)

• Project leader 75% of time on the project
• Team members 25% of time on the project
• Non-salary budget: €120,000
• Other resources negotiated on a requirement and supply basis

**Team member responsibilities**
• Carry out the research and data collection needed
• Participate in development of business cases, source plan and strategy
• Work with stakeholders to develop business requirements
• Attend meetings and work as part of the team
• Assist in implementation of the Source Plan
• Promote the Category Management project in the organization

**Team leader responsibilities**
• Facilitate the development and activities of the team
• Provide an overall direction of the team's activities
• Negotiate scope, targets and requirements with the sponsor and the business at large
• Manage the project and report as necessary
• Maintain appropriate records
• Lead in the development and implement ation of the Strategy and Source Plan

**Sponsor responsibilities**
• Agree clear objectives with the team and update as required
• Communicate any changes in business expectations of the project
• Provide guidance
• Remove barriers to progress
• Ensure resources are available
• Wider senior management communications, for example at board level

realized they need to attend the team meetings but may not have appreciated that there is also an expectation for them to go back to their function and communicate project progress, engage with colleagues to gain input and data, and so on. This open discussion will ensure that there is no doubt or confusion regarding the role of team members on this project. Therefore there should be no excuses for not contributing.

- *Team leader responsibilities*. The team leader will probably have a good idea what the role is about. However, discussing and debating the role with the wider team serve to ensure the team is clear about the leader's role. This helps to cement the team leader as the authority for the project.

- *Sponsor responsibilities*. This section needs to be discussed and agreed with the sponsor, as described in the earlier section.

# Stakeholder mapping

This step is a *Tool* and is *Essential*

A stakeholder is someone who has an interest in the project or can help achieve project goals. This person may stand to lose or benefit from the change or may have some responsibility or accountability for the area in question. If we do not understand and engage with our stakeholders, we could miss out on support from those who could help us; and those who are not supportive could impede progress. In any organization and for any project there will be a vast range of levels of support or even levels of resistance. Stakeholder mapping is an essential step and is a structured process to understand who the stakeholders are and the degree to which they are in support of the project (or will resist it), and what specific actions need to be taken to win over or increase their support.

The first step is to identify and make a list of all the stakeholders. It should start with individuals but it might also be appropriate to include groups of people, eg a department or specific area of a business. Stakeholders should be identified by considering the project or category and asking, 'Who in the business is responsible for this area, who is accountable, who needs to be consulted here, and who needs to be kept informed?' We call this the RACI Model (see Figure 4.6) and this will give us our starting list of stakeholders.

**FIGURE 4.6**   The RACI model

Inform only

**Inform**    *Those who need to be kept up-to-date on progress*

**Consult**    *Those whose opinions should be sought and with whom we would need two-way communication*

**Accountable**   *The one ultimately accountable for what happens; the final approving authority. 'Accountable' sign off what 'Responsible' does*

**Responsible**   *Those responsible for doing the work or achieving the outcomes within the area in question*

Active Involvement

Once we have our list of stakeholders we need to identify a series of specific actions to engage with each of them, depending on the level of support or otherwise each has for the category management project. If we consider a continuum that ranges from 'against' the project to 'fully supportive', or someone who can make the project happen, then it is possible to map our stakeholders onto this range, as follows:

- *Against it happening (AIH).* As we learnt previously, resistance to change is the single biggest cause of project failure. If we do not attend to this and work to minimize resistance, we are setting ourselves up to fail. To avoid this we must first understand the sources of and reasons for the resistance. Resistance can come in many guises, for example: 'Let me help you – what you're suggesting was tried a couple of years ago and failed; don't waste your time,' or 'If it isn't broke, don't fix it.' Stakeholders may resist for many reasons: they may stand to lose out if certain changes go ahead, they may not want more work, or their control over an area of the business may be threatened by the project. Such stakeholders will clearly be AIH. Actions should be centred on converting them and winning their support, for example through engagement, use of facts and data, getting them to participate, gaining executive support to win them over etc.

- *Lets it happen (LIH).* These are people who are neither against nor for the project. They don't stand to gain or lose by it and have no reason to help make it happen, but equally they have no reason to stand in the way. LIH stakeholders should not be allowed to become AIH, but actions should centre on moving them to a better position so that they can help the project.

- *Helps it happen (HIH).* These are stakeholders who are generally supportive towards the project, believe in it and feel it is a good thing. They will typically be good advocates for the project. Actions here need to centre around maintaining them as HIH and maximizing their support by getting them to help cascade communications etc.

- *Makes it happen (MIH).* These are the stakeholders who are not only supportive but can help enable the project, perhaps through the provision of resources, removal of obstacles, or general positive communication. These stakeholders should be loved and cherished, and a close relationship should be established to maintain their MIH positioning.

There are many alternative models for stakeholder mapping but they all perform a similar function, that of identifying the stakeholders and then mapping the positioning of each in a way that allows specific actions to be tailored to either maximize their support and engagement or move them to a more favourable position. It is essential that an active approach is used, but it doesn't matter which. Some mapping approaches use words like 'Supporter', 'Blocker' or 'Resister' to label individuals. Such words can be highly emotive, especially if the individual gets to know.

Be very cautious about who has access to a completed stakeholder map. A single inadvertent publication of the stakeholder map could lead to a catastrophic project setback if stakeholders get to see how they have been labelled. Stakeholder maps should be regarded as very sensitive documents, especially where emotive words or labels are used. The category management team should therefore consider the requirement for confidentiality when developing a stakeholder map and make appropriate arrangements.

Figure 4.7 gives an example of a stakeholder map for a packaging category. A template is also provided in the Appendix. Note that the map has a date to reflect its dynamic nature and indicate when it was published. Here the map is shown with six stakeholders; in practice the list is likely to be longer. This is a simple example of a map and could be expanded to include the RACI determination also if required.

**FIGURE 4.7** An example stakeholder map

### Stakeholder Map: Packaging category – Updated 12th July

| Name & Role | AIH | LIH | HIH | MIH | R | A | C | I | Comments | Action |
|---|---|---|---|---|---|---|---|---|---|---|
| John Parsons – Production Manager | | | X | | | X | | | Currently positive and very important for success | Invite to be part of the project team |
| Sam Merton – Technical Manager | | X | | | | | X | | Can facilitate the work or slow it | Regular interviews and meetings |
| Billy Williams – Finance Director | | | X | | | X | | | Supports and controls the budget | Weekly detailed updates, including projected finances |
| Sheila Smith – Logistics Manager | X | | | | X | | | | Resisting the change, disruption will make her task harder in the short term | Convert if possible, use sponsor to 'reach out'. Repeatedly highlight long-term benefits and existing support |
| Peter Ayres – Sponsor | | | | X | | | X | | Behind the change but demands to see results fast | Weekly positive updates, use to remove obstacles |
| Trisha Norton – Stores | | X | | | | | | X | Limited supporter, sees no need and a lot of work | Interviews and regular communications |

The completed stakeholder map is revealing. A general spread of stakeholders from AIH to MIH is typically expected. If there are no MIHs or AIHs it is worth challenging – are the team being realistic? Equally, if the list is skewed to one side or another, question it, and remember that every project needs some MIH for success!

# Communications planning

This step is a *Tool* and is *Optional*

Category management project communications are a bit like changing your diet to a more healthy one. You don't really want to do it and it feels a bit unnecessary at the time, but by doing it you will feel better. In a category management project communication will mostly be internal but could also be external and serves five key purposes:

1 to secure project buy-in, support and participation from the wider business;

2 to help condition those in the organization or externally that something is going to change;

3 to help manage change and ensure everyone knows what is expected of them, especially if we need people to do something differently in order to implement a change;

4 to keep the project as high profile as possible and thus maintain support and momentum; and,

5 to share success stories that help reinforce the overall programme.

Effective communications in category management will ensure a healthy project and will prolong its life; after all, it is rare that the high-visibility projects that deliver results are cancelled by organizations.

Communications planning is an essential process step and is about a structured and planned approach to communicate both specific and general information across a number of areas. These may include information about the category project, its progress, the benefits and what will happen next; but it may also be very focused on communications relevant to one individual. The actual message will vary throughout the process according to the specific needs of the category and the target group or individual. Part of the process of developing a communication plan is therefore to identify at the outset of the project what messages need to be communicated, to whom and when. The communications plan is also one of the dynamic activities that should continue beyond Stage 1 and flow through the entire process. It should be regularly reviewed and updated as the project progresses.

A single point of ownership for the communications plan can help ensure that communications activities are properly executed. Nominating a team member to assume the role of communications manager is the most effective way of ensuring that actions are delivered. The choice of individual should be considered; someone with experience or an aptitude for internal communications should be chosen.

There are two types of communication that need to be planned for:

- *Narrowcast communications*. These are specific communication activities with a defined message or focus in response to the stakeholder map, and probably on a one-to-one basis with key stakeholders. Narrowcast communications are used to help reduce and eliminate resistance among individual stakeholders and to win support and even positive contributions. Narrowcast channels include face-to-face, phone, e-mail and informal networking.

- *Broadcast communications*. These are general communications with a broad message to groups of people or even the entire business. Broadcast communications are required where the scale, complexity or reach of potential changes will impact on many people or on groups. The aim of broadcast communications is to help minimize future resistance to change and potentially to invite participation. Examples include newsletters, in-house road shows, noticeboards, intranet/extranet, conferences, group e-mails, video, audio, team meetings and SMS messaging.

In a corporate environment where people are subjected to ever-increasing demands on time and attention, reaching people to tell them about your category management project is a challenge. At the narrowcast level the challenge is probably about getting time in people's schedules. However, at the broadcast level effective communications are nothing short of an art form. This is where some creative communications, ideally from someone who has experience in this field, can work wonders in a project. A wordy article in the company newsletter is unlikely to be read, especially if the key message is way down the text somewhere. Multicast e-mails are rarely read past the first line unless recipients perceive that the rest of the e-mail contains something that is personally important or relevant to them. So creative communications are essential if the message is to be received in people's heads.

We can learn much from how professional communicators get a message across and stimulate interest. This is often completely different to how we are taught to write in business; for example business reports perhaps provide some introduction, background, a summary of current position and what we are hoping to do moving forward and so on. This communications structure might work for a business plan, but will fail in the world of effective communication. Instead if we turn to how the experts capture our attention our project communications will be more successful.

Newspapers grab us with a headline, then a sub-message, then some key messages and if we are still interested we can read on to the detail. Advertisements don't explain things, they convey an idea or aspiration. Some of the most successful category management projects I've witnessed try to emulate what professional communicators do as a means to secure buy-in and support for a project. Succinct e-mails or articles in company publications with attention-grabbing title lines such as *'Packaging project team predict $1m savings within six months'* or *'New cellphones for all next month'* can make people want to read the next few lines at least. Simple, low-budget gimmicks such as having some project branded mugs or mouse mats made up and giving them to key stakeholders can be impactful and help keep the project high profile. These things might seem at odds with how projects are traditionally run in organizations, and that's great – just what is needed to make a difference and drive exceptional communication for a category management project.

## CASE STUDY    Changing cellphone carrier

A global company initiated a category management project to identify a new sourcing strategy for mobiles/cellphones across the UK division involving thousands of users located across a wide geographical base. The project communications plan involved two key phases:

- general awareness communication using the company magazine and intranet site;

- communications direct with company mobile/cellphone users to gain their views and then later roll out the new arrangements.

Initially, staff received an e-mail questionnaire asking about the service, international roaming needs, desire for separate billing for personal calls etc. This was followed by a series of SMS text messages reminding people to submit their questionnaire and counting down the days left. Later in the project the category management team identified a new sourcing strategy that would overall give greater business benefits, new features including significant savings for international roaming, and a personal-use option with separate billing (which was used as a selling point to staff to help generate support).

The new strategy involved switching to a new provider. Individual phone numbers were retained and moved across to the new provider but this had to coincide with handset replacement. Arrangements briefed out by e-mail gave people 30 days to organize their individual switchover. A series of SMS text-message reminders were used only for those who failed to respond. By the end of the 30 days only a handful of users had not moved across. They were easily tracked down and the process was completed.

The change was a success and there was little resistance; every user was clear about what they needed to do.

In developing a communications plan, thought should be given to any cultural differences, especially if the category management project scope is across geographical boundaries. Different communications approaches are relevant in different countries. For example, in the United States and the UK, staff are generally accustomed to the majority of business being conducted via e-mail, but in Ireland, Italy, Spain and many other countries the only way to communicate is to 'go and talk to people'; if you fail to do this you will not gain the required buy-in or support. It is therefore essential to understand the prevailing culture for communication and engagement of individuals and groups.

A communications plan requires a simple framework such as that shown in Figure 4.8 (a template is provided in the Appendix). There should be a natural relationship with the stakeholder map, perhaps even a mirror image, and it would typically identify the planned communication activities at both individual and group levels. It should identify the messages that are relevant to the individual or group, the communication channels that will be used and the timing. Most importantly, there must be assigned owners (or a single overall owner) for the communications activity.

**FIGURE 4.8** The Communications plan

| | Packaging category Communications Plan –Updated 17th July | | | | |
|---|---|---|---|---|---|
| Stakeholder or group | Comments | Key messages/what we will communicate | Channel | Frequency/ importance | Owner |
| John Parsons – Production Manager | Currently positive and very important for success | Plans and progress | Face-to-face meetings and e-mail updates | Weekly | Category manager |
| Sam Merton – Technical Manager | Can facilitate the work or slow it | Summary of planned changes, benefits, updates on progress | Face-to-face meetings | Monthly, not to be missed | Sam Way |
| Billy Williams – Finance Director | Supports and controls the budget | Benefits and investment case | Meetings or telecons | No more than monthly | Mike Condoza |
| Sheila Smith – Logistics Manager | Resisting the change, disruption will make her task harder in the short term | Case for change, sponsor support | Only face-to-face | Every 2 weeks reducing after October | All |
| Peter Ayres – Sponsor | Behind the change, tends to get bored quickly | Summary of plans, high-level progress updates and likely benefits | Short e-mails, quick meetings & 'phone call updates' | At least twice a month | Category Manager |
| Trisha Norton – Stores | Limited supporter, sees no need and a lot of work | Case for change, sponsor support, long term benefits | Face-to-face followed by papers | Two or three times early in the project | Robyn Frith Sam Way |
| Wider business | General awareness is required to minimize resistance to change | General awareness level introduction and progress updates | Articles in company newsletter | 3 monthly | Category Manager |
| Group Purchasing | Synergy opportunities, support is important | General awareness level introduction and progress updates | Monthly reports and present at annual purchasing forum | Monthly and six monthly | Category Manager |

Finally, remember that the communications plan is a dynamic document. It should therefore be reviewed and updated regularly to reflect the changing nature of the project. It should include a date or version reference.

# Project time planning

This step is a *Tool* and is *Optional*

As the category management project begins to take shape, the team will have a clearer idea of what the project is, together with its goals and scope. It is now appropriate to develop a plan that leads us to the start of Stage 4, implementation.

Project time planning is about developing a simple view of the project ahead in a way that enables the whole team and stakeholders to fully understand what will happen and what their roles are, thus providing a basis for communication to the wider business. The plan should be simple but effective. Most importantly, it should be a dynamic document that is regularly reviewed, updated, adjusted and republished, reflecting the changing needs of the project.

Project planning should be kept simple if it is to be effective. Complex plans, with many detailed activities generated by software planning tools such as Microsoft Project, are unlikely to be internalized by recipients. For the category project team to understand and embrace the plan it should be developed collaboratively and ideally worked up by the team as part of the first workshop. However, the project leader may also present a proposed plan for discussion and development.

All that is required at this stage is a simple plan, possibly using a format such as a Gantt chart, or an action plan where listed activities need to be completed by set dates, or perhaps plans in a combination of formats.

Figure 4.9 shows a typical plan for a category project (a template is also provided in the Appendix). This was created using Microsoft PowerPoint and gives a simple overview of all the tasks and key activities that make up the project. It also shows key milestones and events such as workshops, with dates agreed.

**FIGURE 4.9** An example project plan

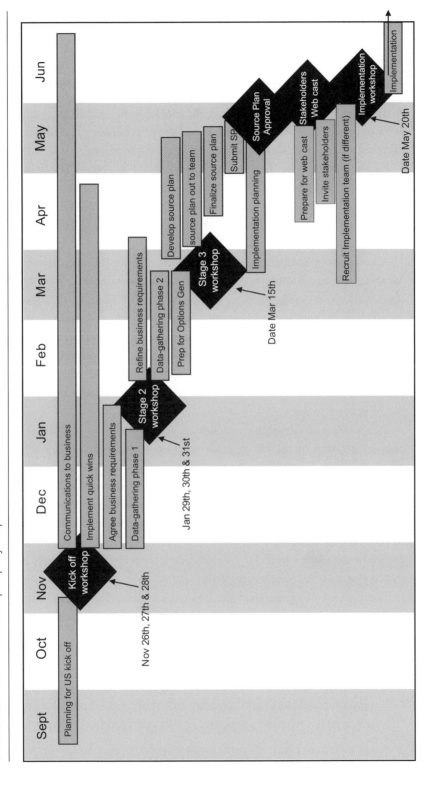

# Securing quick wins

> This step is a *Tool* and is *Optional*

A quick win is, as the name suggests, some form of benefit that can be achieved quickly or easily. If such benefits are available early on with little difficulty, then effort should be put into their realization.

Earlier we explored the opportunity analysis tool and the potential for this to identify some quick wins. At this stage of the process we once again consider the opportunity for quick wins, but here we are looking beyond category or sub-category prioritization level to specific actions within our category that might bring immediate benefit.

A category management project can take many months before a new sourcing strategy is identified, and many more months before implementation of the new arrangement is complete. This means that the business is investing time and resources in the promise of future benefit realization. Early opportunity analysis work, sponsor and stakeholder engagement and ongoing communication activity help to keep the project firmly in the minds of key decision makers in the business. However, delivering some early benefits in the form of quick wins can help to shore up the success of the project early on.

The process of identifying quick-win opportunities is not difficult. When you get a group of people together who have some sort of knowledge or involvement in a particular area of a business, they will all undoubtedly have ideas for how things could be improved. Often the ideas will offer sizeable benefits and represent things that have been in people's minds for some time, but there has been no appetite, opportunity, time, forum or inclination to do anything with the idea. Until now! The reality in any business is that there are usually at least 10 great ideas right in front of people's noses if they'd just take the time to see them.

The process of identifying quick wins is simple. The activity should be performed by the cross-functional category team, following these steps:

**1** *Brainstorm.* Brainstorm ideas for quick wins and make a list of all the ideas.

**2** *Prioritize.* Sort and prioritize according to the potential benefits they represent and the ease of realization. Figure 4.10 shows the quick-win analysis matrix (a template is also provided in the Appendix),

**FIGURE 4.10**  Quick-win analysis matrix

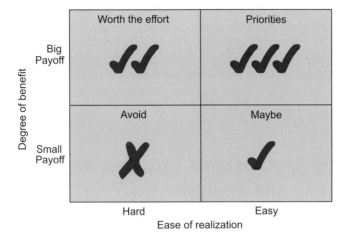

which uses a similar approach to the opportunity analysis to consider both the potential benefit and ease of realization. This matrix can be used to identify the potential way forward, or not, for each idea.

**3** *Quantify*. Where possible, quantify the benefits somehow, ideally in terms of cash. Benefits can be savings, improvements in process or product efficiency or effectiveness, reducing or eliminating spend – basically anything that adds value.

**4** *Action plan*. Finally, draw up an action plan, with clear owners and timescales for the quick wins that have been identified as priorities. Some quick wins may be worth progressing but insufficient resources may be available within the team to progress them. In circumstances like this there is potential to develop a mini business case to secure additional resource, perhaps using the sponsor to help if the benefits are worth the effort. This action plan should not be a once-only event but should be managed, reviewed and updated on a regular basis. The project leader should check progress regularly and maintain sufficient pressure on action assignees to ensure there is no slippage.

**5** *Report*. As benefits are realized, they should be recorded and reported in line with any benefits tracking arrangements within the organization.

# FIRST INSIGHTS AND DIRECTION SETTING

This part of Stage 1 is concerned with using three key tools to understand what is happening in the category, how and where we might secure benefits, and about developing the first definition of what we need and want to source for this category. These three tools help frame what we will do through the rest of category management.

## Gaining first insights into the category using day one analysis

This step is a *Tool* and is *Essential*

The category management process has a robust logic with a series of activities organized in a well-proven sequence. However, in its purest form the analysis of the information we collect as part of the process does not take place until later, when much effort and resource have been spent to get there. An early insight is therefore required to understand what is happening in the category, any factors that hinder freedom of sourcing, and what type of activity might be required to overcome them or gain benefits. Getting this insight early can confirm that the project is worth the effort, or in some cases may suggest a rethink of approach.

The STP (situation, target, proposal) tool helps to give some early insight, as it collects the thoughts regarding the current position and aligns future direction, but in developing the STP the contributors may not fully appreciate factors that might be hindering freedom of sourcing. The key questions that we are seeking to answer here are: 'Can we switch supplier easily? And if not, why not?' It is the 'Why not?' insights that can open up potential ways forward to achieve breakthroughs.

For example, consider a category to examine machined components used in military applications. Within this category many of the components are made to drawings developed 15 years ago during the original design process. In some cases manufacturers and their part numbers are specified on the drawings. The drawings cannot be changed without requalification of the overall product containing the components. This is both expensive and impractical. The challenge is not about finding a cheaper source of machined components; it is about overcoming the sourcing restrictions imposed

**FIGURE 4.11**    Day one analysis

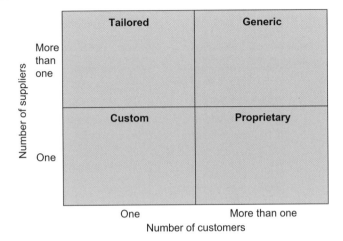

by historical design practices for these components within the category. This early analysis is aimed at identifying such constraints and shaping the direction and areas of focus of the category project team accordingly.

A simple tool that can be used here is *day one analysis* (see Figure 4.11). Day one analysis is used by plotting on the matrix categories and/or areas of spend (or even individual products) according to the number of suppliers in a particular marketplace that could supply the category or item, against the number of buyers. Any organizational constraints which limit the number of potential suppliers should be ignored at first by using the tool to look at the whole marketplace, but any constraining factors, such as current contracts, should be noted. Also, different geographical market boundaries may give different insights into what is happening.

The axes for day one analysis need to be understood clearly. They are not sliding scales. There may be either one supplier or buyer or more than one supplier or buyer, but there is no middle ground.

To use day one analysis we plot our category, area of spend or product on the respective quadrant according to the number of suppliers and buyers in the marketplace. Day one analysis is best worked in a group, as use of the tool will typically spark discussions regarding differences in outcomes or positioning, depending on how people view the category and its boundaries, or the product and how it is sourced. This discussion is good and differences will often reveal insights into what is happening. For example, the view of a category looking at the in-country market might mean the category is positioned as 'proprietary' if there is only one supplier, while a global view might make it 'generic'.

**FIGURE 4.12**    Day one analysis with examples

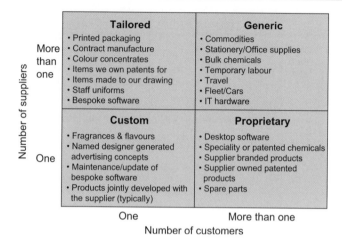

Using examples of categories that might be found in each quadrant helps to given an insight into how the tool works (see Figure 4.12). Let's consider the quadrants in turn:

- *Generic* (many suppliers, many buyers). In this quadrant the buyer has the greatest choice and ability to switch; so the buyer has the power. The supplier's mindset is about beating the competition, so leveraging the best price in the market in this case is relatively straightforward.

- *Tailored* (many suppliers, one buyer). Here the products and services are made uniquely for the organization. Anything that is branded or made to a unique, business-owned specification or drawing fits here. The supplier's focus is on selling its process and capability (see Figure 4.13). As there is more than one supplier, the buyer has the power, so in theory it is possible to switch suppliers to gain the best value. However, it should be noted that switching here is not as straightforward as in the generic quadrant and there may be issues around transition or acquainting the new supplier with specific requirements and manufacturing/service provision process.

- *Custom* (only one supplier and only one buyer). As the name suggests, this quadrant features the things that are custom-made for one company by only one supplier. Either party may have a unique process or patented component and the arrangement is such that it can only be made by/sold to the other party. In the custom quadrant

**FIGURE 4.13** Day one analysis: power balance in each quadrant

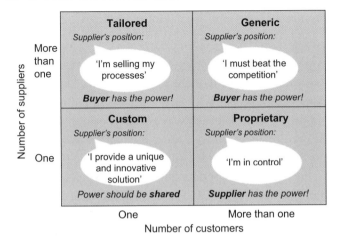

there is likely to be some form of strong relationship between buyer and supplier and the supplier may have accumulated certain know-how regarding the manufacture/service provision. For example, consider fragrances used by big perfume companies: to prevent copying, the fragrance houses that specialize in the development of these ingredients produce unique formulae that are protected by patents and complex chemical compositions that inhibit easy cloning. Global brands may wish to secure exclusive rights to a particular fragrance to confer uniqueness on their products, meaning only one customer and one supplier. In such an arrangement there would most likely be a strong, well-managed long-term relationship, which is a typical consequence of custom positioning. The balance of power between the buyer and supplier would therefore most likely be shared, although this is not always the case, and if the relationship has not been managed well the supplier may have gained ground.

- *Proprietary* (one supplier, many buyers). This is where suppliers want you to be, as it gives them the power and a degree of control. They are very clever and will work to identify ways in which you can only come to them for their products. Convincing a design team to specify make and part number on a drawing or specification will secure a proprietary position, as will differentiating a generic product to make it unique in some way, and thereby convincing a buyer it is better. Supermarket shelves are full of 'proprietary' products with expensive advertising to convince us of their added value. An everyday household chemical with an additive creates a 'unique formula' with the promise of being improved, kinder to the environment, gentle on your hands or better in some way; this moves its positioning from generic to proprietary. Buying a specific brand has the same effect.

Once the positioning on the day one analysis matrix has been established, the next stage is to consider why and what the implications are, or what needs to happen to unlock benefits. A generic position suggests ways forward might need to focus on leveraging the market as well as the need to stay in control and prevent 'added-value' repositioning by the supplier that might move the category or product down the matrix. A tailored positioning would suggest the need to look at how the overall value could be improved, perhaps by considering value engineering, improved transparency of costs, efficiency gains etc. In a custom positioning the focus should ideally be on value, not just price or cost, with initiatives to strengthen the relationship and perhaps work together on new product development. In a proprietary positioning the key questions to ask are, 'How did we get there?' and 'What do we need to do to move to generic?' This might involve challenging the specification or looking for generic substitutes. If it is not possible to move, then the focus needs to be on what is possible to gain benefit, for example by aggregating spend with other products or commodities from the supplier to gain leverage. Finally, the interpretation of the entire analysis should be summed up and recorded in a single paragraph so that there is a record of the outcome of the discussion and use of the tool.

There is a final note on 'bundling'. Suppliers love to bundle things together to convert a collection of generic categories or products into a unique bundle that only one supplier can provide, thus moving themselves to proprietary. For example, consider a facilities management company that began its relationship with the client by providing cleaning services (see Figure 4.14). As the relationship progressed, and under the guise of 'We're here to help', the supplier offered to take on and manage other support areas including running the staff restaurants, looking after the multitude of photocopiers around the buildings, carrying out building maintenance and running the reception desks. One by one these areas were outsourced to the provider, each decision seeming logical as there were inefficiencies that needed to be addressed and the supplier had already proved very capable. However, as time passed, the cost of the outsourced contract kept increasing and service declined, and so an initiative was launched to look at the market. Providers for each of the individual elements of the overall service

**FIGURE 4.14**  Day one analysis: bundling

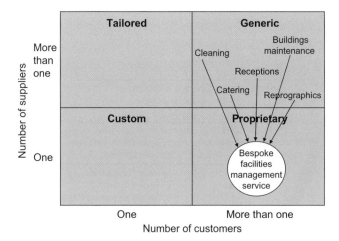

were in abundance but there was no single provider of that precise bundle. This prevented switching.

Furthermore, the supplier had managed to achieve a position that prevented easy unbundling without significant disruption because of the know-how it had accumulated. Such bundling typically moves to proprietary rather than custom because if the supplier is making a success of one particular mix of offering, it would also work to provide it to other clients.

Therefore beware the bundle. Often the group that is most susceptible to bundling is to be found in a company's boardroom; through established relationships with a key supplier they may have approved and endorsed a series of sourcing decisions that have expanded the supplier's scope of supply. Day one analysis should be used to identify any components of the category or product being examined, in order to understand if bundling has taken place. If it has, the focus needs to be on what needs to be unbundled, so as to gain leverage.

# Value levers

This step is an *Tool* and is *Essential*

We now come to the first of two of the most pivotal tools of the entire category management process: value levers. 'Value levers' are a checklist of

**FIGURE 4.15**    The value levers model

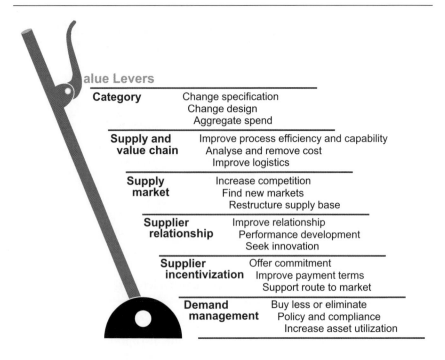

**Value Levers**

| **Category** | Change specification |
| | Change design |
| | Aggregate spend |

| **Supply and value chain** | Improve process efficiency and capability |
| | Analyse and remove cost |
| | Improve logistics |

| **Supply market** | Increase competition |
| | Find new markets |
| | Restructure supply base |

| **Supplier relationship** | Improve relationship |
| | Performance development |
| | Seek innovation |

| **Supplier incentivization** | Offer commitment |
| | Improve payment terms |
| | Support route to market |

| **Demand management** | Buy less or eliminate |
| | Policy and compliance |
| | Increase asset utilization |

all the potential sources of value and should be used as a prompt and check to consider what opportunities to investigate and pursue. Value levers are not a once-only activity but something that continues through the entire category management process. At the outset the project team may have an idea what value could be realized and where it might come from; however, as the team gathers data and gains insights new value-adding possibilities emerge and regular reviews against the value levers provide the basis to identify these.

The value levers model is given in Figure 4.15 and there are six headings, which are expanded further in Table 4.1:

- category levers;
- process levers;
- supply market levers;
- supplier relationship levers;
- supplier incentivization levers; and;
- demand management levers.

**TABLE 4.1**   Value levers explained

| Value lever | | Intervention to drive value |
|---|---|---|
| **Category** | **Change specification** | • Change, consolidate or standardize specifications<br>• Make generic<br>• Add some feature or function to drive growth |
| | **Change design** | • Review 'fitness for purpose' and value-engineer<br>• Incorporate innovation to drive growth |
| | **Aggregate spend or demand** | • Aggregate spend or demand across the business<br>• Consortia buying with partners<br>• Consolidate volumes |
| **Supply and value Chain** | **Improve process efficiency and capability** | • Understand the end-to-end supply and value chain (including our internal process) and identify areas for development<br>• Drive in improved efficiencies<br>• Improve capability (process, and skills of people)<br>• Use Lean or Six Sigma approaches<br>• Reduce or eliminate waste<br>• Eliminate unnecessary steps<br>• Improve transactional effectiveness (e-catalogues, e-billing, invoice consolidation) |
| | **Analyse and remove cost** | • Understand the total cost of ownership<br>• Understand where cost is introduced in the supply and value chain<br>• Identify and pursue improvement objectives to tackle specific cost areas |
| | **Improve logistics** | • Optimize packaging (size, spec, number of components, quantities, pallet load, reusable etc)<br>• Ullage reduction for packaging and transport<br>• Optimize logistics (trailer/container fill, back hauling etc) |

**TABLE 4.1**    *continued*

| Value lever | | Intervention to drive value |
|---|---|---|
| **Market** | **Increase competition** | • Switch suppliers<br>• Run a tender or competitive market exercise<br>• Use e-auctions or competitive bidding |
| | **Find new markets** | • Look beyond current market – global sourcing<br>• Low-cost country sourcing<br>• Look at new/other markets where similar capabilities exist |
| | **Restructure the supply base** | • Make vs buy/insource vs outsource decision<br>• Rationalize supply base<br>• Create new suppliers<br>• Backwards integration (start doing what your suppliers do) |
| **Supplier relationship** | **Performance development** | • Supplier performance measurement<br>• Drive in supplier improvement plans<br>• Set improvement objectives and targets<br>• Provide support to develop supplier capability<br>• Introduce performance incentives or penalties |
| | **Improve the relationship** | • Change or develop the relationship<br>• Agree a structure for how the relationship works<br>• Manager supplier interfaces better<br>• Joint working and collaboration to drive joint improvements<br>• Drive in shared objectives and values with common aim and purpose |
| | **Seek innovation** | • Check for potential innovation and 'value add' opportunities with suppliers<br>• Collaborate and align innovation initiatives<br>• Offer incentives, seek exclusivity<br>• Look for new capabilities for growth |

**TABLE 4.1** *continued*

| Value lever | | Intervention to drive value |
|---|---|---|
| **Supplier incentivization** | **Offer commitment** | • Offer potential or firm contractual commitment in terms of volumes, spend or length of contract<br>• Promise of future volumes of spend<br>• Introduce pricing mechanism linked to agreed commodity tracking (where the category is heavily linked to raw material fluctuations) |
| | **Improve payment terms** | • Offer improved payment terms<br>• Offer stage payment<br>• Prompt settlement discount |
| | **Support route to market** | • Help the supplier improve their route to market through your organization |
| **Demand management** | **Buy less or eliminate** | • Reduce need or buy less<br>• Eliminate need |
| | **Policy and compliance** | • Introduce new policy to manage demand<br>• Change existing policy<br>• Align and consolidate multiple policies<br>• Track and manage compliance to policy |
| | **Increase asset utilization** | • Improve/optimize asset management<br>• Optimize asset disposal<br>• Consider lease vs buy<br>• Understand and maximize the return on investment |

We use the term lever because using a lever is a positive action that delivers a result and a significant result is possible with only a small force applied in the right way using the lever. Value levers therefore represent a series of possible positive actions or things we can do to achieve the result of increased value. Remember, securing value is not just about getting reduced pricing or costs but can be many things including improved efficiency, reduced risk or brand enhancement through innovation.

There is a series of steps in using the value levers model effectively, as follows:

**1** Consider the category in question, review the list of potential value levers in turn and ask, 'If I did this (ie applied this value lever) what value would this bring? How much value would this bring?'

**2** Review all the potential opportunities and prioritize those that offer the most potential (the opportunity analysis matrix can be used here).

**3** Instigate data-gathering and research activities to verify the priorities.

**4** Update the business requirements (outlined in the next section).

**5** Develop actions to pursue value opportunities.

In the 1970s one word added at the end of the usage instructions on a bottle of shampoo transformed the industry, nearly doubled profits overnight and represented a breakthrough. In category management this same word will help find breakthroughs when applied to the way value levers are used. The word is: repeat. And 'repeat' is exactly what you should do with value levers, right through the entire process. The model should be used as a checklist and prompt to continually look for new sources of value and consider what things you can do to find it.

Value levers should not only consider intervention that could unlock value to us but also value to the supplier, as value to the supplier can present value to us. Buyers tend to opt to push the risk onto the supplier; suppliers tend to seek to protect their position. However, changing the approach here can unlock further value. For example, if a product is sensitive to raw material price volatility and we demand a fixed price or specific level of discount then the supplier carries all the risk. They will protect themselves within any pricing they offer. However, if we recognize this and can share this risk, say with a price review mechanism should commodity prices fluctuate outside agreed limits, then this has great value to the supplier and so could be sufficient incentive to provide further price improvements. Similarly suppliers value certainty of future commitment so they plan. Breakthrough benefits are possible by considering what the supplier values but more importantly by being able to organize ourselves so as to make and deliver on any commitment we make.

**CASE STUDY**    How a group of healthcare organizations used value levers to secure nearly 60 per cent lower prices for one category

Compression stockings are widely used in the healthcare profession to prevent DVT (deep vein thrombosis) – one of the most common hospital-preventable deaths. They are stockings worn on the lower leg (or garments worn on the arm) that are tight around the limb so exerting a squeezing that reduces the pooling of fluid, reducing swelling, improving blood flow and preventing dangerous blood clots forming. They are worn as a preventative therapy post surgery but also by at-risk patients during and after a hospital stay.

Compression stockings are used by healthcare organizations the world over. In the UK, these are either purchased by the NHS by individual healthcare trusts (responsible for one or more individual hospitals) or by buying groups acting on behalf of the NHS.

A category management project at one trust looked carefully at compression stockings and identified a significant potential opportunity. This healthcare trust had already identified significant opportunity by working together with six other trusts to aggregate spend and develop a consortia buying approach across a series of categories including DVT stockings. The category team comprising procurement and key stakeholders from across all the trusts involved met and started to work through the category management process, beginning with an STP worked as a team to gain alignment. The STP revealed some interesting facts about the current situation:

- Total spend of £872,000, of which about 60 per cent was with one just one dominant supplier, 30 per cent with a second, a third small supplier and the remaining spend spread across a handful of different suppliers.

- Of the three main suppliers, two were original manufacturers and one outsourced manufacturing.

- Brand loyalty was strong to one or another supplier at most trusts.

- Analysis showed dramatic price variations for the same product across trusts, in some cases twice that of the lowest average price previously negotiated by one trust.

- The spend was distributed across 184 SKUs and the team was interested to discover that suppliers had allocated different product codes to the same product when supplied to different trusts in order to hide different pricing approaches. Analysis showed that 14 SKUs accounted for 90 per cent of spend (£777,000) and three SKUs made up 50 per cent of category spend.

- The team considered the raw materials used to manufacture the stockings (primarily oil-based raw materials, cotton and silk) and identified recent falls in polymers (around 10 per cent) and cotton (around 20 per cent) suggesting this fact alone showed all trusts were overpaying for these items.

- All products across all suppliers met the required British or international standards and there were no strong clinical preferences so quality could be regarded as comparable.

Initially, based upon these findings the team talked to the market asking for revised pricing proposals that reflected the new combined spend, and would address price fluctuations and shifts in raw material costs. Responses suggested a saving of around 22 per cent was achievable. However this didn't quite seem like the right level of breakthrough for this category so the team worked through the value levers to consider how further benefit might be secured as follows:

- *Aggregate spend.* The team aggregated spend across seven hospital trusts.

- *Change specification.* Standardization and rationalization of products and SKUs.

- *Analyse and remove cost.* Moving to only suppliers who were original manufacturers (not outsourced).

- *Increased competition.* The team created competition between incumbent suppliers to secure future business, offering 90 per cent business across trusts in return for the lowest price.

- *Offer commitment.* In addition to the promise of market share the team offered a 12-month contract but also committed to a shared risk mechanism to permit price reviews if raw materials prices fluctuated outside agreed limits.

- *Policy and compliance.* The team worked at trust level to ensure that only the agreed supplier and products were used for 90 per cent of applications and there was no leakage to previous suppliers.

In the end, the application of these different value levers enabled the category team to achieve a total saving of 58.9 per cent, representing a £514,000 reduction in price. Whilst a proportion of this is clearly attributable to the effect of aggregation, raw material fluctuations and creating a competitive tension (perhaps the initial 22 per cent), the team realized that the full scale of benefit was due to the team considering what the supplier might value and what would be needed to secure further benefit.

Prior to this point trusts just bought what they needed individually under a framework agreement; suppliers engaged individually and had no basis to have any confidence in the future. Their tenure was only as strong as the preferences of ward-level professionals specifying their products. The key breakthrough here is that the category team identified what the supplier would value and that the seven trusts involved were able to organize themselves so as to offer commitment and deliver on their promise. It is possible that 37 per cent of the total savings here are attributable to this factor alone.

# Defining the business requirements

This step is a *Tool* and is *Essential*

Business requirements form the second most pivotal element of the entire category management process. Defining them is an essential step and informs many other activities. Their definition comprises a structured description of what the business needs and wants from the supply base for the category.

Imagine you are with a supplier, talking about working together, and the supplier says, 'Tell us what you need from us and how we can help.' You might respond by describing the product you require, its specification, the required lead time and how it must be delivered, and you might even have a target price that must be satisfied. In its simplest form the process of defining business requirements is just this – but it is about having a predetermined answer to this question as opposed to letting the supplier propose what they can sell. Crucially, however, business requirements cannot come from purchasing alone; the requirements must be a consolidated and aligned definition of what the entire business needs and wants. The process of defining requirements therefore has to engage the business and find ways to work through the different or conflicting individual requirements to arrive at a single, aligned list.

To be effective, the business requirements must also be about what is right for the business. This may seem obvious, but often companies end up buying a particular grade, nature and type of goods or services as a result of historical factors or what the supplier said they needed, as a result of preferences from technical or marketing functions, or for a variety of other reasons. In developing business requirements it is therefore important to challenge established ways; it is also important to make a distinction between what the business 'needs' and what it 'wants', since breakthrough opportunities may come from switching to what is needed rather than by accommodating what is wanted. The process to get there may involve pain of conflict between functions, but this should not put off the category team from applying the necessary rigour to arrive at the optimum set of business requirements.

The model for defining business requirements is the RAQSCI model (Regulatory, Assurance of supply, Quality, Service, Cost/Commercial and Innovation): see Figure 4.16. These are the different themes or headings under which we will define the requirements for the category in question. There is a sequence or hierarchy to business requirements, and for this reason the model is shown as a staircase. With a staircase you have to step on the first step, then the second and the third before you can get to the fourth. In the same way with business requirements, it is pointless considering *service* requirements such as account management or delivery conformance reporting if *assurance of supply* cannot be met and the goods may not turn up. This hierarchy is crucial as it refocuses attention in a prioritized order on what is important. This hierarchy helps disarm concerns from stakeholders and potentially suppliers. I often hear, 'You purchasing people are only

**FIGURE 4.16**    Business requirements RAQSCI model!

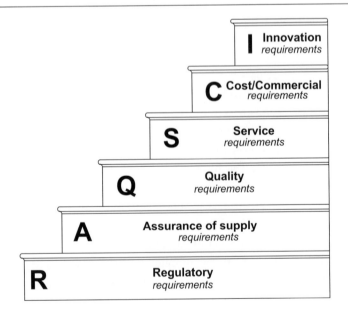

interested in cost!' to which I reply, 'Actually, no, cost is fifth on the list; first are regulatory, assurance of supply, quality and service, and then we'll consider cost. And if that goes well, we'll look at innovation.' The RAQSCI model helps to structure the definition of the business requirements in a way that reflects the overall needs of the entire business. The logic of the model is also instantly recognizable as relevant and appropriate in all camps.

There are many variants of the RAQSCI model around. You may see them as the AQSCIR or AQSCI, or variants including QCLDM (Quality, Cost, Logistics, Development and Management) and other similar models, each with a different label.

It is worth investing significant effort in working up the business requirements. Defining them is not a once-only activity. In fact, like value levers, looking at business requirements is an activity that runs through the entire process. This is because it is necessary and appropriate to review the requirements and update them regularly in the light of new information, consultation, value opportunities, breakthroughs and general progress. Even once the category reaches maturity and new sourcing arrangements have been implemented, the business requirements then become the reference point that can be reviewed regularly in light of changes in the organization and marketplace. This helps determine when the category management process should be started again for the category.

Business requirements are pivotal to the entire process and many later activities depend on the rigour with which requirements are developed. These include:

- development of evaluation criteria to evaluate strategic sourcing options identified in Stage 3;
- basis to develop an RFP or RFQ or run an e-Auction in Stage 4;
- development of supplier selection criteria in Stage 4;
- basis for negotiation planning in Stage 4;
- basis for structuring contracts with suppliers in Stage 4;
- basis for developing performance measurement framework in Stages 4 and 5;
- basis for ongoing management of the supplier and category in Stage 5;
- basis for triggering a review of the category in Stage 5.

If we consider what is included under each of the six business requirement headings, then the staircase concept begins to make more sense. Table 4.2 explores each heading and what it is concerned with, and defines the scope or typical areas where specific requirements might be developed.

**TABLE 4.2**  Business requirements explained

| Requirement | Concerned with... | Scope |
|---|---|---|
| **Regulatory** | Acting in accordance with stipulated laws and regulations | • Complies with relevant and/or forthcoming current legislation or regulatory obligations |
| **Assurance of supply** | Factors associated with the availability and accessibility of goods and services when required | • Financial stability of supplier<br>• Coverage<br>• Risk<br>• Capacity<br>• Delivery<br>• Problems or incident management<br>• Corporate Social Responsibility (CSR) including environmental obligations (from any stated corporate policy) |
| **Quality** | Factors associated with the consistency and fitness for purpose of the goods or services and the ability of the supplier to ensure repeatability. | • Design<br>• Consistency, repeatability and fitness for purpose<br>• Compliance with specification<br>• Reliability<br>• Measurement<br>• Quality management systems or accreditations of supplier (eg ISO9001) |
| **Service** | Factors associated with the way the goods or services are supplied or provided and any support activities | • Lead times and flexibility<br>• Inventory holding, staging, allocating etc<br>• Processes and procedures<br>• Response times<br>• Account management<br>• Communication<br>• Information<br>• Support (eg help desk, hotline number etc)<br>• Training and education |

**TABLE 4.2** *continued*

| Requirement | Concerned with... | Scope |
|---|---|---|
| **Cost/ Commercial** | All factors associated with cost or price including commercial terms, conditions and arrangements to comply | • Acquisition cost goals and objectives eg target cost, lowest benchmarked market cost etc<br>• Implementation costs<br>• Continuous improvement (future cost, cost reduction, cost avoidance)<br>• Terms and conditions<br>• Charging methodology<br>• Cash retention in the business |
| **Innovation** | Continuous improvement within all parts of the customer experience, intended to reduce costs, increase value or create competitive advantage. | • Capabilities and areas of focus<br>• Supply chain<br>• Market driven<br>• Internal<br>• Use of emerging technology<br>• 'First point of call' for supplier's new ideas<br>• Arrangements for sharing and collaboration |

Business requirements are the vehicle that connects organizational mission, vision, aims, objectives and strategy to the supply base. We may be aware of, and understand, corporate goals but it is all to easy to assume that it is someone else's job to deliver on these while we get on and look after our suppliers and what we buy. It seems this is a common yet restricting mindset. When I work with purchasing teams a question I sometimes ask is, 'Whose job is it to translate corporate policy and objectives into specific actions within the supply base?' Sometimes teams have a robust answer; more often people look at each other with thoughtful expressions. The reality is that in most organizations it is the purchasing function that needs to pick up the mantle here and sometimes this comes as a surprise to those involved. Remember the 3S model back in Chapter 2 (Figure 2.2) illustrating the

**FIGURE 4.17**    Business requirements as a key enabler to connect *sourcing*, *satisfying* and *strategy*

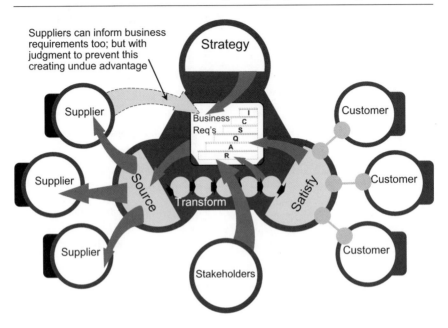

high-level principle for an effective organizational structure? Purchasing looks after how we *source*, sales and marketing look after how we *satisfy* our customers and there is a flow of value through the organization from one to another with *strategy* informing and being informed by both. Business requirements are one of the key enablers to connect *sourcing, satisfying* and *strategy* (Figure 4.17). It provides the framework and means to convert current and future customer needs and aspirations into definitions of what we need from the supply base. Similarly it is the place where corporate policy and intent is turned into real statements of requirement for suppliers to deliver against. For example, if the organization sets a policy that all significant suppliers must comply with a specific health and safety policy or must observe the company's corporate social responsibility then these requirements must become statements within our business requirements alongside the needs and wants of internal stakeholders.

Business requirements cannot be developed in isolation if the project is to succeed. There are many areas that need to be examined through a process of extensive research and stakeholder consultation. A good set of business requirements should be like a tree with roots extended far and wide throughout the organization and grown through engagement with the various functions to understand and define the complete needs and wants of the organization.

**FIGURE 4.18** Business requirements: inputs

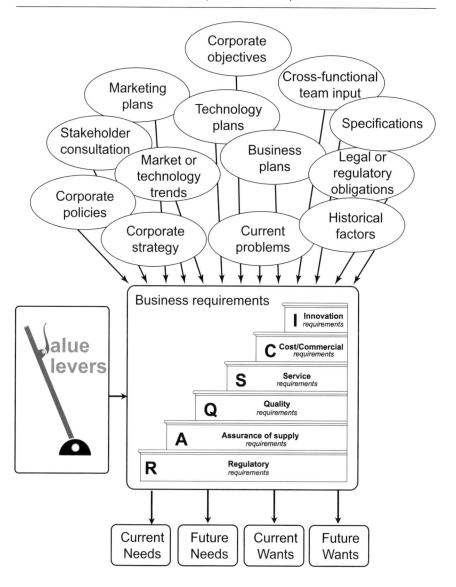

It is here where we first attempt to convert potential value levers into specific requirements that will shape how we will source. For example if we are using a *change specification* lever to drive standardization or rationalize a range of products then our requirements should define the new specification and how we intend to buy. Figure 4.18 gives a view of the typical inputs that help shape business requirements. The steps involved in reaching a definition of business requirements are:

1 *Gather data.* Gather data regarding corporate strategy, policies, objectives, marketing plans, business plans, technology plans etc. Here it is important to establish the intended future direction and aspirations of the business. The results may not make specific reference to the category in question, and so it is the role of the category team to make the connections between where the organization is heading and how this category is sourced both now and in the future.

2 *Convert value levers.* Review the value levers identified and determine how these can convert into business requirements.

3 *Consult internally.* Consult with stakeholders to understand their requirements. This process is not as straightforward as might first appear. Within it, it is necessary to establish what has been sourced in the past, what is believed to be required in future and, crucially, to challenge why. I will explore how this challenge needs to happen more fully in a moment.

4 *Consider external factors.* Understand any external factors that should be considered but have not been identified as part of 1 and 2 above. These might include emerging technologies or new processes, for example.

5 *Build requirements.* Distil the knowledge and understanding reached into a set of business requirements.

6 *Share and refine.* Communicate back to key stakeholders to secure their buy-in; refine, optimize, develop and update as required.

7 *Review ongoing.* Review and update the business requirements as appropriate ongoing throughout the category management project.

To be successful here, one of the most important elements in developing business requirements is the process of challenging, of asking the question, 'Why does it need to be that way?' It is this process that can make the difference between small incremental improvements and breakthrough results. This activity, however, is unlikely to be met with waves of support or empathy from the wider business. It is more likely it will lead to questions as to why purchasing and the cross-functional category team appear to have assumed the remit to question marketing, technical or other functions that believe they have the monopoly on specifying what is sourced. This is the first point in the category management process where conflict emerges. This is good, and should be regarded as a sign that inroads towards achieving a breakthrough change are being made. The conflict does, however, need to be carefully managed.

The mindset required is to disregard what has gone before and begin to think about the underlying purpose the category needs to satisfy and, if there were no constraints, the most effective way to achieve it. Looking back at the breakthrough bottle example, the underlying need was to get the product to the consumer using a means that preserved recognition of the brand. The process of consultation with stakeholders should therefore use questioning that allows this kind of key issue to be explored, taking thinking away from the constraints of 'What we have always bought' to 'If we could do anything, what would we do?'

Table 4.3 provides some typical stakeholder questions that help to open up thinking. It is only by challenging that you begin to move beyond the constraints of historical practices, individual preferences, resistance to change, ignorance, intransigence etc. The '5 Whys' technique can help here (see below).

**TABLE 4.3**  Sample questions to establish business requirements

| Requirement | Sample stakeholder questions |
| --- | --- |
| Regulatory | • What industry, customer or company working standards exist here? How do they affect what you and your suppliers do? <br> • What restrictions or guidelines do your suppliers place on you for operating with them? |
| Assurance of supply | • Have you ever gone without the product when required? Why is that? <br> • What are the greatest risks associated with the continued availability of the product? Why? <br> • Are there any goods or services your suppliers cannot provide? |
| Quality | • Who defines the quality standards you work to? <br> • Which standards do you agree and disagree with? Why? <br> • Which standards do suppliers find it hardest to deliver consistently? Why? |

**TABLE 4.3** *continued*

| Service | • What supplier information would enable you to work effectively? Why? |
| | • What frustrates you about the way your suppliers service the account? |
| | • How do you rate your supplier's personnel? |
| **Cost/Commercial** | • What cost pressures are you under with regard to this category? |
| | • What cost targets do you have? |
| | • How have your suppliers helped you to drive down costs? |
| | • What contractual terms are needed for this category? |
| Innovation | • How much of your supplier's goods or service capabilities are you using? |
| | • What could the category team do to help create competitive advantage in this area? |

**General questions**

| General questions that will help 'unlock' key business requirements | • What are the factors which stop you doing your job effectively? |
| | • Who are your best and worst suppliers and why? |
| | • Are the best available suppliers in the market being used? How can we be sure? |
| | • How do your suppliers perceive your department/company? |
| | • What concerns do you have over the work the category team is doing? |
| | • Does your department miss, meet or exceed its targets? How and why? |
| | • What influence if any does this category have on your department's targets performance? |
| | • If you had the power to change anything about the category, what would it be and why? |
| | • How do other organizations manage this category? |

It is also important to be cognizant of the role of the cross-functional team to combine and rationalize the requirements as viewed by multiple functions, each of whose needs from a category may be different.

As an example, consider the category 'temporary labour'. HR will be interested in factors such as compliance with employment law requirements, single contact point for requesting new staff, account management and reporting. Purchasing will be interested in lowest benchmarked rates, finance will be interested in payment cycles and timing, and operations will want to be assured that the provider can supply the best people when required. Sometimes the requirements of different functions will naturally combine to give the full picture. Sometimes, however, they may conflict, and so active stakeholder management is required to broker agreement between functions to arrive at an agreed statement of requirements.

The process of engaging with the business is not just about reaching an agreed definition of business requirements. The process itself is an essential component of change management. Securing agreement along the way will reduce resistance to change later and will even facilitate support to roll out the changes.

As the final list of business requirements emerges, the difference between 'needs' and 'wants' and the timing of the requirement should be agreed. This will require challenge, as it is unlikely there will be agreement regarding what constitutes needs and wants, as well as which wants are relevant. For example, consider the category of travel. The process of stakeholder consultation might involve consulting staff regarding their needs from corporate travel. Responses might typically be the need to fly business class, stay in comfortable hotels and benefit from points and Air Miles. These, however, are not needs; they are wants. That doesn't mean they should be ignored, but the distinction must be clear. The business need is to enable staff to travel in the best value-for-money way that is just comfortable enough to maintain overall staff contentment with the employer. Within business requirements the distinction between needs and wants opens up possibilities for creative solutions or for suppliers to gain an advantage if they can provide the wants where others cannot.

It is also relevant to consider the time dimension. There may be requirements that are not possible today but must be met at some point in the future: for example, emerging legislation. Or perhaps there is emerging technology that, once available, is desirable. It is appropriate to give business requirements a time dimension stipulating whether the need or want should be satisfied now or at some time in the future. Figure 4.19 gives an example of a simple set of business requirements for a packaging category that illustrates how this works.

**FIGURE 4.19** Business requirements example

| Business Requirements – Packaging Category | | | | |
|---|---|---|---|---|
| Requirement | Need? | Want? | Now? | In 3 years? |
| **Regulatory** | | | | |
| • Supply solutions comply with all industry environmental and recycling standards | ✓ | | ✓ | |
| • Meets all internal regulatory standards | ✓ | | ✓ | |
| **Assurance of supply** | | | | |
| • Just-in-time delivery requirements for sites A, B and C | ✓ | | ✓ | |
| • Site lead time requirements from 5 days to 6 weeks | ✓ | | ✓ | |
| • Must support primary and secondary packaging, labels | ✓ | | ✓ | |
| • Must have robust problem management procedures | ✓ | | ✓ | |
| **Quality** | | | | |
| • Suppliers compliant to our needs – confirmed by audits | ✓ | | ✓ | |
| • No product recalls driven by print supplier performance | ✓ | | ✓ | |
| • No print component-driven production stoppages. Product delivery tolerances (+/–10% tolerance) | ✓ | | ✓ | |
| • Capable of meeting clients Lean Sigma targets | ✓ | | ✓ | |
| **Service** | | | | |
| • Supplier Managed Inventory System capabilities to manage relevant categories and line items | ✓ | | | |
| • Order tracking capabilities available to operations | | ✓ | | ✓ |
| • Account management personnel available 7 days a week | | ✓ | ✓ | ✓ |
| • Supplier must be highly responsive to changes | | ✓ | ✓ | |
| **Cost/Commercial** | | | | |
| • 20% PPV reduction over 3 years across total spend of 4.8 million Euros | | ✓ | ✓ | ✓ |
| • Capable of identifying and delivering cost out projects | | ✓ | ✓ | |
| • 60 days payment terms | | ✓ | ✓ | |
| **Innovation** | | | | |
| • Electronic Artwork Transmission facilities | | ✓ | | ✓ |
| • Digital printing capability | | ✓ | | ✓ |
| • Capable of leading innovative pack designs | | ✓ | | ✓ |

Finally, as I said earlier, business requirements are not a 'once only' activity but once defined should be regularly reviewed and updated as new insights, opportunities or threats emerge. Here the relationship between business requirements and value levers is important. As we progress through category management it is likely we will identify new value levers that we could use representing new sources of potential breakthrough or new market possibilities; similarly identifying new business needs and wants requires us to consider which value lever we might use to secure benefit. Value levers and business requirements therefore go hand-in-hand with one informing the other cyclically throughout the entire process. It is this ongoing cyclical relationship that is the primary source of breakthrough within category management. Category teams therefore should actively provide for regular review and reappraisal of both value levers and business requirements throughout the project.

## The 5 Whys

The 5 Whys technique can be useful to help challenge what people want and get to the real business need. This is a technique that children learn early on and thankfully we leave behind in adulthood, but is good for getting to the bottom of things. 5 Whys is as simple as asking the question *why* five or even more times when presented with a problem or scenario and the answers progressively get closer to the real reason, for example:

*The scenario:* The product is specified as needing to be gold plated

*Category Manager why #1:* 'Why?'

*Stakeholder answer #1:* 'Because that is what the specification says.'

*Category Manager why #2:* 'But why does it need to be gold plated?'

*Stakeholder answer #2:* 'Because we've always had them like that.'

*Category Manager why #3:* 'Why?'

*Stakeholder answer #3:* 'Well, there would have been a good technical reason for someone to specific them like that.'

*Category Manager why #4:* 'OK, so what is it... why do we need gold plating?'

*Stakeholder answer #4:* 'Perhaps marketing insisted on it?'

*Category Manager why #5:* 'Why does it need to be gold plated?'

*Stakeholder Answer #5:* 'Truth is I don't think we've ever stopped to think about it.'

It is a powerful approach, but it is also problematic because asking why repeatedly can appear a bit condescending. A more subtle approach is to mix why questions with questions like 'How does it do that?' Or 'In what way' or 'How does it make that happen?' and so on.

---

### Chapter 4 summary

Recap on the key points from this chapter:

1   The first stage within the category management process is *initiation* and is concerned with kicking off the category management project. This includes forming the team, verifying the opportunity, engaging with stakeholders, identifying potential sources of value, defining the business requirements, delivering early benefit and planning the project.

2   It is essential to define clearly the scope of the category that will be worked on.

3   We can use the opportunity analysis tool again here to verify the opportunity and to prioritize the sub-categories that we will work on.

4   Recruiting an executive sponsor can help the project, elevate its profile and provide support, resources and remove obstacles.

5   Category projects are generally most impactful when delivered by a cross-functional team who work through the process and help implement new sourcing arrangements. We start by recruiting the right team and ensuring team members are committed, available and have the support of their superiors.

6   The STP (situation, target, proposal) tool is an essential tool to understand and gain team alignment to the current situation and begin to identify where we need to be and what we are going to do to get there. It is as relevant here as it is for any stage in category management.

7   The team charter, compiled by the team, defines the project, team composition and the agreed roles and responsibilities for each contributor.

8  Key to project success is the identification of all the stakeholders (people who have an interest in the project or could help achieve project goals) and determining how we will engage with them.

9  Category projects benefit from effective communications planning, delivering tailored communications to stakeholders and stakeholder groups in order to secure buy-in, help prepare the organization for change and maintain project momentum and support.

10  Once the team is formed and we have kicked off the project a project time plan can help plan the rest of the project and the key activities the team will be involved in.

11  It is important to look for early benefits to show success as soon as possible as it might take some time for the project to deliver its ultimate benefits. It is therefore worth looking for quick wins and agreeing actions to deliver these. The quick-win tool can help to prioritize which initiatives to pursue.

12  The *day one analysis* tool is used early on to provide essential insight into the category and understand where benefit might come from.

13  Value in category management can come from many different sources so we consider the different *value levers* that we will use to secure benefit.

14  We define what we need from a category using the *business requirements* framework in RAQSCI format. Arriving at a definitive set of requirements requires us to engage with the wider business and look at all the different factors or influencers that shape what the organization needs to buy. Here there is potential for breakthrough but it requires us to challenge what we buy and consider what the organization 'needs' versus what the organization 'wants'.

# Stage 2: Insight

In this chapter we will explore the second stage, insight. We will examine the need and process for gathering rigorous and detailed market, supplier and organizational data to gain a greater understanding of the category and potential opportunities. We will look at how we can make sense of all the information collected, using a series of strategic analytical tools. Finally we will consider the vital contribution this stage can make to the identification of breakthrough sourcing strategies.

Pathway questions addressed in this chapter:

**8** For each and any category, what is my current position?

**9** How can I identify the optimum, and ideally breakthrough, future sourcing strategy for a category?

**10** How do I ensure all our future sourcing strategies are based upon a robust understanding of all market and external drivers and factors?

## The insight toolkit

Insight comprises a series of research activities followed by the use of strategic analysis tools to gain some insight that can help inform the subsequent development of a recommended sourcing strategy. The toolkit is shown in Figure 5.1. It is important to remember that not every element is essential; some steps are optional. The following sections give some guidance in its use.

**FIGURE 5.1**  Stage 2: Insight

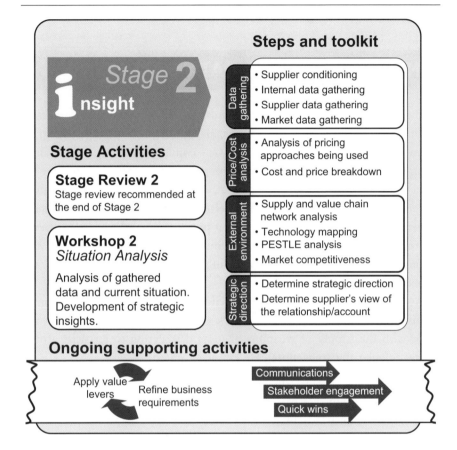

# Developing category insights

Stage 2, insight, seeks to achieve a number of key objectives:

- Gather data in three key areas. This is data about:
  - the category and how the organization uses the category;
  - suppliers and potential new suppliers;
  - the marketplace and potential other or new marketplaces.
- Analyse the data and gain insight using a series of analytical tools and techniques.

This stage is about gaining a rich and detailed understanding from which a future strategy can be formed. This is one of the most crucial parts of the category management process. The more complex a category is, and the more stakeholders who are involved, the greater the need here.

# INTRODUCTION TO DATA GATHERING

It is the depth of understanding gained during this stage that can make the difference between identifying a breakthrough future sourcing strategy or just a small incremental improvement. One common mistake often made in using category management is the assumption by the project leader or the team that, from the outset of a project, they already possess an adequate understanding of the category and therefore already know the way forward. This misguided belief is a blind spot that prevents breakthroughs. However, approaching this stage with an open mind, rigorously carrying out data gathering and applying the strategic analysis tools can reveal significant, hitherto unseen, opportunities.

At a news briefing in 2002 the then-US Secretary of Defence Donald Rumsfeld attempted to defend the lack of evidence linking Iraq's government with the supply of weapons of mass destruction to terrorist groups (**www.defense.gov/transcripts**). He famously stated:

> There are known knowns; there are things we know we know. We also know there are known unknowns; that is to say we know there are some things we do not know. But there are also unknown unknowns – the ones we don't know we don't know. And if one looks throughout the history of our country and other free countries, it is the latter category that tend to be the difficult ones.

Rumsfeld subsequently came under attack from a number of camps for what some regarded as gibberish or nonsense (Girard and Girard, 2009), yet others praised how he concisely described the complexities of identifying things we don't know we don't know (Bennet and Bennet, 2004). Within category management it is our focus on the things we don't know we don't know that holds the greatest importance as here is where the game-changing new sourcing strategies might be found. This is illustrated in Figure 5.2 where the complete pie represents the sum of all knowledge for a category project or indeed any area we are working on. The area called 'I know what I know' represents things we are aware of, data or information we have in our possession (or know where to find). This segment represents the basis of our current understanding.

We can also articulate the things we are aware we do not know ('I know what I don't know'). This represents the data, information or understanding

**FIGURE 5.2**   Data-gathering 'knowledge pie'

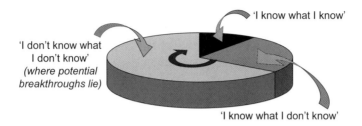

we know we are lacking. In a category project this might be, for example, spend data, specification details, usage data, or information about suppliers. We can identify and find this information.

The final segment, 'I don't know what I don't know', is often ignored, yet this is where the biggest prizes may lie. 'I don't know what I don't know' contains all the data, information, ideas, understanding and knowledge we are not aware of. The way to reveal this information is through detailed research.

If you've ever been involved in any research, perhaps for a dissertation or within a research and development function, then the concept of exploring the unknown will not be new. The insight stage of category management is fundamentally about research and analysis, and good research looks beyond what is currently understood. It is about deep, rigorous and inquisitive data collection and analysis that, if done properly, will naturally cause a breakthrough future sourcing strategy to emerge.

Practitioners often take shortcuts at this stage, but if this part of the process is not attended to thoroughly, the results will be suboptimal.

**CASE STUDY**   The war room

Figure 5.3 shows a 'war room' for a particular category management project. This room had been provided specifically for the duration of the project and the walls had been progressively filled with documents, data, workshop outputs, papers, analysis and anything and everything to do with the category and the process of data gathering. The room was used as the base and working area for the cross-functional team. Key stakeholders would be brought in and walked through the entire project. Over time the information on the walls painted a rich picture of the

**FIGURE 5.3**    A war room example

category. The team lived and breathed the entire contents of the walls for several months. When the time came to determine options for the future sourcing strategy, the potential ways forward became obvious. It was simply a case of the group standing in the middle of the room and suggesting approaches. This example shows the level and depth of data gathering typically needed for effective category management and how a means of 'immersing' the team in the data can help to open up new possibilities.

Throughout the category management process there are a number of places where data is collected. Some of these are dedicated data-collection activities, which are explored in this chapter, whilst others are not but will naturally yield valuable information. The collection and analysis of data is fundamental to Stage 2; however, it is also an activity that runs through the entire process.

Data-gathering outputs take a number of forms ranging from reports, spreadsheets and technical papers to scribbled notes from a discussion with key individuals in the business. One critical activity is to identify and share the insights along the way. If you were the person who gathered the data, perhaps involving an interview with a key stakeholder, you will have a pretty good idea of what is happening in that area of the business. You may even have some good ideas in terms of what could be done differently. But it is important to find a way to share learnings. This is actually quite straightforward, but within the team you must adopt the discipline of routinely doing it. There are four steps for success here:

1  For every piece of data you gather, ask yourself, 'So what does this tell me?' and write it down in no more than one simple paragraph and a few bullet points. If you're using a war room, then write it beside or on the report or notes before posting it on the wall.

2 Share the 'So what does this tell me?' question and its answer with the rest of the team at the earliest opportunity.

3 Make sure that the rest of the team also write up and share their own 'So what does this tell me?' questions and answers.

4 Collect all your questions and answers together with everyone else's. These can be used later to quickly remind the team of what you and they learnt along the way. The STP tool can provide a means to capture new insights as you go. This is a vital step prior to determining any future sourcing strategy.

There are some key data-collection methods that will help with research across the three key areas (category/internal, supplier and market data). These exist at various stages throughout the category management process and are shown in Table 5.1.

**TABLE 5.1**　Data collection sources and methods

| Means to gather data/ sources of information | Type of data that can be gathered | | |
| --- | --- | --- | --- |
| | Category and internal data | Supplier data | Market data |
| Defining business requirements | Yes | | |
| RFI (Request for Information) | | Yes | Yes |
| Internet and desk-based research | Yes | Yes | Yes |
| Stakeholder interviews | Yes | Yes | |
| Supplier visits | Yes | Yes | Yes |
| Engage expert | Yes | Yes | Yes |
| Tradeshows and exhibitions | Yes | Yes | Yes |
| Books and published papers | Yes | Yes | |
| Governmental bodies | | Yes | Yes |

Whilst data collection should seek to keep expanding the sum of knowledge to open up previously unseen opportunities, it should also be planned as realistically as possible. Therefore one of the activities for the second workshop should be to develop a data-gathering plan (see Figure 5.4 and a template is provided in the Appendix). This is a simple action plan specifying all the data that needs to be collected and who will collect it.

These actions should be shared among the category management project team. In order to create such a plan the team first needs to understand what data exists already and what further data is needed. This may seem obvious, but often when a group of individuals works together on projects there is no common understanding of what already exists. In organizations people are not good at sharing information. A particular report, some analysis or some industry data that one person is familiar with and regularly consults may be perceived as a data gap by another individual. We need an early pooling of information to determine what needs to be collected, then the data-gathering plan can be developed.

Today good data gathering is in reach of us all and the internet is a fantastic source of information, much of it free, if we know where and how to look. In addition there are many professional companies and websites who can provide a paid service to supplement our data-gathering activities. The basics of internet searching are known to almost everybody these days; however, it is important to remember that just as in a supermarket when the products at eye level are the ones they want us to buy, popular search engines can present results that they want us to have – perhaps those listings determined by companies paying to get there or as a result of the prevailing algorithms determined by the search engine to limit website designers from gaining a free advantage through incorporating too many search engine optimization features.

Developing advanced skills in internet searching can allow us to access information of a greater quality and often free. There is no right or wrong way to carry out internet searches and experimentation is the best approach. Ten tips for advanced internet research are provided below to help here (incorporating suggestions adapted from *Information Literacy Toolkit*, 2009). Furthermore, it is worth considering using a selection of search engines and desktop search tools that access the internet, especially those focused on business such as **www.copernic.com** or **www.hoovers.com**. The rest is down to clarity of search terms and thinking about all the potential sources of the information needed. Table 5.2 provides a range of suggestions here.

**FIGURE 5.4** An example data-gathering plan

| Data-Gathering Plan | Plan Type: Category/Internal ☐ Supplier ☐ Market ☐ | Category: Hot beverage cups | | | | | Date: 23rd Aug | |
|---|---|---|---|---|---|---|---|---|
| | | How data will be collected | | | | | Who | By when |
| Data to collect | RFI | RFP | Desktop research | F2F with Stakeh'dr | Other (specify) | | |
| 1 Spend (total and for cups and lids for each business unit) | ☐ | ☐ | ☑ | ☑ | Run report | HS | 1 Sep |
| 2 Range of cup sizes, lids and specifications | ☐ | ☐ | ☐ | ☑ | Internal Quest'naire | HS | 1 Sep |
| 3 Current volumes by supplier and part number by bus' unit | ☐ | ☐ | ☐ | ☑ | Internal Quest'naire | HS | 1 Sep |
| 4 Future volume projections by bus' unit | ☐ | ☐ | ☐ | ☑ | Internal Quest'naire | HS | 1 Sep |
| 5 Global and regional manufacturers and suppliers of cups/lids | ☑ | ☑ | ☑ | ☐ | | JW | 14 Sep |
| 6 Current and future market product offerings (cups and lids) | ☑ | ☑ | ☑ | ☐ | | JW | 14 Sep |
| 7 Business requirements for 'generic cup' cross bus' units | ☑ | ☑ | ☑ | ☑ | | HS | 14 Sep |
| 8 Sleeves (volumes, cost of sleeves and where used) | ☐ | ☑ | ☑ | ☑ | | HS | 14 Sep |
| 9 Brang requirements for generic cup | ☐ | ☑ | ☑ | ☐ | | JW | 7 Sep |
| 10 Recyclability by product | ☑ | ☑ | ☑ | ☐ | | JW | 7 Sep |
| 11 Product cost PPCA breakdown for top 5 current products | ☐ | ☐ | ☑ | ☑ | Team at workshop | Team | 23 Sep |
| 12 Commodity trends for cardboard, plastic, wax coating | ☐ | ☑ | ☑ | ☐ | | JW | 23 Sep |
| 13 Market trends for cups and lids | ☑ | ☐ | ☐ | ☐ | | JW | 23 Sep |
| 14 Drivers and forces (PESTLE and Porter's five forces) | ☐ | ☐ | ☑ | ☐ | Team at workshop | Team | 23 Sep |

**TABLE 5.2**    Suggestions for what to search for and potential sources for internet searches

| Type of data | What this will provide | What to search for |
|---|---|---|
| General information | General information that will help understand markets. | Consider using multiple search engines and desktop search tools. National statistics sites (eg **www.statistics.gov.uk**), Government trade sites (eg **www.trade.gov** in the US, **www.cbi.org.uk** in the UK). |
| Market overview and trends | Business and financial news provides insight into world events, changes in sectors and what is happening with big corporations. How global stock markets view a sector or institution is a good insight into what is happening in a marketplace. | Find the websites for all the key news providers (eg *Financial Times*, *The Economist*, *Harvard Business Review*, *Wall Street Journal*, BBC, CNN, Bloomberg, Reuters etc). Market intelligence and market research sites (eg Keynote, Market Research). |
| Sector and category-based market information | Insight into what is happening in a particular sector or the forces that are likely to drive change. Indices, pricing and trends for specific sectors, categories or commodities. | Websites providing white papers by sector; try the World Trade Organization, sites offering sector-specific information (eg Kompass, Company Sleuth), sites offering sector-specific pricing and trends (eg **www.icispricing.com** for the chemical sector), sites offering industry reports and sector data (eg **www.cbi.org.uk**, **www bizminer.com**). |
| Financial, stock indices and currencies | Insight into value and trends of companies and currencies. | Currency conversion sites (eg **www.xe.com**), financial market and exchanges (eg Dow Jones, *Financial Times*, FTSE, London Stock Exchange, Bloomberg). |

**TABLE 5.2** *continued*

| Type of data | What this will provide | What to search for |
|---|---|---|
| Commodity intelligence | Current commodity price information and insight into how trends across multiple commodities can impact your business. | Websites offering commodity pricing or sites offering a full detailed 'on demand' reporting service (eg **www.mintec.ltd.uk**). |
| Company information | Insight into individual companies, which when combined with other information helps establish an overall understanding of the market. | Search for details of the company; use one or more of the sites who offer company and market information (eg Hoovers, Dunn and Bradstreet, OneSource, Skyminder). |

## Ten tips for advanced internet research

(incorporating tips adapted from *Information Literacy Toolkit*, 2009).

1 Get familiar with several search engines – different search engines will return different results for the same search term so read the online help files for the search engines – they contain great detail about how to search effectively.

2 Think carefully about the search terms you use – repeat searches using alternative words or phrases that hold the same meaning, eg purchasing, procurement, sourcing, buying etc.

3 Limit results for a given search using the search options feature within the search engine (refer to the online help files to find out how).

4 'Double quotation marks' – use to find phrases or terms in the exact order specified and so limit results.

5 AND (+) – use the plus sign to combine search terms so only results featuring both keywords will be returned, eg *cleaning+chemicals*

6 NOT (–) – use the minus sign to limit a search so as to exclude a concept, issue or person eg *syringe-medical*.

7   OR – use OR (in capital letters) to find related words or synonyms, eg supplier OR vendor.

8   Truncation – use to search for different endings to a specific word, eg buy, buy-ing, buy-er. Some engines do this automatically, others might require the use of a 'wild character' to indicate different possible endings to the word, eg buy*.

9   Geographical limits – many search engines are set by default to first return results relevant to the country you are in, which may be unhelpful for global research. Use advanced search options to widen or lessen the scope here.

10   Check the number of hits for your results to see whether you are getting more or less information relative to the highest-ranking result.

Finally, a word about depth of data gathering. Gathering lots of data far and wide and immersing ourselves in as much different knowledge as we can will help us to see new breakthrough opportunities. But breakthroughs can also come from depth of research into a single area. If we are buying in volume, then a very small change somewhere to the product (or service) we are buying could yield a breakthrough result overall. If we are buying many similar products (or services), or buying from multiple sources, then the ability to make like-for-like comparisons in terms of performance or effectiveness across the range could reveal opportunities for rationalization and improvement. To do this a deeper analysis into the product or service is required. Here we need to use attribute analysis to examine the individual features or attributes of the product (or service) and identify the things we can measure that will allow us to make direct comparisons. As consumers we do this every day without thinking about it. If we go to buy a desktop printer for home, we might first ask what features it has: Does it just print? Can it print and scan? What size document can it handle? We might then move on to look at specific areas of performance: How many pages per minute will it print? What do the consumables cost? How many pages do the inkjet cartridges (typically) produce? Finally, we can combine our analysis together with some usage and life-expectancy assumptions to give us a single measure or set of measures that will allow us to make an unbiased comparison across printers: the cost per print. Prudent buying here might save us $50 a year in consumables, so imagine what we could do if we were responsible for buying inkjet printers for an entire university where hundreds of students needed to be equipped with their own individual printer and consider the difference our campus-wide intervention would make against individual purchases.

Our personal buying choices are informed by a similar measure based upon product or service attributes: supermarkets now display 'cost per kilo or pound', car fuel consumption ('mpg' or 'kmpl') gets more important to us all every year and the 'rate per hour' for the builder we employ needs careful consideration. Finding the equivalents within our data gathering will enable us to make direct comparisons and could help us find breakthroughs. Doing this is a very simple process but one that is often missed, but requires us to consider four key questions:

1 What attributes does it have? What are the individual features or characteristics? List everything you see.

2 What does it do? What function does it perform overall, what function do the individual features or characteristics perform?

3 How well does it do it? What comparative measures can you use to allow you to compare this to other similar products (or services)? Here you are looking for the 'something per something' measure.

4 How does it compare? Here you should look for differences and identify areas where there are opportunities for improvement.

---

**CASE STUDY**   How depth of data gathering helped H J Heinz

A global category management project within H J Heinz examined the category of metal cans used across the entire canned product range. It was no surprise that there were multiple suppliers around the world, each aligned with a particular canning plant and the consumer expectations in that region. This presented an immediate opportunity to benchmark and align pricing and some features. However, the team started to look further and identified that there were subtle differences in the cans that different plants were using and the specifications that suppliers were working to. The team tackled this by identifying all the features or attributes a can has: eg steel thickness, plating thickness, lacquer thickness, ridged or unridged, easy open or traditional etc. Deep data gathering to look at what was being supplied across all of these features revealed a significant range of differences and with no apparent need or reason for such differences. It seemed that in some regions the specification was based upon manufacturing methods and good practice some years ago; however, the team also identified that advances in technology meant a leaner specification could still deliver the required can quality. This breakthrough led to a global rationalization and alignment of can specifications (with some regional variations where needed) together with a project to implement the changes across the key suppliers. The small changes in specification for a project used in very high volumes delivered significant value to the organization.

# Supplier conditioning

This step is an *Enabler* and is *Optional*

Conditioning is about convincing the suppliers we mean business! It is the process of setting boundaries in the mind of another party so that they respond in a particular way, usually to further our cause. You might call it a mild form of manipulation; indeed, some of the approaches used are often the same.

Supplier conditioning is about signalling to the other party that we are seeking a particular outcome. The aim is to achieve a greater overall benefit while reducing the amount of effort we have to expend to get there. It is not a once-only activity but something that happens right through the process, using any and every opportunity to apply it.

There are two types of supplier conditioning:

- *Offensive.* This is where we strike first with a conditioning message. For example, when we meet with a supplier we might say something like 'We are under huge pressure to reduce our costs and become more competitive. Our competitors have already done this by sourcing from low-cost countries.' This is a powerful message, as it tells the supplier that we want a cost reduction. It also gives a credible reason, and there is an implied threat here suggesting if we don't get what we want, we too will be moving sourcing to low-cost countries.

- *Defensive.* This is where the supplier seeks to condition or counter-condition us (buyer conditioning). Do you recall a supplier dropping remarks into a conversation such as 'Despite rising prices for raw materials, we're currently doing everything we can to hold our prices'? This means they are gauging your reaction to see if they can send in a price increase. This is just one example of many ways in which suppliers attempt to condition buyers. The most powerful defence to buyer conditioning is to condition the supplier before they can condition us and to keep doing it. But if you do find yourself on the end of some buyer conditioning, it is important to quickly counter-condition so that you retain the power in your favour.

Supplier conditioning is not an activity that should be confined to purchasing people. For it to be effective, any stakeholder across the business must also condition the supplier, using the same conditioning messages. This means that supplier conditioning must be planned, and stakeholders need to be engaged to ensure they are 'on message'. The first step here is to determine the conditioning message that will be used. There are many conditioning messages. Some are shown in Table 5.3.

Sometimes it is more powerful if the conditioning message is delivered by a stakeholder rather than purchasing. For example, if the supplier has a

**TABLE 5.3**   Possible themes for a supplier conditioning message

| What is happening in the business | Possible conditioning message |
| --- | --- |
| **Difficult financials** | Ask for direct contribution, reduced pricing immediately, increased payment terms |
| **Major changes** | Impact of acquisition process, restructuring or closures |
| **We're creating new products (or services)** | New projects or services are driving growth creating the potential to expand the volume of business |
| **We're entering new markets** | New markets drive growth |
| **Competitive challenge** | There are new international suppliers and/or low-cost producers, the market is changing |
| **New management team** | New people, new ideas, new challenges, new approaches – change is coming! |

good relationship with the marketing director and the relationship with purchasing has always been around the commercial aspects of the relationship, it would be very powerful if the marketing director begins to tell the supplier that the company is urgently looking for significant cost reduction. However, long-standing relationships between suppliers and stakeholders often breed resistance amongst the latter to being the messenger for this sort of conditioning. This is where stakeholder education is vital, so that they can understand the game being played and ensure they are playing the right role within it.

If we do no conditioning and then invite suppliers to make proposals, they will inevitably aim as high as they can. However, if we have been repeatedly conditioning them that the solution needs to be much more cost effective or value rich and the organization is under pressure to deliver reduced operating costs or secure more from the supply chain etc, then the supplier's starting point is likely to be tempered. It is also important to make sure any conditioning is credible and believable or the supplier will simply see it as a tactic.

# Internal data gathering

This step is an *Enabler* and is *Essential*

This is the first of three essential areas of data gathering. It concerns research and information gathering for the category, and is centred around both the category and how the organization uses the category and intends to do so in the future. The questions that this activity and subsequent analysis work is attempting to answer are:

Informing questions:

- What have we bought in the past?
- What do we need to buy in the future?
- How much have we bought in the past?
- How much do we want to buy in the future?
- Who buys this?
- Why do they buy it?
- How do they use it?
- Where is this category within the product life cycle?

Opportunity questions:

- Are we buying the right thing?
- What scope is there to buy something different that fulfils the same need?
- Are there any opportunities for improving efficiency in the way we buy and use this category?
- Are there any technological advances now or coming that will present opportunities to us?

It is important to note that the raw data gathering alone will not necessarily answer these questions, but the rich picture gained through analysis of this data using some of the later process step tools will help to answer these questions. Table 5.4 gives some potential areas of data to collect, and their possible sources.

**TABLE 5.4** Internal data gathering and possible sources

| Potential data to collect | Possible sources of data |
|---|---|
| **Organizational usage data** | |
| • Business requirements – RAQSCI | • Business requirements |
| • Volumes, now and future | • Purchase orders, invoices |
| • What are we buying? | • Ledgers |
| • Where are we buying? | • Interviews with key internal staff eg production managers |
| • How the product is used | |
| • Sourcing process | • Logistics managers |
| • Value of sales or revenue dependency for this | • Sales information |
| | • Quality records |
| • Current performance or satisfaction | • Internal R&D or NPD experts |
| • Usage or process requirements | • Organizational strategy and objectives |
| • Future needs (linked to organizational strategy) | |
| | • Internal product plans |
| • Inventories and logistics | • Internal RFI |
| **Category data** | |
| • Product life cycle | • Technology roadmap |
| • Technical and specification data | • Industry publications |
| • Related categories (potential synergies) | • Websites |
| | • Technical papers |

# Supplier data gathering

This step is an *Enabler* and is *Essential*

This second essential data-gathering area concerns research on current and previous suppliers. The questions that this activity and subsequent analysis work are attempting to answer are:

Informing questions:

- Who and where are the suppliers and what can they do?
- Where are these suppliers headed?
- How do we currently buy from these or other suppliers?

Opportunity questions:

- Who else could supply this?
- What do we know about these suppliers? How are they organized?
- What things could suppliers do differently to make a difference?
- How could suppliers bring innovation or help us achieve new competitive advantage?

One potent means of collecting supplier information is to use a request for information (RFI). An RFI is typically a questionnaire sent to many suppliers asking for information to be provided, usually in response to a series of tailored questions. RFIs were historically paper documents, with suppliers submitting their responses by return of post. Today most RFIs are conducted electronically, using one of the many web-based portals or providers that offer this facility. We will come back to RFIs later in this book.

Table 5.5 gives some potential areas of data to collect, and their possible sources.

# Market data gathering

This step is an *Enabler* and is *Essential*

This is the third and final essential data-gathering area. It concerns the market-place for the category and any potential alternative marketplaces that could

**TABLE 5.5**  Supplier data gathering and possible sources

| Potential data to collect | Possible sources of data |
|---|---|
| • Range of products<br>• Geographical coverage<br>• Sales volumes<br>• Financial information<br>• % spend to suppliers sales<br>• Quality performance history<br>• Accreditations (eg ISO9001)<br>• Directors' interests<br>• R&D pipeline/where they're heading<br>• Other key customers<br>• Other suppliers in the marketplace<br>• Suppliers who do not currently supply this category but could adapt easily<br>• Possible new entrants | • Request for Information (RFI) (and later Request for Proposal/Quotation RFP/Q)<br>• Purchase orders/invoices<br>• Supplier's literature<br>• Supplier's website<br>• Industry publications and experts<br>• Quality records<br>• Supplier visit or interview<br>• Alliance organizations<br>• Benchmarking activity |

open up breakthrough opportunities. Such alternatives might include emerging markets (alternative geographies offering low-cost sourcing) or other alternative markets that might be opened up through fulfilling the fundamental needs of the category in a different way. The questions that this activity and subsequent analysis work are attempting to answer are:

Informing questions:

- What is the marketplace?
- What is happening in the market and why?
- What is likely to happen in this market in the future and why?
- What are the trends in the market?

Opportunity questions:

- What alternative marketplaces exist and will any of these allow us to fulfil the needs for this category?
- Are there any risks or issues in this marketplace we need to understand and provide for?

**TABLE 5.6** Market data gathering and possible sources

| Potential data to collect | Possible sources of data |
|---|---|
| • Market conditions and factors driving these<br>• Trends<br>• Suppliers in this market today<br>• Potential future suppliers in this market<br>• Competitiveness within the market<br>• Technology trends/emerging technology<br>• Market segmentation (geographical, by product/service etc)<br>• Possible future opportunities<br>• Possible future threats to this market<br>• Our relative power within this market | • Industry publications<br>• Interviews/discussions with suppliers<br>• Interviews/discussions with experts<br>• Financial reports<br>• Business newspaper articles<br>• Specialist consultants<br>• Published indices (eg commodity prices)<br>• Trade shows |

It is important to differentiate between market and supplier data gathering. Within market data gathering we are interested in establishing a picture of what is happening in the market, what is likely to happen and whether the market dynamics are changing. We do not need a detailed picture of all individual suppliers; this should be covered as part of supplier data gathering.

Table 5.6 gives some potential areas of data to collect, and their possible sources.

Market data gathering can be one of the most difficult areas, as gaining insight into a marketplace is not always easy; the pieces of the jigsaw that make up a picture of the marketplace may be scattered far and wide. There are dedicated research companies that will provide insight into markets, and even some companies who specialize in providing ongoing reports and insights into one single marketplace (eg energy, car fleet, commodities etc). Such companies may well save you a lot of time and effort. Alternatively, some time spent doing a thorough research activity will also yield good results.

If the category is a commodity (ie a raw material or primary agricultural product) or the products within the category largely comprise one or more commodities, then an understanding of the market trends here is essential. In their purest form commodity prices are driven by market forces, based upon supply and demand at a global level. There are various organizations, cooperatives and regulatory bodies that help this process along. Here there is no or precious little influence on the market so it is essential to understand it or we could get caught out by it. Understanding the ongoing commodity market trends, and the impact each has on the overall category or individual products, allows effective market and category modelling. This in turn can help determine when to buy and how to buy, so as to minimize risk of exposure from commodity price hikes and optimize our buying position. Understanding commodity markets and commodity price modelling is a whole subject matter in its own right, each area worth an entire book on the subject. In this book all I will say is if the categories being bought comprise or are heavily based upon commodities it is essential to establish and maintain an ongoing understanding of these individual markets and use this intelligence to determine when and how to buy.

# PRICE AND COST ANALYSIS

## Understanding the supplier's pricing approach

This step is a *Tool* and is *Optional*

Many people think a price is a real number. In some cases 'price' is simply what was made up by someone in the supplier's marketing department, and which keeps being made up each time a new price list is released – linked, of course, to some sort of assessment of what the market will pay. 'Cost', however, is a real number. Any product or service will cost a certain amount to produce or supply before the supplier adds their margin. Whilst it may be possible to reduce the cost by making efficiencies, the cost remains a real number and a real and determinable part of what we pay. Understanding the cost will allow us to understand if the price is fair – and if not, what it should be. Later we will look at a specific tool to understand cost more thoroughly, but first we need to better understand the supplier's approach to pricing and the different types of pricing used.

Why is 'price' so powerful? Well, simply because suppliers want to maximize their revenues. They therefore put huge amounts of effort into conditioning us that their price is the right price for what we are buying. A walk around a supermarket with a food sector expert would reveal many shopping-basket items where the price bears little relation to the actual cost of the goods. This means that we are all overpaying for our groceries every day, even though we may be buying at the best price possible (or even at below competitors' best prices if we take advantage of some of the supermarket offers designed to get us through the door). So how can we tell? The answer is to understand the pricing model or approach that is being used for any given item.

As we saw in the previous chapter, suppliers prefer to be able to differentiate their products in some way so that we can only buy from them. In the supplier's marketing department, as a new product is being developed, we might hear people ask, 'What can we sell this for?' or 'What price will the market stand?' To answer these questions, suppliers commission extensive research to see how consumers react to different price points. The aim of this is to determine the price that will maximize both sales and profit.

If more proof is needed that 'price' is not a real number, then consider how often you hear phrases such as 'Buy one, get one free,' or '30 per cent off our published list price'. If price was a real number, these offers would not be possible.

So we have looked at price and then cost. But there is a third area that we cannot ignore, one that is even more revealing. This is 'value'. As we have established in the last chapter, value can take many forms. It can mean many different things, at different times. How value is seen also depends upon the perspective of the beneficiary. Our perception of value therefore depends upon our circumstances.

The mature purchasing perspective is to consider buying as the acquisition of value of some sort in exchange for some form of consideration. This is much more than simply considering purchasing as 'buying goods (or a service) for a given price'. If we think about the total value we are acquiring, then we are best placed to determine the optimum sourcing approach. The value is not necessarily limited to the goods or service but could include the wider supply experience. For example, if we buy insurance, then the low price of the premium is one source of value, but the real value might come from a 'no quibble' payout or from good call-centre support. Indeed, these value areas may be more important than the premium cost itself. It is therefore important to define, from the buyer's perspective, the value we are attempting to acquire. Within category management we do this by using our value levers to determine where value might come from, then updating our business requirements (both explored in Stage 1, initiation).

The supplier's perspective regarding value is simple. The supplier's objective is, if possible, to find new sources of value or even perceived value that they can convince us we need, and then lock us in. In developing countries value is about improving access to the basic utilities, perhaps followed by acquisition of some of the basic possessions that we in the West take for granted, such as a refrigerator or a TV. In developed countries our expectations have far exceeded this, and suppliers now concentrate on selling value as part of creating desirable brands, latest fashion, cutting-edge technology, unique selling points etc.

In order to make sense of the relationship between value, cost and price in the context of buyer and seller perspectives, we need to understand how the price we pay is determined in the first place. This will in turn help us understand what response or intervention is needed to optimize how we source.

In order to analyse the pricing approaches being used we need to understand each pricing type. There are six in total (Figure 5.5) and most of them, but not all, are 'supplier determined', ie based on what the customer is prepared to pay for some sort of value or, in some cases, based on what the supplier can get away with. Some pricing approaches are 'buyer determined' or even 'market determined', both giving the buyer the advantage of power over the supplier. We now look at each pricing approach in turn. A price model template is provided in the Appendix.

## Greed pricing

This is the most extreme example of supplier-driven pricing. As the name suggests, it is where the supplier has the ability to charge pretty much whatever he wishes, and yet customers will still buy the product, sometimes reluctantly but often willingly. Here the supplier firmly holds the power.

Greed pricing applies where the customer has no choice, cannot go elsewhere, and must make the purchase. The supplier knows this and has accordingly set the price high, often to a level far in excess of what the goods would otherwise cost. On a hot day at the beach, the only cold drink vendor for miles around can easily double his prices and still have a queue of desperately thirsty people ready to buy. A few years ago a dispute in the UK by oil company tanker drivers meant that fuel stations started to run out of fuel. As cars began to queue round the block, many outlets doubled and tripled their usual prices, and the queues only got longer.

While we're talking of oil, consider how it has been priced historically. It has not, as might be thought, behaved like a commodity whose price is

**FIGURE 5.5** The price model – summary of different pricing approaches

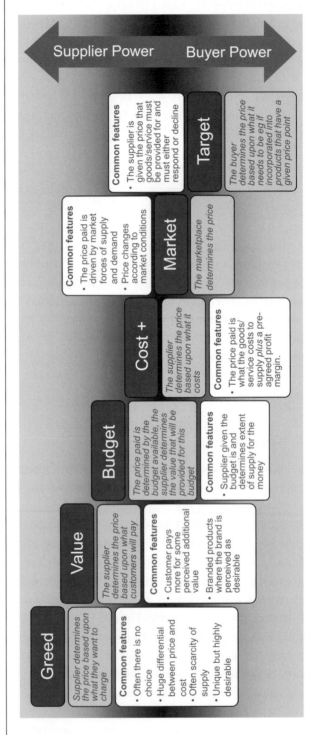

Supplier Power     Buyer Power

**Greed**

*Supplier determines the price based upon what they want to charge*

**Common features**
- Often there is no choice
- Huge differential between price and cost
- Often scarcity of supply
- Unique but highly desirable

**Value**

*The supplier determines the price based upon what customers will pay*

**Common features**
- Customer pays more for some perceived additional value
- Branded products where the brand is perceived as desirable

**Budget**

*The price paid is determined by the budget available, the supplier determines the value that will be provided for this budget*

**Common features**
- Supplier given the budget is and determines extent of supply for the money

**Cost +**

*The supplier determines the price based upon what it costs*

**Common features**
- The price paid is what the goods/service costs to supply plus a pre-agreed profit margin.

**Market**

*The marketplace determines the price*

**Common features**
- The price paid is driven by market forces of supply and demand
- Price changes according to market conditions

**Target**

*The buyer determines the price based upon what it needs to be eg if incorporated into products that have a given price point*

**Common features**
- The supplier is given the price that goods/service must be provided for and must either respond or decline

driven by market forces. Instead, the price we have been paying for oil, gas and oil derivatives has been indirectly determined by OPEC limiting or increasing supply and thereby determining price for the given demand at any particular point in time. In these circumstances oil can be regarded as an example of greed pricing. This situation shifts with increased oil supplied by non-OPEC member countries and with it the price model therefore shifts too.

Another is where we have no choice but to buy a spare part for a machine or piece of equipment from the original equipment manufacturer (OEM).

## Value pricing

Value pricing is when the customer pays more for some sort of additional or perceived value. Here the supplier holds the power. This is the place that most suppliers aim to be and is the pricing approach that lies behind brand theory. We are in a good position if we can establish our product or brand so that customers will pay more to own it because of the tangible and intangible brand attributes that it brings. For example, it would be hard these days to buy a poor car, as quality and reliability across the entire automotive spectrum have reached levels that are hard to surpass. In the UK I could choose to buy a Ford, Toyota, Renault, Volkswagen or other make and I would pay a price that is reasonably consistent from one manufacturer to another for a similar type and specification. But if I choose to buy a BMW or Mercedes, then I'd be paying a significant premium to have an equivalent-specification car. I'd be paying for the brand value associated with owning and driving a prestigious car. In the UK these manufacturers work hard to enhance the experience of owning their cars and maintain their brands as 'high end', 'exclusive', 'well engineered' and so on. This distinction is also firmly implanted in the minds of the British car-buying public, but the picture varies from one geographical area to another. For instance, in Germany, as we might expect, BMW and Mercedes are more in the mainstream.

Value pricing also applies where the supplier has differentiated the product in some way or other so that the customer will pay more for the difference. Where the developed world now has more disposable income per capita than ever before, companies are always on the lookout for new ways to make people pay more for an old product. As I write this I am distracted by a commercial on TV for toilet tissue from one of the well-known brands, but this toilet tissue is of course a new, 'improved' product. It is softer, thicker and quilted with the promise of being 'kind to your bottom'. Understandably, it costs more than standard tissue.

There are degrees of value, and it is worth exploring 'high-end value'. This is when customers are prepared to pay a price that is hugely disproportionate to the cost of the goods. This type of pricing at the high end is often debated by purchasing people, and many class this as 'greed' rather than an extension of value pricing. It is value, but at the high end. Where value stops and greed starts is not as important as the discussion itself regarding how the goods are priced.

An example of high-end value is premium luxury goods with high price tags. Consider designer handbags: a leading designer handbag, positioned as an exclusive 'top end' product, might sell for US $2,000. Products like this originate from a time when luxury was only available to the privileged few, when family-owned businesses were dedicated to integrity and quality, and produced exceptional goods. Teams of artisans would handcraft fashion accessories, using the finest materials, and it was not uncommon for the creation of a single handbag to take eight days of loving care and attention. There are still specialist companies like these, but as the demand for high-end luxury goods has increased, many of the leading brands have called in the consultants and have found ways to speed up and streamline the production process, in some cases by moving production to low-cost countries. These same brands have also cut out intermediaries and sell through dedicated outlets in premium malls, thus further increasing profit.

Thomas (2007) suggests that the retail price of certain designer handbags is typically 12 times the production cost, yet these products are in great demand. Buyers undoubtedly have some feel for the disparity between price and cost, but still desire and buy designer handbags simply because of the value of the intangible attributes associated with the brand. In other words, when we walk down the street with the right designer handbag, it makes a statement about us to the rest of the world. We could also include high-end brands such as Ferraris and Lamborghinis, where the product is highly desirable and deliberately made scarce with a price tag only a handful can stretch to; even then the buyer would probably have to join a waiting list.

If value pricing is identified, then it is important to qualify this value and determine if the perceived value and the price match up. If there appears to be a gap, or the value has declined over time, then we may wish to challenge the basis of the pricing or indeed question the value we actually need.

## Budget pricing

This is where there is a budget to achieve a particular outcome, and the supplier is provided with the details of the budget and asked to determine what can be provided within it. To a purchasing professional the notion of telling the supplier our budget might appear somewhat misguided. This is usually the correct response, as such an action is effectively handing power over to the supplier, yet this happens in organizations more than we might think. Those who share details of their budget with a supplier are often oblivious to the implications.

For example, budget pricing is often applied in the purchase of marketing creative design and agency services. When the marketing executive calls in the agency to discuss a campaign, the first question the agency asks is 'What is the budget for this?' The agency then determines what is possible for the amount. This is normal practice in this area. The supplier clearly holds all the power and may even appear to show support by offering a price that is just under budget; yet the breakdown of how this price is developed will remain hidden. Purchasing teams in large businesses have struggled to make inroads into improving marketing spend areas, while the suppliers have leveraged their relationships with the marketing teams to keep purchasing away and perpetuate the use of such approaches. Yet significant benefits are usually possible in this area with the right approach.

In contrast, consider an example from the world of construction, specifically the fit-out of a new building. Here budget pricing can be used more legitimately. The budget available determines the specification and quality of the fittings that are possible. Here budget pricing is effective, as the hard work to identify what is possible within the money available is shifted on to the supplier. Furthermore, given the nature of this spend, there is little scope for the supplier to use this to his advantage: all of the individual prices of the various components that form the fit-out can be clearly benchmarked within the marketplace.

## Cost-plus pricing

Historically this type of pricing would be found within the public sector for large areas of spend such as defence projects. The price paid is whatever the cost is plus a pre-agreed profit margin. It is not surprising, therefore, that there is a history of cost overrun in governmental projects around the world – because within a cost-plus environment, the more something costs, the greater the profit will be. Cost-plus is used less and less these days, as government bodies have been required to be more accountable and effective in the way public money is spent, and have moved to other procurement approaches.

Cost-plus is an effective pricing model for circumstances where it is not possible to establish the detailed specification at the outset. The supplier therefore takes the risk of establishing this detail along the way. Success here depends upon the ability to be clear that the costs the supplier incurs are fair and appropriate. Transparency and benchmarking by the buyer are essential to have any degree of control of power. Theory suggests that the balance of power within a cost-plus-based project should be shared between the two parties, assuming the arrangement is well managed. However, caution is required here. I regularly encounter purchasing professionals who support the use of cost-plus, providing there is good transparency of cost with the supplier: in other words, a full and detailed understanding of the cost breakdown, so that there is no opportunity for the supplier to artificially increase the costs. In my experience, working in such an 'open book' arrangement with a supplier does not automatically provide this transparency. Interrogating a supplier's financial information with any degree of thoroughness requires a very special capability beyond that of most good purchasing professionals. To illustrate this, consider how fraud investigations track down anomalies within a company. Teams of specialist forensic accountants would be sent in for several weeks to examine the business and find out where money is being hidden/diverted. These are people who have an exceptional accounting background and have specific training to track down the flows of money within a business to find the true picture. How effective then can a single purchasing professional be within the context of a supplier review meeting?

## Market pricing

This is the first of the six pricing models where the buyer has the power and the supplier has very little scope to determine the price, or the value that is provided for a given price. Instead the market determines price and the dynamics of supply and demand drive this. Market pricing is therefore not a strategy that we can freely choose to adopt. It either applies or it doesn't, depending on the nature of the product. Market pricing applies to similar commodities or generic products where there are multiple sources, it is easy to switch supplier and there is competition within the marketplace between suppliers.

As we might expect, commodities such as metals, grains, fruit, vegetables, coffee, tea and electricity all have market pricing. However, non-commodity items and services such as computers, real estate, cleaning services, stationery and mobile phones also utilize market pricing. This reflects the generic nature of the product, ie we could buy an equivalent from many manufacturers. The moment we shift from buying a standard computer for business applications to a high-end titanium-cased laptop utilizing the latest technology components, we can expect to pay a premium above market price; in other words, the model changes to value pricing.

It would be easy to think that if the market determines the price, there is little we can do to influence price. That is true to a degree but there is still great opportunity in areas where market pricing is being used:

- *Understand the market price.* There are whole industries that rely upon the fact that the customer does not understand the true market price, and which successfully manage to apply substantial mark-ups, often under the guise of providing some 'added-value service' or a 'pleasurable buying experience'.

- *Responsiveness of markets.* In any marketplace the forces of supply and demand will naturally work to balance each other and reach a point of equilibrium. However, markets change all the time and any equilibrium will not last long. Supply markets are like large ships set on a course at a given speed: they cannot simply change speed in an instant; instead they slowly respond and eventually the ship reaches the new speed. Opportunity often exists within the time it takes to respond to demand changes that can create oversupply in the marketplace. A smart buyer watching such a market will spot these opportunities and take advantage of them. The same buyer will also know when not to buy.

- *Understanding the market trend.* Market prices can go up and down. If we can spot the trends, we know when to buy and when not to buy and, in some cases, how to buy. Here trends are determined by input costs, changes in technology, competitiveness in the marketplace, changing consumer preferences etc. If we can understand the trend, we can respond with different buying approaches.

Market pricing is often the approach that is hardest to determine. If we buy a nice house in a highly desirable location is this 'value pricing' because we are paying more for the location or 'market pricing' because market forces still determine the price? The answer is that every price approach listed here is a form of market pricing in some way; it is just that the boundaries of the market we are looking at are different or constrained in some way. It is not so much the classification of the pricing that is important but the debate we have to determine how we classify it as this will provide insight into our position.

## Target pricing

Target pricing is the ultimate 'buyer power' pricing approach. We identify the specification of what needs to be supplied and then tell the supplier the price it must be supplied for. Clearly target pricing is only possible where the buyer has a strength of position within the marketplace. We might not get a favourable response if we tried to instigate a target pricing approach with Microsoft! But if we are a large automotive manufacturer, then target pricing with our suppliers is entirely possible.

Target pricing is usually driven by the ultimate end-product pricing. If the market research suggests a small family car with a defined level of specification needs to retail at £9,999, then it is possible to work back from this and identify what each component must be sourced for. After allowing for a reasonable profit margin, the automotive company might determine that the steering wheel needs to be sourced for £5.85, fully assembled and meeting a tough specification. But what if an ambitious target price results in suppliers not being able to supply? However, any supplier to the automotive industry offered the potential of supplying parts for a new model would not just walk away. Instead the supplier's technical R&D teams would work hard to find ways to meet both the specification and target price demands. If the target price was truly unachievable, then dialogue around an alternative specification or increased price would be entered into. The end result would be the supplier working closely with the automotive company to arrive at the optimum balance between price and specification, with full transparency of the cost breakdown.

There are similarities between budget and target pricing, as in each case the supplier is being given the price that the goods need to be provided for. However, the key difference here is around the specification. With budget pricing the supplier determines the specification and the degree of value that will be provided for the price, thus offering scope for that supplier to gain advantage. With target pricing the supplier is given a clear specification of what must be achieved for a given price, thus keeping the balance of power firmly with the buyer.

# Developing a cost vs price breakdown

Now we consider an approach that helps to identify what a product or service should cost. This in turn enables any significant differential between cost and price to be challenged. The approach is called purchase price cost analysis (PPCA) and is concerned with analysing all the costs that go into making a product or providing a service. This can highlight differences between the actual cost of the goods or service and the price being paid, which might mean the supplier is making excessive profits. Armed with this information, we can challenge the supplier in negotiation. This tool is sometimes also called a should-cost analysis or a cost breakdown analysis.

Purchase price cost analysis is not suitable for every scenario. If we hold little power over the supplier, for example because we are sourcing something unique, perhaps in low volumes, then PPCA will do little more than provide the supplier with some amusement, followed by a polite rejection of our demand for a reduced price. It is therefore essential to decide if PPCA is an appropriate tool for the situation. To do this, we use day one analysis. Figure 5.6 shows the applicability of PPCA for each quadrant.

PPCA will work well for products or services in the *tailored* and *custom* day one analysis quadrants. For example, an assembly that is made to our drawing is perfect for PPCA. Some *generic* items can benefit from PPCA but only if they are non-complex and can be done as a 'quick test'. For example,

**FIGURE 5.6** PPCA and day one analysis

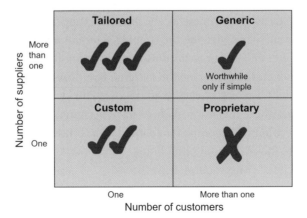

if we were buying buildings maintenance, to understand the cost we might calculate what the service should cost based upon the hours worked at known market rates, together with any materials used. There is, however, little point spending much significant time on items in this quadrant, because if we are buying well, then market forces have in theory already driven price as close to cost as the market will allow. Nor is there any point using PPCA if we are in *proprietary*. Here we are paying for something unique that only this supplier can provide, and the supplier is probably using a value price approach. Instead our efforts should be directed at understanding why we are in the proprietary quadrant in the first place, and attempting to change this.

Developing a PPCA is really straightforward, but it is one of those activities that buyers seem to shy away from. It seems there is a commonly held misconception that to develop any sort of credible cost breakdown we need to have some highly developed ability or access to special information. This is not the case. The most that is needed is a basic understanding of what goes into a product or service; the rest we can work out along the way or ask experts. Table 5.7 shows the types of information to collect when developing a PPCA. The steps to achieve this are as follows:

1 Sketch out all the direct cost components that sit behind a product or service. If it's a product, take it apart if possible and look at all the bits that make it up. For a service, list all the different activities that happen, any materials used and any expenses incurred.

2 Next make a list of the indirect cost components. These are all the costs that support the overall running of the business.

3 For both the direct and indirect cost components, identify or estimate the cost of as many as possible, leaving the difficult ones for later. This activity is best done in a group, as in many cases it will be possible to do the estimate in one pass. For other items consider some research such as reviewing the supplier's annual report, visiting the factory etc. This is not as hard as it might seem. If the PPCA relates to a product, then examine the material composition of each part, the size, weight, volume of each material used, the degree of processing involved, where it is most likely to have been made, and from this estimate what each component should cost. If it is a service, then calculate the cost based upon hours' effort, market rates and the cost of associated consumables, travel etc.

4 Finally, for the areas that could not be completed, agree actions to do the further work and research and complete the analysis.

**TABLE 5.7**    Types of information to collect to support a PPCA

| Cost area | Data to collect | How you might find this out |
| --- | --- | --- |
| Material costs | What is it? How much is used? Where does it come from? How is it made? | Visit the factory, talk to experts or material suppliers. |
| Labour costs | How many man hours does it take? Who is involved? What do they do? What is the hourly cost? | Local labour rates, trade associations, contracts, internet. |
| Process costs | What is the process? What equipment is used? Does this supplier invest heavily in this area? | Annual reports, trade associations, experts. |
| Distribution costs | How is it shipped? Who does it? What special needs exist? | Talk to logistic companies. |
| Overheads | Cost of the factory, offices, buildings, people, benefits, depreciation, sales, admin etc | Annual reports, visit, talk to experts, take a guess. |
| Profit | What is the profit? What is returned to shareholders? What is reinvested? | Annual reports, talk to shareholders. |

When the PPCA is complete, review it and ask, 'so what is it telling us?' and check back through assumptions if it doesn't feel right. This is not an exact science, but a crude means to test the differential between cost and price. So if you don't know what something costs, make an assumption and take an informed guess, then make a note that this is an estimate only, to be revisited later if the PPCA throws up anything of interest.

When working through a PPCA it is worth keeping in mind day one analysis together with the different pricing models suppliers use. These same tools are, of course, relevant to the supplier's sourcing of the component parts. If the PPCA breakdown is simply a series of generic and market-priced items, then estimating the cost is straightforward. However, if one or more of the components is a specialist part, perhaps incorporating some patented technology or unique in some way, then establishing a cost estimate is more difficult and may even be impossible. If you encounter an apparent 'special component' within a PPCA, then this may be the area of opportunity, so the only option is to be as creative as possible about finding out the facts.

In my experience, suppliers do not like being presented with PPCAs, as this forces them into a position where they have just two possible responses:

**1** The game is up and they are forced to lower their prices.

**2** They can reject the PPCA as incorrect, in which case the counter-response is to ask them to show where the error lies; in other words, the supplier is forced to provide transparency of pricing.

Determining the direct material and labour costs is usually straightforward, especially if people with the right experience are available to help; however, determining the cost of overheads is much more difficult. It is here where accuracy is least likely, so the key is to take a view. A typical manufactured product comprises direct costs, overheads and hopefully some profit (see Figure 5.7) with the following key elements:

- *Direct costs.* All the costs that contribute directly to the product or service. This includes material costs, labour costs relating to producing the product or delivering the service.

- *Direct overheads.* Often called 'variable overheads' and includes all the cost of running the production line or keeping the service going, eg electricity for plant and machinery, consumable tools and materials, labour to keep things operational.

**FIGURE 5.7** Typical cost, overhead and profit structure

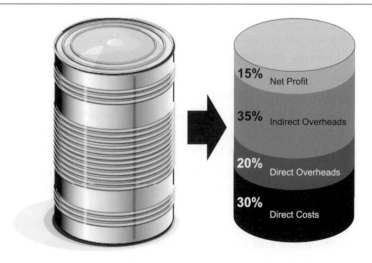

- *Indirect overheads*. These include all the other costs associated with maintaining the organization and not included elsewhere. These might include rent, rates, cost of equipment, depreciation, cost of indirect functions such as purchasing, marketing, sales force costs, cost of buildings, R&D, admin and support staff.

- *Profit*. Unless we are looking at a not-for-profit organization there should be a profit element and as we saw in Chapter 1 the proportion here varies with sector.

Research into indirect overhead costs can help gradually build up the picture. Indeed, if the supplier is suggesting the cost lies in the indirect overheads and we believe that this may be used to hide costs, it is worthwhile spending time here. Sources of information to establish overheads include:

- *Annual accounts*. These glossy annual publications developed for shareholders hold vast amounts of information. CEOs boast about how much was reinvested in R&D, and interrogation will soon determine costs of administration, depreciation etc. With private companies, ask for a copy of the accounts. They may not be in the form of a glossy brochure but should still tell a story that helps identify the cost of overheads.

- *Factory tour*. Visit the supplier, understand how many people work in the different functions, look at the buildings and their location to decide if this is a low- or high-overhead business. Gauge throughput and how much labour time is spend processing each product or delivering a service, examine how much has been invested in capital equipment.

- *Realtors/estate agents*. These can provide great insight into the cost of commercial property in the area where the supplier's facility is located. Five minutes on the internet will reveal a range of commercial rental rates ranging from 70 cents per square foot per month in Shanghai to $250 in central London.

- *Ask the supplier*. Information such as marketing and R&D costs are usually readily available and the supplier will happily share this.

- *Desktop research*. Carefully chosen internet search terms can sometimes help turn up the unexpected gem of information or there maybe experts who could be consulted, perhaps people with experience of running similar businesses.

The alternative and simpler approach is to estimate all the indirect overheads using a simple rule of thumb. First consider the overhead loading. Is this a high-overhead business, requiring expensive facilities and with high costs associated with sales and R&D and getting the product to the customer; or a low-overhead business such as an internet-based company? As a general rule, for most businesses the indirect overheads would be less than the direct costs and direct overheads combined. Two good rules of thumb here to help with 'fast and approximate' PPCA determination are as follows:

- Direct costs including direct overhead represent 60 per cent of the total cost (including some profit margin).
- Indirect overheads represent 50 per cent of the combined direct costs and direct overheads.

Finally, let's look at a simple example. Dispatch departments often use hand-held stretch-wrap dispensers. These comprise a plastic handle upon which a roll of stretch polythene is mounted on a cardboard tube. The wrap is free to rotate, allowing the user to walk around large items, stretching the wrap over and round the object as they go.

If we do a simple PPCA on this item (see Table 5.8), we can quickly take it apart and estimate the cost of the individual items. We can guess the direct labour element. There is minimal intervention needed as these items are produced on a highly automated line. We can assume one minute of time per dispenser by a factory worker (loading machines, removing from machines, packing into boxes etc).

In this case the total PPCA cost estimate suggests that there is a significant differential with the price being paid per item. This intelligence can now be used with the supplier to drive a price reduction. Of course, this is only feasible if we are buying in high volumes. We might also want to consider reusing the handles and having the supplier just supply replacement rolls of wrap. But it is clear the PPCA has revealed an opportunity for improvement. A PPCA template is provided in the Appendix.

**TABLE 5.8**  Example PPCA for stretch wrap dispenser

| PPCA for stretch wrap dispenser | | | |
|---|---|---|---|
| **Cost component** | **Basis for calculations** | **Firm or estimate** | **Cost ($)** |
| *Direct costs* | | | |
| Handle | 80g MDPE, moulded | Firm | $0.36 |
| Core | Cardboard tube | Firm | $0.11 |
| Film | 100m stretch film | Firm | $1.49 |
| Carton | Holds 24, cost = $2.16/24 | Firm | $0.09 |
| Direct labour | 1 minute per dispenser, assuming hourly pay of $15 per hour | Estimate | $0.25 |
| | | **Total direct** | **$2.30** |
| **Overheads and profit** | | | |
| Overheads | Guessed at 100% of direct cost | Estimate | $2.30 |
| Profit | Estimated at 10% of total | Estimate | $0.51 |
| | | **Total overheads and profit** | **$2.81** |
| | | **Total PPCA cost estimate** | **$5.11** |
| | | **Price being paid for this item** | **$9.99** |
| | | **Differential** | **$4.88** |

# UNDERSTANDING THE EXTERNAL ENVIRONMENT

So far we have concerned ourselves with the category, our internal requirements and what we might need from the supply base. However, we will now spend some time considering the external environment beyond our business and immediate supplier relationships in order to identify drivers, forces, opportunities or threats that we might need to understand and respond to within our sourcing strategy. We will begin by looking at the supply and value chain.

# Supply and value chain network (SVCN) analysis

This step is a *Tool* and is *Optional*

In this tool we look beyond the immediate relationship we hold, or plan to hold with specific suppliers to the entire supply chain. However, first we need to be clear what we mean here as the term 'supply chain' is a broad term and one that holds different meanings; there are multiple concepts here to help understanding:

1 *The simple supply chain* (often represented as a linear chain) – one where materials flow from the original raw material or plantation, and are progressively transformed by a series of firms to create goods (or services) that are supplied to an organization. Mentzer *et al* (2001) call this the *direct supply chain.*

2 *The end-to-end value chain* – In practice few supply chains are simple but have many players. Most definitions of 'supply chain' or 'value chain' conclude that this encompasses the flow of materials or services through a number of suppliers to us and on through to the end customer, each hopefully adding value in some way. A firm is therefore typically part of a chain rather than the end of it, and the focus is on how value is added throughout the entire chain, end-to-end rather than just the flow of materials prior to reaching us. Mentzer *el al* (2001) calls this an *extended supply chain.* The concept of the 'value chain' as defined by Porter (1985) was touched on in Chapter 1.

3 *Supply chain network* – The traditional view of supply or value chains as a linear bears little relationship to how most are actually structured. There are in fact only a handful of scenarios where the linear chain might exist; in practice our suppliers might also be linked to other suppliers, or even directly with our customers and our customers might be linked to suppliers further back upstream and so on. In fact the value chain is typically quite a complex affair. Christopher (2011) suggests that the word 'chain' should be replaced with 'network' to reflect the fact that there will normally be multiple suppliers and suppliers to suppliers as well as multiple customers and customers' customers in the total system. Mentzer *et al* (2001) call this the *ultimate supply chain.*

To cover all bases and avoid confusion I will use the term supply and value chain network (SVCN) from this point on. SVCN analysis is about developing an understanding of what the SVCN looks like so as to identify and act upon opportunities or threats relevant to our category, either now or for the future, that might lie upstream closer to the original plantation, raw material, processor or producer or downstream closer to the end customer.

Mapping an SVCN is no small task so we should be clear it is worthwhile before embarking on creating one. It is worthwhile where this effort will bring insight that we can turn into actions or incorporate into a sourcing strategy so as to realize new value or find a breakthrough. What value is relevant or desirable of course depends upon our overall objectives – both macro corporate objectives and targets for this category. Reasons to embark on SVCN analysis might include:

- cost reduction – if we believe there are opportunities to remove cost from the SVCN by analysing where cost is introduced and either restructuring the SVCN as far as our influence permits or identifying a new sourcing approach;
- to improve value, reduce inefficiencies, waste or excessive inventories held by those involved;
- to improve logistics and flow of material – faster, more agile and responsive;
- to understand and mitigate risk exposure or put contingency arrangements in place;
- to achieve compliance with CSR policy.

There is no definitive test to decide if an SVCN analysis would be worthwhile; instead we need to make a judgment based upon whether we believe the effort might lead to a breakthrough opportunity and start small by making quick sketches of the SVCN before moving to a more comprehensive analysis. For example if we believe the SVCN is more complex or lengthy than it needs to be, or we suspect some of the practices that lie with producers many steps removed upstream are in conflict with our CSR policy.

Even if we manage to fully map and understand our SVCN it doesn't follow that we can change it. Our contractual relationship, and our immediate influence, is with the immediate players upstream and downstream of us. Changing what lies beyond these is not easy, yet not impossible and typically requires the brokering of relationships with players in the SVCN to improve information flows, share details of forward demand or change poor practice. This is typically the way companies are driving in CSR compliance by developing relationships and working directly with original producers or plantations. However, we can also use our understanding of the SVCN to source differently, perhaps sourcing direct from producers cutting out unnecessary agents, transport companies, wholesalers and warehousing intermediaries or even vertically integrating so we own the entire supply chain. Figure 5.8 gives an example of a SVCN map and some of the insights gained.

## SVCN mapping

SVCN mapping is best accomplished by a group of individuals carefully selected for their knowledge and expertise. We map the SVCN based upon how the category is currently sourced but we could equally do this for potential new ways to source the category. The process has five steps:

1 *Map the physical structure.* This is, put simply, about creating a big diagram that shows all the players in the network and who is connected to whom. A big sheet of paper is essential and unrolling some brown paper onto a large table around which the team can assemble is ideal. Start at the point where the goods are used (or the service is delivered) then work back and identify each step and activity prior to this. Identify each player, each interface or handoff, each transport or movement, who supplies or interfaces with whom and how material, information, demand, value and money flows. Once underway it is likely the team will identify a number of areas where further information and investigation is required in order to complete the map, so creating a complete network map may take several workshops to get it right. This mapping activity has many names. You may know it as process mapping or business process re-engineering and it is an approach that is used in many areas including lean manufacturing.

2 *Environment and context.* Consider the environment and context the SVCN exists in. This includes countries and geographies involved, cultural differences, prevailing political and economic climates, end-customer changing needs and aspirations and environmental considerations (the *PESTLE* analysis tool, covered next, can help here). Identify any unique factors that might hamper making change or equally could present opportunity such as complexity, variety, differentiation, market difficulty etc. This step is important to gauge the degree to which we have influence here. For example if, in a developing country, it is accepted and normal practice for children

# FIGURE 5.8  An example SVCN map

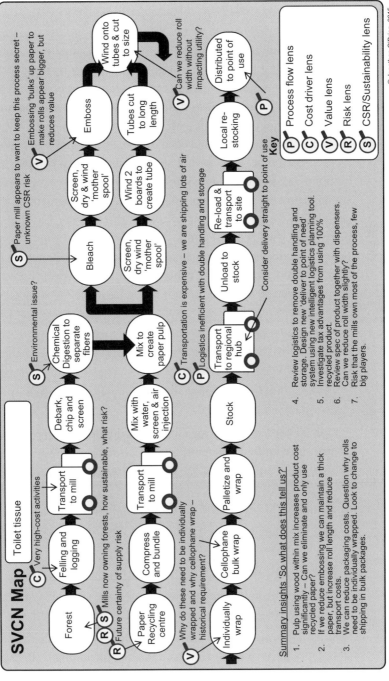

**SVCN Map** Toilet tissue

Individually wrap

Cellophane bulk wrap

Palletize and wrap

Stock

Forest

Paper Recycling centre

Felling and logging

Compress and bundle

Transport to mill

Transport to mill

Debark, chip and screen

Mix with water, screen & air injection

Chemical Digestion to separate fibers

Mix to create paper pulp

Bleach

Screen, dry & wind 'mother spool'

Screen, dry wind 'mother spool'

Wind 2 boards to create tube

Emboss

Tubes cut to long length

Wind onto tubes & cut to size

Transport to regional hub

Unload to stock

Re-load & transport to site

Local re-stocking

Distributed to point of use

**(C)** Very high-cost activities

**(R)(S)** Mills now owning forests, how sustainable, what risk?

**(R)** Future certainty of supply risk

**(V)** Why do these need to be individually wrapped and why cellophane wrap – historical requirement?

**(S)** Environmental issue?

**(S)** Paper mill appears to want to keep this process secret – unknown CSR risk

**(V)** Embossing 'bulks' up paper to make rolls appear bigger, but reduces value

**(V)** Can we reduce roll width without impacting utility?

**(C)** Transportation is expensive – we are shipping lots of air

**(P)** Logistics inefficient with double handling and storage

Consider delivery straight to point of use

## Key

**(P)** Process flow lens
**(C)** Cost driver lens
**(V)** Value lens
**(R)** Risk lens
**(S)** CSR/Sustainability lens

Summary insights 'So what does this tell us?'

1. Pulp using wood within mix increases product cost significantly – Can we eliminate and only use recycled paper?
2. If we reduce embossing we can maintain a thick paper, but increase roll length and reduce transport costs.
3. We can reduce packaging costs. Question why rolls need to be individually wrapped. Look to change to shipping in bulk packages.
4. Review logistics to remove double handling and storage. Design new 'deliver to point of need' system using new intelligent logistics planning tool.
5. Investigate tax advantages from using 100% recycled product.
6. Review spec of product together with dispensers. Can we reduce roll width slightly?
7. Risk that the mills own most of the process, few big players.

© Jonathan O'Brien, 2015

to work in a factory, and factory owners will exploit this given the chance, then this context suggests that driving in compliance to a CSR policy that excludes child labour will require robust intervention and ongoing local level policing.

**3** *Find the hot spots.* A pragmatic approach is essential if we are to gain meaningful insight for our efforts. We do this by using a series of different *lenses* and searching for *hot spots*. Successively examine the SVCN map from a series different perspectives, as if looking through a series of different lenses, each enabling the network to be viewed in different ways and each time identifying opportunities and threats. Each time, look for hot spots to cut through complexity and pinpoint areas to focus on without having to analyse a complex system, ie focus on where we might expect to find something. For example, if we are looking at a network through our CSR lens then there are known processes, industries, practices, geographies where there is, according to historical understanding, known potential issues or risks we should be concerned about and where hot spots are likely to exist; so we look there at these first. The lenses we can use are as follows and Figure 5.9 gives a typical insight box that can be used to aid mapping and capture insights – print out, number and stick onto the big paper map at all the key points and have the team complete as they apply each lens.

– *Process flow lens.* Examine the flow of materials, information and how demand is managed.

– *Cost driver lens.* Look for all the cost drivers and where they are introduced into the network.

– *Value lens.* Consider where and how value is introduced or added, where innovation might come from or how quality is created, assured or possible. Value in a SVCN might include processing, transport, assured supply, innovation or things the customer would pay more for.

– *Risk lens.* Look for sources of risk or potential risk.

– *CSR lens.* Examine the network specifically for CSR impacts or potential risks against a corporate policy or framework.

**4** *Identify opportunities and risks.* Translate the insights gained during Step 3 into a list of opportunities and risks (including CSR risks), consolidate and prioritize so as to make sense of the SVCN map. Areas to consider include:

– eliminating unnecessary or non-value-adding steps;

– adding new activities to reduce risk;

– combining activities;

– reassigning activities elsewhere to reduce cost/become more effective;

– backward integration (ie we do it);

– vertical integration (ie we own it);

– forward integration (ie we get our suppliers to do more).

5 *'So what'*. Summarize the SVCN map and ask 'so what' is this map telling us and how might it influence our future sourcing strategy for this category? Consider how the opportunities can be exploited and what specific actions might be needed to address risk. If the value added is unique, then this product is most likely within the custom or proprietary quadrants of day one analysis, and attention should be directed to how the product could be made more generic. Remember that the purpose of this exercise is to identify opportunities for improvement or even breakthrough, rather than to develop a perfect supply chain map.

In practice, an effective means to accomplish SVCN mapping is to map the network on a large piece of brown paper, then to use different-colour Post-it notes for each lens to identify the risks and opportunities. Figure 5.10 shows a full SVCN in a retail category management environment. Here the high-level SVCN is relatively simple and is given across the top of the sheet. Underneath each step the team identified a range of risks and opportunities for each lens from which a list of priorities for action were identified.

Supply chain management (SCM) and logistics are an entire topic all of their own with a wealth of publications, knowledge and education available out there so it is impossible to do any justice to this topic in just one section. This topic and this specific tool are expanded more fully in one of my other books, *Supplier Relationship Management*, also published by Kogan Page.

**FIGURE 5.9**   SVCN mapping insight summary box

| Lens | Risks | Opportunities |
|---|---|---|
| Process flow | | |
| Cost drivers | | |
| Value lens | | |
| Risk lens | | |
| CSR lens | | |

**FIGURE 5.10**   An SVCN map using different-coloured Post-it notes for each 'lens' identifying the risks and opportunities

**CASE STUDY**    How SVCN mapping enabled supplies to field
technicians to become more effective

A category management team working on the category *electrical equipment* – an umbrella category containing a vast range of sub-categories, some significant and many small – suspected benefits might be found by examining how individual parts got to the place of use. The company's business involved the installation of large electrical equipment items at remote locations. Installation costs appeared excessive, the most significant item being the labour costs of the installation technicians, which were charged by the hour. The team developed a SVCN map of the supply chain and researched some of the steps by talking to the technicians, spending time with them to observe what they did, and talking with suppliers. The SVCN map revealed three key opportunities:

1  Eliminate the need for technicians to collect parts and equipment from the local depot/hire shop through improved job planning so large or 'job-unique' parts could be sent directly to site, with consumables delivered to the technicians' vans at a set time and place each day when required.

2  Remove local depots which had become mini stores carrying (often badly controlled) inventory and providing a base for the technicians to start and finish their day, thus increasing overall travelling time. Technicians were switched to being van based.

3  Eliminate the need to hire equipment. The study revealed that much of the equipment was hired because technicians were not being properly equipped or broken equipment was not being repaired. Technicians were re-equipped with a new maintenance regime and an arrangement was introduced by which hire equipment was delivered to site.

These improvements in efficiency delivered a 12 per cent increase in productivity and reduced costs of stockholding.

# Technology mapping

This step is a *Tool* and is *Optional*

Things don't stand still. Technology is constantly changing. Sometimes new technologies improve the old ways, make things cheaper, more environmentally robust, perform to higher standards. Sometimes new technologies can completely change the game. It is appropriate to consider the rate of change of technology, as both opportunity and prevention of risk can be achieved through better understanding. If the category is 'IT hardware' or 'batteries' or 'video conferencing', then in each case the history over recent years shows an ongoing advance in technologies, and it is relevant to understand this more. However, not all categories have a significant technology element; if the category is 'flour' or 'cleaning services', then there are not too many advances in technology to speak of. However, that doesn't mean processing technologies have stood still. We therefore have the option to develop a technology road map for certain categories to help identify our future sourcing strategy and be ready to take advantage of breakthrough opportunities.

We are interested in shifts in technologies, not small improvements. It is when a technology changes that incredible opportunity may be possible, especially if we can utilize the new technology before the competition or we have some sort of exclusive rights. This is one of the reasons why it is so important to have a close relationship with our key strategic suppliers who are developing new technologies, so that we can benefit first. Equally, if we fail to fully understand the technology landscape, then we could be exposed to the risk of relying on old technology that our suppliers one day decide to make obsolete.

Adoption of new emerging technology as soon as it appears does not necessarily make sense. NASA has made no secret of the fact that right up until its final mission in 2011 the space shuttle ran on computer processors and versions of Microsoft Windows we all used in the early 1990s. This is because their primary focus was to use something well proven and understood: it did what it needed to do. The key point here is not which technology we are going to use but being clear about how technologies are changing and using this intelligence to make an informed decision about what we want to use now, and how we want this to change in the future.

First, let's consider the life cycle of any technology using the marketing approach of a product life cycle (Figure 5.11). Remember, advances in technology don't come from some special governmental body set up to advance

**FIGURE 5.11**    Product life cycle

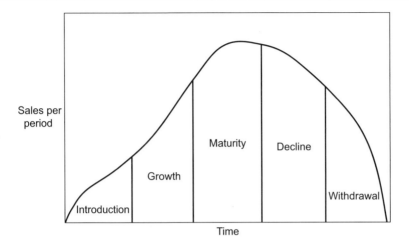

the quality of our lives; they come from suppliers who are investing in research and development to find that next thing they can convince us to buy. When new technologies emerge there is a gradual take-up until the technology becomes mainstream. When technologies get superseded, they steadily decline.

The technology road map is a simple tool that combines multiple product life cycle views for historical, current and future technology into a single view, allowing the identification of our overall position and desired position (Figure 5.12). A template is provided in the Appendix.

**FIGURE 5.12**    Technology road map

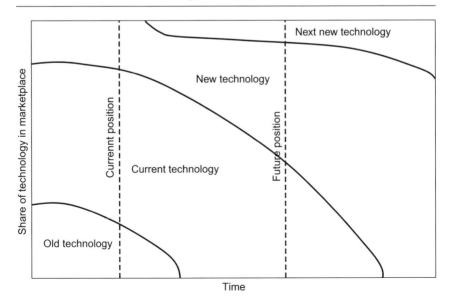

At any point in time, for any given technology, there is likely to be a mix of old, current, new and future technology with at least the first three, maybe even all four, available on the market. Just look around you at something that feels 'fast moving' and attempt to do the categorization. I'll use the example of television monitors. The cathode ray tube (CRT) is dead but we can still find the occasional big old box TV still in use if we try hard enough. Standard plasma and LCD panels soon became established – and soon became out of date due to two successive grades of higher-resolution, cheaper LCD technologies, backlit at first by fluorescent tubes and later by LEDs. Then 3D panels emerged and TVs became thinner, more curved, with faster processing and, as if we didn't have enough resolution, 4K or Ultra HD arrived. The future promises bigger panels, even higher-resolution, 'glasses-free 3D', new panel technology using LED pixels and no backlight technology. You can easily decide the mix today for yourself. If we are in a developing country this mix would be very different and CRTs are still commonplace with new technologies some way off.

The technology road map is divided into the four technology types. It is unlikely these lines will need to change, as pretty much all technologies develop in this way. Furthermore, it is just possible to have all four at the same time. For the category in question, plot the different types of technology in each of the areas. When this is complete, decide where you are today by drawing a vertical line. You may want to include different perspectives here to reflect different parts of the business. Then decide where you want to be and why (and any risk associated with not moving). It is this last step that is vitally important and should feed into the development of a sourcing strategy later in the process.

## PESTLE analysis

This step is a *Tool* and is *Optional*

If we came up with a great idea and went about setting up a business to turn the idea into action, we would be crazy if we didn't take time to properly understand the marketplace that we are attempting to get into. For any company considering entering a particular marketplace, a full understanding of the changing face of that market, and likely future changes, is essential. It doesn't stop there because we would also want to understand how customers' needs are changing, what impact changes in society or technology might have on our idea or if current or future legislation might affect us. In marketing, teams will use a tool such as PESTLE analysis to help here. Within purchasing category management this essential tool is equally valid and helps us to better understand the marketplace we are sourcing from together with the forces that are driving change in our external environment. PESTLE analysis helps us see the issues, trends, risks, changes and market direction that we need to be mindful of when developing our sourcing strategy and could present both future opportunity and/or future risk we need to mitigate against. Essentially PESTLE helps us understand the forces of change that are important to us.

PESTLE (Figure 5.13) stands for *Political, Economic, Sociological, Technological, Legal* and *Environmental* and each of these are individual headings under which we consider the forces or drivers that might be relevant to our category. A template is provided in the Appendix.

There are many variants out there – these include PEST and STEP (dropping the legal and environmental elements), or STEEP (no legal), or STEEPL

**FIGURE 5.13**   PESTLE analysis

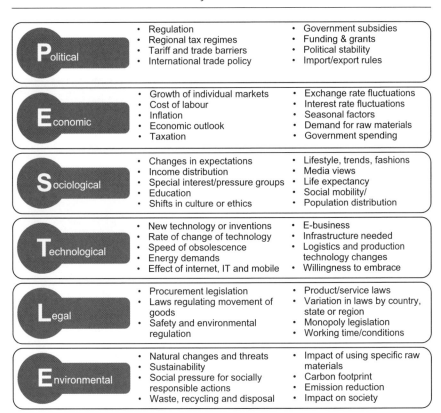

or STEEPLE (with an added 'E' for 'ethical'), DESTEP (with legal replaced by demographic), or PESTLIED (with added 'international' and 'demographic'). If that wasn't enough there are further versions out there with an additional 'R' (regulatory) or another 'E' (environmental) which as far as I can tell don't spell anything recognizable. It really doesn't matter what model is used; they all serve the same purpose.

Completing a PESTLE analysis is very simple. It can be done by an individual but is best worked in a group. Once the team understands the tool and what it does, simply brainstorm each heading and record the findings. Then, once complete, ask the 'So what does this tell us?' question and note down the answers and this insight will help shape the future sourcing strategy.

Table 5.9 gives an example of a completed PESTLE analysis for the pharmaceutical industry. Here we find a 'clinical studies' category and marketplace where suppliers recruit groups of suitable people to participate in the final stages of new drug testing. Understandably this activity is well regulated and the PESTLE shows this; however, this analysis also reveals both an increasing cost in this market countered by the opportunity to look at different approaches for clinical trials including considering developing countries and better use of technology.

**TABLE 5.9** Example PESTLE analysis for clinical trials marketplace

| PESTLE heading | Issues, risks, opportunities and forces of change |
| --- | --- |
| Political | <ul><li>Government approval is required.</li><li>Studies must align within each trial country's healthcare model.</li><li>FDA (US) or similar body control trials and has a legal remit.</li></ul> |
| Economic | <ul><li>Cost of studies is increasing – participants want more money!</li><li>Healthy participants demand higher fees.</li><li>People with no healthcare insurance participate more willingly (US).</li><li>Cheaper to run studies in developing countries.</li><li>Poor people will volunteer.</li><li>Doctors increasingly requiring payment to approach patients who might participate (country specific).</li></ul> |

**TABLE 5.9**   *continued*

| PESTLE heading | Issues, risks, opportunities and forces of change |
|---|---|
| Sociological | • Often trials need a specific demographic group. <br> • Studies cannot be run in any country, depends on trial conditions required. <br> • Easier to conduct studies where there is high concentration of population. <br> • Risk of reputation damage if a trial goes wrong. |
| Technological | • New technology for data collection, measurement, analysis and management of trial information (trials are faster/cheaper). <br> • Electronic submission to FDA and other bodies now possible. <br> • Increasing use of biomarker technology makes trials easier, more reliable and cheaper. <br> • Increasing option for simulation to avoid or delay need for clinical trial. |
| Legal | • Legislation is country specific. <br> • Legislation for trials is generally getting tougher. |
| Environmental | • Increasing disposal cost and requirements for trial products. |

# Understanding market competitiveness

This step is a *Tool* and is *Optional*

In 1979 a young up-and-coming economist called Michael E Porter published his first article in the *Harvard Business Review*, entitled 'How competitive forces shape strategy'. Since then 'Porter's five forces' have helped to shape corporate strategy and business practice. Fundamentally these are a market-ing tool used by companies to understand and cope with competition and the forces that dictate competition within any marketplace. Similarly to PESTLE, Porter's five forces are concerned with examining the external

**FIGURE 5.14**    Porter's five forces adapted to purchasing

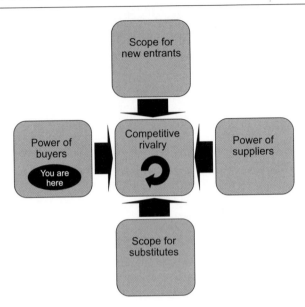

environment or market. Within purchasing and category management the model is adapted slightly to understand the dynamics relative to the buyer (Figure 5.14).

Porter's five forces are concerned with determining the competitive forces acting on and within a specific marketplace. To illustrate what competitiveness means, imagine we plan to set up a business. We would need to understand the degree of competition or we might find we can't get our idea off the ground. Let's say we've developed a new cola and we believe its taste is superior to both Coca-Cola and Pepsi. How easy would it be for us to establish our new cola in the global marketplace? It would be nearly impossible. No matter how exceptional our product, there are other forces at work that would prevent us from gaining any sort of foothold. The players in this market hold massive power because they work hard to own and manage the routes to market. Branded dispensing equipment and keen prices in return for exclusive long-term supply agreements secure and lock in customers. Brand positioning helps keep the products firmly in consumers' minds so they don't ever want for anything else. And with cola dominating a large percentage of the 500 billion litres of soft drink consumed per annum (equating to around 77 litres of soft drink for every person on the planet), it is no surprise that the companies in this marketplace put intense effort into maintaining their market shares. Whilst the ongoing rivalry between the two big players might suggest this is a competitive marketplace, it is not. A truly competitive marketplace will naturally drive margins down. For cola, and indeed the soft drink market overall, typical margins are high (as high as 38 per cent in the United States). If we compare this sector to others where the degree of competition is more intense, such as airlines, margins elsewhere are much less, typically around 6 per cent. Michael Porter described this industry competition and therefore the overall level of profitability as an outcome of the underlying structure of the sector resulting from the five forces he identified, not from the product itself.

In the version of the model used within category management, there are some subtle differences with Porter's original 'marketing perspective' model. His 'threat of new entrants' becomes 'scope for new entrants', to recognize that from the purchasing perspective a new entrant is a good thing and helps reduce overall market competitiveness. Similarly 'threat of substitutes' becomes 'scope for substitutes'. This tool is often applied incorrectly in a purchasing context because there is one important consideration when working this model; we place ourselves in the 'power of buyers' box and consider our relative position as a buyer within a given marketplace and the 'power of suppliers' refers to suppliers to the marketplace in general for the category, not the suppliers to our business. In other words our supplier's suppliers. This is crucial to understanding the forces acting on a marketplace; otherwise if we were to map the power of our suppliers this would merely be a reverse of power of buyers and so would be meaningless. These subtle shifts are important or the tool will fail to provide the purchasing insight required. We will now look at each of the five forces in turn.

## Power of buyers

In the purchasing context this is you and other buyers like you. Powerful buyers can capture more value by using leverage to force down price and cost, demand improved quality or ongoing improvements and innovation.

Factors that create buyer power within a marketplace include:

- There are few buyers.
- Buyers purchase in large volumes relative to the size of a single supplier.
- Buyers have the ability to switch supplier at minimum risk and cost.
- The product or service is generic (day one analysis) and undifferentiated, allowing buyers to play one supplier against another.

- There is scope for backwards integration. Can you or other buyers easily start doing what your suppliers are doing? Even if you don't want to, can you credibly threaten this? If so, power of buyers is increased.
- There is an absence of control of distribution channels, thus increasing choice.

## Power of suppliers

Remember, these are the suppliers to the marketplace, not the suppliers to your business. Powerful suppliers can increase their value gained through charging higher prices and by controlling quality and choice; and they can squeeze profitability if the market is unable to pass on cost increases.

Factors that create supplier power within a marketplace include:

- Locking in customers: creating the inability for buyers to switch to alternative sources of supply.
- Differentiation: the product is differentiated or unique in some way, such as branding, patented design, unique features.
- The nature of the supply market: is it concentrated with a few dominant players or highly fragmented? Concentration will increase supplier power.
- Threat of forward integration: if the suppliers to the market can credibly threaten to enter the market in their own right and become another producer (not just a supplier), then they have power.
- There are no substitutes for what the suppliers provide.
- Suppliers rely on multiple marketplaces for their revenue and are therefore not afraid to push their position within individual markets to the limit.

## Scope for new entrants

How easy is it for new suppliers to enter the marketplace and establish themselves? A new entrant will bring new capacity, with forcefulness to secure market share, and will have an effect on price within the market.

Factors that increase the scope for new entrants are fundamentally around low barriers of entry and include:

- low cost of entry: low capital investment required;
- regulatory: minimal or no regulatory requirements;

- distribution channels: ability to gain access easily to existing distribution channels or create new ones;

- little expected retaliation by existing players;

- absence of any advantages for incumbents: the current players do not have established advantages that new entrants cannot also secure (eg preferential governmental incentives, unique access to technology);

- size: if size is needed in order to gain the economies of scale required to compete, this could deter new entrants. Scope for new entrants is increased where size is not critical.

## Scope for substitutes

A substitute is something that performs the same or a similar function as the product the market is supplying. For any product in a particular market, different types of substitutes must be considered. For example:

- generic substitutes, eg instead of buying Coca-Cola, buy another sparkling soft drink;

- brand substitutes, eg Pepsi instead of Coca-Cola;

- product substitutes, eg bottled water instead of Coca-Cola;

- need substitutes, eg don't buy a drink.

It is within 'substitutes' that potential breakthroughs lie and we are concerned with identifying what the substitutes are. Consider what it is you are buying and alternative ways in which the same need could be fulfilled. The scope for substitutes is high if:

- substitutes are emerging and being adopted;

- there is a price and/or performance advantage that a substitute brings which might compel consumers to switch;

- the buyer has low or no cost when switching to a substitute.

## Competitive rivalry

This is the degree of rivalry among existing competitors. Rivalry can take many forms but fundamentally it is when you experience the suppliers having to work hard to win or retain your business. On a daily basis we are surrounded by examples of competitive rivalry, be they an advertising campaign or a discounted product in a supermarket. The greater the competitive rivalry, the less the profit potential within the marketplace, as the suppliers are effectively each working to out-manoeuvre the other, often by price cutting. The factors that drive competitive rivalry are:

- The number of competitors. The more there are, the greater the rivalry (assuming competitors are roughly equal in size).

- Industry growth is slow, meaning that each player has to fight to keep their market share and avoid being taken by a competitor.

- The players want to remain in the market and perhaps even have desires to dominate.

- Markets that are growing attract more entrants and thus introduce rivalry.

- Capacity has to be added in large increments, thus leading to overcapacity as each new facility comes on line.

- There are high exit barriers, meaning that suppliers hang in there rather than exit a marketplace, thus making all the other suppliers work harder.

The power in using Porter's five forces comes from the analysis of what is behind each force. It is entirely possible that some forces are nonexistent, whilst others are much more important. Where an important or powerful force is identified it should be examined as deeply as practicable. The analysis should also consider the trends and future projections. If there are no substitutes today, are there any developments on the horizon that will give substitutes tomorrow? Porter's five forces are best worked in a group to maximize the opportunity to debate the relevant factors behind each force. Once the analysis is complete each force should be designated as high, medium or low, and the net overall position recorded. Finally ask 'so what does this tell us?' and extract the relevant insights. A template is provided in the Appendix.

**CASE STUDY**    Using Porter's five forces to help determine how to progress a mobile phone category

The mobile or cell phone industry has become a huge global concern. The individual markets, however, remain very much in-country due to the way the networks are regulated. A Porter's five forces carried out as part of a category management project in a European division of a global company revealed the following interesting results:

- *Buyer power: low–medium.* It is possible to switch within the boundaries of the marketplace, but there are multiple buyers. Even the giant buyers may enjoy good pricing and attentive account management, but such accounts are still one of many.

- *Supplier power: high.* The suppliers to this marketplace are primarily the handset providers and the regulatory body that grants the licence to operate a network: in other words, government. Power here is therefore very high.

- *Scope for new entrants: low.* Unless new licences to operate a network are made available, new entrants are not possible.

- *Scope for substitutes: medium.* New technologies are gaining momentum. These include VOIP (Voice over IP) handsets using wi-fi technology to route the call via the internet instead of the mobile telephone network.

- *Competitive rivalry: medium.* Markets continue to grow but there are limited players. There is a reasonable degree of rivalry.

So what insights did the company gain? Essentially, this analysis suggested the company had little power or leverage in this marketplace. Even if they were a huge buyer, they would just be one of many. The analysis suggested a degree of competitiveness but always within the overall structure and constraints of the market. This suggested that potential sourcing strategies should attempt to negotiate the best possible terms within these constraints but focusing on securing additional value.

# DETERMINING STRATEGIC DIRECTION

## Determining potential sources of leverage

This step is a *Tool* and is *Essential*

Finally, a strategic analysis tool designed for purchasing! But before we get to that, let's explore 'leverage'. We began to explore leverage in the last chapter when we looked at value levers. Leverage is a word that is used a lot within purchasing, and for good reason: if we have leverage, then we have the sway, the control, the advantage necessary to get the results we need. But this is not the entire story. Leverage on its own is no use if we don't know we have it. Even if we realize it but are unable to use it to any advantage, then it is equally ineffective. Even worse if we think we have leverage but we don't really, and suppliers are merely humouring us. Worse still, we have no leverage and what we are buying is critical to us but we are entirely at the mercy of the supplier. Over the years suppliers have done a good job in retaining the leverage or preventing buyers from obtaining it, and even where the buyers have had the leverage, suppliers have often managed to behave as if it was the other way around. Maybe you have come across instances where the supplier seems to act as if you need them more than they need you.

Within category management we are searching for leverage, as this will help us achieve good results or even breakthrough. The value levers help us identify where leverage could potentially come from, but we still need to understand if we have the ability to use this leverage. The tool we use here is portfolio analysis and this is an essential tool to help us determine if we have the scope to use leverage or what we need to do to secure it.

Peter Kraljic (1983) developed the portfolio approach to enable buyers to determine the specific approaches required for each area of spend according to the potential profit impact and supply risk or market difficulty. Over the years there have been many adaptations of and variants on Kraljic's original work, with different interpretations of both axis and quadrant labels and even a switching of the axis. But the underlying principles remain unchanged. The version of portfolio analysis we shall use is the one that appears to have become the most established within the purchasing community. This is shown in Figure 5.15 and a template is provided in the Appendix.

The portfolio analysis tool provides the buyer's perspective. There are three key steps in its use, as shown in Figure 5.16.

These three steps are critical, as portfolio analysis is frequently misused by attempting to combine steps one and two. For portfolio analysis to work, the initial classification of the category of spend using the matrix must first be done without considering the relative strength of position within the marketplace. Initial classification must be inward focused in terms of the quadrant that reflects the position of the category within the organization. In many instances, and this is where confusion arises, the initial classification naturally reflects the strength of position in the marketplace. For example, if a large organization is buying from global markets and the buyer is in the *leverage* quadrant, then they have leverage. However, this correlation fails

**FIGURE 5.15**  Portfolio analysis

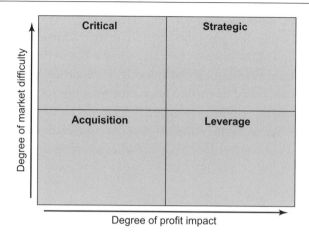

**FIGURE 5.16**  Three steps of portfolio analysis

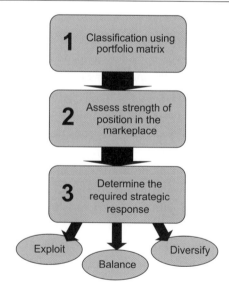

for small businesses, small spends, and for companies with very large buying power. I will expand on this shortly. It is therefore essential when using portfolio analysis that the steps in Figure 5.11 are followed and kept distinct. I will expand on the three steps in turn.

## Step one: classification using portfolio matrix

Let's begin by working through the first of our three steps shown in Figure 5.16. Using the portfolio analysis matrix shown in Figure 5.15, map the position of the category (or categories) in one of the four quadrants, avoiding placing anything on the lines. It is important to note that the portfolio matrix should be used to map categories, not suppliers.

The interpretation of the axis is crucial. First, 'degree of market difficulty' (called 'supply risk' in Kraljic's original paper) is concerned with all the factors that might restrict our freedom of choice when sourcing the category. These include:

- inability to switch suppliers easily;
- only one or a small number of suppliers can supply this;
- the category is complex, therefore it is necessary to work closely with suppliers before they are able to supply;
- availability, eg there is limited supply or capacity in the market, or storage and distribution channels introduce risks in supply;
- competitive demand.

In some versions of the matrix, the second axis, 'degree of profit impact', is changed to 'spend'. However, considering spend alone can introduce some difficulties in using this model and begins to blur the distinction between steps one and two in Figure 5.15. We might spend very little on a category that contains component parts, but the quality of a particular component may be critical to the quality of the final product. Thus, if we encounter any quality problems with the component, this could dramatically impact our overall profit. Using spend alone for the component would be low, but this becomes high when using Kraljic's original 'profit impact' approach. Profit impact is concerned with the degree to which a small benefit per unit purchased would have a significant and positive impact on the overall profit of our organization. This could be a saving per unit, dramatically multiplied due to high volume or high spend, but could equally be mitigation of risk, improved effectiveness or something that will improve future profit potential. Therefore it is relevant to look beyond simply how much is spent on a category. Factors that heighten the degree of profit impact are:

- spend on this category relative to the overall spend of the organization (not the market or size of individual suppliers);
- the percentage that this category represents against total purchase cost of the final goods or service;

- volume purchased;
- impact on final product quality;
- impact on business growth.

Using the correct application of market difficulty and profit impact, the category or categories should be classified on to the relevant quadrant of the portfolio matrix. Portfolio analysis is not a tool to prioritize the categories to work on, but it is a classification tool. No quadrant can be ignored, but rather the distinctive purchasing approach that each quadrant suggests begins to help identify our future sourcing strategy and how we can improve our overall position. If the category is on the right-hand side in either *leverage* or *strategic*, the high profit impact means it is worth putting energy into maximizing our overall position. For *leverage* this might mean securing the best price or terms in the market. In *strategic* it could mean working in a long-term relationship with the supplier to secure optimum value and minimize risk.

If we are on the left-hand side, then things are different. For categories in *critical*, we are experiencing sourcing in a difficult market where this category represents little profit impact. It is therefore likely that the sourcing process is consuming effort and energy for little return. There is also likely to be risk here. For example if, in this difficult market, the supplier decides to cease supply, we may have limited alternatives. Furthermore, if we are in *critical*, it is entirely possible (but not a given) that our spend is low and we have little leverage in the marketplace. If the category or individual components are essential to the operation, then there is a problem.

We cannot just ignore categories in *critical*. Instead, we need to understand why we are there and what we can do to change it. I will come back to this.

Equally, a category within *acquisition* warrants little effort and energy, as the potential returns are small. However, here the market is easy, so switching suppliers is easy and there is scope to simplify the purchasing process, perhaps even automating it entirely. Of course, at this point in the use of portfolio we have yet to consider the strength of our position in the marketplace and the degree to which specific courses of action are possible.

If we think back to business requirements in the last chapter, the headings (with the exception of regulatory, as it is a prerequisite) can be mapped directly on to the portfolio matrix to correspond with the distinct purchasing approaches that each quadrant suggests (see Figure 5.17). This does not mean the rest of the requirements do not apply in that quadrant; they do, but it helps to understand our prime focus for each quadrant. For example

**FIGURE 5.17**    Portfolio analysis and business requirements

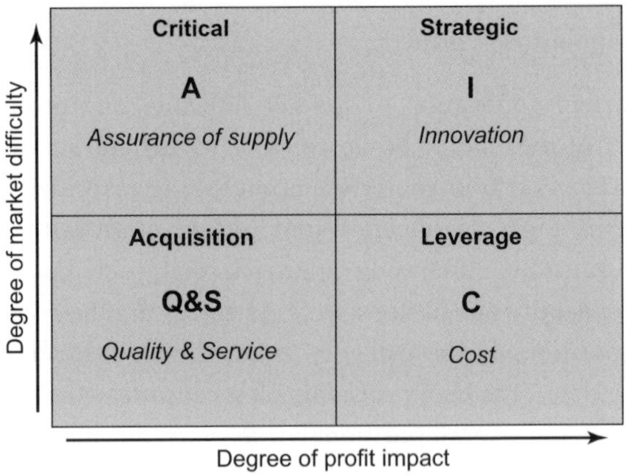

in *critical*, assurance of supply and minimizing risk are paramount, in *leverage* the market is not difficult, so assurance of supply issues is greatly reduced, but we potentially have a strong opportunity to improve profit by securing best cost. Regulatory requirements are essential in all quadrants.

## Step two: assess the strength of our position within the marketplace

Portfolio analysis is not naturally scalable without understanding the strength of our position in the marketplace. Portfolio analysis works well for a large organization with a sizeable spend and sourcing in a global marketplace, and the purchasing approaches that each quadrant suggests are feasible. However, things change for organizations with very small and even very large buying power, and portfolio analysis can work only if we understand the classification on the matrix, together with our overall strength of position in the marketplace. I'll give a couple of examples to help illustrate this point.

Consider a small restaurateur. His biggest spend area apart from staff costs is food and other ingredients. The cost of ingredients represents the most significant percentage of the menu price his customers pay. His source for the vast majority of supplies here is a national company that supplies part-prepared food to the trade. In portfolio analysis the market for this category is easy, as there are many alternatives, and in this case the profit impact would be high because the spend represents a significant part of the overall price paid. Therefore portfolio analysis would suggest that this category is in the *leverage* quadrant. However, the restaurateur does not have any leverage. His is a small restaurant dealing with a huge national company. The prices he pays are set by the supplier and there is no real ability to negotiate, although the supplier has to remain competitive against other similar suppliers. The restaurateur could switch suppliers but would end up in the same position. No matter what he did, he would be too small to have any significant strength of position in the marketplace.

Conversely, consider a multinational giant corporate with huge buying power and which is buying a category that sits in *critical*; the market is difficult and there is little potential to impact profit. There is still likely to be leverage here. Even if the overall spend or volumes purchased are low relative to the overall size of the buying entity, they may be significant within the marketplace. And even if this is not the case, the prestige associated with supplying this giant global customer would not be overlooked by a supplier.

Within portfolio analysis, when we consider our strength of position relative to the market, the distinct purchasing approach that each quadrant might suggest can shift. There are natural power brokers for each quadrant, assuming that we have a good strength of position or strong buying power in the first place, so for such a scenario the power brokers are shown in Figure 5.18. If the category is in *leverage*, then not only is the potential to impact our profit high but so also is our ability to leverage our position in the marketplace. This is because the market is easy, we can switch suppliers if we are not getting the price or terms we desire and, because the strength of our position is also high, we have actual leverage. Assuming we are able

**FIGURE 5.18**   Portfolio analysis: power balanced

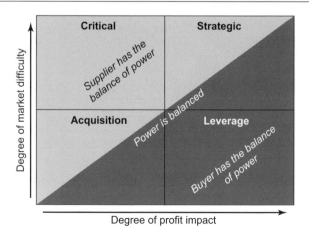

to negotiate well and capitalize on the strength of our position, leverage means we have the potential to push suppliers to extremes in terms of price points or favourable terms because they want or need to win or retain the business.

If the category is in *critical*, then the market is difficult and so the supplier has the balance of power. Furthermore, the degree of profit impact is low and there is little benefit in focusing on this category. It is also possible we are not buying this category in great volumes (which could be the reason why profit impact is low), thus heightening the supplier's power.

If the category is in *strategic*, then although the market is difficult, so too is the degree of impact of profit. This category would attract our focus and we would most likely be working closely with the supplier. The supplier would ideally also recognize the supply of this category as an important part of their overall business and thus would put similar effort into the relationship. In this case the power would usually be balanced between buyer and supplier (although there are exceptions here).

Similarly, in *acquisition*, power is usually balanced. However, it is also diluted, as the market is easy and it is easy to switch suppliers. There is little supplier power. Profit impact is also low, so the degree of focus on categories in this quadrant is limited. Perhaps the spend or volumes purchased are low also.

The diagonal in Figure 5.19 shows the shift of power in different situations. Where the strength in the marketplace is low, for example in the case

**FIGURE 5.19**    Portfolio analysis: power shifting

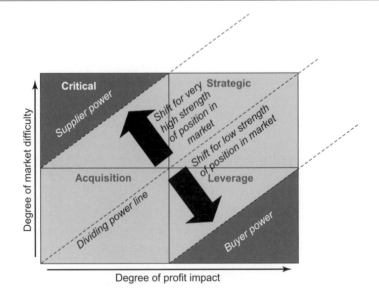

of the restaurateur, this diagonal effectively shifts to the right, increasing supplier power into *leverage* in some or even all circumstances. Similarly, for a giant global buyer with huge buying power the line shifts to the left, increasing the overall buyer power into *critical*.

To help identify where we should draw this power line, we need a means to determine our relative strength of position within the marketplace. At the crudest level this could simply be volumes purchased or even spend. However, adopting this approach alone has flaws. Remember the restaurateur. Say the restaurant was bought by a celebrity chef who turned it into an outlet bearing his name. The new restaurant would be no bigger than the original and would not be purchasing in any greater volumes, but the same suppliers might offer much greater levels of discount just to claim the prestige associated with supplying the celebrity. Strength of position in the market is therefore not just about degree of spend, although this is a major element; there are other influencing factors. Porter's five forces give us the most definitive assessment of the strength of our position within the 'power of buyers' dimension relative to the other dimensions.

In Kraljic's (1983) original work, the link with Porter was not established. Kraljic offered his own basis of determining strength of position. This included:

- large volumes purchased relative to size of suppliers;
- low utilization of capacity in the market;
- ability to switch suppliers;
- non-differentiation of products.

It does not matter which approach is used. The important thing is to assess strength of position within the marketplace for the category. On balance, Porter's approach has greater depth, as it seeks to relate the power of buyers to the other competitive forces that exist within a given market scenario. The output here should simply be an assessment that indicates if our strength is good, low or very high.

## Step three: determine the required strategic response

The third and final step is to determine what we are going to do in response to what the portfolio analysis classification tells us and the degree of leverage we actually have. This is the key output from the use of this analytical tool and is often overlooked; practitioners often work the tool, then pin the finished matrix up on the wall as a completed piece of work. Unless we take what portfolio analysis tells us and turn this into a strategic response, it is worthless.

Portfolio analysis is one of the key activities for shaping future sourcing strategy. It can help determine what things need to happen to shift from a vulnerable position, where the supplier is in control, to a position of leverage and power. In Kraljic's (1983) original work he suggested three strategic responses:

- *Exploit*: maximize the strength of our current position and use this to our advantage to leverage results.
- *Balance*: maintain the current position.
- *Diversify*: do something that enables us to move away from the current position to a more favourable position.

If we consider these three potential responses for each of the quadrants against the three potential strengths of position in the marketplace, the results are given in Table 5.10.

## Shifting position

Once portfolio analysis has been completed and the strategic response determined, the next step is to use this, together with the insights gained from all the other analytical tools, to determine the specific course of action. Clearly, if the response is 'exploit' or 'balance', then the position within portfolio must be maintained. However, where 'diversify' is identified, we need to identify the actions required so that we can shift into another quadrant.

For example, consider the purchase of electrical spare parts within a maintenance category. Here the category sits within *critical* (Figure 5.20). First, the market is difficult, as the spare parts have to match the original equipment manufacturer (OEM), so there is only one source. Second, there is little profit impact potential as these things are purchased in relatively small volumes. However, across the business the overall spend on these and similar items is significant. Third, our assessment of the strength of our position shows that the suppliers have the power. Consequently they inflate prices because they know that only they can supply the OEM parts. This is a common problem, and often the response is to accept the situation as beyond influence.

But sometimes there are responses that can shift the position. If there was scope to aggregate spend with suppliers of this category, we could increase both our overall attractiveness and strength of position, giving us leverage.

**TABLE 5.10**   Purchasing approaches in each quadrant of portfolio analysis

| Portfolio quadrant | Low strength of position within market | Good strength of position within market | Very high strength of position within market |
|---|---|---|---|
| **Leverage** | ***Exploit where possible*** <br><br> • Do your best to use what power you have <br> • Shop around for the best deal <br><br> ***Where possible build relationship with supplier to get best discounts*** | ***Exploit*** <br><br> • Target pricing <br> • Short-term commitments <br> • Spot buying <br> • e-auctions <br> • Use competition to the full <br> • Hard negotiations <br> • Maintain 'generic' (day one) specification <br> • Maximize profits <br> • Retain full flexibility (and ability to switch easily) <br><br> ***Arm's-length supplier relationship managed by tough and even slightly aggressive buyer style*** | |
| **Strategic** | ***Balance*** <br><br> • Build best relationship possible <br> • Work to keep supplier focused on your account <br> • Sell your potential as a good and long-term client <br> • Pursue the supplier for early access to innovation <br><br> ***Work to build and maintain the best relationship possible, don't allow the supplier to overlook you*** | ***Balance*** <br><br> • Develop and nurture relationship <br> • Focus on joint cost reduction, perhaps even open book costing <br> • Jointly agreed continuous improvement programmes <br> • Pursue innovation <br> • Share risks and opportunities <br><br> ***Collaborative supplier relationship focused BUT maintaining degree of 'arms length' and ability to switch away (move to Leverage) if necessary*** | ***Balance*** <br><br> • Balance use of competitive strength against developing a relationship according to need <br> • Manage relationship <br> • Agree continuous improvement programmes with supplier incentivization <br> • Possibly use open book costing <br> • Pursue innovation <br><br> ***Managed 'prime supplier' relationship BUT maintaining degree of 'arms length' and ability to switch away (move to Leverage) if necessary*** |

**TABLE 5.10**    *continued*

| Critical | Diversify | Balance or Diversify |
|---|---|---|
| | • Seek alternative or ways to move out of Critical<br>• Secure maximum value until alternative becomes available<br>• Manage risk and supply exposure carefully, consider contingencies<br>• Increase attractiveness to supplier, perhaps through bundling<br>• Keep close to supplier and anticipate their plans for this category<br><br>*Careful and diplomatic Supplier Relationship Management focused on maintaining and growing overall attractiveness* | • If necessary seek alternative or ways to move out of Critical OR work to balance and maintain position and manage risk<br><br>*Manage supplier closely to ensure power advantage can be maintained, if not diversify or develop attractiveness* |
| Acquisition | *Exploit where possible*<br><br>• Do your best to effect best prices and terms, consider standardization of products and consolidation of suppliers<br>• Simplify ordering and payment process, automate where possible<br><br>*Basic supplier relationship* | *Exploit*<br><br>• Simplify ordering and payment process, automate where possible<br>• Use competition, standardization of products and consolidation of suppliers to effect best prices and terms<br>• Minimize intervention of purchasing resource<br><br>*Basic supplier relationship, possibly managed by a junior buyer* |

Within portfolio this would shift the classification into the *strategic* quadrant. This is because the aggregation of spend would increase the potential for increased profit impact, so the strategic responses in this quadrant would shift to those appropriate for *strategic*.

We could consider changing the specification and finding a way to use generic or non-OEM parts (day one analysis). Such a move might require intense stakeholder agreement, risk assessment and even re-qualification of processes or re-certification of design; but it might not be as impossible as it

**FIGURE 5.20**    Portfolio analysis: *critical* to *strategic* to *leverage*

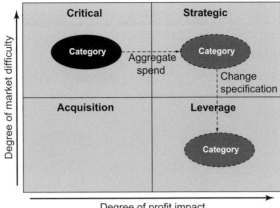

Degree of profit impact

might first seem. A change of specification to a generic part immediately moves the degree of market difficulty to easy and opens up competition and the ability to switch suppliers. Our portfolio classification would shift to *leverage*, as would the strategic responses associated with this quadrant, and we are free to broker the best price and terms possible.

Here there were two distinct actions to diversify from our original position: aggregate spend and change specification. There may be others and they may be done in a different sequence; the value levers tool here helps us to open up possibilities to shift position. The point is the identification of what is needed to shift from one portfolio quadrant, with the strategic responses associated with that quadrant given the strength of position in the market, to a more desirable quadrant. This is one of the key strategic enablers within category management.

Consider a slightly different example as shown in Figure 5.21. Here the category is strategic outsourcing of a printed circuit board (PCB) assembly. The category represents both significant volumes and significant spend, and the quality of assembled PCBs is critical. Any defects will require expensive rework; thus impact on profit is high. The market for PCB assembly is easy as there are many providers. However, the single outsource supplier for this category has amassed a considerable amount of process know-how, thereby placing them in a unique position – they have in fact accumulated the balance of power – and increasing the market difficulty. The category would therefore be classified as *strategic*. Despite a pre-agreed fee structure, the overall cost of the outsourced arrangement has crept up, and the supplier

**FIGURE 5.21**    Portfolio analysis: *strategic* to *leverage* to *strategic*

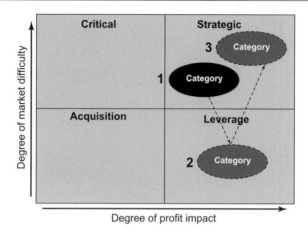

appears to be charging for activities beyond the core activity, claiming that issues within the relationship are introducing delays. Even though the category is *strategic*, maintaining the balance of our position, as would usually be expected in this quadrant, is not appropriate. Instead we need a course of action that will rebalance the power.

Portfolio can help. Work to understand the process, and cost breakdown will open options for competition, switching suppliers, dual sourcing or even just the threat of these actions. This will reduce market difficulty and the category will move to *leverage*, with the response shifting from balance to *exploit*. Once new supply arrangements are in place, this time with better supplier management to prevent the balance of power shifting too much into the supplier's favour, the category moves back to *strategic* as the supplier amasses know-how and switching becomes unattractive. Figure 5.20 illustrates this shift from *strategic* to *leverage* and back to strategic, showing how portfolio analysis can help to identify the key steps that are required to address problematic categories.

## *Behaviours can be deceptive*

Finally, it is worth a brief word on the difference between an actual classification using portfolio analysis and the supplier's behaviour. Remember that suppliers are adept at making us feel we need them and they add great value. This behaviour is akin to a category that might sit within the *critical* quadrant, but in actual fact the category in question would be classified in

**FIGURE 5.22**   Portfolio analysis noting supplier behaviour

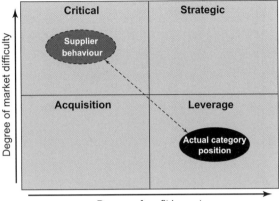

*leverage* (see Figure 5.22). When using portfolio analysis, the classification should be strictly based upon an assessment of the position, using the axis definitions. Supplier behaviours should not influence the classification. However, where there is a disparity, the behaviour should not be ignored but rather should be noted using the portfolio matrix as shown in Figure 5.22. This helps to identify strategic courses of action. In this example we would seek to exploit our position, which might include addressing the factors that are allowing the supplier to project power or influence key stakeholders.

# Understanding how the supplier views the relationship/account

This step is a *Tool* and is *Essential*

Imagine you could sit invisibly in a supplier sales meeting. What would they say about your company, you and the stakeholders in your business they interface with? Suppliers' sales planning meetings are often like planning battlefield tactics, except the meeting takes place in an office, not a tent in the middle of a field. Suppliers have just one objective and that is to grow and maintain the accounts that are important to them. If this includes our company, then we will be the subject of discussion at sales meetings. Suppliers will debate what they need to do to develop the relationship

**FIGURE 5.23**    Supplier preferencing

| | Development | Core | |
|---|---|---|---|
| Attractiveness of account | | | |
| | Nuisance | Exploitable | |

Relative value of account

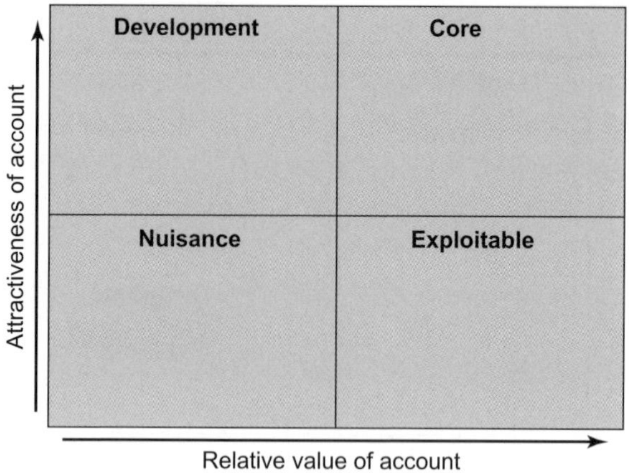

so that they are in prime position. This will include tactics for engaging with us and our key stakeholders.

Not every account is of interest to a supplier, and the supplier has only so much resource to put into growing and maintaining their accounts, so this will be directed at the accounts that are seen as priorities. There are accounts where the supplier will not be hugely interested, perhaps because they are difficult to service, unprofitable or have poor terms within the contract. In this case suppliers may adopt a deliberate strategy to either do the minimum to maintain the account or even manage the account out of the business. It is vital we understand how the supplier sees our business, because there is great risk if we see the account as *strategic* (portfolio analysis) but the supplier sees the account as one to manage out.

The analytical tool we use here is called supplier preferencing, and it should be used in conjunction with portfolio analysis. This essential tool, like so many within category management, comes from the world of marketing. You might see this, or similar tools with other names, in marketing textbooks. It is shown in Figure 5.23 and a template is provided in the Appendix.

When we used portfolio analysis, our perspective was that of the buyer considering specific categories. Supplier preferencing is the supplier's perspective and to use the tool we need to put ourselves in the supplier's shoes. Here we are mapping not categories but suppliers on the matrix.

First, let's consider the axis, 'attractiveness of account'. This is concerned with the degree of attractiveness our account presents to the supplier. Attractiveness here is not just about how much we spend with the supplier (that is a factor, despite also featuring in the bottom axis) but it includes all the factors that might make a supplier interested in growing and maintaining their position as a supplier to us. Attractiveness is a function of the following factors:

- purchase is in high volumes or there is a high spend;
- our brand is well known and would give kudos to the supplier to be able to claim they supply us;
- good payment terms and payment on time;
- degree of profit margin;
- ease of servicing the account;
- the fit of our type of business and the associated supply lines with the supplier's future strategy and direction;
- the fit of our operating locations with the supplier's future planned geographical supply footprint;
- finally, and this should not be overlooked, we have developed a good relationship with the supplier and they enjoy working with us.

The power of attractiveness should not be underestimated but it often is. To truly understand how attractive our account is, we need to get close to the supplier. Review meetings with suppliers are a good opportunity to test this with a few simple, well-structured questions such as 'Tell me how you find our company to deal with; what could we improve?' or 'What are your future plans and strategic direction, and how do we fit with those?' Find an opportunity for the supplier to give their general introduction to someone new in your business. Chances are they will show a few PowerPoint slides, and one will contain the logos of all the companies they supply. If yours is there in prime position, you know they value your account. If it is not there at all, you might want to 1) ask why; and 2) be concerned and re-evaluate your position.

The bottom axis is 'relative spend of account'. This means how much we spend with this supplier relative to their overall annual sales or turnover. If our total spend is a high percentage of the supplier's turnover, say 30 per cent, then we would place this supplier on the right-hand side of the matrix. However, there are no absolute numbers, and overall scale of the relationship can change how we use this matrix. For example, consider a supplier with annual sales of $400 million, of which our business represents 12 per cent ($48 million). This is a relatively high spend for the supplier and they would ensure we would receive their attention. However, if we are a large global business spending $48 million each year on Microsoft software (and that's a lot of software!), the relative value of the account would be 0.0011 per cent of Microsoft's annual $45 billion sales revenue. In this case it would be hard for any customer to become a relatively high spender. Instead there is a spend point that certain customers will reach, and that will attract the highest level of account management and discounting. In terms of how supplier preferencing is used, in these circumstances the relative value of account should be regarded as high. This bottom axis therefore requires some interpretation.

We use supplier preferencing to plot how we believe a specific supplier views our account on the matrix. Each quadrant operates as follows:

- *Development*. Here the account is attractive to the supplier but the relative spend is low. The supplier would seek to develop this account and increase the overall business. This is the type of account the supplier would see as future business and thus it would feature firmly within their future sales pipeline with sales personnel tasked with finding ways to grow the account. The supplier would put their best salesperson on the account, the phone would ring regularly, requests for meetings would be frequent and, if our company permits such things, the invitations to golf events would be in abundance.

- *Core*. This is the heartland for the supplier, the accounts they need to maintain at all costs. Maintaining an account is not simply a case of doing nothing. It requires ongoing care and attention, keeping close to customers, filling gaps in their requirements, maintaining the relationships. *Core* accounts represent a significant percentage of the supplier's turnover, so the supplier will not do anything to jeopardize the account. These accounts will be managed by a 'safe pair of hands', ie the seasoned salespeople who are very capable of maintaining such an account.

- *Nuisance*. This is not a great place to be as a buyer. The supplier really does not want to do business with us. They may not tell us this and keep up the pretence that everything is fine, but behind this the supplier would be entirely happy if we stopped placing orders with them. In fact, they have probably flagged this account as one to put little or no effort into and to be prepared to lose. It seems rare that a supplier will explicitly tell a customer the account is undesirable. Such a move would undoubtedly anger the buyer, who may tell other buyers in other customers, and this could be damaging. So suppliers seem to deal with the accounts they don't want with a more subtle approach. The reason why this quadrant is called *nuisance* is that suppliers will often allow the arrangement to continue so long as the nuisance factor is tolerable. But the moment it becomes unbearable for them, they will make doing business very difficult. In practice this manifests itself in suppliers not returning phone calls, putting a less than competent account manager on the account, imposing aggressive pricing or charging, or being unavailable for supplier review meetings. There are situations where the supplier will end the relationship, but we may find the true reasons are kept secret. A colleague received a letter from a key supplier that simply stated, 'We are very sorry, but we have decided to cease production of miniature attenuators with effect from one month from now, as falling demand has meant that this area of our business has become unfeasible for us. We wish you every success in finding an alternative supplier.' Once we picked my colleague up off the floor and considered the problem, we realized we had failed to understand the supplier's position and had not realized our vulnerability. Buyers who fail to understand when they are sourcing from a supplier in this quadrant may find themselves pushing hard, because that is the instinctive thing to do, only to find that this tips the supplier to want to shake off the account. *Nuisance* accounts may not appear to be managed by the supplier at all; or if they are it will be by the least capable sales individual.

- *Exploitable.* This is also not a great place to be as a buyer. The account is not attractive to the supplier, but as long as we continue to spend significant money with them they will continue to service the account. In *exploitable* the supplier will not, as is the case in *nuisance*, set out to deliberately lose the account, but instead will have planned to do just enough to keep it, as long as the revenues are strong. At the point where revenues decline, this account would switch to *nuisance* and become one to shake off. 'Doing just enough' sums up the supplier's overall approach to management of this account. The account manager will be someone who squeezes in the management of the account in their spare time when not working on other more important activities. Our phone calls will be returned, but maybe not immediately, and the supplier will make us feel they are interested and responsive. However, if we start asking for commitment from the supplier in participating in regular review meetings to look at future innovation, we may find they are uninterested.

**FIGURE 5.24**    Preferencing: *nuisance* to *development* to *core*

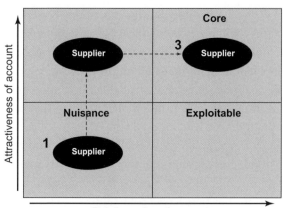

Once we have classified the supplier and how we see their positioning of our account on the matrix, the implications need to be considered. If we are in an undesirable quadrant it doesn't follow that this is where we need to stay. It is possible to identify actions that will shift our account from one quadrant to another.

Imagine discovering that an account with a particular supplier is sitting in *nuisance* (Figure 5.24), but this supplier provides some fairly important components that we cannot easily get elsewhere. The first step is to understand why this account is not attractive to the supplier. This may be easy to fix and it may simply be a case of changing payment terms, allowing a price increase, or offering our company as a reference site. Or it may require some more substantial action, such as opening discussions around this supplier taking on new areas of supply. If we can understand the source of unattractiveness to the supplier, actions such as these can remedy the problem easily.

The difference, when we take steps to make our account more attractive, is often very noticeable. Suddenly we get a new account manager, they call us up frequently and are very interested in what we are doing.

The story doesn't have to end there. A second shift from *development* to *core* will shore up our position and protect supply. This might involve increasing the overall spend with this supplier and moving other business to them, perhaps bundling together similar categories. Supplier preferencing therefore allows us to understand how the supplier views our account, and if we find we are in a vulnerable or undesirable position, the analysis of the underlying reasons can help us develop actions to resolve this (which we will explore shortly).

**FIGURE 5.25**    Preferencing: *nuisance* or *core*?

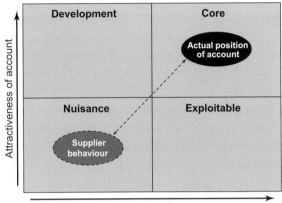

Supplier preferencing requires one final explanation regarding supplier behaviour. As with portfolio analysis, it is possible that the actual position and the way the supplier behaves are entirely different, perhaps deliberately, but often simply through incompetence on the part of the supplier. A large global company I worked for had a key supplier that provided process technology components. This supplier enjoyed a spend of around £1.2 million per annum, but despite this the account and the way the supplier interfaced with the company felt like *nuisance*, with the account manager neglecting to return calls and showing little sign of being interested (see Figure 5.25). Supplier preferencing suggested the actual position would undoubtedly be *core*. The difference between actual position and behaviour was a puzzle. In the course of working through category management, a meeting was convened with the account manager, his boss the sales director, and the managing director. During this meeting the category manager actually showed the supplier preferencing matrix and asked the supplier to explain why there was a difference. Within one week the account manager had been taken off the account and replaced with a new individual who was immediately more attentive and shifted the behaviour back to that expected within *core*. Often if there is a disparity between actual position and behaviour, there is a simple reason behind it, and it may be down to one individual who is demotivated or not doing the job properly.

Of course, as with all the other tools, once the analysis is complete it is essential to review the outputs and ask, 'So what is this telling us?' and note the insights gained.

# Portfolio analysis with supplier preferencing

Combining the portfolio analysis with supplier preferencing gives a powerful insight into our position. By examining the combination of positions we can begin to identify the most appropriate way forward in terms of strategic sourcing. The use of these two tools together is fundamental to category management.

Imagine a category that is mapped in *strategic* in portfolio analysis. The category has a good degree of importance to our organization, and the supplier or suppliers view it as *core* within supplier preferencing, meaning it is equally important to them (see Figure 5.26). This is a good position to be in, as there is a shared mutual dependency, probably with a good relationship between buyer and supplier. Risk associated with potential loss of supply or loss of account on either side is mitigated by the shared mutual dependency.

**FIGURE 5.26**    Preferencing: *strategic* and *core*

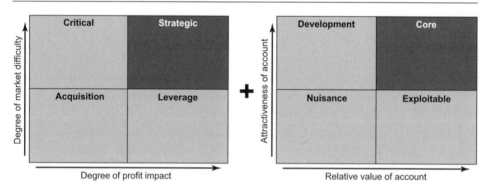

Now imagine a scenario where a category is classified as *critical* in portfolio analysis but the supplier (or suppliers) views the account as *nuisance* in supplier preferencing (Figure 5.27). Here we are in a very risky situation and need to take action quickly to change things. The market is difficult, so our ability to switch suppliers is limited, and the degree of profit impact is low – which might also mean we lack any sort of leverage if the spend is low. The supplier sees this account as *nuisance* so could potentially cease supply at any time or might refuse to resolve any delivery or quality issues. With this combination we are highly vulnerable and our only way out is to either

**FIGURE 5.27**    Preferencing: *critical* and *nuisance*

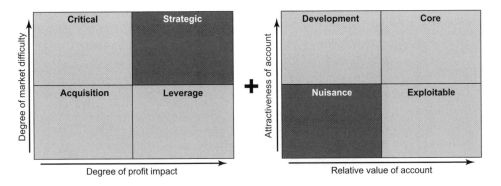

make the account more attractive to the supplier or remove the market difficulty, perhaps by switching specification to a generic alternative; or both of these things. This combination of quadrants in portfolio analysis and supplier preferencing is not uncommon, but it is often not fully understood, and supply vulnerabilities are not considered and planned for until it is too late. If the 10-cent gasket made from a material for which only one supplier holds the patent suddenly becomes obsolete because the supplier doesn't seem interested in us, we have a supply problem. If the unavailability of that gasket is grounding a commercial flight packed with fare-paying passengers, the impact is much more than a supply problem. The use of these two tools is not just about identifying leverage but also about understanding vulnerability, and is a key step in developing a strategy for future sourcing.

There are 16 possible combinations of portfolio analysis and supplier preferencing, although the potential responses are often the same across a number of combinations. Figure 5.28 shows each tool mapped against the other. To this I have added the three strategic responses identified by Kraljic (1983) (exploit, balance, diversify). This shows both good and unfavourable combinations and the potential response that is appropriate. It is this insight that can then be used to determine the nature of the strategic supply strategy that is appropriate for the category in question.

**FIGURE 5.28**    Portfolio analysis plus supplier preferencing

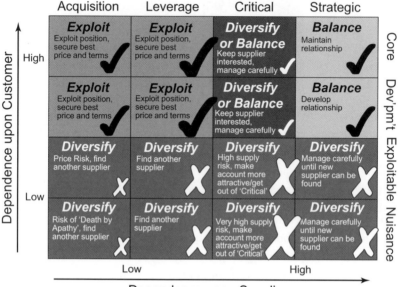

### Portfolio Analysis Quadrant

Chapter 5 summary

Recap on the key points from this chapter:

1   The second stage within the category management process is *insight* and is concerned with a series of research activities and application of strategic analysis tools to gain insight that will help inform the development of a sourcing strategy.

2   At the heart of the *insight* stage is effective data gathering where we attempt to expand our knowledge and gather information, facts and data beyond that we know already, beyond that we know we don't know and gather data extensively to inform 'what we don't know we don't know.' It is here where we are likely to find breakthroughs.

3   We gather data in three primary areas; data about the category, about suppliers and potential suppliers, and about the marketplace.

4   Supplier conditioning is about using different offensive or defensive messages with the supplier to signal to the other part that we are seeking a particular outcome. Conditioning early on in category management helps to prepare the supplier for what we want.

5   Different pricing approaches exist for what we buy, determined by either the supplier, market forces or perhaps even us. Price model analysis enables us to understand how price is determined and this insight helps determine how we might influence price.

6   A purchase price cost analysis (PPCA) is a tool to develop an estimate of what goods or a service 'should cost' and this insight allows us to check for a significant disparity between the actual cost and the price we pay, which might highlight opportunities for a new sourcing approach. PPCA is appropriate within *tailored* or *custom* quadrants in day one analysis.

7   Supply and value chain network (SVCN) analysis is a tool that enables us to identify potential opportunities or risks beyond immediate supplier relationships. It can provide useful insights that can shape future sourcing approaches where cost or risk reduction, or improved value and logistics within SVCN might yield significant benefit.

8   The technology mapping tool is relevant for categories that are technology dependent to understand and determine which mix of old, current, new and future technologies might be appropriate.

9   Within category management it is important to understand the external environment including the marketplace we are sourcing, or plan to source the category from. Here two tools from the world of marketing, the PESTLE tool and Porter's five forces, help bring insight that can shape our future sourcing strategy.

10  The two tools that help us determine our overall strategic direction, and are informed by all the insights gathered thus far, are portfolio analysis (based around the matrix originally developed by Peter Kraljic, 1983) and supplier preferencing. Together these tools enable us to classify both the category and supplier relationships to determine the strength of our position, the balance of power and the specific actions needed to improve our overall position.

# Stage 3: Innovation

This chapter explores the third stage, innovation. We will examine how the outputs from Stage 2 begin to suggest different solutions or ways forward in terms of how this category can be sourced in the future. We will explore how a single way forward can be selected from these options and how this single strategic option is then developed further into a solid plan for execution. We will consider how business agreement for the way ahead is secured before we move to the implementation phase in the next chapter.

Pathway questions addressed in this chapter:

9  How can I identify the optimum, and ideally breakthrough, future sourcing strategy for a category?

10  How do I ensure all our future sourcing strategies are based upon a robust understanding of all market and external drivers and factors?

11  How can I effectively implement new sourcing strategies so they become a reality and we realize the benefits?

## The innovation toolkit

Stage 3 (Figure 6.1) differs from Stage 2 in that it contains few tools but a series of steps or activities. Most of these capitalize on the benefits of working as a group and use the cross-functional team to generate the outputs required. The stage culminates in the completion and sign-off of a source plan defining the proposed future sourcing strategy.

**FIGURE 6.1**    Stage 3: Innovation

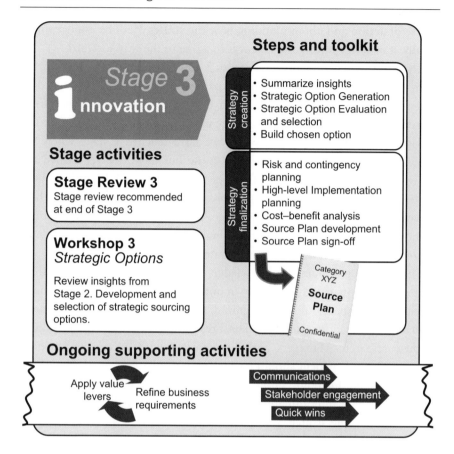

A third facilitated workshop supports this stage, in which the cross-functional team meets and determines the future sourcing strategy. In this section we will explore the key steps to achieve this, including the sessions that would be run in the third workshop.

# The steps towards innovation

This stage is about determining the future sourcing strategy. It is called innovation simply because the best sourcing strategies are the innovative ones that represent a significant breakthrough. Innovation is the bridge between the analysis gained from data gathering and the implementation of a way forward. It is about identifying a handful of potential ways forward which are informed by the outputs of the insight stage, selecting the most suitable and then building and developing the result into a well-defined sourcing strategy. It is about understanding the risks associated with this course of action and about planning how the strategy will be implemented. Finally, it is about getting the business to agree to the way forward.

The process that runs through Stages 2 and 3 takes us from our starting point of limited understanding and expands our knowledge through data collection to reach a point where we have much data, but not yet in a form that easily makes much sense. This stage in the process is called the point of maximum ambiguity. In other words, we have reached a stage where we know as much as we can practically know but have not yet turned the knowledge into something that can shape the way forward. From this point, strategic analysis helps us begin to make sense of the mass of data, and then, as we progress into the innovation stage, we can identify potential options for how we will source in the future. Finally, we select and develop a single option to arrive at a future sourcing strategy.

This widening of data and knowledge, followed by a narrowing to form strategic direction, is a core concept in implementing category management, and its importance should be recognized. Practitioners of category management should pay close attention to ensure, within reason, the thoroughness of their research. Managers and those tasked with overseeing category management deployment should be challenging, wherever possible pushing practitioners on this point; good research can make the difference between more of the same and dramatic breakthrough.

Determining the strategic sourcing options is not an automatic step; it requires informed brainpower from those involved in the project. It is here that practitioners can often lose their nerve and are tempted to settle for a small improvement in the current position. However, real step-change benefits come only from making bold steps, so the potential for a breakthrough solution should not be discarded easily.

# CREATING THE SOURCING STRATEGY

## Summarizing the insights

This step is a *Tool* and is *Essential*

This is an essential step, as there is little point in mindlessly working through a series of analytical tools if the implications are not going to be considered.

In category management it is not the tool or step in the process that is important but what the tool tells us, and what we do with this knowledge. Remember each piece of analysis and insight should therefore be concluded by asking the question, 'So what does this tell us?' and noting the answer. 'So what' sounds similar to 'SWOT', which is a happy coincidence, as SWOT analysis (strengths, weaknesses, opportunities and threats) is the final analytical tool we will use to combine all the 'So whats' gained from working through the process so far.

By this stage we will have a vast number of files and documents. Now we need to make sense of the combined story these begin to tell. This is unlikely to just appear (although we may have some idea what the story is), but by finding a way to immerse ourselves and fellow team members in all of the outputs thus far, the story will begin to emerge. Here the 'war room' concept that we explored at the start of Chapter 5 can help. SWOT is a useful tool to help marshal insights into a cohesive form. It should only be used to record the most important findings, not every piece of detail, otherwise there is a risk of the story being missed.

An example of a SWOT analysis matrix in its completed form is shown in Figure 6.2. It is a simple set of headings under which we can summarize the individual insights gained from all of the work so far, as well as our overall position. Strengths and weaknesses should have an internal focus, while opportunities and threats are outward looking.

# Strategic option generation

This step is a *Tool* and is *Optional*

The overall aims of the innovation stage are to determine the nature and shape of the recommended future sourcing strategy, and to secure business agreement to proceed. The sourcing strategy is a definition of the way forward. It is by nature a short high-level statement that encapsulates the goal and how it will be reached, while options generation is a means to develop a number of potential sourcing strategies for subsequent selection. Before we explore options generation, some explanation of what constitutes a good sourcing strategy is worthwhile.

The sourcing strategy needs to be accompanied by supporting detail that explains how it was determined, why it is the most appropriate course of action and precisely how it will be achieved in a step-by-step form. Statements

**FIGURE 6.2**   Completed SWOT analysis

| Strengths | Weaknesses |
|---|---|
| Internal focus | • Good understanding of future volumes<br>• Scope to change specification to generic equivalents with trials<br>• Good understanding of category, suppliers and market<br>• Willingness by key stakeholders to drive change | • Our arrangements for supplier management has allowed suppliers go gain undue balance of power<br>• Current relationships with suppliers unduly favour certain suppliers<br>• Specification has restricted free choice for certain parts |

| Opportunities | Threats |
|---|---|
| External focus | • Strong leverage if we aggregate spend across entire category<br>• Market competitiveness is increasing with many new entrants<br>• Potential to use emerging markets<br>• Scope to optimise supply chain<br>• PPCA suggests we are overpaying by 30% | • One prime supplier views us as 'exploitable'<br>• Risk to other business areas if a supplier pulls out before we are ready<br>• A change in import duties might preclude use of emerging market |

that describe high-level sourcing strategies where the way forward can be summarized in a series of simple sentences might include examples such as:

- outsource facilities management to a third-party provider;
- consolidate our spend on packaging with two providers;
- switch supply of electronic assemblies to a provider in a low-cost country;
- develop the relationship with The Widget Corporation to become our sole provider of widgets.

There could be many more. Potential sourcing strategies will naturally emerge from good data gathering and analysis. However, there will undoubtedly be more than one potential option. For example, analysis and team brainstorming might suggest a way forward such as 'Run a tender exercise to find a new supplier', but others may also be proposed, such as 'Switch the business to an existing supplier to give aggregation of spend and leverage', or 'In-source and make in-house', among others. To determine the correct sourcing strategy we need first to determine all the potential sourcing strategy options that emerge from the data gathering and analysis, and then use a structured approach to select the most appropriate one based on what the business needs.

Potential strategic options must be at the highest level; a long list of ways forward will be unworkable. As a rule, around five potential strategic sourcing options is about right. If the list is much larger it is likely that many options are variants of the others. This should be avoided, with more thought being given to defining the high-level options by consolidation where many options emerge.

The identification of the handful of sourcing options to be considered is about using two key points of reference: first, what will meet the needs of the business (identified as business requirements, informed by the value levers); and second, what will generate or leverage the most value and benefit. Remember, value and benefit are linked to what the business needs to achieve, be it reducing cost, reducing risk or increasing effectiveness, or enabling innovation from the supply chain.

At this stage within the category management process, the cross-functional team may believe they are able to describe a list of the potential strategic options. However, this might not be as easy as it seems. To generate the options effectively – and ensure we don't miss any – we need a more structured approach.

Strategic option generation is a group-based activity to identify a handful of potential ways forward. This is an important activity and is not something that should be just squeezed into a meeting. It requires careful planning and the right environment. A strategic option generation workshop demands a degree of creative thinking. Participants should be asked to remind themselves of all of the insights gained so far and, using these as reference points, identify the potential ways forward. Ideally the session should be away from the distraction of the normal day in the office and in comfortable surroundings that allow team members to concentrate fully on the activity, with maximum potential for creative and breakthrough thinking. Figure 6.3 shows the process of options generation and evaluation. We shall explore each step in turn.

## Step one: develop option evaluation criteria

Before we can begin to generate strategic options, the criteria against which the options will be evaluated must be identified. If the evaluation criteria are

**FIGURE 6.3**    The Options generation process

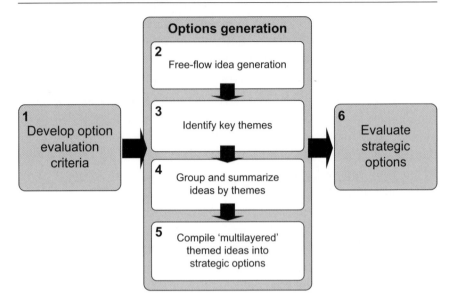

developed post-option generation, there is a risk that they will be shaped, consciously or subconsciously, to select favoured options. Figure 6.4 shows a typical options evaluation matrix and a template is provided in the Appendix. Options are across the top, the evaluation criteria are on the left, and the resulting grid gives the facility to assign scores and a weighting system for each option against each criterion.

There are two areas where criteria should be developed:

- *Business requirements criteria.* Where the requirement is defined as a 'need' – in other words, compromise is not acceptable – then we can use a Go/No-go evaluation approach rather than a numerical weighting and scoring system. If the requirement is a 'want', then each option can be evaluated based on the degree to which the option will deliver the want. Here a numerical weighted scoring approach is relevant.

- *Implementation criteria.* A particular strategic option might appear to be the ideal solution when matched against the business requirements, but if it cannot easily be implemented, would cost too much or would introduce unacceptable levels of risk, then clearly such an option is unworkable.

**FIGURE 6.4**    The options evaluation matrix

| Options evaluation | | | | | | |
|---|---|---|---|---|---|---|
| **Evaluation criteria** | Weighting | Max Score | Option 1 | Option 2 | Option 3 | Option 4 |
| Meets business needs | G/NG | – | | | | |
| Business want No 1 | 40% | 400 | | | | |
| Business want No 2 | 10% | 100 | | | | |
| Business want No 3 | 30% | 300 | | | | |
| Business want No 4 | 20% | 200 | | | | |
| **Business requirements TOTAL** | 100% | 1000 | | | | |
| Ease of implementation | 20% | 200 | | | | |
| Low implementation risk | 30% | 300 | | | | |
| Scale of benefits | 50% | 500 | | | | |
| Low cost to implement | G/NG | – | | | | |
| **Implementation TOTAL** | 100% | 1000 | | | | |

Implementation criteria might include:

- ease of implementation internally;
- ease of implementation externally (ie with supply base);
- potential value of benefits that will be achieved;
- the overall cost to implement (it may be appropriate to set boundaries here);
- minimum risk;
- timing for implementation within set boundaries.

In Figure 6.4, both business requirements and implementation evaluation criteria have been identified in this simple evaluation matrix. Note that as a general rule, for the process to be workable, around 7 to 10 evaluation criteria are about right for each.

Once developed, the evaluation matrix should be put to one side for later use when the process of options generation is complete.

## Step two: free-flow idea generation

Strategic options don't just appear. Some might, but the best option may not naturally emerge and instead needs to be coaxed out from the myriad of analysis and insights. Free-flow idea generation is, as the name suggests, simply about allowing the team to share all their existing ideas and hopefully generate new ones, using a brainstorming technique. This step works on the principle that all the team members are fully familiar with the outputs and insights from the analysis work so far, and therefore their minds are equipped with the understanding of the environment, challenges, risks, needs and opportunities that will prompt ideas. It is important to note that we are using 'idea' and not 'strategic option' here. That is because it is unlikely that people will consistently make the leap to a strategic option, but rather may have a series of ideas, some of which are strategic and some tactical, and some are just good ideas that should be considered anyway. Some may just be crazy. The activity is about capturing all of these without prejudice or constraint.

Free-flow idea generation requires the presence and participation of the cross-functional team familiar with the outputs so far, a comfortable room with no interruptions, a flip chart and a facilitator. The group first needs to be introduced to the process of what will happen, what is expected of them, and the ground rules for the brainstorming activity. Next, the group simply lets the ideas flow, each being captured on the flip chart along the way. A good brainstorming approach here is vital and the session should not be rushed – in fact, brainstorming should continue once all the initial ideas have begun to dry up. It is in the silence that emerges that people begin to think further and reach for new, more creative ideas. Then the idea from one person triggers a thought and a new idea from another. The result is a rich, varied and often long list of brainstormed ideas. It is not unknown for an option generation session to take a whole day and end up with 15 or 20 pieces of flip-chart paper on the walls, packed with hundreds of ideas.

## Step three: identify key themes

This long list is, of course, completely unworkable in its current form. Not only are there too many ideas to be processed easily, but it is likely that the list will naturally contain a mix of contributions, typically:

- strategic options and ways forward;
- good ideas that can be incorporated into specific strategic options;
- good ideas that can be incorporated into any chosen strategic option;
- quick wins;
- other ideas and crazy thoughts where no one can work out what to do with them.

Furthermore, some ideas will be opposite to others, while some would naturally complement and could be incorporated with whatever way forward is chosen. Also, similar ideas may appear several times with slightly different wording.

To begin to make sense of the long list, the entries should be divided according to a handful of common themes or headings that summarize the nature of the idea. Between five and 10 common or key themes is about right. To identify these, look down the list and ask, 'What type of idea is this?' and try to determine the handful of themes into which all the ideas could be categorized. This may take some time. If you are struggling or keep coming up with too many themes, then you are not thinking in terms of the type of idea, but of the idea itself. Instead aim for five to 10 themes; if more are identified, then combine some.

A typical list of themes is given below. Note that it looks very similar to the list we saw just above:

- strategic options and high-level statements of future direction;
- good ideas linked to a specific strategic option;
- good ideas we might want to incorporate into whatever strategic options we choose;
- supplier management/supply chain ideas;
- internal changes or improvements;
- policy or procedure changes;
- quick wins to do now;
- 'off-the-wall' ideas;
- things to park.

## Step four: group and summarize ideas by key themes

The long list of ideas should now be sorted according to the themes that have been identified. This must be completed by the group; initially, if working

**FIGURE 6.5**   Themed and summarized ideas

| Strategic options | Ideas linked to a specific option | Good ideas to do whichever option | Policy and procedures |
|---|---|---|---|
| Summarized idea 1 | Summarized idea 1 | Summarized idea 1 | Summarized idea 1 |
| Summarized idea 2 | Summarized idea 2 | Summarized idea 2 | Summarized idea 2 |
| Summarized idea 3 | Summarized idea 3 | Summarized idea 3 | Summarized idea 3 |
| Summarized idea 4 | Summarized idea 4 | Summarized idea 4 | Summarized idea 4 |
| Summarized idea 5 | Summarized idea 5 | Summarized idea 5 | Summarized idea 5 |

on flip charts, it might be achieved by using a symbol, letter or colour system to categorize each entry on the list. However, to preserve full team engagement and begin to make sense of the new themes, the entire sorted list should be rewritten, with each entry appearing under its new theme. This will take some time but it is an important step. An alternative approach here is meta-planning (using Post-it notes for each idea, then conducting affinity sorting). In the course of doing this, it will be apparent that many ideas are similar or even the same. With group agreement, they should be combined to reduce the overall list as far as possible.

The result (Figure 6.5) is a series of new, reduced and themed lists that should be placed on the wall for all to see.

### Step five: compile multilayer themed ideas into strategic options

If this seems a little hard to grasp, hang in there. It is a complex process that really needs to be done for real to see how it works in practice.

Although we have been working with something called 'strategic options', this is just a place to put the ideas that fall into this category. We have not yet fully developed a definition of the formed options. Finalizing the definition of a strategic option requires us to consider what the option involves, what is excluded and exactly what we are going to do. If the strategic option idea is 'Outsource all spend to a single provider', this is great as a high-level statement, but we may want to combine it with other ideas that have emerged from the work so far. These might be ideas such as 'Redefine internal policy for committing spend in this area', or 'Reduce inventories and implement a call-off system'. It is at this stage that we combine compatible ideas under each theme to build up our strategic option.

**FIGURE 6.6**   Multilayer ideas into strategic options

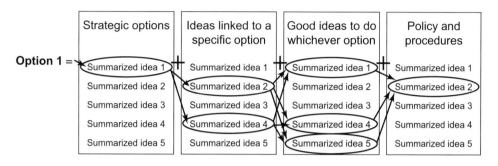

This part of the process is where creative thinking is required. Although some ideas will naturally be compatible with others, there will also be areas where ideas are opposites and cannot be combined. The aim of this step is therefore to work through each list, starting with the highest-level ideas (ie those we can term strategic options) and combine ideas that will fit together. Figure 6.6 represents how taking one or more idea from each list and combining them might happen.

The output from this should be no more than five strategic options that are sufficiently well defined and understood by the team so that the team can progress to step six, the final step. This evaluates the options generated. If you struggle to distil the thinking to this number, then there are probably too many variants of each option. The focus should be on identifying the high-level option itself with the potential variants within it as a subset. Typical strategic options might include:

- do nothing;
- outsource;
- in-source;
- switch supplier;
- go to the market;
- centralize;
- decentralize;
- aggregate spend;
- joint venture;
- acquisition;
- develop relationship.

You might notice some similarity with the value levers from Stage 1. This is because here we are effectively searching for the strategic value levers, or combination of different sources of value that will determine our future sourcing strategy and deliver the outcomes we need. Value levers are therefore an important input in shaping our strategy but also in helping clarify our definitions of the strategic options.

# Strategic option evaluation and selection

This step is a *Tool* and is *Optional*

Organizations can make decisions in a variety of ways. A group of executives might take a vote or even hold a secret ballot, the leader might impose a decision or a first idea might be routinely chosen. A decision might even be based on little more than a hunch. Such approaches to decision making do not fit with category management, which is structured around providing a robust basis for key sourcing decisions, made by a team with cross-functional representation and based on facts and data. The category management approach makes for a compelling recommendation that is difficult to ignore, and the process naturally provides an audit trail to show how the decision came to be made.

If the future sourcing recommendation is a breakthrough idea that involves hard changes, there is a risk that resistance by key stakeholders could prevent the idea going ahead. A facts-and-data approach is essential. The strategic option that is presented as the recommended way forward therefore needs to support this with a clear audit trail back through the process, showing how the analysis resulted in the recommendation. The options generation and the evaluation process provide this.

Following from the evaluation criteria identified as part of the options generation process, the actual evaluation activity simply uses the previously identified criteria and weightings to evaluate each option. Figure 6.7 shows an example of a completed matrix.

In the example the matrix evaluates four strategic options (outsource, centralize spend and supplier management, in-source and do nothing). The business requirements criteria and the implementation criteria have been set, each with provision for separate totals. Go/No-go evaluations together with weighting have been set to reflect the 'must haves' and the desired degree of importance of each area. The maximum possible score assumes a maximum score of 10 against any criterion for one or more of the options.

**FIGURE 6.7**   Options evaluation matrix

| Options evaluation | | | | | | |
|---|---|---|---|---|---|---|
| **Evaluation criteria** | *Weighting* | *Max Score* | *Option 1 – Outsource* | *Option 2 – Centralize* | *Option 3 – Insource* | *Option 4 – Do Nothing* |
| Meets business needs | G/NG | – | Go | Go | Go | No Go |
| Business want No 1 | 40% | 400 | 10(400) | 7(280) | 6(240) | – |
| Business want No 2 | 10% | 100 | 8(80) | 10(100) | 5(50) | – |
| Business want No 3 | 30% | 300 | 8(240) | 10(300) | 6(180) | – |
| Business want No 4 | 20% | 200 | 10(200) | 9(180) | 3(60) | – |
| **Business requirements TOTAL** | 100% | 1000 | 920 | 860 | 530 | |
| Ease of implementation | 20% | 200 | 5(100) | 4(80) | 10(200) | – |
| Low implementation risk | 30% | 300 | 10(300) | 8(240) | 3(90) | – |
| Scale of benefits | 50% | 500 | 10(500) | 3(150) | 4(200) | – |
| Low cost to implement | G/NG | – | Go | Go | Go | – |
| **Implementation TOTAL** | 100% | 1000 | 900 | 470 | 490 | |

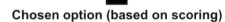

**Chosen option (based on scoring)**

Evaluation is simply a case of working down the evaluation criteria for each strategic option and allocating either a Go/No-go or a numerical score response.

This should always be done by the team, and full discussion and debate should be allowed about individual scores. It is useful to record some of the rationale and arguments along the way. There are some basic rules to ensure that this step is successful. They are:

1 Where a No-go is recorded, there is no point in conducting any further evaluation for that option. It should be ruled out (as option 4 is in Figure 6.7).

2 Make sure the team understands the scoring system; for ease, use a 1–10 scoring approach, with 1 being very low and 10 being very high.

**3** At least one option must score 10 or the weightings allocated will not work. More than one option can score 10 as long as there is always at least one 10 for each of the criteria. The best approach is to start by asking, 'Which option most meets this criterion?' Then allocate 10 to it and work back through the remaining options, scoring them in relation to this high benchmark. This is an important point in the process and removes the need to pre-agree guidelines for scoring at a particular level.

Add up the scores and see what you have. If the result doesn't feel right or if it is at odds with what you thought the outcome would be, go back and check the calculations. If all is well, then try to identify what has led to this result. Be careful not to work backwards and manipulate the results, but some small post-scoring changes are often required to ensure that each option is fairly ranked against the others. Once you have checked and finalized the scoring and if the result still seems at odds with what you thought the way forward should be, then maybe the result is the breakthrough you've been searching for and it should be taken seriously.

Figure 6.7 shows two options scoring highly against business require-ments, but only one of them scores highly against implementation criteria, thus ruling the other out. The result appears conclusive. Sometimes this type of result will emerge from the options generation and evaluation process and give a clear and robust recommendation of the way forward. At other times the conclusion is not so obvious, and further discussion, debate and engagement may be required with stakeholders to finalize the decision. In this case the evaluation output provides the basis for this discussion and new, more detailed criteria may need to be added and evaluated to arrive at a final decision.

# Building the chosen option

This step is an *Activity* and is *Essential*

This essential step follows from strategic options generation and evaluation. It should be done immediately after the evaluation is completed and while the team is still present. This step is about better defining the strategic option that has emerged as the way forward from the evaluation activity. By now, the team that conducted the evaluation will have a good, well-aligned understanding of what the option is, and what it does and doesn't include.

This would have been naturally gained in the course of discussions. However, outside this group there is likely to be little or no understanding of the chosen option, unless a team member chooses to impart the details. It is vital that the chosen strategic option and therefore the future sourcing strategy are defined in a series of statements under headings as follows:

- *Definition of strategic option.* A single paragraph describing the option, what is included and what is specifically excluded.
- *Features and benefits.* What this option features or what makes this option what it is, including any benefits that might be known at this stage.
- *Specific short-term activities.* A simple bulleted list of all the specific activities that need to take place within the next six months to support this way forward.
- *Long-term activities.* A simple bulleted list of anticipated longer-term activities together with a time frame.
- *Immediate next steps.* These might include any data gathering required to validate elements of the proposed option, or stakeholder engagement before formally circulating the proposal for comment and approval.

The level of detail required should be just enough to capture the essence of what this option is, to enable its communication to others not present in the workshop where the option was decided. Crucially it should be sufficient to answer the question 'what will we do differently tomorrow when compared to how we source this today?' If any areas are not yet clear or require further work, they should be noted and revisited later, to try to finalize every last piece of detail. Figure 6.8 shows two typical definitions of strategic options and the appropriate level of detail required, a template for strategy definition is also provided in the Appendix.

# FINALIZING THE SOURCING STRATEGY

In this next section we shall finalize and define our sourcing strategy, with a summary of all the work done to date, the resultant insights and a precise definition of what we recommend in terms of the sourcing approach moving forward. We will also begin to plan how our strategy can be implemented so as to present a fully formed and costed recommendation and summary

**FIGURE 6.8** Examples of strategic option definition

---

**Strategic option – *Consolidation in the UK***

**Definition of option**
*Consolidate UK flywheel supply to a single source for all except a small package of medium volume flywheels*

**Features and benefits of this option**
- *Target saving of $1.8m*
- *Achievable within six months*
- *Low risk if any of prime vendors is selected*

**Short-term activities**
*Drive supplier down through focused negotiation based on:*
- *Leverage against European/Far East pricing*
- *Consolidation of spend*
- *Tier 2 developments*
- *Efficiency improvement*

**Medium- to long-term activities** *(18 months)*
- *Evaluate longer term move of business to Far East*

**Immediate next steps**
- *Verify the prime suppliers that have adequate capacity*

---

**Strategic option – *Low-cost country sourcing***

**Definition of option**
*Move all supply of flywheels to a single source in china*

**Features and benefits of this option**
- *Target saving of $2.4m*
- *Achievable within 12 months*
- *Phased transition away from current vendors whilst managing risk*

**Short-term activities**
- *Initially move 3 medium volume parts from UK as a start up*
- *6 months later move 3 high volume parts from US*

**Medium- to long-term activities** *(12 months)*
- *Move entire flywheel business to China*
- *Negotiate improved arrangements with logistics provider*

**Immediate next steps**
- *Evaluate potential partners in China*
- *Find an expert in this area*

of projected benefits to our sponsor and stakeholders to approve. This the pivotal milestone within the entire category management process and is the basis to determine whether the project ends or will continue through to implement our strategy. We start by considering risk and contingency planning for our chosen strategy.

# Risk and contingency planning

This step is a *Tool* and is *Essential*

Now we have our strategy, what could possibly go wrong? Well, the bigger the change, the greater the scope for things to go wrong. If we have identified a breakthrough change that will deliver dramatic benefits, perhaps involving moving supply to new providers, or outsourcing something that was previously done in-house, or any other significant change, then there is scope for much to go wrong. New suppliers have to become familiar with the intricacies of the category they are supplying, the new logistics and how our organization works. The move of an in-house operation to an outside provider will result in all sorts of challenges. If a new supply arrangement fails or transition takes longer and there is no contingency, the activities of the whole organization could be placed at risk.

Many of the challenges associated with changing supply arrangements can be provided for through good project management and attention to detail. The eventualities all have to be identified, and that can be done only through a structured approach. Risk and contingency planning is such an approach. It is about considering and assessing all the things that could go wrong and identifying appropriate actions in response to each. If you have experience of project management or safety-critical industries, then it is likely you will be very familiar with this concept. There are many different techniques and approaches that can be used, all of which are valid. Here is one very simple approach for working up a risk and contingency matrix within a team (Figure 6.9 shows a completed example and a template is provided in the Appendix):

1 With the team assembled introduce the tool and concept, then brainstorm all the things that could go wrong, otherwise known as risks. Enter in the left-hand column. This is an important step and care should be taken to ensure all key risks are identified.

**FIGURE 6.9** Risk and contingency matrix

| Risk assessment and contingency planning | | | |
| --- | --- | --- | --- |
| **Risk** | **Likelihood of occurrence** | **Severity of impact** | **Action required** |
| Team become overloaded. | H | M | Renegotiate workload with managers. Push sponsor for more resources. |
| New supplier becomes insolvent. | L | H | Two credit checks. Investigate switching costs. |
| Demand increases beyond forecasts. | M | M | Check demand calculations and monitor trends. |
| Users reject the new product. | L | H | Carry out trials first. |
| Supplier fails to manage transition to plan. | M | M | Detailed project planning and ongoing management. |

2 For each identified risk, determine the likelihood of occurrence and severity of impact. A simple high/medium/low rating system should be used, with the group discussing and debating what rating to award. Likelihood of occurrence is best interpreted as the chance of the risk happening. It is hard to predict the future, but discussion within the group should enable a view to be formed.

3 Finally, for each risk, determine the action (or actions) required. Actions may be specific mitigations to prevent the risks from happening and included in overall implementation planning, or, if the risk is unpreventable, the actions would centre on putting contingency arrangements in place. The actions to address the risks should be prioritized, with high likelihood of occurrence and high severity of impact placed first.

# High-level implementation planning

This step is an *Activity* and is *Essential*

The next activity to finalize our recommended sourcing strategy in a source plan is to plan the strategy's implementation. Here we are aiming to develop a time-based plan for the sole purpose of better communicating what is involved in implementing the strategy. At this stage it is only possible to have a macro-level view of the individual activities that will take place. Developing a detailed plan is not possible, since much of the detail will not yet have been worked out. However, it should be possible to identify broad activities and timelines.

The most effective type of high-level plan is a simple Gantt chart. This type of chart was developed by a mechanical engineer named Henry Laurence Gantt in about 1917 and has become the standard for project planning. A Gantt chart (see Figure 6.10) provides a graphical overview and schedule of all activities, elements and dependencies of a project programme.

A Gantt chart is easy to develop and starts with activities down the side and a timeline along the top. For a sourcing strategy, a high-level timeline of more than 12–18 months is unlikely to be needed at this stage. Next, brainstorm all the activities that are required to turn the sourcing strategy into reality, and list them down the side. At this stage avoid getting into the detail; that will come later. Just list the headline activities. To help, consider the activity of *making a cup of tea*. You might be tempted to list activities as: get cup, put tea bag in cup, boil water, pour water in cup, let it brew, and so on. However, this is too detailed at this stage in the process. Instead, the headline activities might simply be: *make tea, drink tea, wash cup*.

Once all the activities have been identified, identify the time it will take to complete them by placing a bar on the chart against the timeline. Before some activities can begin, they may depend on others being finished (this is referred to as project dependencies), so the activities must be listed in sequence. Other activities may be able to happen irrespective of the state of others, as in Figure 6.10.

**FIGURE 6.10**  A simple Gantt chart

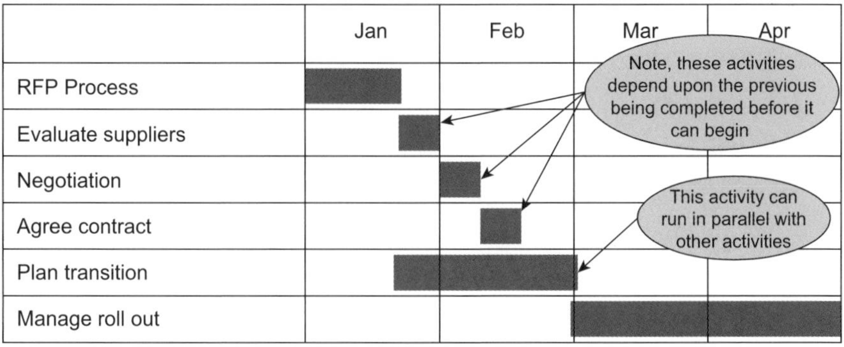

Remember that the aim is a simple plan to show our stakeholders that we have thought about what needs to happen and the timescales within which events will occur. More detailed planning will come later. Once agreed by the team, the completed high-level implementation plan should be incorporated into the strategic source plan.

# Cost–benefit analysis

This step is a *Tool* and is *Optional*

The final activity before documenting our recommended sourcing strategy in a source plan is to develop a cost–benefit analysis. The primary purpose here is to articulate a summary of all our work so far throughout category management into a recognizable format to support executive decision making regarding our proposed category sourcing strategy. You may be familiar with the use of a cost–benefit analysis as a means to evaluate multiple options; however, effective options generation and evaluation should have already accomplished this. Furthermore there is little new here, so instead we gather some specific outputs from previous work we have done. By now the category team will be very familiar with what the strategy will deliver and what is needed to realize it, but executives, key stakeholders or sponsors may not be able to readily pick out the pieces of information from the various category outputs. This step is therefore about succinctly summarizing these vital bits of information to help ensure our proposed strategy has the best chance of securing agreement. Figure 6.11 gives an example of a cost–benefit analysis a template is provided in the Appendix.

We develop a cost–benefit analysis by simply identifying all the costs and the benefits so we can make a comparison between the two. In its simplest form a cost–benefit analysis might comprise a value for each enabling us to calculate the net benefit and viability of a proposal. In practice however there are some challenges here:

- Costs and benefits might occur at different times throughout the implementation of a sourcing strategy, perhaps through the life of a new contract.

- We are unlikely to have firm figures as we have not yet implemented our strategy, so we may not know what the market might offer or what actually be involved.

- Many costs or benefits might not be hard numbers, but might be time involved, intangible benefits, etc.

We are therefore aiming to build a cost–benefit analysis to cover a period of time and to include all the factors that are relevant, building estimates that are as accurate as our current insight permits and quantifying as much as possible. It is entirely normal for a cost–benefit analysis to include a mix of hard numbers together with a list of the additional things that are less easily quantified. However the less things are quantified the harder it is to make any decision as the list of costs or benefits will be subjective and will require interpretation, increasing the risk of the proposed sourcing strategy being rejected. So a good cost–benefit analysis seeks to quantify as much as possible. For example the cost of time for persons to implement a new arrangement can be converted into a number if we can estimate how many hours they will need to spend and what their hourly cost to the business is (usually fully loaded to include an apportionment of overhead costs also). Similarly an efficiency gain benefit can be quantified in terms of the hours saved and the monetary value of these hours. There is a watch-out here as it is very easy to construct a cost–benefit analysis where all sorts of things are converted into a suite of hard numbers that paint a picture of a fantastic net gain. Most decision makers, especially those with a financial background, will immediately look at the assumptions and calculations behind the numbers. If these don't stack up, are unrealistic or unfounded then it will cast doubt over the entire strategy and may risk rejection. The cost–benefit analysis must not only be well quantified but also must be believable with the basis for the proposed benefit clear and credible.

The organization may have adopted a preferred style for cost–benefit analysis and so may expect a specific format, or conventions such as NPV (net present value) to be used; this should be checked. Furthermore, chances are there are people on hand who have vast experience of using tools such as these and building financial models where intangibles need to be quantified. These people may well be found in the finance function of an organization so calling on some help and support from others with experience here could make a big difference to getting this right.

We build a cost–benefit analysis by listing all the costs and benefits separately then quantifying them much as possible. A cost–benefit analysis might include:

*Costs*

- cost to implement new arrangements (direct costs, time, resource requirements);
- capital cost of new equipment needed;
- penalties or cost to exit current sourcing arrangements.

Costs are informed come from our data gathering and our analysis as part of *options evaluation*.

*Quantifiable benefits*

- direct price savings;
- rebates or one-off payments;
- reduction in administration;
- reduced inventory;
- reduction of transactions;
- increased efficiency or time saved.

Benefits are informed from our early *opportunity analysis,* the targets we have identified in our *STP* and *Team Charter* and refined following data gathering and use of *value levers* as well as our analysis as part of *options evaluation*. Notwithstanding my earlier comments on quantifying as much as possible, there will typically be additional benefits that a sourcing strategy will deliver that have great value to the business, are not easily quantified or where decisions would not be made on cost factors. These should be brought to the fore through a supporting commentary. These might include:

*Other benefits*

- improved assurance of supply;
- reduced risk;
- compliance with CSR policy;
- increased time to market;
- price certainty predictability;
- competitive advantage or differentiation.

Later, in Chapter 9, we will explore how we track category management benefits and here a fuller definition of potential benefits is provided.

**FIGURE 6.11** Example of a cost–benefit analysis

## Cost–Benefit Analysis

| | Cyrogeta | Toilet tissue paper | | Deta | Jan 15th |

Summary of category strategy — *Switch from multiple providers engaged locally to one single provider managed centrally on 3-year contract. Remove supplier-owned dispensers and switch to generic dispensers at all facilities in EU.*

| Costs | Immediate | Year 1 | Year 2 | Year 3 | Year 4 | Year 5 |
|---|---|---|---|---|---|---|
| *Penalties to exiting current contracts* | £75k | | | | | |
| *Removal of existing supplier's dispensers (over 1 year)* | £25k | £25k | | | | |
| *Capital costs for new dispensers – 1700 units* | £15k | £15k | | | | |
| *Installation of new dispensers (over 1 year)* | £35k | £35k | | | | |
| *Time to support implementation (assumes £30/hour)* | £12.5k | £7.2k | | | | |
| **Totals** | £162.5k | £82.5k | | | | |

**Total costs over term – £245k**

| Benefits | Immediate | Year 1 | Year 2 | Year 3 | Year 4 | Year 5 |
|---|---|---|---|---|---|---|
| *Contract signing rebate* | £250k | | | | | |
| *Annual savings (price reduction – estimated)* | | £338k | £338k | £338k | | |
| *Reduced transaction and inventory management costs* | | £20k | £20k | £20k | | |
| *Generic dispensers – (removal of supplier 'lock in')* | No lock in – ability to go to market at contract renewal | | | | | |
| *Future predictable pricing* | Contractual price mechanism controls price fluctuations | | | | | |
| **Totals** | £250k | £358k | £358k | £358k | | |

**Total benefits over term – £1.34m**

# Creating the strategic source plan

This step is a *Tool* and is *Essential*

Innovation is also about finalizing the source plan. This is the pivotal document and key output within category management. It is a detailed summary of the work to date, the key findings from the analysis, the recommended future sourcing strategy and how the recommendation was arrived at. Source plans can take many forms – paper-based documents created in Word or PowerPoint, or entries in an online electronic system designed for the purpose.

The source plan is an internal document. It must not go to suppliers – that might give away tactics and confidential intentions. The source plan may vary from a few pages to hundreds of pages, depending on the complexity of the category and the number of stakeholders involved. However, the purposes of a source plan remain the same; it aims to:

- get business and stakeholder sign-off and agreement to the recommended course of action;
- provide the facts and data necessary to make a compelling business case for the recommended course of action;
- provide a documented record of the journey through the category that can both act as an audit trail and support future work on this or other categories;
- provide a communications vehicle to key stakeholders.

This is the first time that the source plan appears in the category management process, and all preceding activities culminate in it. However, a good category management practitioner would not wait until now to begin work on it. Ideally, work on the source plan should start during the early stages of the project, with outputs from analysis being added along the way, leading to a finalized document at the end of the innovation stage. The document is then submitted for sign-off – with the potential risk that the entire project stops if this cannot be achieved.

The source plan seeks to answer three fundamental questions:

- What are the current situation and the proposed future sourcing strategy?
- Why was the proposed sourcing strategy selected?
- How will the strategy be executed?

In addition, the source plan needs to serve the following further purposes:

1 *A basis for agreement and go-ahead.* This is perhaps the most important use for the source plan. It gives decision makers and the executive sponsor the basis to give the go-ahead for change.

2 *Communication to stakeholders.* The document serves as a vehicle to communicate the strategy and future direction to key stakeholders. These might typically include decision makers or those who will be involved in or affected by what is implemented.

3 *A catalogue.* The source plan serves as a comprehensive record of all the work done and the decisions made in a way that can be accessed in the future.

4 *A check for process rigour.* The full record within the source plan is a demonstration that the category management process has been followed with appropriate rigour.

Figure 6.12 shows just some of the potential inputs to a source plan document. However, while all the tools and outputs would typically be incorporated, there is little point in simply presenting these in a sequence. Instead, the combined story told by these outputs needs to be extracted, summarized, optimized and further developed to create a compelling document and business case for change. It is usual for the full outputs of each activity gathered along the way to appear in a source plan, but typically within an appendix or separate supporting document, with the essence or insights gained appearing in the main body of the text.

As we have worked through each step in the process, I have concluded with a reminder of the need to ask, 'So what does this tell us?' to help extract the insights and to summarize these in the SWOT analysis. This is a great starting place to begin to marshal together all the threads of the story the source plan needs to tell.

A source plan must have a structure if all the work done is to make any sense. A suggested outline structure is given in Table 6.1. The key outputs and insights gained so far will help to inform each stage. There are natural points in the source plan structure where each output is relevant and so Table 6.1 also indicates the key tools, outputs and sources of insight and information that should be used to help inform each section.

# FIGURE 6.12   Source plan inputs

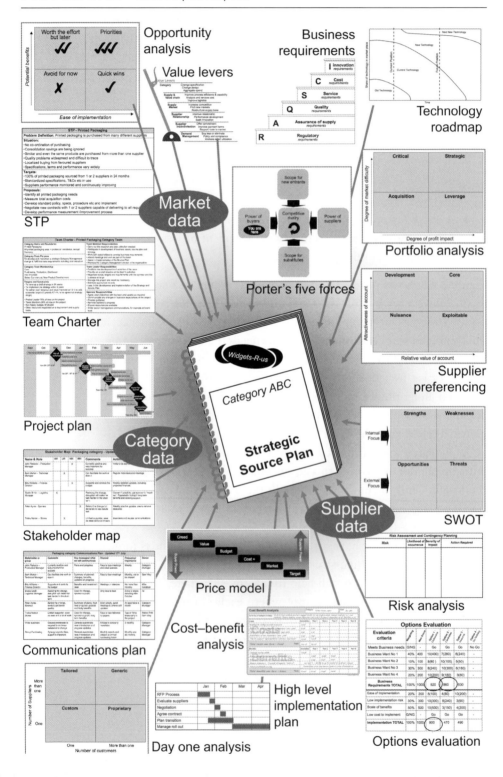

**TABLE 6.1** Typical source plan sections, content and sources

| Source plan heading | What this should contain | Sources and insights that inform this section |
|---|---|---|
| Executive summary | Once the rest of the document has been prepared, the executive summary should be the last thing to be written. Ideally it will summarize the entire document and the recommended sourcing strategy in just one or two well-crafted pages. | • Building chosen option<br>• Cost–benefit analysis<br>• Summary of other outputs as required |
| Background | Background to the category management project. Here the source plan should introduce the reader to the project including scope, team members, stakeholders, project timeline and a summary of the process followed. | • Opportunity analysis<br>• Team charter<br>• Project timeline<br>• Stakeholder map<br>• Communications plan |
| Current situation | This section is not only about describing what is happening currently but also areas that are suboptimal. The section must be based on fact, not opinion, and must also clearly show the problem or problems that the source plan is attempting to address. This section could include:<br><br>• internal/category – total volumes, spend, how it is used, who buys, how it is being bought and issues identified;<br>• suppliers – who they are, what they do, where they are, where they are headed, our spend with them, how they see us, what problems we have had historically, what alternatives exist and issues identified;<br>• market – the nature of the marketplace, market size, what alternative markets there are, what is happening in the market, eg is it expanding or contracting, are there new entrants or factors that will change the market dynamics in the future? | • STP<br>• Category data summary<br>• Supplier data summary<br>• Market data summary<br>• Technology road map<br>• Day one analysis<br>• Cost and price breakdown<br>• Supply value chain network analysis |

**TABLE 6.1** *continued*

| Source plan heading | What this should contain | Sources and insights that inform this section |
|---|---|---|
| Business requirements | Definition of the agreed business requirements in terms of needs and wants, and current and future requirements. Details of value levers that have been considered. | • Business requirements<br>• Value levers |
| Strategic analysis and insight | A section that builds on all the factors identified within the current position, as well as the business requirements, to provide analysis and insight into the position we are in and what needs to change to realize benefits and move forward. This section should draw on each of the insights gained from the strategic analysis tools (eg portfolio analysis, supplier preferencing, Porter's five forces and many others), but crucially must knit all the individual insights together to provide a single overall insight that forms the basis for identifying strategic sourcing options. | • Porter's five forces<br>• Analysis of pricing approaches<br>• Portfolio analysis<br>• Supplier preferencing<br>• SWOT |
| Options for change | The shortlist of strategic sourcing options that were identified in direct response to the strategic analysis and insight, together with the evaluation details and evaluation methodology used. | • Options generation<br>• Options evaluation |
| Recommended sourcing option | The recommendations in terms of the chosen strategic sourcing option and sufficient supporting detail to adequately describe what the recommendations are. | • Options evaluation<br>• Building chosen option<br>• High-level implementation planning |
| Risk and contingency planning | Summary of the risks identified with implementing this option, plus potential mitigating and contingency actions that need to be provided for. | • Risk and contingency planning |

**TABLE 6.1** *continued*

| Source plan heading | What this should contain | Sources and insights that inform this section |
| --- | --- | --- |
| High-level Implementation plan | A simple high-level plan that describes the headline activities and timing required to execute the recommended strategic sourcing option. This is also a good place to include quick wins. | • High-level implementation plan<br>• Quick wins |
| Cost–benefit analysis | The indicative cost and resource requirements to execute the strategic sourcing option and the resultant anticipated benefits and their timing. | • Cost–benefit analysis |
| Next steps | Immediate next steps and action required from the stakeholder or sponsors. | • High-level implementation plan |
| Appendices | All the supporting detail including data gathered and the outputs from each of the key tools worked through the process. It may be appropriate to make the appendix section a separate supporting document. It is important that the appendices are comprehensive, as this serves as the catalogue for future reference. | • All tools and outputs |

Source plans can vary in complexity according to their nature. If the new sourcing strategy is a complex change that will affect many people within the organization, the source plan will need to be a detailed and thorough document. It must tackle the complexities of the proposed change with great precision, and must be able to secure buy-in from the many stakeholders. If the source plan is in document format it will most likely be a weighty publication of many pages. However, if the proposed sourcing strategy is a simple change affecting only a few people, then the document (and indeed the way the category management process is used) need only be simple. I have even seen a one-page source plan, although this would normally be an extreme simplification. Figure 6.13 shows the suggested focus and typical length of source plans for different situations.

**FIGURE 6.13**   Source plan complexity

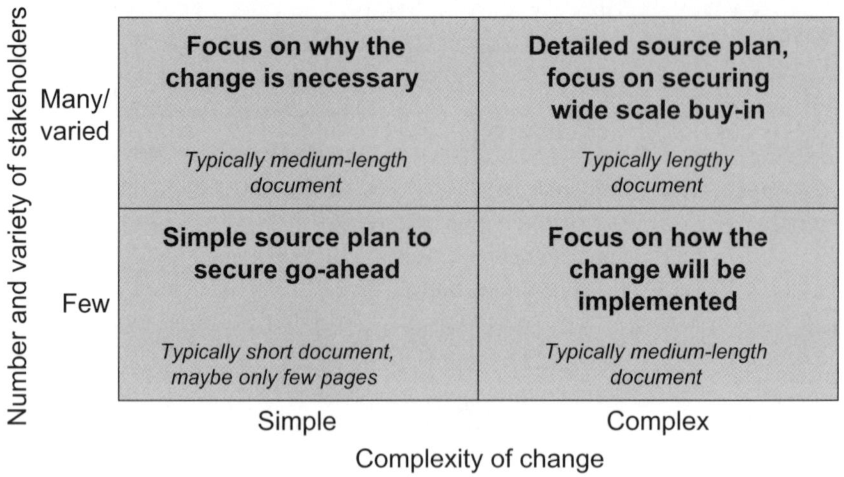

So far we've discussed the source plan primarily as a document. While this is currently its most common form, there is a growing use of online source plans as part of either a bespoke software platform or a wider purchasing e-enabling platform. The advantage of online systems is that the information is available to all who are given the authority to view it. This promotes knowledge sharing and helps to drive rigour into the process. These systems can range from simply posting an electronic version of the source plan document online, to a platform that allows the lead manager to complete each step of category management online, progressively uploading each tool and key outputs along the way, with a summary and recommendation to complete the plan. The format used is not important; it is the content and how it serves the purpose that matters. However, I have observed more often than not that where the organization is using an online solution the quality of the category management, deployment is suboptimal. This is because many of the online tools are built to provide real-time management information about category project status, requiring individuals to simply complete fields in order to achieve a good progress status within a management dashboard. The problem here is that it compromises process rigour and promotes a 'tick box' approach to category management that will fail to shoot for the big breakthroughs. We will return to this again later. Therefore any organization adopting an online solution to source plan creation should be clear that the tool is recording and reporting on the outputs from real team and business engagement with the required degree of rigour, not a desktop box-ticking exercise. The governance approach needs to provide for this and we will cover that in Chapter 9.

# Source plan sign-off

This step is an *Enabler* and is *Essential*

The end of Stage 3 is a pivotal point. It is now that the source plan and its recommendations are complete, and the business needs to decide whether or not the recommendations should be implemented. It is therefore entirely possible that the project could stop right here and simply die. Of course, this must be avoided, and this section aims to help ensure this.

By the time we reach this point in the process, there must be clear agreement as to who has the remit to sign off the source plan and its recommendations. If we do not have this clarity, then the project could stop because no one appears to have the authority or accountability, or those who do are unwilling to make such a decision. Here the work we did at the outset of the project begins to bear fruit. If we think back to the early part of Stage 1 when the team was established, we appointed an executive sponsor and identified the stakeholders. Our sign-off authority most likely lies within this group (depending on the nature and structure of the organization), and ideally the precise arrangements have been agreed and recorded in the team charter. The structure and decision-making nature of the organization usually shape how source plan sign-off takes place, but one of the following approaches is likely:

- the sponsor signs off the source plan by consulting with key stakeholders;
- the key stakeholders and sponsor sign off the source plan collectively;
- the sponsor takes the source plan and solicits sign-off from the relevant authority (or the executive team).

If the individual or individuals who are to sign off the recommendations are not bought in, or if the recommendations are a surprise and cause them to question the proposed strategy, then all the work thus far may have been a waste of time. This is especially true for breakthrough or radical changes.

Again, the work we do at the early stages of category management is crucially important.

Success here requires the team to have identified and engaged with all relevant stakeholders previously and to have executed an ongoing programme of communication. By the time the final source plan has been created, sign-off should be more a formality than a major event. Notwithstanding this, it is not uncommon for senior individuals who have been supportive and involved thus far suddenly to doubt and procrastinate when faced with actually putting their name to a radical way forward. Facts and data and the support from other key stakeholders will help, together with an understanding of the specific nature of any obstacles. If the recommended strategy is sufficiently compelling, it is hard for any individual to procrastinate for too long, and even if there are genuine issues they can almost certainly be provided for.

If for some reason the source plan is not approved, then find out why and work out what is required to address the problem, and resubmit the source plan.

When sign-off is accomplished, the team has the remit to proceed to Stage 4, the implementation of the category management process.

## Chapter 6 summary

Recap on the key points from this chapter:

1   The third stage within the category management process is *innovation* and is concerned with building our recommended sourcing strategy and securing approval from the business to implement it.

2   *Innovation* begins by summarizing all the insights gained across Stages 1 and 2, particularly focusing on the 'so whats?' we identified as we worked each tool.

3   Strategic options generation is the process of identifying a handful of potential future strategic sourcing options. We accomplish this by immersing the team in all the outputs from our work so far, then brainstorming potential ideas and options. Through a process of affinity sorting, theming and combining ideas we arrive at our shortlist of strategic options, each perhaps containing many more tactical ideas that emerged from the process.

4  Our list of strategic options is evaluated using a set of evaluation criteria we determine prior to identifying our options (to prevent bias). Our *business requirements* form the basis of our evaluation criteria together with some new criteria to judge how easily the strategy might be implemented. Options are evaluated using a scoring matrix.

5  Once we have selected our chosen option, we first validate that our evaluation has been robust, then we define what we mean by our option, listing a definition of what it involves together with features, benefits, short- and long-term activities and next steps.

6  We finalize our sourcing strategy by developing a risk and contingency plan for the identified option together with a high-level implementation plan and a cost–benefit analysis.

7  Our recommended sourcing strategy is then defined within a strategic source plan. This is a document that contains all of the outputs from our category management project so far, but structured so as to make clear recommendations supported by summary insights, plans and cost–benefit analysis.

8  The primary purpose of the source plan is a means to secure approval to proceed to implement our proposed sourcing strategy. However it also provides a means to communicate details of our project to stakeholders and secure business buy-in. It also forms a catalogue of our project that helps share knowledge and is a means to demonstrate process rigour.

9  The *innovation* stage ideally culminates in the approval of our source plan and if we achieve this then we can proceed to Stage 4.

# Stage 4: Implementation

This chapter explores the fourth stage, implementation. We will examine how we respond to the signed-off source plan from Stage 3 and begin to prepare for the execution of the chosen sourcing strategy. We will explore some of the implications of managing change within organizations as well as the steps involved in identifying a new supplier and agreeing the final arrangements with that supplier. Finally, we will examine what we need to provide in developing a contract with a supplier.

Pathway question addressed in this chapter:

**11** How can I effectively implement new sourcing strategies so they become a reality and we realize the benefits?

## The implementation toolkit

The elements within the implementation stage now become more activity and concept based instead of the tools and output-based format we saw in previous stages (see Figure 7.1). When combined, these activities and concepts are crucial to the overall success of the project. The last cross-functional workshop may take place in this stage, although others may be instigated if needed. The implementation planning workshop is where the team meets to plan the detail of the implementation. Alignment across the team is essential in terms of the required activities and the roles the team members will play.

There is a point in time when the project could be regarded as a success and where the majority of the benefits can be demonstrated. It is important to identify this point, as beyond it the project might appear to simply fade

**FIGURE 7.1** Stage 4: Implementation

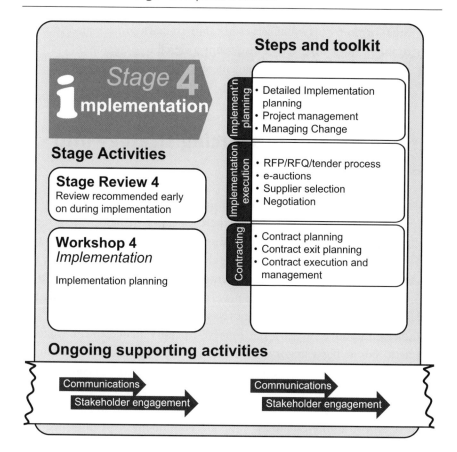

away and team members move on to other things, leaving purchasing to take the project into Stage 5. Until this key point there will have been much hard work by the team. For some, involvement in a category management project can be a career- and life-changing experience, as it may be the first time they experience for real the difficulties associated with implementing hard change. Therefore, at the point where success can be demonstrated, two key things should happen; it is the responsibility of the category management team leader, together with the sponsor, to make sure these happen:

- *Communication.* The project success should be communicated far and wide where appropriate, and with due sensitivity to what had to happen to secure the change. This should be with a great fanfare so that the organization can see the benefits of the investment in the category management project.

- *Celebration*. The category management team should celebrate success with a team meal, a night out or whatever is appropriate within the organization. This event serves not only to mark project success and to thank those involved; it also sends a signal to others that involvement in category management projects is recognized by the organization to be of value.

# Turning the future sourcing strategy into reality

Implementation is about turning the future sourcing strategy defined in the source plan into reality, and this is where category management projects frequently stall. Identifying a strategy is relatively easy when compared with the hard work of actually driving change within an organization. But it is not just internal change that presents the challenge. Transferring well-established supply arrangements to new suppliers or new geographies is full of difficult tasks with many inherent risks that need to be overcome.

Implementation is usually the longest category management stage to complete. For a big category, with lots of stakeholders and a complex change, the implementation time could be six months or longer. Together with the time taken to run through the initial three stages, this can make for a long project. There is the risk that stakeholders, the sponsor and the business will lose interest unless they are continually kept informed and benefits flow from the outset in the form of quick wins.

This is the point in the process when the focus, activities and therefore the skill set required by the category management team shift from purchasing to project and change management. Purchasing staff have traditionally not been well equipped with these skills, but they are essential for this stage.

Up to now the cross-functional team has been involved in gathering data, analysing the situation and determining the future sourcing strategy. From this point onwards they will be involved in driving in new arrangements, managing and overcoming resistance to change, and intensive communication with stakeholders and the business – all the activities associated with turning intent into reality.

Changes to the composition of the cross-functional team may now be needed. This stage of the process is an opportunity to remove or replace any team members as appropriate. It is also the time when new skills and energy can be introduced in the form of new team members. Changing the line-up of the team can be a difficult move, especially if the team has formed and bonded together. There is a strong argument to retain team members who are enthusiastic and want to be part of the project but lack experience of implementation, as this phase will give them valuable insight. However, the category management team leader must also balance the overall needs of the project.

## IMPLEMENTATION PLANNING

## Detailed implementation planning

This step is an *Activity* and is *Optional*

Following source plan approval, the first step is to plan the implementation in detail. Earlier we explored high-level implementation planning using minimal detail. In contrast, this essential step is concerned with a much more detailed approach. In fact, level of detail should be sufficient to enable the implementation of all aspects of the strategy to be managed and monitored effectively.

I'll start with a word on terminology. An architect would regard a plan as a drawing; here it is not. In this context the plan is a Gantt chart or other similar approach to define the overall sequence of activities arranged in a structured manner to outline what needs to be done and when; this might also be referred to as a programme.

We previously examined reasons why projects fail, the most common being resistance to change. In developing our detailed planning, it is not just failure we are concerned with but also things that can stop a project or hold back its progress or deliver suboptimal results. These might include:

- inadequate resources;
- lack of focus;
- settling for minor results;
- pulling back when people resist;
- loss of nerve;
- 'injelitus' (initiative jealousy: from those who don't own the initiative but become jealous of its success and want it to fail).

Detailed implementation planning needs to prevent the project from stopping or stalling. This is about both the development of a meaningful plan and its project management, and it includes active stakeholder engagement and good communications. The plan is the document that lies at the centre of project implementation and the management of the changes, but developing an effective plan is not as complicated as you might think.

There is little point in developing a complex plan and then simply handing it to others, expecting them to grasp the intricacies it contains. The reality is often that unless people spend several hours reviewing the plan line by line they will not grasp what it is telling them. Without time to study such a plan it is little more than wallpaper.

Using a tool such as Microsoft Project is great for project planning if we were building a bridge or an Olympic stadium. In fact, managing such a project would not be possible otherwise, as the scale of the project is so complex. Also, because the tools are electronic, generally only one person can work on them easily at any one time. But category management projects rarely need anything quite as sophisticated. An alternative, more collaborative approach to project planning is appropriate.

Imagine getting the category team together in a room for a couple of hours and doing a piece of work that enabled each team member to leave the room with a complete, aligned knowledge of the detail of the implementation required. Any plan developed on paper, either electronically or otherwise, would simply be a representation of what was in the heads of the team members. This would be powerful and would naturally lead to everyone pulling together to make implementation a success. Such an outcome is possible using a technique called 'brown-paper planning' (Figures 7.2 and 7.3).

As its name suggests, this technique involves brown paper, usually about three metres of the stuff laid out on a table around which the team can stand. Post-it notes are placed on the paper in order to develop a plan collaboratively. The process is as follows:

1 Divide the paper into 'swim lanes' horizontally across the paper. Use each lane to represent a different theme or strand of activity and label each one accordingly. Figure 7.2 gives a typical set of labels for four swim lanes that work well for any category management project.

2 Put a timeline across the bottom or top of the paper. For detailed planning there is little point in considering a time horizon beyond 12 months, or 18 months maximum, simply because things will change as the project progresses. If a longer time horizon is required, carry out detailed planning for the first 12–18 months and then high-level planning for the remainder.

**FIGURE 7.2**  Brown-paper planning

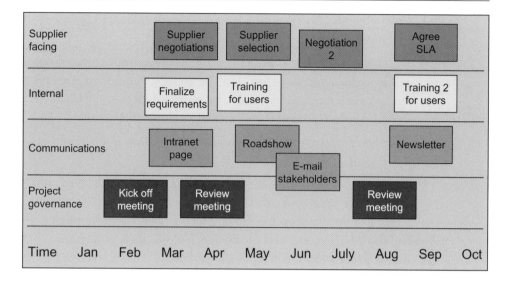

**FIGURE 7.3**  Brown-paper planning in action

**3** Decide on a colour scheme. Post-it notes come in a variety of colours, which means they are very flexible when used as a tool in brown-paper planning. You may decide to use certain colours to represent communication activities or review meetings.

**4** Working with the team, write the activities on individual Post-it notes and place them on the paper. Don't be afraid to move them, remove them, replace them, change them, cut them, adapt them or whatever is necessary to represent the combined thinking of the team.

**5** Once you are happy with the placement of the Post-it notes, you can, if you wish, draw lines to link one to another.

**6** Finally, and of the utmost importance, take a photo of the plan, and then tape all the Post-it notes onto the brown paper with clear tape. I have had the experience of leaving such a plan overnight only to find the next morning that the Post-its had lost their grip on the brown paper and were in a pile on the floor.

When a team works together on a plan, initial progress may seem slow, because the members will want to discuss and debate the plan as it develops. The debate may even get heated. However, the discussion process is critical to gaining not only an effective plan but also alignment and clarity regarding the way forward, even if there is some pain along the way. The outcome will probably be better, since potential issues will have been resolved early.

There are no hard and fast rules regarding how the brown paper is used. Figure 7.4 shows an example where the team was creative by using lots of different shapes cut from Post-it notes, and where time had been taken to make the final result neat and tidy with straight lines. The right approach is the one that works best for the team.

**FIGURE 7.4**    Example of a brown-paper plan

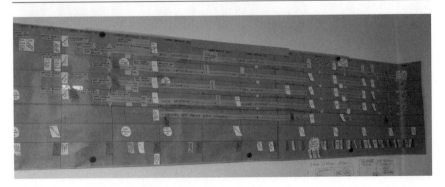

So far we have talked about placing activities on the brown paper where they happen. In effect this is a form of milestone planning, and it is a good technique for a small project. However, the duration of each activity is also relevant, and this might not be well represented visually by a single Post-it note. It is here that we turn again to the Gantt chart (see Figure 7.5). Once the team has populated the brown paper, there is merit in revisiting it and converting each Post-it into a time-bound activity. In Figure 7.4 this had taken place. It is rarely appropriate to do this for every Post-it note. Where the activities are simple or short, they can remain Post-it sized, but longer-running activities should be represented differently.

The completed brown-paper plan is complete, it can either be converted into an electronic format so that it can be e-mailed and used to manage the project, or it can remain in brown-paper format for the entire project. Some of the most successful projects have used live updates on the brown-paper plan to drive review exercises. In a global organization this may not be possible, but the principles of maintaining team alignment to and involvement in the planning process remain paramount. Furthermore, there is something about plans in electronic format that seems to stop people fully embracing the content.

There is scope to be creative if you want the plan to be the pivotal, living document it needs to be in order to make the project a success. The completed brown-paper plan could be redrawn using an electronic tool and, rather than it just being e-mailed, poster-sized copies could be printed and sent by good old-fashioned mail, with a note encouraging recipients to put it up on the wall. Furthermore, don't limit thinking to specialist project planning tools such as Microsoft Project; tools such as Microsoft PowerPoint or Excel or other similar applications can be just fine for the levels of complexity required in the average category management project. Standard desktop tools are usually sufficient, and their use will ensure that others can open the plan without requiring additional software.

If you want to be really creative and abandon technology altogether, then a project plan could be just a simple sketch, hand drawn, placed on the wall and used to manage the project. If you want to share it, use your phone to take a photo and then email it out. This approach opens up scope for artistic creativity to better represent visually what is happening throughout the project. I've witnessed a team use a dynamic brown-paper equivalent with team members gathering around the poster on the wall to physically move activities and add updates; the result was highly effective.

**FIGURE 7.5** Example of a Gantt chart for implementation

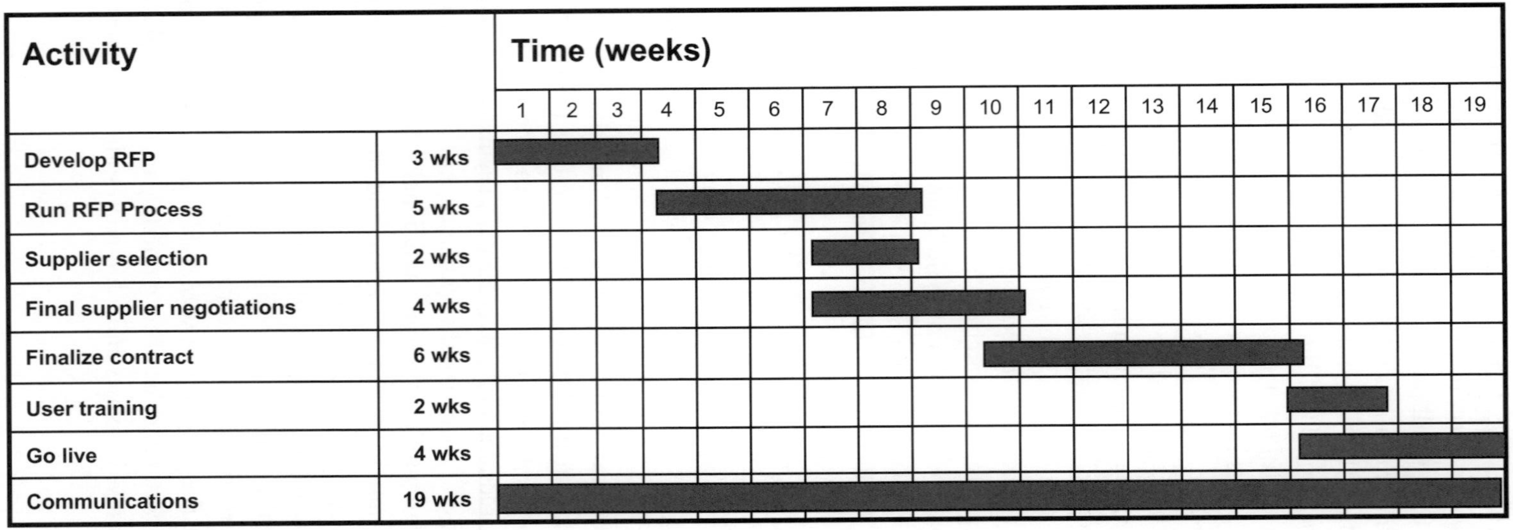

| Activity | | Time (weeks) | | | | | | | | | | | | | | | | | | |
|---|---|---|---|---|---|---|---|---|---|---|---|---|---|---|---|---|---|---|---|---|
| | | 1 | 2 | 3 | 4 | 5 | 6 | 7 | 8 | 9 | 10 | 11 | 12 | 13 | 14 | 15 | 16 | 17 | 18 | 19 |
| Develop RFP | 3 wks | ▓ | ▓ | ▓ | | | | | | | | | | | | | | | | | |
| Run RFP Process | 5 wks | | | | ▓ | ▓ | ▓ | ▓ | ▓ | | | | | | | | | | | | |
| Supplier selection | 2 wks | | | | | | | ▓ | ▓ | | | | | | | | | | | | |
| Final supplier negotiations | 4 wks | | | | | | | ▓ | ▓ | ▓ | ▓ | | | | | | | | | | |
| Finalize contract | 6 wks | | | | | | | | | | ▓ | ▓ | ▓ | ▓ | ▓ | ▓ | | | | | |
| User training | 2 wks | | | | | | | | | | | | | | | | ▓ | ▓ | | | |
| Go live | 4 wks | | | | | | | | | | | | | | | | ▓ | ▓ | ▓ | ▓ | |
| Communications | 19 wks | ▓ | ▓ | ▓ | ▓ | ▓ | ▓ | ▓ | ▓ | ▓ | ▓ | ▓ | ▓ | ▓ | ▓ | ▓ | ▓ | ▓ | ▓ | ▓ |

# Project management

This section cannot do justice to the power a well-planned and coordinated project can achieve, so further reading on this topic is recommended. Unless they have had previous experience, purchasing people are not usually natural project managers. However, in category management the ability to manage a project well is essential if brilliant sourcing strategies are to be turned into reality and the benefits realized. This gap can, of course, be filled with good project management training and support from people who have done it before.

Some of the key techniques used for project management fall under three main headings:

- *Planning.* We have already explored plans and these form a key element within project management. Always plan as if the project was brand new and you didn't know anything about it. Planning should start by assessing the scale of the change, then developing a top-level plan and breaking it down into milestones or points in time by when key activities need to be complete. Never overanalyse, and always plan the detail only to the next milestone. Familiar tools such as Gantt charts should be used, and they should be developed and updated collaboratively with active team contributions. Use both high-level plans to communicate details of the project to key stakeholders and detailed plans to guide the project.

- *People.* There are many people who need to be involved in a project or need to be informed of progress. Beyond the immediate team, others should be identified using 'stakeholder mapping', and should be engaged in an ongoing programme which maintains their support and enthusiasm, and which uses their contribution to develop project momentum. Ongoing and well-managed communications to all involved are essential. Those on the team contributing to the direct realization of the plan need to be managed to ensure no obstacles or delays get in the way and everyone has the support they need to deliver what is required of them. A good project manager can help drive this, supported by intervention from the project sponsor when needed.

- *Performance.* A key part of project management is to maintain project performance. The plan and progress should be regularly communicated to all involved. A regime which collects data on change progress and which monitors the delivery of benefits should be set up from the start. To maintain momentum and visibility of the project, success stories should be published far and wide. Managing expectations is also critical, and ongoing engagement with stakeholders is required to ensure promises are kept but within the agreed project scope.

# Managing change

This step is an *Enabler* and is *Essential*

There is no tool for this activity, no matrix, no mini process to be followed, and no template to be completed. Managing change is an enabler. It is about attending to things that need to be in place if the change is to be successful. It is about ensuring that the principles of good change management are well provided for within the implementation plan as it develops.

Throughout this book so far we have examined many tools and approaches that contribute to good change management. Stakeholder engagement and project communications help prepare the organization for what lies ahead, cross-functional teams help maximize participation, while the support of an executive sponsor helps champion the cause and helps create the felt need for the change itself.

Driving change is one of the foundations of category management, and it is essential to attend to the human reaction to change if implementation is to be successful. It is therefore necessary to understand and make provision for how people react to, and deal with, change along the way. It is here that we turn to the work of Elisabeth Kübler-Ross.

Kübler-Ross was a Swiss-born psychologist. She graduated from the University of Zurich medical school in 1957, moved to New York and began her career working with terminally ill patients. She was appalled at the treatment in hospital of patients who were dying. By giving lectures featuring terminally ill patients she forced medical students to confront those facing death. In 1969 she published the results of her studies in the groundbreaking book *On Death and Dying*, which has become the benchmark for counsellors and carers. Kübler-Ross (1969) identified the 'five stages of grief', which describe the sequential stages humans go through when faced with the prospect of their own death; in order, they are denial, anger,

**FIGURE 7.6**   Change curve adapted from Kübler-Ross

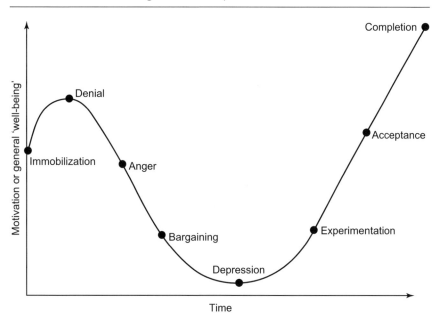

bargaining, depression and, finally, acceptance. Later, she proposed that those who have lost loved ones go through the same stages. In fact, the stages apply in any loss or threat of loss.

There is a very good reason why the stages of grief are here in a business book. Within organizations, changes represent potential or actual loss. This might be the loss of a job, the loss of a way of working that feels comfortable, the loss of a seat by the window, and so on. In different ways we experience a grieving process, even if the loss is not yet realized and is only the threat of a loss. Kübler-Ross's five stages are therefore entirely appropriate to understanding the human side of change within organizations. The stages reflect swings in the individual's overall well-being and, in the case of an organization, its motivation. The change cycle shown in Figure 7.6 is adapted from Kübler-Ross's work to give an interpretation more suited to organizational change. Here the stages are immobilization, denial, anger, bargaining, depression, experimentation, acceptance, completion.

Taking each of these in turn:

- *Immobilization.* This is the event that changes everything, the shock we receive or the news that we are facing a loss. This might be an announcement that the company is to be restructured and that jobs will be lost, or a whole area of the business is to be outsourced or relocated to another site.

- *Denial*. This is a conscious or unconscious refusal to accept facts, information or the reality relating to a situation. It is a natural human defence mechanism designed to protect us from the shock of a traumatic event. Many animals don't have such sophisticated defence mechanisms, and often a severe shock may kill an animal. As humans we have developed the ability to delay dealing with the immobilizing event through denial, and our overall feeling of well-being actually increases for a short period of time immediately following the event. This may be a conscious act of putting off dealing with the situation, or an unconscious response triggered by release of endorphins within our bodies that give a temporary boost to our feeling of well-being. Denial can last minutes, hours or even days, and during this time we simply do not accept or believe that the immobilizing event is real. We may even laugh about it and exhibit some unusual behaviour that others around us might find inappropriate to the situation.

- *Anger*. Denial doesn't last long and soon the individual is overwhelmed by feelings of frustration that turn into anger. This is directed in many directions: anger at the cause of the immobilizing event, anger at oneself, or anger at colleagues for no apparent reason. It may be manifested by out-of-character emotional outbursts; people will often not understand why they are behaving in this way but will feel unable to stop it. When observing someone going through change, anger is the most obvious stage to identify and it helps prepare us to provide the right support for what follows.

- *Bargaining*. In Kübler-Ross's original work, bargaining was identified as the stage where the individual attempts to broker a deal to get out of the inevitable. This might be 'making a bargain with God' in the case of a terminally ill patient or, in the case of a relationship breakdown, asking, 'Can we still be friends?' Within organizational change, bargaining is just as evident, and when the reality of the change hits, people will attempt to exert any power they might have to secure a more favourable outcome. This might be requests such as, 'If I go along with the move to the new office, can I sit by a window?' or, 'If you need to make redundancies, can I get a good package to go?' Bargaining rarely provides a sustainable solution, and it gives way to a growing feeling that the change is inevitable.

- *Depression.* In an organizational context this is not depression as in the clinical definition of a psychiatric disorder characterized by a pervasive low mood, loss of interest in the person's usual activities and diminished ability to experience pleasure. In our context it is a stage that people go through and is often referred to as a dress rehearsal for what comes next. It is natural for there to be a confused mix of emotions including sadness, regret, fear and uncertainty. Depression is a sort of acceptance of the change but with an emotional attachment.

- *Experimentation.* In organizational change it is relevant to include a stage between depression and acceptance where individuals tend to experiment with ways to come to terms with the change. An example might be, 'If I have to move to work in another part of the building and lose my seat by the window, at least I'll be nearer to the canteen.' Experimentation is the beginning of acceptance.

- *Acceptance.* Here the individual has finally accepted the change and has managed to achieve a degree of objectivity without emotional attachment to the new position.

- *Completion.* Following acceptance, overall well-being continues to develop as any residual emotional detachment finally subsides. When people reach this state in organizations they will be talking of the 'new place' being much better than the 'old place'. The final dynamic is that, on reaching completion, the overall motivation and well-being are at a higher level than at the start. This is because the individual is stronger as a result of the pain and experience of going through the curve.

Knowing what people are going through when they are involved in organizational change helps with making robust provision for change management. Spotting where people are on the curve is usually obvious; providing the right response takes rather more thought. Figure 7.7 illustrates the typical responses required to support people throughout the curve.

With any organizational change there will be pain; even in the most resilient of organizations where change is the norm, there will still be pain somewhere for someone. An awareness of how humans respond to change helps us understand and react to those going through this. However good change management is in practice, it is also about a series of proactive measures aimed at smoothing out and accelerating the change as well as the duration. In essence, good change management is about preventing the pain as much

**FIGURE 7.7** Responses through the change cycle

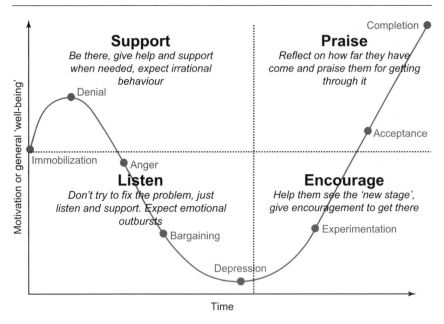

as possible, which in turn will enable wider change and organizational objectives to be achieved faster and with less resistance.

There are some crucial elements that must be in place to support the management of change. These are:

- *Strong executive support*. Clear executive support visible to the organization and those affected by the change. This is where the sponsor's role comes into its own, and the sponsor needs to either provide this support directly or secure it from peers. At this stage the support is much more than participating in cross-functional workshops and motivating the team. Instead, executive support and backing should be an integral part of all change communications, and support should be actively secured from peers and colleagues across the organization, from the boardroom down.

- *Involvement and participation*. Not everyone can take part, but through good communication and stakeholder engagement it is possible to involve a representative cross-section and make others feel involved or at least consulted.

- *Providing the necessary resources*. Implementation without resource is difficult. If the organization fails to resource implementation adequately, it will simply fail. Within the process of planning, the category team needs to identify the resources required and use the sponsor to help secure them. In busy organizations, simply loading up busy people with yet another action to support implementation is unlikely to help. Instead, people need to be freed of other commitments so that they can provide the necessary implementation support.

- *Creating a felt need*. This is achieved by helping the people affected to see the vision and why it is important. There is no single event or activity that will achieve this, but rather the combination of all the project activities, communication messages and stakeholder engagement should have the ongoing aim of creating a felt need for the change. If there is a felt need, people are much more likely to buy into the change than resist it.

## IMPLEMENTATION EXECUTION

# Running an RFP, RFQ or tender process

This step is a collection of *Tools* and is *Optional*

Implementing a new sourcing strategy may well involve getting a supplier (or suppliers) to start supplying goods or services. This might involve bringing on line new suppliers or developing existing suppliers. Here we need to find the best supplier with the most appropriate products or solutions and the most competitive pricing who can meet all the business requirements we have previously defined, and who will provide precisely what we need, not what they want us to buy.

RFPs and RFQs (defined below) form part of the tendering process and are where the buyer solicits specific information from the seller or a number of sellers in order to identify the best solution and/or provider. An RFP, RFQ or tender is either a document (either hard copy or more usually electronic) or an internet-based exchange using one of the many platforms available. Contained within is a series of questions to the supplier or requests for specific information relating to the buyer's requirements and the supplier's capabilities and ideas, or a quotation for supply of a defined service or product.

Irrespective of terminology this step is about tendering and its role within the category management process is important. There are many businesses that wouldn't claim to use any tendering processes, or small businesses that select and appoint a supplier as a result of an established relationship or recommendation – the supplier is invited in, there is a discussion regarding what is needed and the price, and an agreement is made. This is in fact a form of tendering but it is informal and relationship based. Examples of this type of tendering can still be found within large companies, often at senior level when executives bring in a consultancy or specialist they have previously worked with or in countries where the culture of commercial dealings is relationship based. However, for the rest of us, such an informal approach lacks the expected structure and necessary transparency that organizations require. This is for good reason, not just to protect the individual, but also to maximize the chance of the best outcome for the organization.

High levels of formality and strict arrangements to assure no opportunity for foul play are sometimes required within a tendering process. Historically, construction companies bidding for work in the public sector would be required to supply their tenders in a sealed envelope to arrive at a specified location by a given date and time. All the tender responses would then be taken to a small, often smoke-filled, room and opened together in the presence of an independent body. This ensured that there was no scope for a tender submission to be opened early and information about the bid to be passed to any of the competing bidders, who could then change their bid in a last-minute submission.

Where the selection of the winning supplier bid is based only on price, such arrangements are necessary. However, good tendering is about examining all aspects of how the supplier could potentially meet the requirements and provide the overall best-value solution. Price is a consequence of this and just one component in the overall solution. For this reason, tender processes typically have less formality these days. Within certain sectors there are specific obligations on buyers. For example, as we saw in Chapter 2, public sector procurement around the world is often bounded by comprehensive rules, set processes and requirements for any tendering activity. In Europe in the public sector (and some regulated private sector businesses) the buying organization must follow strict rules regarding tendering as provided for by European Union legislation. According to this, all contracts that are valued above a certain threshold must be advertised so any potential supplier who can meet the basic pre-qualification evaluation criteria can submit a tender.

In the commercial sector the rules around tendering are typically less prescribed, defined according to company policy, good practice and, more often than not, the imperative to act ethically. It is therefore incumbent on the buyer to operate a tender process where the basis for selecting and appointing a supplier is transparent, especially if the buyer's actions could be later audited if required. For this reason we select an appoint suppliers using a formal a tender process as follows:

1 *Definition of requirements.* To provide proposals or pricing, the supplier needs to know what we want. This is the stage within the process where we formally define our needs. However, this definition may not be fully formed but should flow from the requirements identified within the business requirements.

2 *Solicitation.* The suppliers are asked to provide their responses to the questions or requests for specific information relating to the stated requirements. This is the suppliers' chance to impress and they will often spend a lot of time perfecting the responses.

3 *Analyse responses.* The suppliers' responses are reviewed and analysed. The design of tendering process will determine how easy it is to make comparisons between one response and another.

4 *Select supplier/choose solution.* From the analysis of responses the supplier or suppliers who offer the best solution can be selected. How selection works and the criteria used here are important and should be informed by the business requirements. This stage may have a number of steps before the chosen supplier or suppliers are determined.

Across the different tools and approaches associated with tendering, a range of terminologies can be found which seem to change according to the organizations or industry sector we are in. Even the word *tender* is not universally recognized and, for example, is less common in the United States. It is therefore important to be clear what we are talking about here, so here are the most common terms with an explanation of each.

- *RFI (request for information).* The RFI helps early on in the category management process as part of the data-gathering activity, and we briefly mentioned this earlier. The RFI is a solicitation tool that is sent to multiple suppliers and potential suppliers to gather general information such as capability, products, geographical coverage, company set-up and so on (Figure 7.8). The RFI is not part of this

**FIGURE 7.8**   Differences between RFI, RFP and RFQ

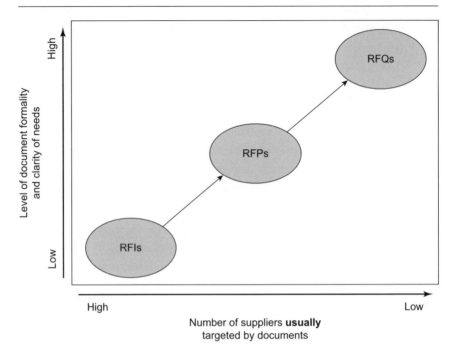

Number of suppliers **usually**
targeted by documents

tender activity but I have included it here for the sake of
completeness within this section.

- *RFP (request for proposal).* A solicitation tool issued by a buyer to
  a supplier, the RFP is designed to ask a small number of suppliers
  to make specific proposals regarding how they would meet some
  stipulated requirements. The sourcing strategy might describe at a
  high level what we are going to do but may not have sufficient
  detail to describe precisely what we want. For example, if we
  were attempting to find a supplier to develop and manage a large
  corporate website, we might be clear about what we want to achieve
  but chances are we will not have developed the detail regarding
  how the site will be built and maintained. Here we need some ideas
  and expertise. Those who know all about doing this work, ie our
  suppliers and potential suppliers, are the best source of ideas. The
  RFP is a way both to qualify the supplier and to gain valuable ideas
  regarding how our overall needs might be met. Therefore any good
  RFP should always include the option for a supplier to make an
  alternative proposal in case they see a better way to fulfil our

requirements. However, a word of caution is needed here: some buyers use the RFP process to gather together all the best ideas from different suppliers and then combine them into a new statement of requirements that is sent out as an RFQ. While this is a valid tactic, suppliers will soon resent having spent lots of time giving us all their best ideas only for them to be passed on for a competitor's use. If there were plans to engage any of these suppliers for future work, they might not be as forthcoming next time. Furthermore, if there is a non-disclosure agreement in place between buyer and seller that affords the seller some protection, then this tactic could breach the agreement. Be very careful about the use of this tactic. An RFP therefore:

- invites a supplier to bid for business;
- seeks a solution to a problem or need;
- conveys key business requirements;
- is focused on the supplier's experience, qualification and proposals.

- *RFQ (request for quotation).* The RFQ is a solicitation tool issued by the buyer to a small number of suppliers and designed to ask for specific commercial or pricing proposals. An RFQ might typically follow an RFP to further refine the definition of what is required and to invite a smaller number of suppliers to respond again. However, this time the suppliers are asked to provide a quotation against a firm specification. Sometimes the RFQ is combined with the RFP as a subsection on pricing. In summary RFQs:

  - request pricing and availability for specific goods or services;
  - have a very clear specification and definition of needs;
  - are highly competitive in approach.

- *RFx (request for x)* This is a generic term used to describe any or all of the 'request for' approaches.

- *e-RFI, e-RFP, e-RFQ, e-RFx.* These are electronic-based solicitation and assessment tools that support, expedite and optimize the benefits that can be obtained and can provide automated analysis of responses. Electronic can mean a simple e-mailed document but more typically today refers to the use of one of the many internet-based platforms. Here the e-RFx is set up on the secure platform and suppliers are invited via e-mail to participate. Providing a response requires the invited suppliers to log on and provide responses online to a series of questions. The advantage of e-RFx platforms is, if used effectively, questions can be configured to maximize the use of value-based or yes/no responses, allowing rapid and automated analysis and direct comparisons between respondents.

- *Invitation to tender (ITT)*. An alternative, and more traditional, name for the RFQ.

- *Competitive process*. Another name for the RFQ.

- *Bid process*. Another name for the RFQ.

- *Pre-qualification questionnaire*. A form of RFI typically used in public sector procurement to pre-qualify suppliers prior to running an ITT.

The most common terminology used today for tendering is RFP and RFQ. The design of questions in the RFP, and to a lesser degree in the RFQ, is important in order to solicit precise responses that allow easy comparisons between them. Also, if quality responses are required, the RFP or RFQ should be kept as short as possible.

From the supplier's perspective, if the RFP/RFQ is so long and complex that it takes a team of people to answer all the questions and provide the necessary supporting information, there is a risk that the quality of the response is compromised and the essence of how the supplier can actually help gets diluted within the need to answer all the questions. Even worse, the supplier may even decline to participate so they can redirect their efforts towards other opportunities. Therefore, when designing an RFP/RFQ it is good practice to challenge the purpose and relevance of our questions. For each one, ask, 'Why am I asking this; what will it tell me?' Another useful approach is to start off by asking yourself, 'If I could only ask 10 questions, what would they be?' In addition to keeping RFPs and RFQs simple, they should be structured so that the suppliers know what is expected of them. Consequently there are some key elements that must be included. Table 7.1 lists the sections that an RFP or RFQ might typically contain. It also illustrates some of the differences for both combined and separate documents.

Traditionally, RFPs and RFQs have been based around paper processes but it is e-RFPs and e-RFQs that are most commonly used today.

The focus of the RFP/RFQ, and therefore the type of questions asked, should be adapted according to our requirements and the nature of the category. For example, if we are running a tender process to select a provider of catering services, then the RFP would need to focus on the service, how the

**TABLE 7.1**  Sections that an RFP or RFQ might contain

| Section | Details | RFP | RFQ |
|---|---|---|---|
| **Introduction and background** | Introduction to the business, the RFP/RFQ, the purpose of the RFP/RFQ and how the business got to this stage. | Yes | Yes* |
| **Scope and boundaries** | The scope and boundaries of the category or area in question including geographical boundaries. | Yes | Yes* |
| **Points of contact** | The address for responses to be sent to and points of contact for any questions that can be raised during the tendering process. Note that if a point of contact is given in an RFP/RFQ then arrangements should be made to ensure this individual is available when the process is running. | Yes | Yes |
| **Confidentiality** | A confidentiality statement that obliges the supplier to keep details of the RFP and its dealings with you secret (unless provided for separately). This may also be a two way statement assuring the supplier of confidentiality also. | Yes | Yes |
| **Commitment** | A statement that makes it clear that by submitting the RFP/RFQ there is no obligation to use the supplier or further commitment. | Yes | Yes |
| **Tendering/ RFP/RFQ process** | Details of the tendering process and instructions for respondents and required format. This should include: <br>• timescales and deadline for responses; <br>• how to submit responses; <br>• how to ask questions or seek clarification <br>• how selection will work including the evaluation criteria that will be applied. | Yes | Yes* |
| **Requirements** | A definition of requirements and any assumptions made (these can usually be taken straight from the business requirements). Perhaps a vision of the future and how this area of spend could develop. | Yes | Yes* |

**TABLE 7.1**   *continued*

| Section | Details | RFP | RFQ |
|---|---|---|---|
| **Anticipated volumes/size of contract** | The supplier will need to gauge the anticipated volumes or size of contract. This could involve presenting current volumes with a projection to the future or outlining the scale of service provision required. Remember at this stage that there is no commitment to provide the supplier with exact volumes, but artificially over stating here could introduce difficulties later at the contracting stage. | Yes | Yes |
| **Main questions** | A series of specific questions and requests for information or proposals. | Yes | Maybe |
| **Alternative proposal** | Opportunity for the supplier to make an additional alternative proposal. | Maybe | Maybe |
| **Pricing** | Request to provide pricing or fees. To allow effective comparisons between providers and to get behind the price. Proposals allowing the supplier to provide 'all inclusive pricing' should be avoided. Instead suppliers should be requested to quote against a pre-defined breakdown of the cost elements, or if this is not possible to provide a breakdown of their all-inclusive pricing. | No | Yes |
| **Terms and conditions** | The terms and conditions that will apply (and the supplier's response to either accept these or state areas where further discussion is needed). | Yes | Yes |
| **Appendices and attachments** | Appendices, attachments and further information | If required | If required |

* Would be required in an RFQ unless this had previously been covered within a separate RFP, in which case the RFP can be referenced.

**FIGURE 7.9**    Aligning RFPs and RFQs with day one analysis

| | | **Tailored** | **Generic** |
|---|---|---|---|
| **Number of suppliers** | **More than one** | **Typical pricing**: Cost-plus<br>**Focus**: The service<br>**Qualify**: The supplier's process<br><br>**Value**: RFI ✓ RFP ✓ RFQ ✓ | **Typical pricing**: Market<br>**Focus**: The price<br>**Qualify**: The products<br><br>**Value**: RFI ✓ RFP ✗ RFQ ✓ |
| | | **Custom** | **Proprietary** |
| | **One** | **Typical pricing**: Target<br>**Focus**: Innovation<br>**Qualify**: The supplier's capability<br><br>**Value**: RFI ✓ RFP ✓ RFQ ✓ | **Typical pricing**: Value<br>**Focus**: Your vulnerability<br>**Qualify**: The specification<br><br>**Value**: RFI ✓ RFP ✗ RFQ ✗ |
| | | One | More than one |

**Number of customers**

supplier can meet our particular needs, and on any ideas the supplier might have to make the service appeal to users. The RFQ would solicit specific price detail once the details of the service have been finalized. However, if we are buying OEM spare parts and we have no choice but to buy them and we can use only one supplier, then running an RFP or RFQ that is asking for creative input and best pricing is unlikely to have any benefit. Instead we should focus on the degree of vulnerability and, if there is opportunity to redefine the specification, aim to open up alternatives. An RFI may also be useful in this case, as there may be suppliers who provide alternative generic equivalents that meet the same specification. To determine the focus we use day one analysis; Figure 7.9 shows how this changes in each quadrant, and what our RFP/RFQ should seek to qualify. Day one analysis also helps determine when these solicitation tools are worthwhile: for example, there is little point running an RFP/RFQ if our category is in the proprietary quadrant.

The nature, appropriateness and design of RFP/RFQ shift in public sector procurement where rules govern certain aspects of how a buyer can approach the market. For example in the commercial sector using an RFP to solicit ideas and creative input from suppliers is normal practice. However in public sector procurement this is less straightforward. In the EU, procurement bodies must uphold the fundamental principle of *equal treatment*, which demands carefully managed approaches to soliciting input from multiple suppliers. The subsequent tender process is required to follow one of a small number of set contracting approaches where the total aggregated spend with the supplier will be above a set threshold. Public sector procurement doesn't typically limit what can be done at the tendering stage, but it does demand it is done differently so as to satisfy the specific underlying principles set by the prevailing legislation. Most often, success within public sector tendering demands that buyers direct more effort upfront so as to define a clear and certain set of business requirements. This means that at the point when the market is approached, it is to solicit bids against a precise and fully formed requirement, not only for the goods or service, but extending to how the contract and relationship will operate over the term.

The final stage of the tendering process is to select a supplier (or suppliers). Within category management this is shown later within the overall process (and later in this chapter). Traditional tender exercises often selected a supplier based upon predefined criteria, eg lowest price, and then the contract would be awarded. However, today in the commercial sector it is more common for there to be further negotiations, either face-to-face, by e-mail, by phone or via an e-auction before selecting a supplier (this is less so, and more difficult, in public sector procurement).

# Using e-auctions to support a category strategy

This step is a *Tool* and is *Optional*

Auction rooms and eBay are familiar environments where we bid to buy things, and where the price normally starts at a given point and increases depending on the number of bidders, the desirability of the item and so on. In the world of purchasing, an e-auction is exactly the same, except it works in reverse. Initiated by the buyer, an e-auction is an internet-based event where invited suppliers can make bids for the price they are prepared to offer for a defined product or service, or a defined group of products and services (termed a *lot*). It happens in real time over a limited period and the buyer can often watch the action progress live online and see the bids from all the suppliers, but without being able to identify who they are. During the event, suppliers attempt to outbid each other by making bids and counter-bids, each bid lowering the price, so that at the end of the e-auction they are making their best offers. Price decreases during an e-auction, the reverse of

**FIGURE 7.10** Onscreen view of an e-auction

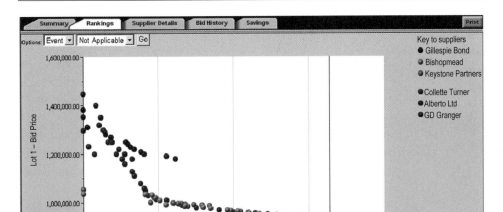

eBay and similar auctions, and for this reason e-auctions are often referred to as reverse auctions or electronic reverse auctions (e-RAs).

Figure 7.10 shows a screen shot of the last stages of a typical e-auction. The auction in question started with six suppliers (in this fictitious case, all identified) and involved multiple bids along the way.

There is no shortage of e-auction providers across the global world of purchasing. Many now offer added-value solutions combining e-auction tools with other purchasing e-tools and even involve consultancy support. Solutions vary from a simple online portal where we can purchase a licence for unlimited use, to fully managed pay-per-event auctions.

The warnings earlier in this book about bundling and of suppliers seeking to provide 'added-value' components in order to maximize price and differentiate the offering are relevant here. An e-auction is simply a tool, just one of many called on by a purchasing function. Many organizations make the mistake of treating e-auction platforms as if they were some magic dust they can buy and sprinkle over the department or category to create instant and lasting results. It is a powerful tool but the power is only realized if e-auctions are integrated into the overall purchasing process. Organizations often buy e-auction platforms or licences and then set them up as an island, with separate external support, isolated from any strategic purchasing processes that might be in place. This just serves to create multiple approaches, which cause confusion and detract from the overall aims of the function. The other watch-out here is around user friendliness.

Within category management, e-auction is an optional tool. It is used where and when appropriate and is typically deployed as part of Stage 4, implementation. With this in mind, use of a suitable e-auction platform must be secured with consideration as to how many auctions will need to be run per year, the initial training required (which, with a good platform, should be minimal) and the commercial arrangements, eg a licence for unlimited use, which is usually the preferred route, or a pay-per-event arrangement. Crucially, signing up to an e-auction provider does not need to be an expensive investment. Work out the business requirement and shop around before committing. E-auction technology is not rocket science and it does not need to be overly complicated; in fact, the simpler it is, the more likely people are to use it.

Once access to a suitable platform is in place, e-auctions can be very successful if conducted properly, on the right categories and with adequate participant training. There are many more variants of e-auction and here are some of the most common ones:

- *Standard reverse auction.* Based upon a single 'lot', the auction happens over a predetermined time-frame and suppliers bid for what they will supply the lot for. The auction either has a hard stop at the end or extends if bidding is ongoing.

- *Cherry-picked auction.* An auction with multiple 'lots'; suppliers can pick and bid against only the lots in which they are interested.

- *Bundled auction.* Here all the requirements are bundled together in one single auction and the suppliers bid for the entire bundle.

- *Dutch auction.* The auction closes upon receipt of the first bid.

- *Cherry Dutch auction.* A multiple-lot auction and each lot closes upon receipt of the first bid for that lot.

- *Japanese auction.* The auction starts at a predefined price point that is reduced in predefined steps. Each supplier must accept each price step or they are out of the auction.

There are many more; in fact, one e-auction provider boasts that over 55 different auction types are available on its platform, enough to cover every eventuality!

In the early days of e-auctions, suppliers made serious mistakes in their bidding. Despite setting a floor bid below which they were not prepared to go, in the heat of the auction and when faced with a lower competitor's bid together with the associated threat of losing the account, they frequently ended up cutting into their profit margins and made very low bids just to win or retain the business. Other suppliers did similar things, and pricing therefore tumbled in e-auctions, often to unsustainable levels. This has now changed and generally suppliers are much more adept at participating in e-auctions. However, there is still the tension of the event that pushes suppliers to make their most competitive offers, thus disarming their tactics to maximize profits. The other key dynamic here that helps the buyer is the way e-auctions work. An e-auction is simply another form of negotiation, except here it is not face-to-face, nor does it require any personal interaction during the event itself. Buyers therefore do not need exceptional negotiation skills in order to hold their position against an experienced and well-trained supplier team. Instead the e-auction and good planning do the hard work here.

If well executed, the e-auction will push price to the lowest level the market will stand. Furthermore, e-auctions shorten the time to decision and enable suppliers to bid regardless of location. Although suppliers were opposed to e-auctions in their early days, now they are viewed as part of the way the game is played. In fact, today suppliers view e-auctions positively as they serve to create a more level playing field, providing both buyer and supplier with a good level of transparency as well as reducing the supplier's sales costs and providing the supplier with intelligence regarding how their pricing compares to that of others in the market.

An e-auction is not, however, a miracle cure; it is only relevant in certain situations, and the way it is carried out is critical to success. There are a number of factors that must be provided for. They are:

- *Lotting strategy.* This is critical to success. 'Lotting' is the way the overall requirement is broken down into discrete packages of work in order for bids to be relevant and comparable to one another. There may be just one big lot that is easier to manage. However, this approach can reduce overall success, as it is harder to establish precise clarity regarding what is included within the lot. A bundle of requirements may also reduce the potential market size. Many lot auctions provide a more flexible and safer alternative but they can be expensive to run, with the risk that suppliers will cherry-pick the lots in which they are interested.

- *Specification.* Closely associated with lotting, the buyer must clearly define and communicate the specification for each product or service, and this is the equivalent of the single of multiple lots. In the absence of e-auctions the understanding of 'what the buyer wants' often comes from a series of meetings through which the supplier gains sufficient information in order to make a proposal. E-auctions negate the need for such meetings and so there must be a clear definition, developed from the business requirements, of what is required. Any ambiguity could result in bids not being comparable.

- *Inviting the right suppliers.* Research the potential suppliers who, where possible, should be pre-qualified. Suppliers who don't meet the minimum technical or commercial criteria should be eliminated before the e-auction. A pre-tender request for information (RFI) may be appropriate here. There must be sufficient qualified suppliers to make the auction worthwhile. While there are no definitive numbers, running an auction with just two suppliers is unlikely to give good results (but there are exceptions). Eight is a good number, while 15 is too many and the event is likely to be difficult to manage and coordinate.

- *Selection criteria.* The basis on which the supplier will be selected should be defined in advance of the auction and published to the participating suppliers. This is an important step. We may choose to bind ourselves to 'Lowest bid wins' or leave flexibility so that we do not need to choose the lowest option, but commit ourselves to validate closing bids before making a decision. This will help if we subsequently have concerns over the lowest supplier's bid. It is also possible that the e-auction may not be the final decider and a further round of negotiation may be appropriate. This should only be the case where the auction itself was not a 'price-only' event. Again, those participating need to understand how the process will work.

- *Training and communication.* Don't just expect the supplier(s) to be capable of participating in an e-auction. Many are well practised and know many different e-auction platforms, but supplier training and good communication are essential both to prepare the supplier in technical and commercial aspects and to eliminate scope for deliberate spoiling tactics. If some or all of the suppliers have little experience in this area, it may be worth running a dummy auction before the main event. Communication in advance is also about selling the benefits of participating to the supplier, to maximize their interest and involvement.

- *Post auction.* Using the selection criteria, select the winning or shortlisted suppliers. All participants should be informed of the results. It is good practice to provide feedback to suppliers as well as to note any lessons learnt from the exercise.

Once the e-auction is complete and the decision made, implementation of the new arrangements with the successful supplier needs to take place. If the post-e-auction implementation was as easy as the event itself and we could just click an 'implement new supplier' button on a website, then managing change in organizations would become a whole lot easier. But there is no such button and no provider offers one, and, as we have seen previously, turning intent into reality is hard work. Although many dramatic price reductions can be achieved through auctions, purchasing teams can struggle to implement new arrangements, for which there is no real way to police compliance. As we saw earlier, an e-auction is just a tool that supports a bigger process, and if the tool is to be effective, careful monitoring is required of the results from its use.

E-auctions do not work for every situation, and there are many cases where they simply should not be used. They are most useful where the supply market comprises a high number of capable suppliers providing highly generic (day one analysis) or standardized products or services. If we revisit portfolio analysis, e-auctions are entirely relevant for categories that sit in leverage and also in acquisition, if there is sufficient spend to make them worthwhile (see Figure 7.10). But they are entirely inappropriate for critical and, in most but not all cases, strategic categories, as the market is too difficult

**FIGURE 7.11**    E-auction viability, using portfolio analysis

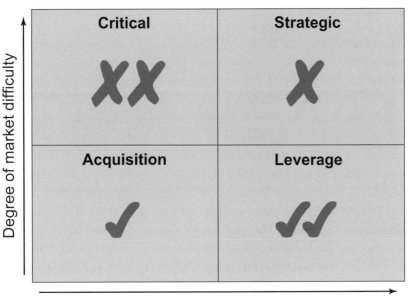

and non-competitive for an e-auction to be effective. Also, don't try to change the market unless you are strong enough to do so. Setting up e-auctions for commodities where the price is determined by market forces and where there is constant price volatility is unwise. For example, an e-auction set up with the only two suppliers in the market whose product was virtually entirely based on a commodity yielded a price increase rather than a decrease, as a result of increasing input costs for the commodity.

# Supplier selection

This step is an *Activity* and is *Optional*

Supplier selection is, as the name suggests, an approach to select one or more suppliers with whom we want to engage. It is placed here in the category management process to provide for when the sourcing strategy requires either a new supplier or current sourcing arrangements need to be opened up to the market with a view to finding the best provider. In this case the RFP/RFQ tendering activity would constitute the majority of our evaluation activity. However, supplier selection is a generic approach and can be used for any scenario where the most appropriate supplier (or suppliers) needs to be identified and engaged.

Selecting a supplier is like putting all the candidates into a funnel (see Figure 7.12) and running a series of selection and evaluation activities that progressively eliminate those who do not meet our requirements whilst positively identifying the suppliers that offer the best solution from those that remain. The aim is to arrive at just one or a few with whom we wish to move forward. The selection process does not need to identify the final supplier but might be used to identify a very small shortlist with which negotiations and contract discussions will take place. This selection process is typical within the commercial sector and could well change mid selection; for example, requirements could still change or the need for additional evaluation might be identified. However, in the public sector this funnel might be quite different, it will need to comply with the provisions of the prevailing procurement legislation. The selection process needs to be clearly defined at the outset and once initiated there is little scope to make changes. Depending upon the contracting approach being used there might be fewer steps with more rigour coming into play at the early stages of the funnel, and less scope for negotiation refinement or optimizing requirements along the way.

**FIGURE 7.12**  The supplier selection 'funnel' process

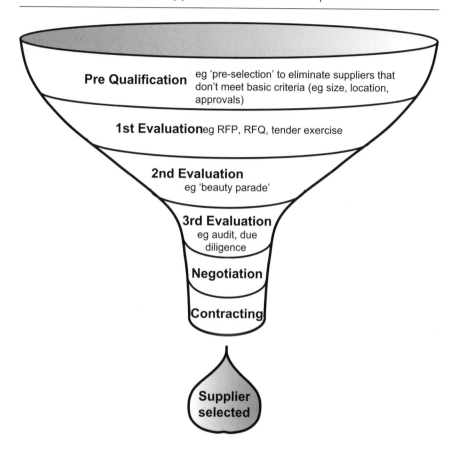

Within category management a full supplier selection process starts right back before the tendering or RFP/RFQ stage and continues on past into negotiation and contracting stages. I will expand each of the selection stages in turn.

## Pre-qualification

This initial stage can prevent us wasting a lot of time and effort. It is about eliminating those suppliers who will not meet some basic or fundamental requirements. For example, if we are looking to select a new corporate mobile phone provider for a large user contract, only a handful of big suppliers exist, so we would most likely involve them all within the tender exercise. However, if we are looking to find a provider of gardening contractors for corporate locations, an online search might highlight many hundreds ranging from 'a man, a van and a mower' companies to large professional businesses geared up to service the business sector. Clearly, sending an RFP to hundreds of providers would be a waste of time; many small businesses would not know how to respond and for those that did the analysis time would be huge. A pre-qualification step is necessary, and for this some pre-qualification criteria are required. In this example, criteria such as number of employees, turnover or accreditation to ISO9001 might be appropriate to eliminate 90 per cent of the companies, leaving only the big players with a quality management system in place. Finding out the information required to apply the pre-qualification criteria might involve a simple RFI earlier in the process, or it might be a case of doing some quick research by internet or phone with each company to establish the basic facts.

## 1st evaluation: tender or RFP/RFQ process

Following pre-qualification the first evaluation would typically be the RFP/RFQ tendering activity. Assuming more than one supplier is identified here, then this shortlist proceeds to the further evaluation stages. Clearly if the RFP/RFQ selects a single supplier, further comparative evaluations are not relevant; however, further due diligence and negotiation may still be needed.

## 2nd evaluation: beauty parade

Following the RFP/RFQ, a further step is often necessary to carry out some further evaluation. For example, if we are buying consultancy services for a large engagement, a shortlisted RFP response might be beautifully crafted, telling a compelling story of how the company can do great things; the RFQ fees may also be favourable. However, until we meet the people who are going to do the work and talk with them about how they will tackle the assignment, it is not possible to gain a full assessment of the supplier's capability. There are other factors also, and the RFP process only requires the supplier to answer our questions in a precise way. When we actually engage with the supplier, we open up the free-flow opportunity for the supplier to tell us what they can actually do, which may not have come across in the answers to our questions.

Furthermore, if we are going to work closely with the supplier, we need to be sure we can work with the people concerned. An RFP response will not tell us this, and the only way we can find out is by meeting them. This next evaluation step is not just about meeting the supplier to see what the supplier can do, but may also be concerned with evaluating a product, a process, capability or approach to a programme of work.

A frequently used supplier selection activity is a supplier presentation, often called a 'beauty parade'. Just like hopeful beauty queens would parade in front of pageant judges the same name has come to be used when short-listed suppliers give a final presentation regarding their proposals, one after another, to an assembled body of representatives and possibly decision makers. This group would typically comprise all members of the category management team.

When organizing supplier presentations it is also a good idea to run these one after another over a day or two so that the team can keep each presentation in their minds and compare one with another. The agenda for the presentation should be set in advance but might include items such as:

- summary of the requirements and the process;
- summary of the proposal from the supplier;
- how the supplier plans to implement new arrangements;
- account management team structure;
- fee proposals;
- questions and answers (two-way).

The supplier presentation or beauty parade helps raise the competitive tension among the participants, as each knows that only the best will win. Suppliers will therefore go to great lengths to project their offer and themselves in the best way, but they will also want to understand what it is we most want and how we will make our decision. This is good, as it is a sign of the suppliers matching their capabilities to our needs. Time should be given in the agenda to describe what we want and for any questions they have for us (ideally at the end of the session).

The supplier presentation is an excellent opportunity for supplier conditioning. It may, for example, be appropriate to ask the supplier to arrive with revised fee proposals. Furthermore, a supplier who arrives and sees a competitor leaving from the previous session is likely to sense the need to raise the game. There is rarely any need to hide this, and even if we tried to, suppliers will attempt to find out the nature of the game by looking at the visitor book if there is one or by asking how many sessions are being run, whether the competition is national or global and so on.

Effective supplier selection requires a structured evaluation tool; Figure 7.13 gives a simple example. This is very similar to the tool used to evaluate the strategic options earlier as the same principles of weighting and scoring are

**FIGURE 7.13** Supplier selection matrix

| Supplier selection | | | | | | |
|---|---|---|---|---|---|---|
| **Supplier selection criteria** | Weighting | Max Score | **Supplier 1** Widgets-R-Us | **Supplier 2** Acme Widgets | **Supplier 3** Widget King | **Supplier 4** Widgets direct |
| Meets business needs | G/NG | – | | | | |
| Business want No 1 | 40% | 400 | | | | |
| Business want No 2 | 10% | 100 | | | | |
| Business want No 3 | 30% | 300 | | | | |
| Business want No 4 | 20% | 200 | | | | |
| **RFP evaluation** | 100% | 1000 | | | | |
| Presentation quality | 10% | 100 | | | | |
| Implementation planning | 30% | 300 | | | | |
| Cultural fit of personnel | 30% | 300 | | | | |
| Understood requirements | 10% | 100 | | | | |
| Innovation | 20% | 200 | | | | |
| **Supplier presentation** | 100% | 1000 | | | | |
| Fees and pricing | 70% | 700 | | | | |
| Terms and conditions | 30% | 300 | | | | |
| **Evaluation of fees** | 100% | 1000 | | | | |

(Row groups at left: **RFP evaluation**, **Supplier presentation**, **Fees and pricing**)

relevant. Here the tool has three sections: the results of the RFP (in this case structured to reflect how business requirements are met), an evaluation of the supplier presentations, and an evaluation of fees and price. In this case a weighted system has been developed to evaluate each section independently, the result being a summary score against each supplier for the RFP, the presentation, and commerciality of proposals.

This is only a simple example. The actual approach to be used should be developed by the category management team around the needs of the business as defined within the sourcing strategy. It should reflect how the team feels it is best to evaluate some of the softer areas, such as the personality fit of the supplier's personnel, if relevant. The approach does not necessarily need to be numeric with weightings as shown in the example, but it does need to be consistent in the way it is used, so allowing a valid comparison of one supplier against another and providing a record of the basis for selection that can stand up to any subsequent scrutiny.

Finally, the supplier selection approach and any quantitative elements, including weightings, should, of course, be worked out in advance to avoid bias. A fully numeric assessment based upon the average of team members' individual scores might prevent some subtle but relevant issues or concerns from surfacing. However, combining quantitative evaluation (as in the example) with group discussion to debate and agree final scores helps ensure the final determination is robust and, more importantly, has the full support of the team.

As we saw in the section on RFPs and RFQs, there is often a requirement for formal, well-structured and transparent approaches. The same applies for supplier selection, and even if this requirement is not driven by public procurement legislation it is good practice to run a supplier selection process in a well-defined way that can hold up to subsequent interrogation by others should the need arise. This is not just to protect the category management team from any allegations of favouritism towards a supplier (though such an approach will provide this protection anyway), but is more to help disarm any last-minute resistance to change from powerful stakeholders. At the point when a key stakeholder learns that their favourite supplier has lost the business, the project could be jeopardized by a barrage of well-thought-through reasons why the category management team's strategy is misguided and should be stopped. If the stakeholder manages to galvanize support for this, the outcome could be dire. Clearly, the work before this point to engage with stakeholders and communicate widely across the business should help to prevent such occurrences, but experience shows that at the point where a strategy is about to become real, people who previously seemed supportive can suddenly rebel. A good, well-documented selection process will therefore provide a facts-and-data record of the journey the category management team has gone through to arrive at the decision. Provided the basis for this decision is robust, it will be difficult to question. A template is provided in the Appendix.

## 3rd evaluation

By now we have selected the supplier or suppliers we hope to move forward with, so this third evaluation is appropriate where there is the need for further checks or verifications. This step is often called due diligence and is about ensuring that the supplier really is who they say they are and really can do what they say they can do. It is about ensuring they have the necessary organizational capability, systems and arrangements in place. This step is like an employer offering us a job subject to taking up references, and here is where we check out the supplier's references. Alternatively this might involve an audit of their facility, checking they have stated accreditations or certifications or financial checks.

## Negotiation and contracting

Whilst our evaluations are complete the selection process is not truly finished until we have concluded any negotiations and contracted with the supplier(s). Suppliers we previously selected could still fail here; there could be points of dispute that our negotiation efforts fail to overcome or a contractual difference that can't be resolved. Worse still, the supplier might pull out at this final stage, which is a real possibility either as a tactic or if, after reflection, they've decided their offer in the RFQ was too low and is unsustainable. The selection process continues right up until the new supplier(s) is or are under contract and therefore we need to be prepared for this possibility and perhaps keep the other suppliers who came close in reserve until we are certain we don't need them. I will explore negotiation and contracting in more detail over the next two sections.

## Supplier selected

With our supplier selected and appointed we are off and running. However there is still work to be done to close out the selection process and we need to inform those suppliers who have been unsuccessful. This step is frequently forgotten or neglected as it is all too easy for the category manager to have his or her mind and focus on the successful supplier and next steps. However, those who have been unsuccessful will most likely have spent considerable time and effort to get as far as they did. They may have incurred costs to support their sales process and attend meetings. Whilst this is part of the game and part of cost of sales, good practice would suggest there is an obligation to take time to provide some good, well-considered feedback to the supplier as to why their proposal fell short. However, there is an even more important reason to do this and this is simply to keep the unsuccessful suppliers 'on side' as we may need them in the future, especially if something goes wrong with our selected supplier arrangement. Furthermore if we demonstrate consistency and fairness we show strength and this is good conditioning for the supplier for any future engagement.

When we inform and give feedback to unsuccessful suppliers caution is needed as suppliers may want to keep a 'foot in the door' or seize an opportunity to open up discussions as to whether the supplier could offer a final new proposal that might change our mind (clearly raising the question of why they didn't do that before). There is also the chance they may want to claim some sort of 'foul play' but this is unlikely as most suppliers will seek to keep future options open. In these discussions it is important to:

- be clear that the decision is made and is final;
- keep the conversation around general points – don't get drawn into a debate;
- give balanced feedback – praise them for everything that was strong and outline the areas where the proposal fell short;
- if possible, offer hope for the future and outline opportunities the supplier might have to make new proposals;
- thank them for their efforts and hard work.

# Negotiation with suppliers

This step is an *Activity* and is *Optional*

Negotiation is a topic all of its own and not one that I can do full justice to in a single section and so further reading, and perhaps training, is recommended here. My second book *Negotiation for Purchasing Professionals* (also by Kogan Page) expands this topic in full and provides the Red Sheet® Methodology for negotiation planning. It is written to work together and compliment this book and the category management process.

It seems the art of negotiation is often viewed as some special skill that only a few posses and yet when I ask those in the various purchasing teams I work with typically only a few have received any sort of formal negotiation training. Probe some more and people will admit that negotiation is the one area where they have least confidence, but admitting this would be tantamount to saying we were no good at our job. The reality here is that across organizations around the world investment in negotiation skills development for purchasing people is sadly lacking. In contrast our suppliers receive on average ten times the training we do, and if more proof were needed just search out the tens of thousands of books, training courses or tools for negotiation; the vast majority are designed and written for the sales community.

So it seems the odds are stacked against us? Perhaps, but actually most of the purchasing teams I train in negotiation are not that far from being great; they just need help with the planning process, developing a good repertoire of tactics and understanding how their personality fits with a specific negotiation. If we are to be good at negotiation we need to recognize that the personality type of the purchasing negotiator is not always that of a competitive, results-driven individual as often found in sales teams. Good planning therefore reduces the reliance on personality-led competitive tactics during the negotiation event itself. If we can attend to these things then we can build confidence in any negotiation to achieve the desired outcomes and remain in control. Negotiation is not a special skill; it is a skill for life and one we all learn early on. There is nothing different about negotiation in business, but the tactics we might use and need to understand change.

Planning a negotiation and understanding the strength of our position relative to the supplier's position requires us to think about what outcomes we want, what leverage we have, and where the supplier has an advantage. The outputs from the category management work up until now provide a rich basis for negotiation planning, way beyond that within any sales-led negotiation. Whilst I cannot do justice to this topic here, I will attempt to provide some guidance to negotiation as part of Stage 4 by providing 10 top tips for negotiation with within category management.

# 10 Top Tips for negotiation within category management

## Negotiation tip #1: Know your personality

Every purchasing team has a rottweiler, the buyer who can go into a negotiation and relentlessly chew up the supplier and the supplier's arguments until what is wanted is achieved. This is usually a combination of personality (someone who doesn't mind upsetting others) and a selection of assertive tactics. Not all buyers can adopt this style. Another buyer might be naturally collaborative and empathic, and be averse to upsetting others. Some scenarios call for an assertive, hard negotiation style. Others require diplomacy and collaboration. If the wrong buyer is put into the negotiation and fails to adapt their style, the results could be suboptimal, even disastrous. Portfolio analysis is the tool that helps determine not only the approach for the negotiation but the optimum buyer personality type. Figure 7.14 gives the ideal personality traits for each portfolio quadrant. The traits given here are

**FIGURE 7.14** Negotiator personality aligned with portfolio analysis

| Critical | Strategic |
|---|---|
| Highly diplomatic personality traits and behaviours required to protect and sell the relationship | Personality traits and behaviours required for relationship building: |
| High *conscientious, outgoing, solution focused, open-minded, agreeable* with good *personal calm.* | High *conscientious, outgoing, open-minded, agreeable* with good degree of *personal calm.* Degree of *will-to-win* and *solution focused* traits also. |
| *Assertiveness* not appropriate but an *Accommodating* conflict style required. | A moderate degree of *assertiveness* with a *collaborative* conflict style. |
| **Acquisition** | **Leverage** |
| Personality traits and behaviours appropriate to execute most effective sourcing approach | Personality traits and behaviours appropriate to hard leverage negotiations to secure the biggest win: |
| High *solution focus*. A degree of *conscientiousness, will-to-win and open-mindedness* are useful. | High *will-to-win* with a degree of *conscientiousness, outgoing* and *solution focused* traits. |
| Good *assertiveness* is essential with a *compete* conflict style. | Good *assertiveness* is essential with a *compete* conflict style. |

*Degree of market difficulty* (vertical axis)

*Degree of profit impact* (horizontal axis)

extracted from the COW SOAP ACE negotiation personality tool that is expanded in full in *Negotiation for Purchasing Professionals*. In *leverage*, the rottweiler will be entirely at home. However, if we put that individual into a negotiation for a *critical* category where the supplier has the balance of power, the results could be awful. Here a more diplomatic approach is needed, one which aims at mitigating risk by working closely with the supplier and/or getting out of *critical*.

The category and the strategic responses suggested by portfolio analysis should therefore be considered and matched against the personality type for the individual(s) who will be doing the negotiation. This doesn't mean that only the buyer type that matches a given quadrant should be used for a negotiation in that quadrant, but instead, where there is not a natural fit, the buyer needs to understand the difference and develop an approach to either avoid or reinforce certain behaviours. You might otherwise call this acting.

## Negotiation tip #2: Be clear about the areas you need to negotiate on

Negotiations should not be just a nice discussion about price, but should focus on what it is we are trying to buy. This is where the business requirements are used to drive the discussions and should form the backbone of the outcomes we want, but not all of them. Many requirements form the basis for pre-qualification of supplier selection before we get in the room; for example there would be little point negotiating with a supplier around a fundamental assurance of supply need. If they can't satisfy this we shouldn't be in the room with them. Instead we need to extract the remaining requirements where we are seeking to maximize our position. Business 'needs' must be secured, and business 'wants' should be aimed for, but also represent areas of potential compromise and trade-off. For any negotiation, pre-planning should identify the MDO (most desirable outcome) and the LDO (least desirable outcome). It should extend beyond price to terms and conditions, speed to implement, account servicing, specification, contract duration and so on. The LDO represents the point that we are not prepared to go below. It is important to define this up front. The difference between the MDO and the LDO represents the areas of compromise or trades that can be made within the process. However, it is also important to aim high and focus as much as possible early in the negotiation on the MDO, since a good negotiator on the other side of the table will soon smoke out our LDO. Finally, if possible, check there is a ZoMA (Zone of Mutual Agreement) before entering the room; that there is a likely overlap between the LDO and the supplier's anticipated LDO (Figure 7.15).

**FIGURE 7.15**    The LDO, MDO and ZoMA

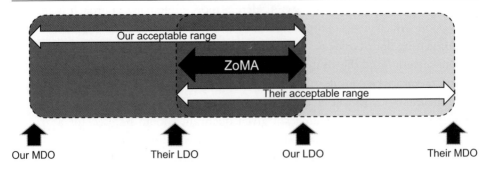

## Negotiation tip #3: Decide at the outset what type of negotiation we are conducting

Not all negotiations are the same. A one-off negotiation to buy a car from someone we don't know is very different to the ongoing daily negotiations with our family and children where our primary objective is to maintain the right relationship with them for the long term. With this in mind the way we approach the negotiation and the tactics and techniques we use are very different. It is a fallacy to say that negotiation is always about seeking a win/win outcome; sometimes this is the case, say for negotiations where the long-term relationship is important, but more often than not parties seek a WIN/win (big win, little win), but will work to make the other party feel like they have the big win even when this is not the case. There are two types of negotiation:

- *Value claiming*. Where parties seek to claim as much value from the negotiation, maximizing their share of the potential benefit, like dividing a pie of fixed size. What one party wins, the other gives up. Value claiming aligns with the *leverage* quadrants in portfolio analysis or are one-off events. Here we might use many and varied tactics, perhaps some hard, delivered by tough negotiators with the sole aim of maximizing our position.

- *Value creating*. Where parties seek to work together to create more mutual benefit. Here the pie is grown so how it is divided becomes less important. Value claiming is about parties working to build outcomes with the interests of both parties in mind. Such negotiations value the relationship more than the immediate outcome and therefore align with the *strategic* quadrant in portfolio analysis. Tactics will be more open and negotiators need to be skilled at maintaining relationships.

## Negotiation tip #4: Have an alternative

The power in any negotiation comes from alternatives. Here we need a BATNA – never leave home without one! (*Best Alternative to a Negotiated Agreement*). If we have got to get a result, all our negotiation efforts will give away the fact that we need to close or reach an outcome. If we have a plan B or an alternative we can accept, then our entire negotiation approach will take the stance of 'I don't need this, I'm going to hold out.' If you've ever been in a situation where you had two job offers at once, perhaps you'll remember how much more confident you felt in pushing hard for a better package than if you had just one offer which you really needed to accept. Always have a BATNA; it works wonders in negotiations, and if you don't have one, find one – there are always alternatives.

## Negotiation tip #5: Do your homework

The best negotiators plan and do their research well in advance. If we try to arrive at a negotiation with the intention to 'wing it' we are handing power to the other party. Negotiation planning is about understanding fully everything about our position and the position of the other party with respect to any and all factors that might have a bearing on potential outcomes. This includes all the potential sources of power each party holds around current market conditions, power of relationships held, time constraints, future opportunity or any current dependencies on one another. Assessing power demands research and engagement with key stakeholders – you can never be over-prepared for a negotiation.

## Negotiation tip #6: Know your opponent

If our personality traits have a bearing on negotiation, it follows that the supplier's do also. We can usually find out in advance the specific individuals we will be negotiating with and with this intelligence we can determine how best to interact with them during the negotiation. Research here is easier than it might seem, as we might know them or we can ask people. However, these days most professional people are proud to boast on LinkedIn about who they are and what they have achieved and for negotiation planning this is a great source of intelligence around who they are and what might resonate with them.

## Negotiation tip #7: Play the long game

Negotiation should not be viewed as a once-only event but a continual process. A single event might arrive at an improved position; however, it is worth considering how the event fits into the overall timeline for our relationship with the supplier. This is particularly relevant for *value-creating* negotiations and this perspective allows us to plan and sequence what we go after. What we can't get today we can work towards getting tomorrow. Where possible, the future option of revisiting other negotiation areas should be retained, perhaps under the guise of 'collaborative working'.

Supplier conditioning helps underpin negotiation, as it provides the right context for the supplier for each and every event.

## Negotiation tip #8: Get your organization on message

Suppliers are clever and will usually put much preparation into every negotiation event. They don't just rely on their relationship with purchasing to decide how to approach a negotiation, but will use all the relationships they have cultivated across the entire organization. If we are working hard to maintain the pretense that we have a wide choice of suppliers and a key stakeholder tells the supplier that it is the only company being considered, we immediately lose some of the strength of our position. Alignment of communication and conditioning messages across stakeholders are therefore required. Effort should be made to brief all stakeholders who have contact with the supplier.

## Negotiation tip #9: Know when to close

When I run negotiation training, one of the biggest mistakes negotiators make is failing to know when to close. There is a point in any negotiation when the other party is convinced and ready to cut a deal. If we fail to notice this and keep ploughing on, perhaps to secure some extra thing or perhaps driven by uncertainty, then we risk compromising the outcome or dashing the confidence of the moment in the other party. Learning when to close is about paying attention to body language, especially the eyes, but it is also about testing if the other party is ready to close with hypothetical questioning.

## Negotiation tip #10: Get the team prepared

If the negotiation is to be conducted in a team then the team must be 110 per cent prepared with signals and ways of working together to handle every situation. This will require a significant amount of pre-event negotiation simulation: trying to predict what might happen and preparing a response to that position. The level of preparation should not be underestimated to make this type of approach successful. However, the outcome, if well done, is likely to be very positive.

With these 10 tips in mind it is possible to begin to plan and execute negotiations. Negotiation is not something we learn once and then become proficient. Like a footballer joining a club who never stops training, good purchasing people should never stop learning how to negotiate. Books and training can help enormously; however, we can also learn a lot by watching others in day-to-day situations and identifying the tactics used, noting what was said and so on. Life is in fact a great training ground for effective negotiation.

# CONTRACTING

## Contract planning

This step is an *Activity* and is *Essential*

The next three sections focus on contracts. This step is about planning the contractual approach that we should use. The next section is about planning for exit and the final step is about determining what goes into the contract and then putting the contract into action and managing it.

Formulation of the contract represents the stage in the category management process where the relevant parts of the agreed sourcing strategy are formally implemented with the supplier or suppliers, perhaps before roll-out of the actual new sourcing arrangements. It is a key step within implementation.

So why have a contract? A contract does many things and at some point in time a contract will be required – or the absence of a contract will become detrimental. Contracts provide:

- a formal definition of what has been agreed by each party;
- a definition of what happens when things change or go wrong;
- a formal definition of the detail of what is to be provided and the way in which it will be provided, as well as key dimensions regarding how the relationship will work.

The role of purchasing in the overall contractual process varies from organization to organization. Some companies, especially US ones, place all aspects of contract development and execution within a legal function. Others place this role within the purchasing function. Some combine both, with purchasing developing an outline of the contractual elements before they are passed over to a legal function to complete the process and make it legally watertight. Whatever the arrangements are it is important to remember that most purchasing people are not lawyers and therefore the degree of responsibility purchasing assumes with respect to establishing and managing appropriate legal arrangements should be considered carefully and should be balanced according to risk, capability, experience and training.

When there seems to be a good agreement between parties, formalizing arrangements within some sort of contract often feels unnecessary. The thing about a contract is that we hope we never need it, but without one we are leaving ourselves exposed to all sorts of risk and misinterpretation. Moreover, the process of establishing a contract helps secure alignment between both parties as to how the arrangement will actually work in practice and creates clear obligations on both parties within the overall legal framework for a stated country.

Contracts are often regarded as dull, lengthy documents written in legal language, and so far I've described them as documents. In fact, the contract itself exists when all the required components that constitute a contract are in place; in many countries a document is not required for a contract to be made and the governing law recognizes a verbal or oral contract as legally binding. However, such contracts are open to wide interpretation from the parties involved, and without witnesses there is scope for the parties to change their stories. Within category management the use of verbal or oral contracts is not recommended, and care is needed within the dealings and discussions with suppliers by category teams so as to not inadvertently enter into such a contract. A contract can also be formed by custom and practice, for example if a supplier regularly provides, and is paid for, the same goods or service over a long period of time, then a contract could be deemed to have been formed in some countries.

What constitutes a contract and the nature of contract law vary around the world. In this book we can only begin to consider the intricacies of contracts, so some further reading or advice on the matter is recommended. When sourcing from different countries, the subtle differences in legal approach must be fully understood and provided for, and the support and involvement of legal experts with territory knowledge are essential.

Under English law, for a contract to exist, four contractual components need to be in place. To explain these, consider the example of buying a lawnmower from a shop:

- *Offer*. The offer is when we have visited the shop, viewed the range of lawnmowers available and decided which one we want to buy and therefore we make an offer to buy the lawnmower from the seller at a stated price. Note that the advertisement by the seller of the lawnmower in the store with its price tag is not an offer under English law. It is called an 'invitation to treat'.

- *Acceptance*. This is acceptance of the offer, for example the seller agrees to sell the lawnmower. Acceptance can be signalled in a variety of ways. It doesn't necessarily require someone to say, 'Yes, I accept your offer.' That a store allows the buyer to pick up something, wheel it to the checkout and have the checkout attendant initiate the transaction with a credit card, is a form of acceptance by action. In the development of a complex contract for a large outsourcing project, the acceptance might be the signature of a contractual document by one or both parties. It is important to appreciate what constitutes acceptance so as to avoid inadvertently giving it.

- *Consideration*. There must be an exchange of something of value between the parties, such as paying the stated sum of money in return for the lawnmower. When a failing company with no or negative asset value is given away for rescue by another company, it is never actually 'given away'. Instead it will be sold for one pound or one dollar or some small token amount so that a contract can exist between the buyer and seller.

- *Intent*. This is the intent by both parties to enter into, and be capable of entering into, a legally binding agreement and be bound by that agreement. This tends to be clear in a shop-based transaction.

Again, this is how things work under English law, and there are differences around the world. In planning for the contracting methodology, thought should be given to the various options that exist. There are many different documents used to establish various forms of contract, and the following are some of those found in a purchasing environment:

- *Purchase order*. This is a commercial document issued by a buyer to a seller to indicate the types, quantities and agreed prices for products or services that the seller will provide. Sending a purchase order to the seller constitutes an offer to buy products or services. Acceptance by the seller usually forms a once-off contract between buyer and seller, so no contract exists until the purchase order is accepted. It is usual for a purchase order to be accompanied by the buyer's terms and conditions, often printed on the reverse for paper orders or included electronically for e-commerce. Sellers are, of course, very keen that their terms and conditions take precedence in case the buyer's terms are less favourable. It is not uncommon for a seller to signal acceptance of the order formally by return of an order acceptance, which contains the seller's terms and conditions, written in such a way as to supersede those of the buyer. Many buyers are alert to this and will make a subsequent counter. It is here that a 'battle of the forms' can occur. This should be avoided where possible, and for new sourcing strategies that seek to establish a long-term relationship individual purchase orders alone are unlikely to be the most effective method. A broader contractual framework that defines how the arrangement and relationship will operate is appropriate.

● *Master or framework agreement*. Such documents are often used with suppliers to establish the terms governing subsequent contracts to be awarded, or call-offs against the agreement using purchase orders. Master or framework agreements are often used to define agreed pricing, terms, and how aspects of the relationship might work. If the master or framework agreement contains elements such as minimum commitments, perhaps in terms of volumes to be purchased or duration of the agreement, then it becomes contractual. Otherwise, the contract is made when the purchase order or individual contract is placed in accordance with the agreement. This type of contractual approach works well for long-term arrangements with regular and ongoing spend, so umbrella terms and pricing can be negotiated, with or without any firm minimum commitment. It also helps prevent the 'battle of the forms'.

● *Letter of intent (LOI)*. This is a document outlining an agreement between two or more parties before the agreement is finalized. Suppliers generally tend to like to use LOIs. If a negotiation leads to an understanding with the supplier regarding the way forward, the supplier will be desperate to crystallize this into some form of formal agreement to avoid the risk of losing the business, especially when the salesperson has registered their 'win' with superiors. Whether or not LOIs are contractual depends on how they are written. Typically, they resemble written contracts but are not usually binding on the parties in their entirety, as by their nature they signal intent rather than define the detail of the contractual relationship. Often LOIs contain certain provisions that are binding, such as non-disclosure agreements, and if an LOI is written in a way that too closely resembles a formal contract with specific commitments, then it may be interpreted as binding. In general, LOIs should be avoided and instead effort should be directed to working through the detail so that a full contract or master agreement is put in place.

- *Memorandum of understanding (MOU).* This describes a bilateral agreement between two parties and expresses a convergence of will between them, typically to indicate an intended common line of action. MOUs should not be a legal commitment, and these documents generally lack the binding power of a contract. An MOU is often regarded as a more formal alternative to a gentleman's agreement. To avoid any confusion and scope for misinterpretation, as with LOIs, MOUs should be avoided, with effort instead directed towards the detail required for a full contract or master agreement.

- *Non-disclosure agreement.* Also called a confidentiality agreement, this forms a legal contract between at least two parties, and outlines confidential materials or knowledge the parties wish to share with one another for certain purposes but wish to restrict from general use. It is usual for a buyer to put an NDA in place at the beginning of discussions with potential suppliers to ensure the right protection is in place. If a seller presents an NDA for signature by the buyer, then the implications must be understood before it is signed. For example, accepting a term that imposes a heavy penalty for a breach caused by factors outside the control of the buyer or the buyer's organization should be avoided.

- *Formal contract.* There is, of course, also the formal contract, a legal document outlining all aspects of what has been agreed between both parties, provision for what might go wrong and how the relationship will work. These documents usually have a recognizable structure, with a number of sections, each performing a particular legal function or fulfilling a specific need within the contract. Contracts vary enormously from simple, well-structured documents written in English that all can understand, to complex, weighty documents that would make good doorstops and whose development and understanding seem to require separate teams of lawyers. In any agreement there will be a combination of elements including general or umbrella terms, the specifics of what will be supplied, their specification, pricing, quantities and so on. It is good practice to separate these out. For example, the schedule of work would be referred to in the main body of the contract, but it would exist as a separate document so that it can later be revised and updated by mutual agreement without the need to revisit the entire contract.

Thought must be given to the contractual framework that is to be used and which is most appropriate for the sourcing strategy. Then we need to determine what provision needs to be made within this and here the outputs from our category management project so far should shape the structure of the contractual mechanism used. It is essential that the category manager and perhaps the category team are involved here and key outputs such as business requirements, targets, value levers, risk mitigation objectives, implementation requirements and of course the sourcing strategy itself are used to shape contract planning. If the category team simply hands over the drafting of a standard contract to a legal function with no engagement around what the contract needs to achieve then the outcome will dilute the impact of a good strategy. How we view the contracts is important. If we see them as documents created by legal teams then that is what they be; however, if we view them as the means by which we will bring our sourcing strategy to life then this is what will be achieved. This means putting energy into contract planning and what a contract needs to contain. Let's consider an example – the sourcing of many large items of manufacturing process equipment to be installed across a range of sites. These products are complex, are partly customized for us and there are some service needs for installation and maintenance. We have decided to use a traditional contract approach as opposed to a master agreement or any other instrument. This contract therefore needs to make sure that we formally agree how the arrangement will work. Specifically this might include:

- the agreed specification for the equipment;
- the timescales for supply;
- the arrangement for spares supply;
- when and how installation must take place;
- what sort of maintenance is required and for how long after installation;
- the agreed pricing.

However, the contract also needs to embed these factors within a recognized legal framework that will make provision for any and every eventuality. These might include:

- What happens if the equipment is supplied late and it impacts on the business?
- How will the relationship between us work in practice?
- If there is some sort of catastrophe that halts the programme, how do we resolve it?

- How do we make sure that we are aware if the supplier is subcontracting some of the work to another company, and can check that this company is suitable?

- If we want to terminate the contract, how will we do this?

- If we did terminate and the supplier still held our equipment, how do we make sure we have the right to recover it?

- How do we ensure the required service levels are met and what happens when they are not?

- We will need to share confidential information with the supplier to enable them to do this work; how do we make sure this is protected?

- What happens if we fall out with the supplier?

As this example shows, there are many aspects our contract needs to provide for and these need to come together within a legal framework defined in a single document that encompasses:

- *Agreed arrangements for the area of supply*. Details of the product, services, specification, agreed service levels and so on. Earlier in the category management process, much time was spent developing a comprehensive definition of our business requirements and these now form the basis for defining contract structure. The format of the requirements may need to be changed, and some may need to be translated from an internal definition of need to a requirement being placed on a supplier. Furthermore, while it is good practice to separate the specifics of the area of supply from the main body of the contract, some of the requirements may need to be built into other sections of the contract.

- *The required relationship*. Account management provision, reporting, performance reviews, obligations on the supplier and so on. In addition to what has been defined within the business requirements, our work to reach this point may have identified some additional requirements that relate to how the relationship with the supplier must work in practice. Often this is considered not appropriate to be included in the contract and is omitted from it. However, if the relationship with the supplier is going to be a crucial component in the overall delivery, then creating a contractual obligation will surely focus the mind of the supplier on what is required. It is difficult to contract for a relationship, but we can create contractual provision for regular reviews and how parties will interact. Where it is possible to define key aspects of the relationship, they should certainly be included. Nothing focuses the supplier like a contractual obligation!

● *Exit provision.* Covered in the next section.

● *The commercials.* Price, fees, payment terms, minimum commitments, currencies, scope for agreeing a price increase or decrease and so on.

● *Provision for all eventualities.* The legal framework that sits around all of the above and makes provision for any and every eventuality to ensure that we, and indeed the supplier, are adequately protected. This might typically include obligations around insurance provision, limits of liability should something go wrong, arrangements for termination should one party choose to exit and how ownership of intellectual property of the two parties works. It will of course contain provision for circumstances outside the control of parties.

The legal framework described in the last point above is usually the start point for contract development. In this book I do not cover the detailed legal structure of a contract, for which further reading is recommended. However, developing a contract such as the one in this example is usually a case of starting with a standard contract for supply and then adapting it and incorporating the specific details relating to the area in question. Most companies will have standard contracts, called 'boilerplate' contracts, which form the starting point for developing the final contract. If not, rafts of boilerplate contracts are freely available on the internet.

Depending on what is normal practice within the organization, the process of building upon and developing the boilerplate contract into the final contract for the area in question will be a function of either the legal team or the purchasing team or a combination of the two. Irrespective of where the buyer's involvement stops and that of a legal team starts, the category team needs to identify the specific elements that are unique to this area of supply and which must be incorporated within the contract, as defined by the business requirements. This is crucial, because if the final contract omits relevant details that have been identified and agreed along the way within the category management process, there is a risk that the whole intent defined within the sourcing strategy may not be fully realized.

Finally, in structuring the contract think about how contracts will be updated or revisited. Development of the contract for the example above might keep teams of lawyers gainfully employed over the period of a week or two, with repeated exchanges between both parties regarding specific terms. So, once a contract has been agreed, amending it unnecessarily should be avoided and ideally it should provide sufficient flexibility to allow development in the relationship or scope of work to be easily incorporated. Therefore, where possible, the contractual elements relating to how the relationship must work and the areas of the supply arrangement that might change over time should be defined in a separate section or in a document referred to within the main contract (and therefore forming an integral part of the overall legal instrument). It is typical for contracts to have this information defined in an attached schedule or statement of work, with a provision in the contract for both parties to amend this section with mutual agreement and without the need to amend the rest of the contract.

# Contract exit planning

This step is an *Activity* and is *Essential*

Contract exit planning is determining in advance the circumstances and means by which a contract might be terminated. It might seem odd to consider exit planning at the outset, especially if things are looking great; however, this is the one area that is usually overlooked when planning a contract and this can lead to significant difficulties later should circumstances change. There are three reasons to consider exit planning upfront, these are:

1 *Circumstances change.* A relationship with a supplier today might be based around our current situation, but things can change – our world is increasingly volatile and what is certain today can change overnight. Markets can shift, requirements can change and demand can disappear. If our contract planning assumes things will stay the same we are being foolish. Instead we should attempt to anticipate what could go wrong, as far as possible, using the risk analysis tool, but in any case agree provision within the contract for parties to exit in a way that is fair.

2 *Relationships and people can change.* If what we are buying from a specific supplier requires some sort of regular interaction, eg a marketing design agency working with our team on marketing communications, then, as with any relationship, things can go sour and this can make the situation untenable. Similarly if we require certain named individuals to do the work and they are unavailable then we might want the option to reconsider our position.

3 *Keeps power balanced.* Entering into a contract with a supplier without exit provision amounts to handing the supplier power. As I said previously, nothing focuses a supplier like a contract, and if that contract is such that once signed we cannot exit it easily they hold the power, and this can drive exploitative behaviour. Instead, if the contract has good exit provision and we can walk away if things are not right then the supplier is more compelled to ensure this does not happen.

Things to consider in contract exit planning include:

- The predictable circumstances that might trigger termination and exit.
- Dispute resolution and escalation process prior to exit to deal with things that are not right.
- Obligations on parties to manage exit and transition, for example handover of certain, defined information and documents, support for transition to be provided, timescales, requirements for reasonable cooperation, who funds this, and so on.
- Notice to be provided and the mechanism to effect exit.
- Any penalties for exit either way.
- Post-contract obligations on parties.

Exit planning is particularly important for outsourced arrangements where the supplier takes over an entire aspect of an organization's business. Here the provider will typically amass knowledge and know-how about the service provision that can be critically important to a new supplier coming in to take over; if there is no requirement for the incumbent supplier to provide this and support transition then they hold all the cards and can prevent any sort of competitive market exercise being conducted. Good exit planning reduces market difficulty (making it *leverage* not *strategic* in portfolio analysis) so enabling alternatives to be considered.

Within a contract exit planning would be incorporated perhaps within a section on termination, but might also need to exist throughout the contract. A good legal function will be skilled at drafting contracts with sufficient exit provision in, but collaboration here is essential to ensure that the exit provision we identify as part of our category management project is understood and fully incorporated by those drafting the legalities.

# Contract execution and management

This step is an *Activity* and is *Essential*

Once the contract is complete and we are content that all of the key requirements of our category management strategy are incorporated then the contract needs to be executed. Contract execution is putting that which is agreed into action and making the legal instrument that is the contract valid, typically by parties signing or sealing it in the case of a full legal document or a master or framework agreement. Contract execution can represent the culmination of much effort by the category management team and so it is big deal, and one worthy of team celebration as well as a good reason to initiate some internal and perhaps external communications to share the success far and wide.

It is at this point where many category management projects might stop, as if contract execution represents some final step with the contractual document then being filed away in case of future dispute. This should not be allowed to happen. A lot of effort, energy and dialogue are spent getting to the point where both parties formally agree the contract and that contract has been designed to provide for all dimensions of the relationship and what both parties are trying to achieve. The contract ideally encompasses and reflects our business requirements. So if it is resigned to a filing system we are putting away a vital roadmap that can help manage our relationship. When we sign the contract our work is not finished; in fact our work here has only just begun.

Contract management is part of Supplier Relationship Management (covered in the next chapter) and is concerned with taking a systematic approach to ensure that the supplier is working in accordance with the contract. This includes:

- Ensuring any agreed performance targets or KPIs, say within an SLA, are being met.

- Ensuring the supplier is meeting any ongoing obligations, eg to maintain certain insurance provisions, to notify of personal changes etc.

- Ensuring the relationship ongoing proactively supports the fulfilment of the contract, irrespective of whether the arrangements here are formally defined within the contract itself. In practice this might include regular reviews to keep close to the supplier etc.

- Identifying any potential risk or issue that might impede the supplier from meeting contractual obligations.
- Taking action with the supplier where there is a problem or potential problem.

Contract management is also concerned with managing the time dimension of a contract along with any other contracts we might have in place with a given supplier. This could include activities or events that must happen at certain times, and the contract expiry.

Open-ended contracts with suppliers are rare; instead it is typical and good practice for a contract to exist for a set period of time. This limits risk to parties, although within that most contracts provide mechanisms for extension if both parties agree. However, in order for us to be in full control of the contract and our suppliers, and maximize our leverage, we need to be in control of the process of managing contract expiry. If we are taken by surprise or wait until a contract has expired or is about to expire before considering our position then we are giving power to the supplier as we may be left with no alternative but to renew and then it will be on their terms. Remember power in negotiation and in the process of supplier selection comes from alternatives. That means that when a contract is due to expire, and we wish to reappraise our situation and consider what the market could provide, we need to leave sufficient time in order to run a sourcing exercise. Such an exercise can take time, many months in fact to do it well, and so if we are to maximize our choice and stand the chance of securing the greatest benefit, we need to plan to do this early.

Contract management is about planning for contract expiry and directing our resources, in a prioritized way, to the sourcing activities that determine in advance what will happen at expiry. This could be a number of things:

- we simply renew the contract 'as is';
- we negotiate a renewal but with new terms and requirements;
- we extend the contract (perhaps to buy time to complete a sourcing review);
- we terminate, or let the contract terminate, in favour of some new arrangements;
- we start an entire new category management project.

Any of these routes forward at contract renewal could be entirely appropriate depending upon the circumstances; the point here is that we avoid doing nothing but rather we take a decision in good time so we are in control of the process and therefore the decision is the most appropriate one.

Contract management is also about making sure a contract continues to work as needed. Things change and what we might need or want can change; so too could the marketplace or the world around us. Part of the role of the category manager as we move into Stage 5 of our process is to keep a watchful eye on the changing needs of the business, stakeholders and the changing market or environment within which we operate. Where things change around us we may need to act and agree a change to what we source or the relationship we have with a supplier. This might even necessitate a change to a contract. For example, imagine if a change in legislation meant that one of our contract terms was inadequate. We would need to agree a change to this contract with the supplier. Clearly changing a contract, and what was previously agreed, is by mutual agreement and could instigate a whole new negotiation.

There are various systems out there that can help with contract management ranging from maintaining a simple supplier calendar (a calendar with all the contract expiry dates entered on it) to more sophisticated systems online or modules within an ERP (Enterprise Resource Planning) or eSourcing platform.

## Chapter 7 summary

Recap on the key points from this chapter:

1 The fourth stage within the category management process is *implementation* and is concerned with all the activities and actions required to realize our approved and signed-off sourcing strategy. As we begin this stage, we are moving into a new phase within our category management project and so we may require a change to our team.

2 *Implementation* begins by developing a detailed implementation plan for the specific activities required to roll out our sourcing strategy. This builds upon the high-level implementation plan we developed as part of defining our sourcing strategy. High-level implementation planning is most effective when the plan is developed by the category team so all team members are aligned and contribute. Here 'brown-paper planning' can help.

3 To implement our sourcing strategy and realize our plan we need effective project management to manage to our plan, manage the

people who are involved or need to know, and ensure project performance. Good project management, supported by the sponsor's involvement, is essential.

4 Change management is a core consideration within category management. Implementing a new category strategy might demand significant change within a business and this change is likely to fail unless the human aspects of change management are understood and planned for. As humans we naturally fear and resist change, whether consciously or not. Research suggests that an individual faced with a major change transitions through a series of identifiable steps in order to accept and be comfortable with the change. By understanding these we can help those involved to move through the change and we can design an implementation approach to enable this, perhaps involving those affected and helping create a 'felt need' for the change through good communication and executive support.

5 Implementing our sourcing strategy may require us to run some sort of competitive market exercise using a traditional tender approach or an RFP or RFQ, either via documents or online. These tools provide the means to approach a market with either an outline or fully formed set of requirements to solicit either ideas and proposals, or firm quotations from suppliers. The use of these approaches is slightly different within the public sector and forms part of defined contracting processes that comply with the prevailing legislation.

6 Another tool that can help implement a sourcing strategy is an e-auction, where suppliers bid online for what they will provide a defined lot of goods or services for, typically for a set contract duration, and bid against each other in real time. Prices fall and the auction closes with a winner or winners who will get the business or proceed to a final stage depending upon the auction rules. E-auctions are suitable for some categories, but not all and portfolio analysis and day one analysis can help us determine suitability.

7 Implementation and realizing the sourcing strategy may involve selecting one or more suppliers. The process of supplier selection is 'funnel-like' where we might pre-qualify suppliers who meet certain minimum requirements from a marketplace, then progressively reduce the list of suppliers as we conduct a series of evaluations and ultimately negotiations. Once again there are differences within this step in the public sector.

8 Negotiation with suppliers is also part of implementation where we are seeking to agree the best deal considering the nature and type of relationship we need with the supplier for the future.

9 The *implementation* stage culminates in putting some form of contractual arrangement in place with the supplier(s). Contract planning is an integral part of category management and it is essential that for whatever contracting approach we use that the outputs from our category management project defined in our sourcing strategy are incorporated so the contract becomes a key instrument to realize the sourcing strategy ongoing. When we put a contract in place it is important to consider exit planning and then once the contract is executed ensure ongoing arrangements for contract management are in place.

# Stage 5: Improvement

In this chapter we will explore the fifth and final stage – the improvement stage. We will examine how implementation turns into improvement and how our focus needs to shift to supplier relationships and management. We will explore the category manager's role to continue to work on the category and to monitor the ongoing effectiveness of the sourcing strategy now implemented, identifying when it is appropriate to revisit the category and perhaps even start the process again.

Pathway question addressed in this chapter:

**11** How can I effectively implement new sourcing strategies so they become a reality and we realize the benefits?

**12** Once improvements are implemented, how do I continue to drive them?

**13** How should I manage those suppliers who are important to my business?

## The implementation toolkit

As we saw in Chapter 7, there comes a point towards the end of Stage 4, implementation, when the change can be regarded as complete. Often, this is not easily recognizable. Once the main effort associated with implementation is over, it is usually some time before the effects are seen and the benefits realized. By this time the category team is less in demand and its members have probably begun to move to other projects.

Remember it is incumbent on the team leader or category manager to set a time to mark the completion of implementation and celebrate success with the team. Beyond this stage, while the contribution of team members will

**FIGURE 8.1**   Stage 5: Improvement

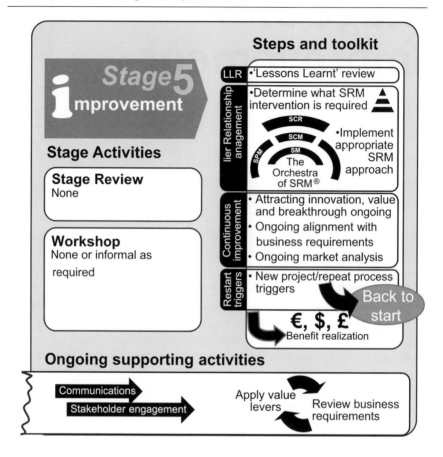

occasionally be required, it is the category manager who largely leads and manages improvement. Before Stage 4, implementation, is deemed to be complete, the team should agree how they will continue to support the category manager, while considering what the organization wants them to do elsewhere. Options range from maintaining an ongoing involvement, with periodic team meetings and participation in supplier reviews, or stepping down and assuming the role of stakeholder to be engaged by the category manager on an ongoing basis. That brings us to the activities that continue into Stage 5 (see Figure 8.1).

As we saw earlier, some activities run throughout the entire category management process. It is therefore essential in improvement that the category manager continues to embrace them and actively ensure that they continue to happen. They include:

- the ongoing search for value, using the value levers concept;
- refinement and optimization of business requirements;
- communication and stakeholder engagement.

These are complemented in Stage 5 by some specific improvement activities focused around maximizing the possible value and the innovation in relation to what the market can offer, and the changing needs of the business. Improvement can also be driven by the effectiveness of the relationship with the supply base, and so in this stage it is necessary to identify and implement the required relationships and put in place arrangements to turn them into reality.

# The concept of continuous improvement

This stage is about making sure the changes that have been implemented remain in place and are appropriate. It is about preventing drift back to the old state and about continually looking for ways to improve the overall sourcing arrangements.

Once a step-change breakthrough improvement has been achieved and implemented, it is important not to simply stop, or all the hard work to get to the new change may be lost. For example, consider a new sourcing strategy that involves a switch of supplier, and where there has been intensive stakeholder engagement and communications across the business to ensure everyone has switched over to the new supplier. If managing compliance with the new arrangements suddenly ceases and if the relationship with the previous supplier was well established, it won't take people long to drift back to the previous supplier, using, as justification, any problem or issue encountered with the new arrangement. The improvement stage is not just about maintaining compliance; it is, as its name suggests, also about improvement. A breakthrough step change takes you to a new, dramatically improved position, but it needs to be maintained, and there are always further improvements that can still be made. Worse, if you allow yourself to stand still your competitors and the world around you will soon overtake you – meaning you start to go backwards in real terms.

This process of continually finding improvements is not a single time-bound activity. It should be ongoing and should continue until the time when it is appropriate to review the entire category sourcing arrangements and begin the process of category management once again. As we saw earlier in this book, the category management process could be regarded as circular and involves periods of working through the process with a cross-functional team (perhaps taking nine to 12 months), moving into periods of continuous improvement while managing the new arrangements (perhaps lasting two to three years) and then beginning another cycle of category management. Eventually a state of category maturity is reached that sometimes allows the duration of the *improvement* stage to be extended, since there is no need to start another category management cycle.

Continuous improvement can relate to value, quality, performance, price, process efficiency, innovation, and indeed any of the factors described within the business requirements and value levers. The concept of continuous improvement was mainstream during the 1980s, with philosophies from practitioners such as Joseph Juran, Genichi Taguchi and W Edwards Deming (considered by many to be the father of modern quality control). It became the subject of many management books. We learned that 'kaizen' was Japanese for 'improvement', and this 1950s philosophy could be applied to the workplace to improve all functions of a business. As the 1990s unfolded, 'total quality management' (as used by NASA) originated in Japan and soon became adopted and adapted as the Malcolm Baldrige National Quality Award in the United States and the European Foundation for Quality Management. Then BPR (business process re-engineering) appeared and continued the quest for improvement.

It is interesting to note that many of these improvement philosophies originated from the need to improve quality, and were largely first used to do so. Quality practitioners would argue that good quality meant considering all aspects of the organization. During the 1980s these concepts were often regarded by organizations as the responsibility of the quality department, with the possible exception of a few forward thinkers. As the years have passed, many of these philosophies have come to be relevant to all functions in an organization and regarded as general improvement approaches rather than those with only a specific quality focus.

Today the concept of improvement continues but is now incorporated within improvement philosophies such as 'lean' (developed around the Toyota production system) and the identification of ways to improve overall customer value and reduce waste. In category management it is embedded as an integral part of Stage 5 but is a core philosophy throughout the entire process. Any and all of the approaches mentioned are relevant, and training · in Lean or Six Sigma principles adds much value to the category manager's skill set.

Within category management, 'continuous improvement' is based around the principle of continually evaluating and analysing our position, identifying opportunities for improvement and designing and implementing the appropriate changes in response. The result is a steady series of small incremental steps that not only prevent an otherwise downward trend in overall performance through inaction, but which positively and steadily increase overall performance and widen the gap between what you do and how things would be if you did nothing.

# CAPTURING LEARNINGS

## Lessons learned review

This step is an *Activity* and is *Optional*

If organizations took the time to review major projects, identify the lessons learned along the way and share them far and wide to help others, I'm certain that the industrialized world would take a major leap forward. The reality is that organizations are, on the whole, very poor at this. When a project is complete, there is often little requirement or appetite to look back and think about what has happened. Some organizations that recognize the value of learning from experience make post-project reviews mandatory, but without such an edict it is often too easy to move on and not look back. Even if a review has taken place, the findings and learnings can only benefit others if they are shared. Sharing knowledge in organizations presents many challenges too, and even if there is a system for the sharing of knowledge, actually getting others to take the time to absorb it is incredibly difficult.

That said, conducting an LLR (lessons learned review) is an essential step in a single category management project. If it is well managed as part of a bigger programme, it can benefit the whole category management process. There are four things that need to happen in order for LLRs to be successful and add value. These are:

- keep it simple;
- conduct the LLR as a team;
- share the knowledge;
- act on the knowledge.

The last two points require some creative thinking. Sharing the knowledge means the results of the LLR should, of course, be communicated in some way. Perhaps this might mean posting it on a department or project intranet site – but this is likely to result in just a handful of people taking an interest. However, there is much more that could be done. For instance:

- Find one or two key learning points and develop ways to share them, eg in the form of a case study or a 'We've completed our project' newsletter.
- Identify other category teams that might benefit from the knowledge, and arrange to go and talk to them or give a presentation.
- If there is a purchasing group meeting or a regular summit, see if there is scope for a slot on the agenda to talk through what you have learned. Often some of the best learning comes from listening to others' experience.

This last method is by far the most powerful, and when those who have completed something can talk about their experience, successes and how they overcame difficulty, it tends to register much more deeply in those who are perhaps yet to follow the same path.

The format for an LLR is straightforward, and the output should be a simple document with key findings as bullets. A suggested format is:

- What did we achieve?
- What worked well?
- Even more effective if...?
- Key learnings summarized.

Remember that if we don't make time to review what we did and what we learned, we will not benefit from improved knowledge and be more effective next time; and if we don't find a way to share what we learned, we are impeding the overall effectiveness of the organization and its ability to deliver category management. One short meeting, some inward reflection and some creative communications are all that it takes. Knowledge is power!

# SUPPLIER RELATIONSHIP MANAGEMENT

This step is a collection of *Activities* and *Tools*. How *Essential* this step is depends upon the category and the degree and nature of supplier importance

Supplier Relationship Management (SRM) is an entire topic all of its own so it is not possible to do justice to it within a single section; however, a summary of the key topics and considerations is provided below. My other book *Supplier Relationship Management,* also published by Kogan Page, expands this topic in full and provides the complete suite of methodologies, tools and techniques. It has been written to work together with this book as part of a complete sourcing approach so securing a copy is recommended.

The term SRM seems to carry different meanings depending who is using it. This is perhaps because for any given organization, different treatments across the vast range of suppliers are needed according to how important each supplier is to the firm. SRM seems to have become a term coined to describe each and every one of these approaches in one way or another. Clarity in understanding and defining SRM comes by considering it as the *overarching strategic philosophy and framework* under which different types of supplier intervention across the entire supply base exist. SRM is therefore defined as:

> The overarching strategic approach to determine and implement different supplier-based interventions, including the development of collaborative relationships with the critical few suppliers who can make the greatest difference; prioritized against available resources, appropriate across an entire supply base to maximize value to the organization, reduce supply chain risk and enable the organization to achieve its goals and enhance value to the end customer.

SRM is about determining *what* the organization needs from its supply base in order to realize strategic goals, with *whom* we need a relationship or some sort of intervention in order to realize strategic goals, and *how* we will deploy specific interventions with the supply base to achieve strategic goals.

A well-executed SRM approach can provide competitive advantage, fuel growth and brand development, reduce cost, improve efficiency and effectiveness and reduce supply-side risk or at least help understand it so it can be mitigated. However SRM is not something that can simply be 'bolted on', nor can it exist as a single step within our category management process. It is an organization-wide philosophy that needs to be embraced by all if it is to deliver these benefits. Just as for category management, in order for SRM to have a purpose and to contribute effectively to organizational success it requires wider terms of reference and cross-functional participation. Remember our *sourcing, satisfying and strategy* model from Chapter 2 and how we explored how value flows from suppliers through our organization to our customers, being transformed by us in some way? Well, if SRM is to have any significant impact then it must also be an integral component in the way the organization connects its *sourcing* with the way it *satisfies* its end customers and the overarching *strategy* of the firm. The relationship between these three is fundamental if an organization wishes to gain competitive advantage by capitalizing on the potential that resides in the supply base. SRM helps to drive a convergence of *sourcing* and *satisfying* customers and *strategy,* and when our category management strategies are aligned with this convergence we are doing true strategic sourcing.

Just as there are some basic principles that make category management effective (our four pillars from Chapter 2) so there are also basic principles for SRM. These include are adopting an 'end-to-end' value focus and working cross-functionally with the wider organization. Notice some similarity to category management? Organizations sometimes regard category management and SRM as separate initiatives, but this mindset can be self-limiting as both initiatives in an organization need to be integrally connected if strategic procurement is to be truly effective. It is for this reason that SRM is included in category management. Its position here in Stage 5 is because this is the point in the process where the nature and effectiveness of the engagement with the supply base become of most importance. In practice, however, SRM doesn't necessarily 'follow on' at the end of category management; instead it can be entirely appropriate to start considering the nature of relationship we might need with our suppliers much earlier. It could even be necessary to stop our category management project altogether and switch to SRM, for example if our data gathering, insights and analysis reveal we have little opportunity to gain leverage in the market for our category, but rather the greatest opportunity is from developing an existing relationship.

So category management and SRM need to be integrated to be effective. SRM can follow, be in parallel to, or even precede, category management, yet these are also very distinct concepts. This is because they relate to separate dimensions of our purchasing function and supply chain. Until now this book has focused on categories of spend and indeed early on we saw how crucial

**FIGURE 8.2**   Categories vs suppliers

| | Supplier A | Supplier B | Supplier C | Supplier D | Supplier E | Supplier F |
|---|---|---|---|---|---|---|
| Category 1 | | ● | | ● | | |
| Category 2 | ● | | | | | |
| Category 3 | | ● | ● | | ● | |
| Category 4 | | ● | | | ● | |
| Category 5 | | | | | | ● |
| Category 6 | | ● | | | | |

the category-based perspective is to leverage value by considering the entirety of the organization's spend in a defined area mapped against how the marketplace is organized. Here our perspective shifts to look at specific suppliers or the supply base, who may provide many products or services and therefore may operate in more than one marketplace and so may supply across multiple categories (Figure 8.2).

Our approach to managing our supply base needs to consider all our categories and the suppliers involved, and determine interventions to manage each supplier across all categories they provide at an organization-wide level. In Figure 8.2 supplier B appears to be a key supplier across a range of categories. This perspective helps us see and use our full leverage. Imagine if category 6 was a concern to us and our analysis placed the category in *critical* in the portfolio analysis matrix and *proprietary* in the day one matrix. If our perspective remains only at the single category level we have no good leverage and are potentially at risk; however, looking at the total business with this supplier we are potentially in a very strong position, which allows us to use leverage elsewhere to reduce our exposure for category 6.

The need to maintain both a supplier and a category perspective has implications for the way purchasing functions are structured and organized. Until now we have described the concept of a category manager, or similar purchasing individual, with defined responsibility across the company for the sourcing of a specific category (or categories). This single point of category ownership or coordination maximizes benefit and increases the likelihood of success, involving others within the wider business as appropriate. The same applies for the way suppliers are managed, coordinated and interfaced with. Where a supplier has multiple relationships across a single business, this wastes resource on both sides and affords the supplier a potential 'divide and conquer' advantage. Therefore a single point of coordination for key supplier relationships is essential in order to dramatically sharpen the focus for those relationships that are important. It can also ensure the engagement with the supplier is on our terms or at least mutually agreed terms. It does not, however, follow that an army of staff is required to carry out these separate category and Supplier Relationship Management activities; instead success here is about clarity of roles and responsibilities, recognized business wide. In practice it often makes sense for a specific category manager to have responsibilities for certain related supplier relationships. Similarly category projects and SRM projects should be overseen by a common governance approach; we'll cover how this works in the next chapter.

---

**CASE STUDY**    How one company competed against itself

---

The marketing category 'television media' is about the purchase of advertising airtime on commercial television channels. Prevailing market dynamics and demand largely influence price; an ad during the Super Bowl is a different proposition to something late at night on a specialist cable channel. Media are often bought as part of a bundled package for an advertising campaign from a marketing agency. However, good category management would seek to unbundle this and treat it as a stand-alone category facing out to a specific marketplace. A global, multi-brand company implementing category management did just this and in doing so discovered that each of the individual brand teams were sourcing from the same suppliers, either directly or via an agency. On the face of it, this seemed perfectly logical; however, with no cross-business supplier management it was apparent that the individual brand teams were, without realizing it, competing against each other for airtime and in doing so driving up prices. As more effective sourcing strategies were implemented resulting from category management, so too were arrangements to manage and coordinate the supplier's cross-brand team, which eliminated this issue.

---

# Introducing the Orchestra of SRM

Within the umbrella concept of SRM, there are different types of supplier or supply base interventions that could be put in place, each serving a different purpose and relevant according to the degree and nature of supplier importance. There is a further concept that helps understand SRM and how it works together with category management and that is the way all the different components of SRM work together. The philosophy of SRM means it is not something that can follow a linear process or a defined series of steps as we find in category management. Indeed, across the plethora of what is written about SRM, it seems there is a common tendency to attempt to squeeze it into some sort of step-by-step approach, possibly explaining the apparent general lack of consistency or agreement as to what SRM actually is and perhaps why programmes can fail to deliver the results needed. The problem here is SRM is not a step-by-step journey to arrive at the ideal supplier relationship. Such a mindset works against us because every supplier is different, and those that are important are important for different reasons, each requiring a unique relationship or series of interventions according to our circumstances, theirs and what each party needs. One supplier may just need some compliance monitoring, whilst another might warrant a full strategic collaborative relationship. One may need intervention to minimize risk, another might hold latent value if we can work with them to unlock it, and so on.

SRM is in fact like an orchestra (Figure 8.3). Each of the sections of an orchestra plays when needed according to the piece of music, all working in unison and taking their lead from a single conductor. Each component of the orchestra of SRM – the areas of focus, the different approaches and interventions – must play as and when needed according to what is appropriate for the circumstances, the current environment and the point in time with the conductor providing a governance framework that guides how the various interventions come in or drop back. Each important supplier has its own piece of music and the melody changes constantly. The Orchestra of SRM has five sections; these are:

- Supplier management (SM);
- Supplier performance measurement (SPM);
- Supplier improvement and development (SI&D);
- Supply chain management (SCM);
- Strategic collaborative relationships (SCR).

SPM, SI&D and SM focus on the direct contractual relationship with a discrete number of immediate important suppliers. SCM considers the entire supply chain beyond the immediate contractual relationship and perhaps even follows the chain further on toward the end customer. SI&D tends to

**FIGURE 8.3**   The Orchestra of SRM

focus on immediate suppliers but could also focus on entire supply chains, and SCR is the most strategic component here and arguably the one that can potentially unlock the greatest value with a focus on a handful of immediate suppliers that are of strategic importance. These discrete approaches are not mutually exclusive. In other words SRM doesn't mean we have to choose one or another; it is possible and often necessary to adopt more than one type of intervention. For example a supplier may require an SM approach but may also need SPM with some SI&D. An explanation of each of these different forms of supply base intervention is given over coming sections, but first we shall explore how we determine which one(s) we might need to deploy.

# Determining what supplier intervention is required

Some suppliers are more important than others and therefore warrant different types of intervention or relationship. At the heart of SRM is the concept that those suppliers who are important in some way warrant special attention. Generally, for any given organization, as importance increases the number of suppliers becomes fewer. This is most commonly represented as a pyramid (Figure 8.4). Organizations of a certain size can usually boast

**FIGURE 8.4** Supplier importance and the different types of interventions

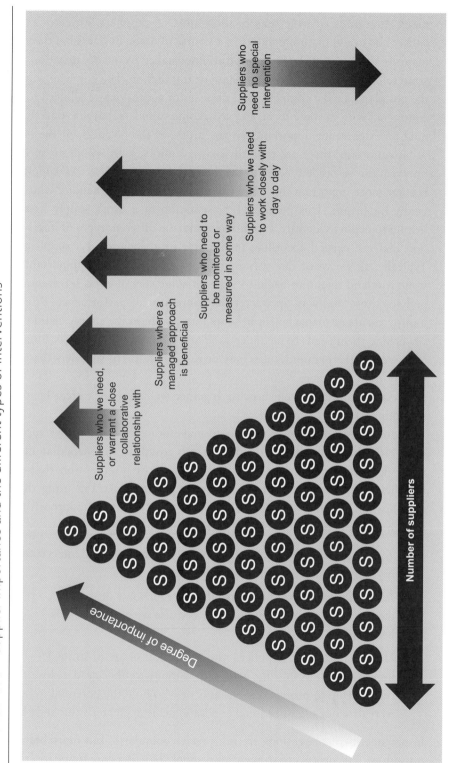

Suppliers who need no special intervention

Suppliers who we need to work closely with day to day

Suppliers who need to be monitored or measured in some way

Suppliers where a managed approach is beneficial

Suppliers who we need, or warrant a close collaborative relationship with

Degree of importance

Number of suppliers

many thousands or even tens of thousands of suppliers. Organizations collect and accumulate suppliers in the course of doing business but the vast majority of these will be of little or no importance to the organization beyond fulfilling a simple order, purchase or transaction. The guy who waters the pot plants or the company that disposes of general waste all need to be contracted with in some form, and so become suppliers, but are unlikely to hold any significant importance to the future of the business. At the level of 'unimportant' there are typically many vendors, with whom no special intervention is needed beyond the immediate transaction. As suppliers become more important they diminish in number to just a handful who are vitally important. This pyramid representation of a firm's supply base is helpful to begin to identify, and differentiate, the different types of intervention that are needed according to how far up the pyramid a supplier is. Typically, as we work our way up, suppliers become more important in some way and therefore begin to warrant some sort of extra intervention; perhaps those mid-way up warrant measurement of performance, driving improvements or management in some form, perhaps the supply chain that sits behind them needs to be understood and managed more closely. Finally, at the top of the pyramid, there may be just a handful of suppliers that are so important that there is good reason to attempt to build a close collaborative relationship with them because together we can unlock great benefits for both parties.

Supplier segmentation enables us to make practical sense of our supply base. Here the supply base is divided up into groups of suppliers that allow us to determine and apply the different types of intervention that are beneficial and worthwhile for each group (Figure 8.5). I'm using three classifications as this seems to be the most widely adopted approach (although there are many models and variants out there), these are:

- *Transactional suppliers.* Suppliers with whom no special intervention beyond the immediate transaction is needed.

- *Important Suppliers.* Suppliers who warrant some degree of management or intervention either because we need to or it is beneficial to do so.

- *Strategic Suppliers.* Suppliers who are critical or are of strategic importance to us in some way, with whom we either need a close relationship to protect our business or who hold the potential to help us realize our organizational goals and achieve greater value together.

In practice the demarcations are not precise boundaries but more blurred transitions. The process of segmenting a supply base is a core foundation for

**FIGURE 8.5** The supplier segmentation pyramid

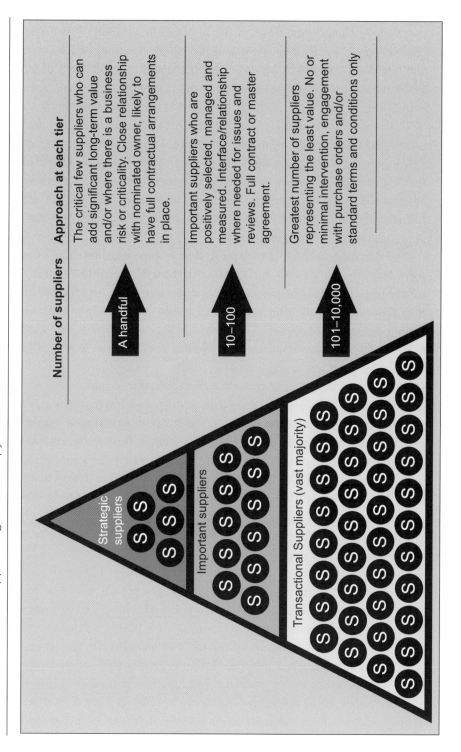

Number of suppliers

Approach at each tier

A handful

The critical few suppliers who can add significant long-term value and/or where there is a business risk or criticality. Close relationship with nominated owner, likely to have full contractual arrangements in place.

10–100

Important suppliers who are positively selected, managed and measured. Interface/relationship where needed for issues and reviews. Full contract or master agreement.

101–10,000

Greatest number of suppliers representing the least value. No or minimal intervention, engagement with purchase orders and/or standard terms and conditions only

Strategic suppliers

Important suppliers

Transactional Suppliers (vast majority)

SRM within an organization. It is concerned with determining which suppliers are important through the application of a set of pre-defined criteria, why they are important and therefore what sort of intervention and relationship would be necessary or beneficial. In our orchestra of SRM, segmentation composes the music we will play with each piece being a unique arrangement specifically for an individual supplier relationship.

Therefore within category management if the organization has already established SRM, has segmented the supply base and is managing the supply base according to this, then our objective is to identify how any supplier(s) that we appoint to deliver our category strategy fits into this established approach. If, however, the organization has no such regime then our objective is to identify how the relationship(s) need to be managed and put the appropriate interventions in place.

One common mistake is to believe that a close relationship is needed more often than it actually is. This is partly because we all like to feel that we are responsible for managing the suppliers that are a bit more strategic than those others look after and partly because suppliers do a remarkably good job at convincing us this is how it should be. It is the supplier's job to make us feel they are important, even when they are not. You may have experienced suppliers saying things like, 'We're working together in partnership, right?' or, 'in the spirit of our collaborative relationship'.

Sometimes these things are even true, but often such statements are conditioning aimed at changing the buyer's mindset so that time is found for meetings and discussions, all with the sole aim of further embedding the supplier into the organization. Yet *we* decide where we need a supplier relationship and, assuming willingness on the supplier's part and objectivity on our part, where we will make one happen. In any organization there is only so much resource to manage suppliers so it is important to direct this where it will have the greatest impact. So here we need a planned approach to determine the nature of the relationship we will have with any given supplier. Without this, organizations would spend time and energy having all sorts of interactions and engagements with suppliers, but not all would be to the benefit of the organization. As the buyer we should choose, and be in control of, the nature and extent of the relationships we have with our suppliers. Indeed in a typical organization, for the vast majority of purchases, we would be unlikely to need any relationship beyond a transactional engagement with an 'arm's length' contract. Putting effort into relationships with suppliers is therefore something that only applies to a small number of suppliers with whom the right relationship can benefit both parties and create and sustain ongoing value improvement.

How we manage a supplier relationship, and the degree and nature of intervention needed are determined by supplier importance. There are many factors that drive supplier importance and these are summarized under five key headings that form a robust set of supplier segmentation criteria:

- Risk (of supply failure, delay, brand damage, loss of competitive advantage, price or cost hikes or quality risk).

- Difficulty (including market difficulty, complexity or inability to switch, proprietary nature of goods or services purchased or the supplier is part of our brand definition).

- Current importance (including spend, contractual commitments, operating locations, knowledge of our business or established relationships).

- Alignment (with our strategic goals, with policies, of ethics and beliefs, of culture and of ways or working).

- Future importance (our future spend or plans, supplier innovation, supplier's future direction and supplier's willingness to work more closely with us).

We can use these headings to determine *why* we need a relationship and this in turn shapes the nature of the relationship we need; for example if we are concerned there is risk of supplier failure for a given supplier then our response would be to implement interventions with that supplier to carefully monitor and manage what the supplier does. If we believe the supplier can bring unique innovation to the category that can create competitive advantage for us we might want to develop a close relationship with that supplier. However, before we consider *why* we might need a relationship, we should first consider *if* we need a relationship and here we turn to the analysis we carried out early on in our category management project, in particular portfolio analysis and supplier preferencing. Our earlier classifications within these two tools help us determine if a relationship is needed, but also help inform the nature of the potential relationship we might need. Using these two tools, together with the segmentation criteria above enable us to determine what type of intervention and how much we might need.

We start with our portfolio analysis insight from Stage 2 (Figure 8.6), but remember here we are taking a 'supplier perspective' and a supplier might provide a series of categories, so a combined view must be taken to determine the nature of the relationship required across all the categories they supply. If our category(s) sit in *leverage* then we have choice in the market, so we may not need any sort of relationship, but if we do it would most

**FIGURE 8.6**    Using portfolio analysis to help determine need for and
nature of a supplier relationship

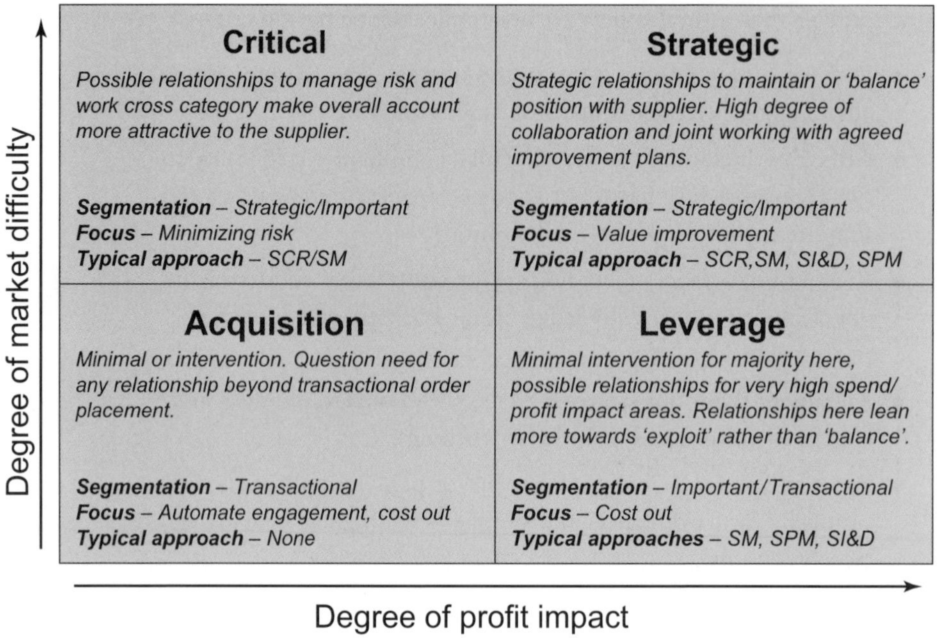

Degree of market difficulty

| Critical | Strategic |
|---|---|
| Possible relationships to manage risk and work cross category make overall account more attractive to the supplier. | Strategic relationships to maintain or 'balance' position with supplier. High degree of collaboration and joint working with agreed improvement plans. |
| **Segmentation** – Strategic/Important<br>**Focus** – Minimizing risk<br>**Typical approach** – SCR/SM | **Segmentation** – Strategic/Important<br>**Focus** – Value improvement<br>**Typical approach** – SCR,SM, SI&D, SPM |
| **Acquisition** | **Leverage** |
| Minimal or intervention. Question need for any relationship beyond transactional order placement. | Minimal intervention for majority here, possible relationships for very high spend/ profit impact areas. Relationships here lean more towards 'exploit' rather than 'balance'. |
| **Segmentation** – Transactional<br>**Focus** – Automate engagement, cost out<br>**Typical approach** – None | **Segmentation** – Important/Transactional<br>**Focus** – Cost out<br>**Typical approaches** – SM, SPM, SI&D |

Degree of profit impact

likely be around managing day-to-day activities to ensure compliance with a contract or monitoring performance. In *critical* however we may be at risk and so attempting to build a relationship with the supplier may be our only means to try and mitigate this. In *strategic* there is mutual dependency within a difficult market and perhaps great future potential and so this is the home ground for developing a collaborative relationship.

Portfolio analysis needs to be considered together with our supplier preferencing (Figure 8.7) as this helps us determine both supplier willingness and what sort of relationship we might need. It doesn't follow that just because we deem a relationship something we believe is necessary, the supplier shares this desire also. If we are in *development* or *core* then the supplier will most likely be receptive; however in *nuisance* or *exploitable* it is a different matter and we risk attempting to build a one-sided relationship that is not reciprocated by the supplier, or worse they pay lip service to it to create the illusion they are interested. There is little point in pursuing a long-term, strategic, collaborative relationship with a supplier that doesn't view our account in the same way.

**FIGURE 8.7** Relationship responses for portfolio analysis using supplier preferencing

Attractiveness of account

| **Development** | **Core** |
|---|---|
| **In Strategic**<br>• *Work to build relationship more and establish mutual dependency*<br>• *Encourage preferential access to new developments and consider growing business*<br>• *Try to establish supplier's motives for 'attractiveness' (check no hidden agendas)*<br>**In Critical**<br>• *Bundle with other spend to increase attractiveness more*<br>• *Pursue actions to get out of Critical*<br>**In Leverage**<br>• *Decide if you need a relationship* | **In Strategic**<br>• *Develop and strengthen relationship*<br>• *Joint improvement programmes*<br>• *Maintain balance*<br>• *See areas of mutual exclusivity for competitive advantage*<br>• *Maintain a watch on supplier's overall strategy and vision*<br>**In Critical**<br>• *Work with supplier to eliminate factors that put this in Critical*<br>• *Challenge the supplier hard*<br>**In Leverage**<br>• *Decide if you need a relationship* |
| **Nuisance** | **Exploitable** |
| **In Strategic**<br>• *Ensure contracts are in place and compliance with business requirements*<br>• *Monitor performance*<br>• *Establish alternative sources*<br>• *Change Nuisance factors*<br>**In Critical**<br>• *Change Nuisance factors*<br>• *Increase attractiveness through bundling with other spend*<br>• *Actions to get out of Critical*<br>**In Leverage**<br>• *Find another supplier* | **In Strategic**<br>• *Challenge the supplier as to why they are behaving in such a way*<br>• *Find another supplier*<br>**In Critical**<br>• *Establish why the supplier is able to exploit.*<br>• *Find out from the supplier if the behaviour is recognized and deliberate*<br>• *Actions to get out of Critical*<br>**In Leverage**<br>• *Find another supplier* |

Relative value of account

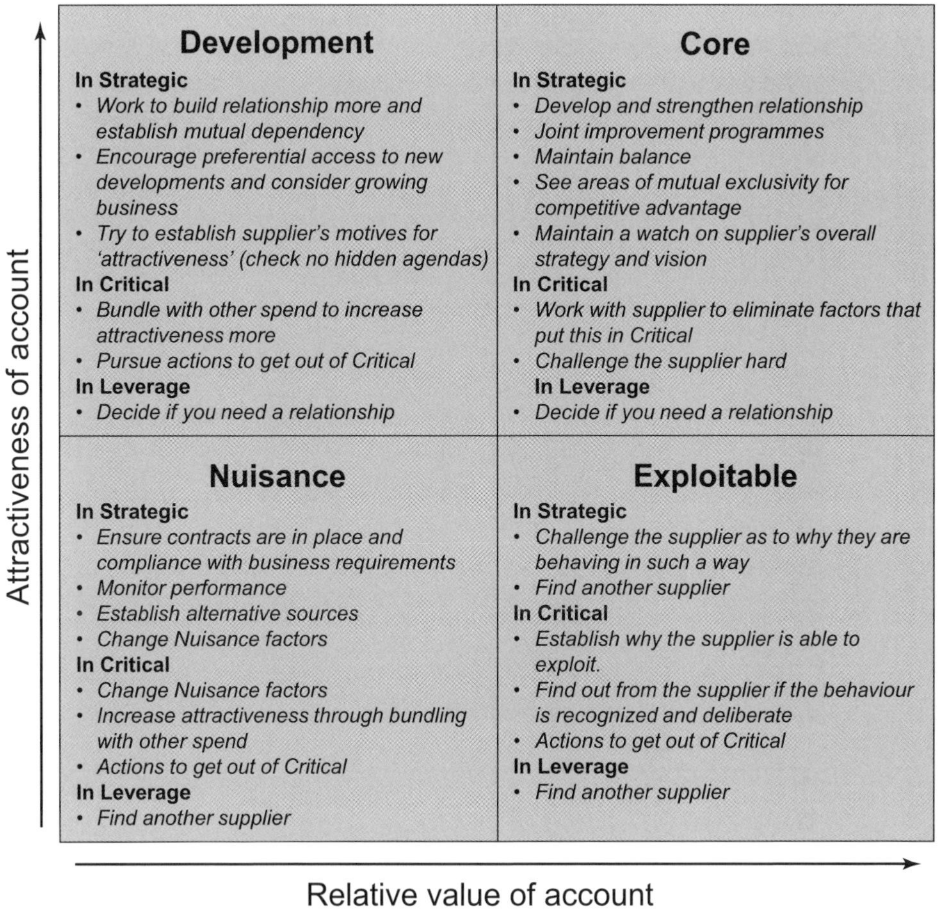

Figure 8.8 shows the combination of portfolio analysis and supplier pre-ferencing and the potential supplier willingness for a relationship.

One final note on segmentation concerns the qualification of suppliers. It would be folly to engage with a supplier without first establishing if they are suitable, reliable, legal and can do what they claim. Any well-developed organization will already do this to a greater or lesser degree. This might involve a simple check of financial standing before a new supplier is added to the purchase ledger; or it could involve a full quality, safety, and environ-mental assessment including a factory audit and taking references from other clients. The degree of qualification will vary according to what the

**FIGURE 8.8** Understanding supplier willingness using portfolio analysis and supplier preferencing

## Portfolio Analysis Quadrant

| | Acquisition | Leverage | Critical | Strategic |
|---|---|---|---|---|
| **High** | **Diluted** Supplier willing to go only so far to develop a relationship | **Willingness** Supplier willing to build a relationship but we don't need one as we are not dependent on them | **Willingness** High dependency on them and whilst supplier has power here they also need us | **Willingness** High dependency on both sides, both are willing to build a relationship |
| | **Diluted** Supplier wants to grow account but willing to go only so far to develop a relationship | **Willingness** Supplier willing to build a relationship but we don't need one as we are not dependent on them | **Willingness** Dependency on them and supplier has the power but yet they want to build a relastionship | **Willingness** We are dependent upon them and supplier wants to grow this account. |
| | **Misguided** Exploitative behaviour from the supplier will drive us to switch suppliers | **Misguided** Exploitative behaviour from the supplier will drive us to switch suppliers | **Opportunistic** We are dependent on them, supplier uninterested in us. Will seize exploitation opportunities | **Not fussed** We are dependent upon them, supplier doesn't need us. Will continue only so long as it works for them |
| **Low** | **No point** We don't need them, they are not interested in us | **No point** We don't need them, they are not interested in us | **Uninterested** We are dependent upon them but supplier doesn't need or want us | **Uninterested** We are dependent upon them but supplier doesn't need or want us |

Supplier's dependency upon us

Low — High

**Supplier Preferencing Positioning**
Core — Development — Exploitable — Nuisance

Our dependency upon supplier

organization does; for most, simple checks will be sufficient but if our business is making aircraft landing gear, then the quality and capability of the casting manufacturer will need intense verification. Qualification is also not a once-only activity and there may be a requirement for an ongoing evaluation process.

Traditional business structures might place this qualification activity within a quality or finance function; however, qualification approaches should be aligned with supplier segmentation and therefore the nature of the relationship to ensure full visibility of the entire supplier engagement and a single approach for coordinating supplier improvements. What this means in practice is a joint and aligned approach with wider business functions as appropriate and if purchasing can be part of the supplier audit it provides a great opportunity to gather intelligence about the supplier.

# Implementing the appropriate SRM approach(es)

Once we are clear about the degree and nature of importance for the suppliers of our category, we can identify how the suppliers should be managed and the appropriate interventions needed. Figure 8.9 shows the five components of SRM within the Orchestra of SRM and how they typically align with the different parts of a supply base represented in the segmentation pyramid. Note for each I have described the focus of the intervention which is with the immediate supplier for all but supply chain management which, as the name suggests, has its focus across the entire supply chain. It is entirely possible that the success of a category strategy might demand intervention beyond an immediate supplier, especially if there are CSR considerations or opportunities by optimizing logistics and flow of information or materials through the supply chain. I will cover each of the five types of intervention in turn.

**FIGURE 8.9**  The different components of SRM aligned to the supplier segmentation pyramid

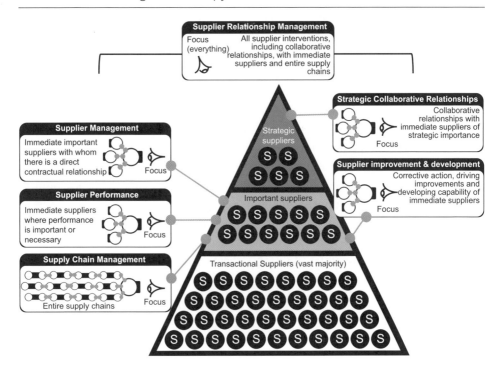

# Supplier management

Supplier management (SM) is relevant for most important suppliers and is concerned with the day-to-day management, interaction, relationship management, contract management, performance management, review and coordination of improvement initiatives. SM is how we ensure all the different engagements with them are effective and is therefore the core component within any SRM approach. Any important supplier will need to be managed in some way to ensure we secure everything we need from a supplier and respond to or prevent problems arising.

Just as in life with a close relationship with a partner, if one party fails to attend to the relationship, fails to communicate, doesn't make time to share then the relationship grows cold and perhaps even comes to an end. Relationships with important suppliers are no different and just because it is a commercial relationship it doesn't mean that we don't need to do anything beyond issuing purchase orders.

If *supplier preferencing* suggests the supplier sees us as an attractive account and one to be developed (*development* quadrant) we will receive their best attention from their best people, but if our account is not attractive, or even not as attractive as other accounts then we can easily end up in the *exploitable* quadrant. Orders will be fulfilled and business will continue as usual but here we simply will not get the most from the supplier. Perhaps other clients will get preference, and we may not benefit from new innovations or developments; furthermore the supplier may be less than interested in our future direction. Perhaps we may even face some assurance of supply risk here.

Irrespective of how the supplier might see us, if we have decided a supplier is important to us then they should be managed; however, supplier preferencing also helps us determine our response. In *development* or *core* our response is to take full advantage of the suppliers interest in us, whereas in *exploitable* we need to manage them hard, leaving them no room to perform averagely but setting high expectations and demanding excellence from them. We must be mindful though that this presents risk to us if the supplier sees us as unattractive, as our demands may simply be too much and the supplier may prefer to distance themselves.

Supplier management therefore has two purposes; to manage the relationship and interface with the supplier, and to provide a single point of coordination for interventions and initiatives. This includes five dimensions; they are:

- *Results*. Managing for results: having clarity regarding what good looks like with any given supplier and defining the outcomes and results we need so we can put in place the right mix of interventions to secure this.

- *Risk*. Supplier risk management: ongoing assessment of supplier and supply chain risk, keeping close to the supplier and watching for anything that might introduce new risk to us. Mitigation of risk where possible and practical, or developing contingency plans. Good ongoing intervention here can prevent us ending up in a position where we are surprised to learn our key supplier has ceased to trade overnight.

- *Review*. Supplier reviews: the right level and frequency of review meetings with discussion points structured around the specific interventions that have been deemed necessary. Meetings for meetings sake to comply with an arbitrary schedule can waste precious resource, but instead appropriate reviews, discussing the aspects of the interventions relevant to that supplier are essential. One supplier review might focus on reviewing performance and checking compliance, whilst another might be a collaborative review of joint progress towards an agreed improvement objective.

- *Contract*. Contract management: this is often overlooked, but once a contract has been agreed it doesn't stop there. Supplier management is about ensuring the supplier is delivering against what was agreed within a contract ongoing, and dealing with any exceptions, but it is also about ensuring the contract provision continues to be effective. Ultimately contract management demands mastery of the contract so we can determine when things need to change and be planning for contract expiry in good time so we retain the advantage.

- *Relationship*. Interface and relationship management: the final, and arguably the most crucial, component of supplier management is how the relationship should be managed. Effective supplier relationships don't just happen. They need to be defined, developed and stage managed, ideally as part of a wider organizational approach that includes the key stakeholders that also need to interface and interact with the supplier. Organizations that develop relationship strategies and do this well attend to a number of areas and put in place appropriate arrangements according to how important the supplier is that, together, form the Supplier Relationship Management approach. These might include one or more of the following:

- *Relationship strategy*. A definition of the strategy for the relationship, encapsulating the aims, objectives and general approach that will be used to achieve these.
- *Relationship charter*. A document that is shared and agreed with the supplier. Typically contains the elements of the relationship strategy that can be shared and a definition of the nature of the relationship and how it works.
- *'Face-off' points*. A defined map of 'who interfaces with whom and why' and nominated points of contact on both sides, as well as escalation routes and arrangements to share details of engagements elsewhere in the business. Here the 'face-off' points across the business should ideally be at a similar level; allowing suppliers' account managers to develop direct relationships with your CEO is often counterproductive.
- *Rules of engagement*. An agreed approach for how the two parties will meet, review progress, discuss and share what the respective businesses are doing and working on, including innovation or the need for specific innovations.
- *Relationship road map*. A definition of the common aims and objectives for the relationship and performance in general together with an agreed road map for the short to medium term. Here agreed supplier improvement initiatives would be included.

## Supplier performance measurement

Supplier performance measurement (SPM) is concerned with measuring supplier performance and perhaps coordinating improvement initiatives in response to findings. Within category management we may have need to measure aspects of the supplier's performance relating to their ongoing supply of the goods and services within the category. We may also have reason to measure how effective our relationship with the supplier is. SPM is therefore a supplier-wide approach that spans all the categories the supplier might provide, yet could include specific measures relating to a single category. Any category specific measurement should therefore be integrated with a broader SRM approach if one exists.

The first step within SPM is to consider what, if anything needs to be measured. This is informed by our previous work to segment our suppliers and determine who is important. However it doesn't follow that just because we have determined a supplier is important, we should embark on a quest of comprehensive measurement of that supplier. There are a number of challenges here that we should consider when putting SPM in place with a supplier:

- *Measuring too many or the wrong measures.* In purchasing we seem to be very keen to measure things but not always the right things. I have worked with companies who proudly show elaborate and complex supplier measurement systems that provide a raft of information about most things at the press of a button or the opening of a spreadsheet. Yet, the response to the question 'So what do you do with all of this?' often proves more difficult. The reality here is only a small proportion of organizations actually do anything meaningful with the results from such measurement, which puts in question the overall effectiveness and the reasons for doing it in the first place sometimes.

- *Only ever looking back.* If we measure suppliers' performance based upon what they have done, this may be useful and even necessary to check compliance, but if we are trying to reach some joint improvement target through collaboration it is less useful. It is like trying to climb a mountain but only measuring how many times you have stumbled so far or taken the wrong turn. It does not tell you how you are progressing towards your overall goal.

- *Measurement demands time and resource.* Any sort of performance measurement demands time and resources in some form, either on our side or with the supplier, and this will have a cost that we will end up paying somewhere.

- *Measurement drives behaviour.* Any measurement system that matters will drive behaviour around satisfying measures first and foremost. For example a SPM approach for a supplier that seeks to verify ongoing that contractual performance targets are being achieved will compel the supplier to organize themselves to satisfy the measures, not necessarily deliver the right outcomes. We can see an example of this in the UK healthcare profession – when you visit a hospital accident and emergency department the hospital must meet a government-set target of making sure you are seen within four hours. Most hospitals meet this target so their performance figures look OK, but in reality 'seen' means a quick check with a triage nurse who then sends you back to the waiting room where you could spend many more hours waiting. Arguably measurement that drives behaviour is OK if the measures reflect our requirements, but another consequence here is that targets that we will measure progress towards achieving frequently get set without really thinking about what has to happen to meet them.

Stipulating that 99.5 per cent of all deliveries must be received on time, in full and to specification might seem like a good number, but in practice might be unachievable without special arrangements and costly supplier buffer inventories. For an automotive company operating a just-in-time supply chain, the target and the measure ongoing would be essential, so they can demand suppliers organize themselves to meet this. But it could be less so for a project-based company where things can be flexed if needed, and it can be questioned whether this precise measure is actually helpful at all or just nice to have.

It is easy to confuse satisfying the requirements of a measurement regime with being effective at supplier measurement. So if we are to put good supplier measurement in place then we need to think carefully about what we measure, how much we measure and the targets or outcomes that we need to meet.

Although we talk of supplier 'measurement', generally we mean and need much more than this and there is much terminology in this space that can confuse so the following are the most common forms of measurement:

- *Measure.* A measure is when we compare and quantify something against a known standard such as 'My speed is 50km/hour' or 'I have 12 litres of fuel left in the tank.' This is useful up to a point but measures alone can require contextualizing to the situation or interpretation so as to be useful to us.

- *Indicator.* By combining more than one measure or adding some interpretation we can create indicators that are more useful, eg 'average fuel consumption has been 10km/litre'. Here the indicator combines measures and does some arithmetic to tell us something about what has happened but is still looking backwards (*lagging indicator*).

- *Leading indicator.* Perhaps more helpful is an indicator that helps predict what will happen, eg '126km until empty', which is using historical information to predict a future outcome. Clearly this prediction is imprecise as the indicator cannot take account of how we intend to drive or the terrain we will cover. Yet this indicator, constantly recalculating as we progress on our journey, could be essential to help us change how we will drive so as to ensure we reach the next gas station. Within supplier measurement it is the use of indicators that helps us focus in on how we can best judge how well the supplier is doing.

- *Performance indicator.* A 'performance indicator' is, as the name suggests, an indicator of performance.
- *KPI.* A 'Key Performance Indicator (KPI)' is one that is decided to be more important than the others.
- *Scorecard.* A scorecard is, as its name suggests, a summary of the current measures of supplier performance or our KPIs. It is a scorecard because, just as a scorecard is used in sport to enter scores, in business it is a card, sheet, book, spreadsheet or electronic measure; a place where a measure of supplier performance is entered.
- *SLA.* Service Level Agreements are also found in the world of SPM. These are not measures although are frequently referred to as if they are; instead an SLA is, as its name suggests, an agreement or a part of a broader contract or agreement where specific targets and basis for measurement with KPIs are defined.

When we are developing a supplier performance measurement approach the aim is to develop just a handful of KPIs that will help us manage and judge supplier performance. Having talked about how indicators are more useful than measures alone, measures are not excluded from that we can use to measure supplier performance, despite the terminology 'KPI'. In practice we might have a mix of direct measures and indicators. The point here is what we use is chosen carefully so as to provide the most meaningful outputs. A KPI could actually be regarded as a 'key performance indicator or measure depending upon what is needed', which is less catchy so let's just stick with the term 'KPI' but appreciate the subtlety of what this might include.

KPIs should be developed as if they are scarce, as if every KPI cost an enormous sum of money to have, so driving a mindset to find the few that will tell us the most. The ultimate test here is to ask, 'If we could have just one KPI what would it be?' A friend of mine runs a small restaurant and often, when he is away leaving his staff to run the restaurant, he will call his restaurant manager towards the end of the evening to find out how the evening has gone. There are many questions he could ask here, but he asks just one: 'How many covers have you done?' (a cover being each diner who eats a meal) and that single piece of information tells him everything he needs to know about how busy his restaurant has been and the likely revenue generated.

We determine what we should measure initially by referring back to our business requirements. Here our various statements of what we need and want for a category form the starting point for a set of KPIs and we just need to translate the relevant requirements into KPIs. Not all should be translated though; for example if we have an *assurance of supply* requirement that 'all suppliers for the category must be financially sound' then this is not something we would seek to measure ongoing with a supplier, but rather something that would form part of a pre-qualification and supplier selection process. Therefore to begin to develop our KPIs we must first extract from our business requirements those requirements that need some sort of ongoing measurement (Figure 8.10). These KPIs are also shaped by any wider requirements for the relationship with the supplier overall, informed by overall corporate goals, for example a policy for CSR set by the organization that all suppliers must meet.

So far we have considered what we might need to measure based upon our category business requirements. The second step is to ensure we match our measures and indicators to the reasons we have deemed a supplier to be important. This might mean supplementing our KPIs, or further developing those we have in response to this. For example if we have determined a supplier is important because they present risk to us, or we need to ensure contract compliance, then our KPIs should incorporate something that will help monitor risk and day-to-day performance ongoing. If a supplier is

**FIGURE 8.10** How KPIs are informed and developed

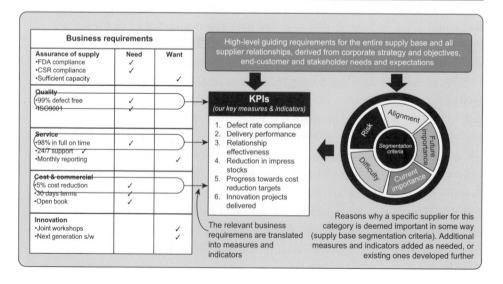

important because they have a unique capability that we believe will help us develop a competitive advantage then we should be measuring how we are jointly progressing towards a mutually agreed goal that will benefit us both. These dimensions informing our KPIs might not necessarily be found within the category of business requirements and it is here that we see the need to ensure a measurement approach considers both what the organization needs for the category but also for the supplier considering their entire engagement with us.

Most SPM systems typically involve some sort of supplier scorecard. The most effective scorecards are in fact quite short, containing only the essential KPIs that help us judge how we are achieving a given outcome; Figure 8.11 gives an example. You may have head the term 'balanced scorecard' which comes from the work of Kaplan and Norton (1996) in the nineties and suggests an approach to measurement that uses more than financial measures alone but rather strikes a balance across all of the measures of what drives value. Effective SPM should not only be balanced but needs to be a business-wide measurement approach measuring how a supplier is contributing to what the business needs overall, involving the supplier as appropriate. Again if we are developing our KPIs from our business requirements then we have already done the hard work here and what we measure should naturally be balanced as it will reflect what the business needs and wants from the category and supplier. KPIs that look back will always be needed but KPIs based around working towards a future goal can be very powerful and no matter what the measurement approach is, it should be developed so it fosters positive behaviour rather than meeting targets.

# Driving supplier improvements and developments

Supplier improvement and development (SI&D) is concerned with supplier-specific interventions to drive some sort of improvement or develop supplier capability. Initiatives here might range from simple corrective action to joint initiatives where parties collaborate to reach a new goal. In category management and SRM there are a number of reasons why we might need to drive an improvement or supplier development. Clearly if we are managing and measuring a supplier who is underperforming then we need to address this and resolve the issue, initially perhaps seeking an improvement or fix from the supplier to correct the problem, perhaps also some action to prevent it happening again, but ultimately, if we cannot resolve the issue we might end

**FIGURE 8.11** An example supplier scorecard

## Supplier Scorecard – For *Entreprise Gadget Logiciel, France*

| Lagging measures or KPIs | Result area and information source | Target | Q1 | Q2 | Q3 | Q4 |
|---|---|---|---|---|---|---|
| **Safety** – Lost Time Injury Frequency Rate | Number of incidents or near misses at supplier, with product or during delivery | Zero | 0 | 0 | 1 | 0 |
| **Assurance of supply** – Delivery on time, in full, in specification (DOTIFIS) | DOTIFIS report from ERP goods receipt + Internal rejections | 98% | 98% | 100% | 99% | 92% |
| **Relationship performance** – delivery of actions, support and communication, | Stakeholder survey results, complaints from stakeholders | 90% Very satisfied | 90% | 100% | 95% | 82% |
| Leading measures or KPIs | Result area and information source | Target | Q1 | Q2 | Q3 | Q4 |
| **Growth and innovation** – supplier contribution to business growth | Number new ideas delivered and total delivered value for both parties from them | 2 ideas €50k/idea | 0 ideas €0k/idea | 3 ideas €78k/idea | 2 ideas €10k/idea | 2 ideas €60k/idea |
| **Waste reduction** – to meet corporate waste minimization goal | Production scrap rates, energy usage, packaging volumes and assessment | 2% | 5% | 4.5% | 4.2% | 3.4% |
| **CSR goals and compliance** – To meet all supply chain CSR policies within 2 years | Audit reports | 100% in 2 years | 78% | 82% | 82% | 82% |

up exiting the relationship and finding a new supplier. We might also need some intervention where we see an opportunity for an improved outcome through development of the supplier or our relationship with them, either as a one-off or ongoing. Here we are not fixing a problem, but unlocking new benefit, perhaps collaboratively with the supplier. Looking back to the outputs from our *value levers* in Stage 1, if we have identified potential sources of value by using levers such as *improve relationship, performance development* or *seek innovation* then these begin to point towards intervention with a specific supplier to achieve this. Reasons for intervention here might include:

*Supplier improvement (reactive)*

- fix a supplier-related problem;
- prevent the problem reoccurring;
- reduce or eliminate a known risk;
- reduce cost;
- improve process effectiveness or efficiency;
- improve performance.

*Supplier development (proactive)*

- develop capability;
- innovate;
- develop a new product or service;
- create a new differentiator;
- increase market penetration;
- enter new markets;
- release new value that benefit both parties.

It doesn't follow that just because we have a need for some sort of supplier improvement or development, that the supplier will necessarily be willing. Perhaps they will respond to a performance issue, but what if we determine that we want to work collaboratively with a certain supplier to find new competitive advantage but they are not so interested, or worse they claim to be enthusiastic but don't really engage. Here, once again, we use *portfolio analysis* and *supplier preferencing* to understand the situation, determine our course of action and anticipate that of the supplier (Figure 8.12). If our category sits in *leverage* but is *core* business to the supplier then we simply seek to drive in an improvement with the supplier, giving them an ultimatum

**FIGURE 8.12** Portfolio analysis and supplier preferencing to determine how we approach a supplier improvement scenario

## Portfolio Analysis Quadrant

|  |  | Acquisition | Leverage | Critical | Strategic |  |  |
|---|---|---|---|---|---|---|---|
| Dependence upon customer | High | **Correct**<br>Corrective and reventative action as needed to issues only | **Improve**<br>Drive improvements. Agree continuous improvement objectives | **Balance**<br>Keep supplier interested, encourage improvements. Build attractiveness and create dependency | **Develop**<br>Ongoing collaboration and agreed programme of improvement and mutual development | Core | Supplier Preferencing Positioning |
|  |  | **Correct**<br>Corrective and preventative action as needed to issues only | **Improve**<br>Drive improvements. Agree continuous improvement objectives | **Build**<br>Build a relationship and encourage improvements. Build attractiveness and create dependency | **Develop**<br>Agree improvement and joint development programme, collaborate towards joint goals. | Development |  |
|  |  | **Don't bother**<br>Price risk and little point in putting effort in. Switch supplier | **Ultimatum**<br>Demand improvements and drive in hard or switch suppliers | **Resolve**<br>High supply risk and supplier interest low. Make account more attractive/get out of 'Critical' | **Resolve**<br>We need them but supplier inerest low. Reduce dependency and switch or increase our attractiveness | Exploitable |  |
|  | Low | **Don't bother**<br>Price risk and little point in putting effort in. Switch supplier | **Ultimatum**<br>Demand improvements and drive in hard or switch suppliers | **Resolve**<br>High supply risk and supplier interest low. Make account more attractive/get out of 'Critical' | **Resolve**<br>We need them but supplier interest low. Reduce dependency and switch or increase our attractiveness | Nuisance |  |
|  |  | Low |  | High |  |  |  |

Dependency upon supplier

to improve or we find a new supplier. Yet if our category is *critical* and the supplier sees us as *exploitable* then we need to resolve this situation, as there is risk to us. The supplier will have some interest to correct a problem, after all in *exploitable* the relative spend of our account is significant, but it is unlikely the supplier will have any interest in engaging in our collaborative development project. However, if our project somehow makes our account more attractive to the supplier, perhaps through the promise of mutually beneficial outcomes, improving ways of working or helping the supplier to strengthen margins, then this might just grab the supplier's attention. Here we are then shifting from *exploitable* to *core*.

The STPDR supplier improvement process (Figure 8.13) is a simple and straightforward approach for driving all types of supplier improvement.

**FIGURE 8.13** The STPDR supplier improvement and development process

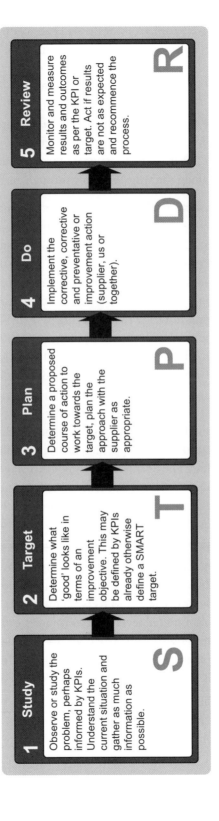

Remember our STP tool from Stage 1? The STPDR tool builds on the principles of the STP tool and is founded on principles from the various improvement methodologies found in the world of Lean, Six Sigma and TQM. It is a five-step improvement process that can be applied to a variety of situations except here we *study the situation* and our proposal becomes our *plan*. The five stages are *Study, Target, Plan, Do* and *Review*. Irrespective of the reason why we need some sort of improvement or development intervention, STPDR helps us to navigate through and provides a means to review progress along the way. We work through each step as follows:

- *Study the situation.* If we are faced with an apparent supplier performance issue it is all too easy to think we understand the problem and cut straight to the solution we think we need. However it is also all too easy to fail to understand the exact issue. A tin of paint bought from a hardware store that cracks and peels shortly after it is applied could be deemed defective and returned for a replacement; however the paint might be just fine, instead the problem could lie with the walls, the temperature of the room or the application. Obvious stuff, but frequently overlooked when faced with supplier problems in business. Across all the established Lean, Six Sigma and TQM improvement methodologies one common principle is the need to first study the situation. This might involve forming a small team, gathering data and developing hypotheses around what might be happening or using techniques such as root cause analysis. The overarching aim of this stage is to really study the situation, to look hard and keep looking until there is a real and insightful understanding of either the problem or what is preventing excellence, and precisely what is causing the problem or what would need to happen to make a change.

- *Target.* If our supplier is underperforming then we will most likely have already set targets for improvement within our business requirements translated into KPIs, so our target either becomes to return to this required level of performance, or a new target if we have reason to do so. Similarly if we are seeking to develop a supplier then here our target is simply the new goal we wish to achieve; again it is most likely we will have already identified this.

- *Plan.* Our plan is the specific actions and steps we will take to achieve the target, who will do these (eg named people in our organization, names people at the supplier or both), when they will be achieved and the arrangement to manage the plan so that actions are realized. For a supplier problem this might involve a series of corrective and preventative actions, and for a supplier relationship we are developing this might involve a series of planned tasks, joint meetings, communications activities and reviews.

- *Do*. As the name suggests, *Do* is concerned with delivering the plan. Here good project management is essential with review points forming a core part of supplier reviews ongoing.

- *Review*. Once an improvement or development initiative is complete, *Review* is concerned with verifying that we have achieved our target. For a problem we once again study the situation, perhaps re-measuring or gathering new data. For a development activity we are seeking to confirm that we have reached our new goal. If our improvement or development is not complete then we can choose to either keep going, or ultimately start over and begin the STPDR process again. If we have reached our goal, then we may need to make new provision to embed the change to prevent drifting back to old ways. This might involve changes to policies, processes, procedures, training and ways of working. It might also demand change management and internal communication. Finally at the end of a complex development initiative a lessons learned review can be beneficial to capture knowledge.

# Supply chain management

Supply chain management (SCM) is an approach to understand and manage the entire supply chain and possibly even the end-to-end supply and value chain network (SVCN) extending to the end customer. SCM is typically concerned with arrangements to ensure flows of information and coordinate logistics, storage and flows of goods right through the supply chain. It is also an approach that helps address risk and realize new opportunities beyond our immediate supplier.

SCM and Logistics are entire topics all of their own with a wealth of publications, knowledge and education available out there so it is impossible to do justice to the topic in a single section here. However, SCM is part of an overall SRM approach, although it has not traditionally been regarded as such, and in category management there could be categories where a game-changing sourcing strategy requires us to understand and effect change within the SVCN. We are used to developing supplier relationships with those immediate suppliers that are important to us but SCM looks beyond these to where there is no direct contractual relationship but to where a different type of intervention can reduce risk or bring competitive advantage, perhaps through improved logistics that enable us to offer 'better, right now and just for you' goods and services.

The logistics dimension of SCM has been around for thousands of years and has been behind any requirement to get the right stuff to the right place in good condition exactly when needed, repeatedly and so reliably. The principles surrounding ensuring an effective flow of materials and information to satisfy a customer have altered little from the building of the pyramids to the relief of hunger in Africa (Christopher, 2011). In organizations the 'running' of supply chains has traditionally been something that tends to sits separate from a purchasing function, perhaps being the remit of a dedicated logistics function, operations, production or even a commercial function.

SCM is no longer just about logistics, it is a practice that can help bring significant value to a business by reducing and managing risk and bringing competitive advantage by enabling a firm to satisfy its end customers. However the greatest impact comes when SCM is connected to, and integrated with, the wider strategic purchasing within the organization and SRM is the means by which to do this. Increasingly SCM is being seen as a strategic enabler alongside and together with purchasing. The two areas appear to be converging to create a single and coordinated approach to managing all aspects of *sourcing* for the business. The factors driving this convergence are all around us:

- The global marketplace drives global supply chains and distribution networks.

- Global distribution drives fewer 'super-sized' production facilities and provides economies of scale over many regional factories.

- Global supply chains drive fewer, 'super-sized' inventories.

- Corporate Social Responsibility means we are now interested in what happens in a global supply chain, but first-hand knowledge and understanding is more difficult to secure.

- Consumer demands for personalization are now being met through clever production technology and good logistics.

- Regional variations and localization can similarly be catered for so one product facility can produce a range of different products for different markets on the same production line in real time.

Therefore when practising category management we need to look further than our immediate supplier with whom we have the contractual relationship to the wider SVCN. As we saw in Chapter 5 understanding an SVCN is no small undertaking so we need to be selective about using precious resources here. Thankfully the need to look beyond immediate suppliers is only relevant for certain categories and we decide which ones by considering if there is a risk or an opportunity that we should respond to. For example a food product producer sourcing the category palm oil and who wishes to protect their brand from negative association with unsustainable practices would need to fully understand and manage ongoing the entire SVCN. For the category leather goods, a luxury goods company offering a 'me too' range of high-specification products, but differentiating the offer by personalizing the products in some way and delivering them next day, will require the category to be part of a highly responsive SVCN.

Ideally, by the time we get to Stage 5 in category management, we are not considering for the first time what, if anything, we need to do with the SVCN, but rather we are driving in arrangements and interventions that we have determined from this insights gained early on in the process as defined in our sourcing strategy. Here insights from *portfolio analysis* and *supplier preferencing* are less useful in determining *when* we might need SVCN intervention, although they should have helped us understand *what* strategic options for change might exist. However other tools within category management that we worked through ideally will have informed our strategy around opportunity or risk in the SVCN and can now direct us as to any SVCN interventions we now need. All of these are part of Stage 2 insight (Chapter 5). They include:

- *Supply and value chain network mapping.* Opportunities and risk identified during the mapping process where one exits.

- *PESTLE analysis.* Considers the wider external environment.

- *Porter's five forces.* Provides competitive analysis around the marketplace from which we are sourcing and as such considers the suppliers to that market.

Driving change within a supplier relationship with a willing supplier is straightforward, but if our category strategy demands that we transform a SVCN then this is much harder. Our contractual relationship extends only to those we immediately interface with so we have no legal basis to engage with or demand something from other players in the network. We could impose a requirement on our suppliers to impose a requirement on their suppliers and so on, and this can work to a degree, but despite good intention and well-drafted contracts the effectiveness tends to get diluted, especially when the original source of supply of raw materials or services exists in less developed countries, where contracts have less worth and shortcuts can be easily taken without being detected. Furthermore all the players in the network will naturally be focused on satisfying their immediate neighbour; after all this is what pays the bills. They are unlikely to have much willingness to do something different for a player many times removed from them unless they can see something in it for them, and often this is hard to see. In recent times, as CSR becomes a key consideration for modern progressive organizations, this very challenge has consumed the brainpower of some the brightest and most experienced purchasing professionals who have sought to find a way to crack this problem. Companies that have made progress here have not done it through contractual means, but by understanding the SVCN in detail; by going and connecting with the relevant players within it, and by getting and remaining close to what happens. Risks get mitigated by visiting plantations and factories or having local representatives visiting and working with the farmers and factory owners to establish and maintain compliance to appropriate policy. Opportunities get realized by establishing relationships with network players to improve forecasting and the flow of demand information, and by establishing groups that work together for the benefit of all to improve the overall effectiveness of the network, perhaps by reducing the need for buffer inventories and improving how material flows. Underpinning all of this is finding ways to incentivize players in the SVCN and make it worth the effort for them to cooperate.

Driving change across a SVCN can become a considerable and specialized undertaking, and one that might be beyond the experience of many purchasing professionals. The good news is help is at hand and what might not be familiar to us is commonplace to others. There are plenty of very experienced supply chain experts and this may be one part of our category management process where our cross-functional team needs the support of such an individual.

Therefore when we consider the SVCN in category management, it is the relationship between *sourcing* and *satisfying*, linked to *strategy* that is key because the SVCN must work to support all of these. It is the underlying principles and pillars of category management that we covered in Chapter 2 that make this relationship deliver results, especially that of cross-functional working and customer focus.

# Strategic collaborative relationships

Strategic collaborative relationships are an approach to establish and improve relationships at a strategic level with the critical few suppliers who can add the most value to the organization. The term *Collaborative Relationship* was popularized by the British Standard BS11000, but this strategic component of SRM is sometimes referred to as *Strategic Relationship Management* (also 'SRM' to really confuse things) or *Relationship Management* or *Strategic Relationships*. Suppliers which are part of SCRs may be called *Strategic Suppliers*, but they may also be called *Partners* or *Critical Suppliers*.

The importance of strategic relationships with the handful of the most important suppliers has, in recent times, become increasingly recognized by organizations, especially since the global downturn. In 1994 research by the US General Accounting Office suggested that effective relationships with supply chain partners may be of strategic importance (USGAO, 1994). Sheth and Sharma (2007) suggest that relationship management is becoming a strategic function and the next generation of competitive advantage may come from an effective relationship with supply chain partners.

As we have seen, competitive advantage can come by connecting end-customer needs and aspirations with supply base possibilities and so if we want to build competitive advantage we need to work with the suppliers who hold the potential to help innovate or make a dramatic difference here. The companies that are creating new marketplaces for things that didn't previously exist or delivering innovative products are not doing it alone; they are working with a few select partners who have the ability to help and want to be on the journey with them.

A strategic collaborative relationship (SCR) is the ultimate level of relationship and one appropriate only for the critical few suppliers who are of strategic importance to us and who hold the potential to dramatically benefit our business and most likely theirs in the process, or with whom there is a critical imperative to maintain a very close relationship. Here we are right at the top of our segmentation pyramid (Figure 8.5) and it is these suppliers that require a higher level of relationship intensity.

In category management we may end up identifying the need for an SCR for three reasons:

- the overall scale and nature of business with one supplier ends up such that it demands strategic intervention;

- our category strategy identifies a future sourcing approach built around developing a strategic relationship with one or more key suppliers;

- we are already sourcing from a supplier with whom we have a strategic relationship and cannot switch easily or we don't want to move away from.

That said, there is a word of caution as it is easy to 'talk a supplier into strategic', or worse for the supplier to talk himself into strategic. Those managing suppliers of any importance will naturally want to think of their supplier as more important than the others, as anything less than this begins to suggest their job is not that important. However, generally the number of suppliers that are truly strategic is usually very small. True strategic suppliers with whom an SCR is appropriate are those who might:

- hold the potential to change something in our business that makes the share price go up (or adds great value to end users in a public or not-for-profit organization);
- have some sort of shared destiny and mutual dependency with us;
- be actively working jointly with us on new developments, innovation, improvements etc;
- be business critical to us.

If a supplier doesn't tick any of these boxes chances are they are not strategic, although they may be very important. In category management and SRM it is essential to challenge thinking here or our belief in and pledge in support of the need to establish the strategic relationship that is not really needed might dilute our leverage, cause us to miss opportunity and misdirect precious resources.

True strategic collaborative relationships are increasingly underpinning today's progressive organization; joint innovation partners, entire functions outsourced, augmenting geographical reach or complimentary product mix are all reasons why companies end up working more closely together than they do with the rest of the supply base. SCRs therefore tend to be defined by a number of typical characteristics:

- Long-term engagement supported by a full and detailed formal contract.
- Clearly defined and jointly agreed goals that will benefit both parties with agreed roles and responsibilities of each party to support this.
- The relationship is collaborative – parties will regularly meet to share, exchange ideas, work towards an agreed outcome and innovate.
- Parties have 'voice' and can raise concerns openly and candidly with the intent of changing objectionable conditions.
- Parties will be readily invest time and money into the relationship, often without counting the cost.

- There will be clear benefits, shared by both, that emerge ongoing.

- The relationship nurtures a new sort of day-to-day working that promotes the realization of inter-company high-performing teams, perhaps involving social interaction amongst players.

Such relationships don't just happen, and traditional approaches to supplier management will do little to help them along. Deciding that a supplier should be 'strategic' doesn't make them instantly operate as a strategic supplier. Instead an SCR is like any human relationship and therefore needs effort from both sides to build and maintain it. Companies don't have relationships with companies; it is the individuals in those companies who have relationships with individuals in other companies. Therefore the personality and experience of individuals who interact together within an SCR are of paramount importance if a relationship is to be built. Trust, consistency and sharing are key here. The wider organization must demonstrate transparency, coordination and effective communication and parties must both be willing, aligned and positioned so to benefit from the SCR.

The process of making SCRs a reality is an entire subject matter of its own and not something I can do justice to in this section. It involves a comprehensive methodology similar to category management in complexity, and approaches to select and support key individuals and to promote and stage manage the right relationship. The steps to achieve this are covered in full in *Supplier Relationship Management,* also published by Kogan Page, which includes the full *5A Strategic Collaborative Relationship Process.*

# DRIVING CONTINUOUS IMPROVEMENT

Once we have implemented our sourcing strategy, and put in place the appropriate SRM arrangements, our work is still not quite complete. In fact in category management our work is never complete as the process doesn't in fact end. If it did we would be setting ourselves up for future decline as what might be a breakthrough sourcing strategy today will soon get overtaken by the world and our organization changing around us. Instead the final phase of category management is concerned with ongoing arrangements for continuous improvement that continue until such point as it is necessary and appropriate to restart the category management process. The category manager therefore has an ongoing role here.

For category management in the public sector continuous improvement is also relevant, but the various legislative requirements might demand this is approached slightly differently. In the commercial sector continuous improvement is just something a good category manager will do, but for public sector contracts we might need to contract for continuous improvement upfront. In other words, at the point we initially approach a marketplace we have defined certain obligations for continuous improvement that are to be subsequently incorporated into a contract – ensuring all suppliers have equal opportunity from the outset and nothing is added in later. This is a subtle shift in the way we approach category management and just requires a bit of thought early on.

# Attracting innovation, value and breakthrough ongoing

This step is an *Activity* and is *Optional*

This section and the next three are concerned with the category manager's ongoing work to make sure the implemented sourcing strategy remains the most appropriate and relevant one. As the world changes around us it is possible that at any point a brilliant leading-edge sourcing arrangement quickly becomes ineffective and outdated. The category manager therefore has an important role to keep a watchful eye on the category and how things change around it. The eye has a lot to look for, as we shall see in this and the subsequent two sections.

If at the outset the category management project was a full-time job for the category manager or team leader, then by now it should be consuming a very small proportion of their time. However, the category should not be forgotten but rather should be regularly reviewed.

The category manager should regularly ask these key questions:

- Is there any new technology development or innovation that would make a dramatic difference in this case?
- What do I need to do to attract new innovation?
- Is there another breakthrough opportunity here?
- How can I add further value?

If these questions are kept in mind, the category manager will spot changes or opportunities in these areas as and when they arise. But this is not enough, and some opportunities will only be found if they are hunted down. The approaches that can help are:

*Attracting innovation:*

- Build the relationship with the supplier. Meet the supplier regularly and open up discussions as to how you can help with future innovation.
- Read the trade press for this area, understand the changes and new ideas that are emerging, then ask for your supplier's view.
- Use the technology road map tool to map and monitor technological changes (Stage 2).
- Show your suppliers that your organization will actively support working with them to help them get new products to market.
- Talk to universities and experts regularly and gain their insights.
- Set up 'best-practice' industry forums to share ideas.

*Finding new breakthroughs:*

- Keep an open mind.
- Regularly challenge and ask, 'Why do we do it that way?'
  Look for parallel or related industry sectors and understand what they do. For example, if you have outsourced your IT helpdesk, visit someone who has also done it and exchange ideas.
- Maintain regular engagement with stakeholders and use their brainpower to help with the ongoing search for breakthrough.
- Look beyond your current supplier, market and organizational constraints to see what else might be possible.

*Finding new sources of value:*

- Keep checking back to the value levers (Stage 1) to see if there are any new potential sources of value.
- If the supply chain warrants it use the supply and value chain network mapping tool (Stage 2) regularly and look for opportunities.
- Visit the supplier and follow the process, looking for areas where improvements can be made.
- Take some Lean or Six Sigma training and look again at the category strategy with fresh eyes.

- Talk to the people who use the goods or service and ask them, 'How could we improve this?'
- Network with peers, share and swap ideas.

Finally, once something of benefit is discovered it needs to be acted upon. This might mean setting up a small project, perhaps supported with a business case to secure resources or funding. Or it might act as the trigger to restart category management in its entirety, or at least to go back and review the sourcing strategy and pick up the process from Stage 3 onwards.

# Ongoing alignment with business requirements

This step is an *Activity* and is *Optional*

If you remember one thing from this book, remember that the business requirements form the cornerstone for the entire category management process (Stage 1). Much work went into getting them right and optimizing them to arrive at a well-honed definition of current and future business needs and wants. Once this definition is correct, then the rest of the category management activities flow from it.

However, things change, and the needs of the organization move on, ideally in line with the needs of the end customer and the changing world around us. What was irrelevant one day might be essential the next. For example, a food manufacturer didn't feel any need to consider where its cocoa beans were sourced from, as they were simply bought on the open market. However, when issues relating to slavery associated with the farming of cocoa beans in Ivory Coast came to light, the company suddenly felt compelled to take note and changed its sources to areas where there were no known problems. The experience made the business recognize a business need, driven by the end customer, to ensure that the source of cocoa beans incurred no unacceptable human, environmental or social impact. The business requirements were hurriedly changed, the sourcing strategy was revised and new arrangements were put in place to remove risk from future sourcing activities.

The category manager should continue to keep an eye on the relationship between *sourcing*, *strategy* and *satisfying* the end customer and watch for any shift in the latter two that might trigger the need to revisit the first. This can be accomplished through ongoing stakeholder engagement and staying in touch with corporate aims, strategy and objectives, and the category manager should continually keep a watchful eye on the business requirements, updating them as things change. If the change is significant enough (as in the cocoa bean example), then this can trigger the need to restart the category management process or at least to go back to Stage 3 and revisit the sourcing strategy.

# Ongoing market analysis

This step is an *Activity* and is *Optional*

Markets are continually changing. Here again our category manager needs to keep a watchful eye.

During Stage 2 we explored the concept of data gathering, including data regarding the market, market trends, players, size, suppliers and so on. In Stage 5 we need to regularly revisit this research and update it as things change. This is not so much a research but a monitoring activity, and so the focus should be on ongoing monitoring and updating rather than wholesale research. For example, if the category incorporates a high proportion of a commodity such as wheat and one year there is a major crop failure, then the market conditions for wheat will change, with an impact on pricing for the category. Being forewarned with such information helps a business to temper and properly understand price increases, and enables risks relating to assurance of supply to be dealt with early.

Ongoing market analysis is not just about tracking changes in prices; it is also about spotting trends and looking for factors that might suggest either risk or an opportunity, and then acting on this information. Sourcing information includes reading trade journals, reading the business press, talking to experts, visiting exhibitions, talking to suppliers – in fact, all those sources originally identified in Stage 2, but here they are used for monitoring. This task should not be onerous and a good category manager would naturally stay abreast of information relevant to the category in question. This stage is no different, and of course the moment a significant change in the marketplace is identified, the need to restart the process or at least return to Stage 3 should be considered.

# STARTING AGAIN

# Determining when to start the process again

This step is an *Activity* and is *Optional*

So, by keeping a watchful eye on a series of indicators, the category manager is able to identify when to act and the degree of action required. As we have seen, this might mean starting the process again, or perhaps going back and updating the sourcing strategy contained within the source plan and implementing the changes. If it is appropriate to restart the category management process, then, depending on the business and the governance structure, the category manager may simply be able to initiate this, or otherwise may need to make some informed recommendations. With any action here it is implicit that there is cross-functional involvement, whether through a new category team or the old team reformed.

There is no hard and fast rule regarding when to act, but if the answer to any of the following questions is 'Yes,' then there is a good chance that something needs to be reviewed:

- Has the risk to the business increased unacceptably?
- Is there some new opportunity, innovation or technology that would bring great benefit?
- Is there a hitherto unseen source of value or breakthrough that would provide a dramatic benefit?
- Have the requirements of the business changed dramatically?
- Has there been a significant change in the market that presents either significant risk or opportunity, or creates a need to act?

Restarting category management is straightforward, and just demands the opportunity and the resources we identified back at the start of the process. Aside from this there is little that stops us doing this; after all such a move is an internal affair. However, at the point where we wish to change our strategy, which might involve approaching the market or considering an alternative supply base, we will of course be constrained by current contracts or agreements that are in place and the degree to which we are prepared to change the nature of a relationship with suppliers. This is especially relevant for category management programmes run in the public sector as we may simply not be able to switch away from a previously established contract. Therefore category management cycles can be planned so they synchronize with contract expiry unless there is a compelling reason and significant opportunity do otherwise, which might involve exiting current contracts, a move that is less possible in public sector procurement.

That said, there is risk with a synchronized approach. I have seen many organizations who have done this, especially in the public sector, and the net result can be that category management ends up getting 'bolted on' to existing contracting and tendering cycles and merely becomes contracting and tendering under a different name with little new strategic or game-changing results. Category management requires the organization to do things differently, yet there can be a rationale for synchronization, so too there is a rationale for programming category management projects independent of contract renewal based solely upon opportunity. It all depends and needs some brainpower to figure out the best approach and a culture change so people don't simply follow old ways.

Finally, with each new category management cycle, category maturity builds. Category maturity means the organization holds a complete understanding of the market, suppliers and the category itself together with the needs and wants of the internal and external customers. Maturity means the degree of new challenge or a sudden and unexpected breakthrough diminish unless something changes as we have, in theory, already found the game changers. If we reach true maturity then we can confidently say we have the most effective sourcing arrangements in place for a category and providing we continue to keep a watchful eye open for a change in something, we can continue to maintain this mature state for some time. In essence, for a mature category where we have run through many cycles, we may remain in Stage 5 for some time until something triggers the need to restart, such as contract expiry or some sort of change in market, technology or customer needs.

## Chapter 8 summary

Recap on the key points from this chapter:

1 The fifth and final stage within the category management process is *improvement* and is concerned with how implementation turns into this improvement. Here our focus shifts to the supplier relationships and supplier management using SRM. We also move into the final phase of ongoing continuous improvement for the category project.

2 *Improvement* begins by first capturing the learnings from the project so far and sharing them as much as possible. A simple lessons learned review (LLR) provides the framework here.

3 Supplier Relationship Management (SRM) is an umbrella term for the various different types of supplier and supply base intervention that are necessary or useful for those suppliers who are important to us in some way. SRM is part of *improvement* as here we identify and effect the required intervention with the supplier(s) for our category.

4 The Orchestra of SRM helps us make sense of the SRM concept. Like an orchestra has different sections which play depending upon the music, SRM is very similar in that it is not a single linear approach but a combination of different approaches that each serves different purposes.

5 We need different sorts of supplier intervention according to the importance and the nature of that importance for suppliers and indeed a supply chain. The vast majority of our suppliers need no intervention and are purely transactional; however, across all categories there is typically a small number of suppliers who are important in some way, perhaps due to reasons of risk, difficulty, current importance, alignment or future opportunity. Within these a handful will be of strategic importance where there is a high degree of dependency which is perhaps mutual. It is these suppliers that hold the potential to make a dramatic future contribution to our business.

6 Our most important suppliers will require some form of supplier management (SM) approach where we are driving interventions around securing the required results ongoing. This typically includes supplier and supply chain risk management, ongoing reviews with suppliers, contract management and managing the relationship between parties.

7   Supplier performance measurement (SPM) might be needed to verify compliance ongoing, provide confidence or to help baseline and measure improvements. Companies frequently overcomplicate SPM, but our simple aim here is to identify and put in place a handful of KPIs that will help guide our relationship and intervention with the supplier.

8   Supplier improvement and development (SI&D) is concerned with intervention with a supplier to effect some sort of reactive improvement (eg fix a problem, prevent a problem reoccurring, reduce or eliminate a known risk, reduce cost or improve overall effectiveness) or proactive development (eg to develop capability, innovate, create new competitive advantage etc). SI&D typically responds to what we measured within SPM and forms the basis for intervention to manage how we, together with supplier, drive the required improvements and development in.

9   SRM is not just about our immediate suppliers, but there might be good reason for intervention back up the entire supply and value chain network (SVCN). Supply chain management (SCM) helps here and is an approach to understand and drive intervention in response to risk or opportunities throughout the SVCN.

10  For the critical few suppliers who are of strategic importance and who hold the potential to add significant value to our business we work to implement a strategic collaborative relationship (SCR) using an established methodology. Here our suppliers have some sort of shared destiny and there is a mutual dependency as we are working towards some sort of shared goal demanding joint, collaborative working.

11  The final phase of *improvement* involves ongoing continuous improvement. Here the category manager moves into a state of ongoing monitoring and keeping a watchful eye on any changes that might trigger a need to revisit the category strategy. This includes looking out for new sources of innovation, value or breakthrough by watching the market and checking for changes in internal needs or a shift in corporate strategy, ideally informed by end-customer needs and wants. This watchful eye informs the category manager when to act to revisit one or more aspects of the current sourcing arrangements but ultimately determines when to restart the category management process.

# Making category management happen

This chapter explores what organizations need to put in place to enable category management. It concentrates on the essential governance and support structure as well as some good practices that will increase the overall chances of success. The aim of this chapter is to describe how category management programmes should be constructed, including organizational design, alignment with corporate objectives, and resources required. This chapter is therefore particularly relevant for senior managers who wish to develop a category management programme.

Pathway question addressed in this chapter:

**14** How does the company need to structure and organize itself to deploy category management effectively?

## Creating the right conditions

There are many things that need to have been put in place before a team can kick off a new category management project. A lone category manager trying to drive in the concept by initiating a project from the ground up will have a tough time making it work. Instead, the organization, or as great a part of it as possible, needs to have signed up to the category management concept. There are many enabling factors that are essential if category management is to be successful within organizations, and we will explore them in this chapter. They need to be combined and work in concert to create a complete programme, which must become so embedded that it is known and recognized across the organization as 'the way we buy'. Category management is therefore a business-wide philosophy and requires business-wide awareness, support, endorsement and participation in order to have the greatest impact.

# Securing executive support

Organizations that conduct category management well begin the process by developing full programmes where, once the necessary capabilities and processes have been put in place, a number of category projects are initiated together, followed by a second wave and so on. Clearly this programme approach requires a wholesale refocusing of resources, not only within purchasing but across the business. It is of course also possible to begin slowly, perhaps with just one category management project and grown from there. However, the gentle approach can often go unnoticed by the wider business, and so fall short of securing the crucial buy-in needed. Where the programme is more 'big bang', it will naturally be high profile and provide the perfect platform to attract support from across the organization. This process begins by securing executive support, championed by one senior individual who can influence peers.

Securing executive support for a category management programme presents a series of challenges. First, few executives actually understand what category management is, and most have little feel for the power of the process. Second, competing demands for resource and immediate priorities make the proposition of a long-term project with the delayed delivery of results difficult to appreciate. This is even more acute if the organization has no prior experience of category management. However, there are organizations out there that regularly make the leap and endorse category management programmes effectively. This usually follows rigorous work to define the opportunity, the benefits and how the programme will work, and to educate the senior team about the concept and the potential it offers. A good business case for a category management programme should show an executive team a dramatic return on investment and a clear road map of how this will be achieved. The business case should therefore be developed around:

- what category management is and what makes it powerful;
- what is possible – examples of the deployment of category management elsewhere and the resultant return on investment;
- the results of an initial high-level opportunity analysis to identify potential benefits category by category, and recommended priorities;

- the proposed programme, including a plan for all the category projects, and the resources required (including resources and commitment required at executive level);

- how benefits will be measured, tracked and reported;

- the additional value and range of soft benefits the project will bring (beyond direct savings);

- the investment required and the anticipated pay-off.

Across the various 'pre-category management programme' boardroom workshops I have witnessed, it seems, more often than not, that unless the executive team has had previous first-hand involvement in a successful category management programme, or understands the potential of strategic procurement, they really don't fully appreciate the potential of such a programme. I've worked with executive teams where eyes glaze over or people check watches at the prospect of sitting through a discussion about a process or tools that procurement people use. However, interest quickly comes back when the scale of hard and soft benefits is revealed (Chapter 1), and where these can be quantified and linked to real examples. A 'dip in' to the process gives executive groups a taster for the toolset category management contains. I tend to use day one analysis (Chapter 4) with executives. This is a great tool to bring about 'light bulb' moments – linking specific supplier actions that on the surface seem appropriate but also seek to push an area of spend into *proprietary* and dilute our power, usually yields a revelation sufficient to change mindsets. I worked with one senior individual in a public sector military organization, who prior to our meeting was highly protective over his so-called 'partner' supplier and had sought to prevent any interference. He stood back from the day one analysis and with a shocked expression said, 'I've been screwed by the supplier.' From that point on he became the biggest advocate for our programme. Not all make the leap. I once described, based upon experience of other programmes, how a 15–20 per cent cost saving could be possible from a specific category with a quality category management implementation. The CFO burst out in laughter, turned to me and said, 'If that sort of return on investment was really possible we would have seen it long ago,' and promptly gathered up her papers and walked out.

It doesn't follow that executive teams will be naturally supportive to a category management project from the off, but if they get it, and come to believe in the power and potential benefits, then it very quickly becomes a 'no brainer' for any executive team. Getting them to this point may not be easy. As with any pitch to an executive team, success depends not only on presenting a compelling business case based on facts and data and comparisons against what is possible, but also on being able to identify and push the hot buttons of the decision makers. Hot buttons are the particular areas an individual knows, understands and gets passionate about. If the business case successfully presents benefits that hit these hot buttons, then support may come more easily. Some examples of hot buttons as if spoken by the CEO and how category management can help are:

- *How can we increase the value proposition to our customers?* A quality category management implementation can connect supply base possibilities with end-customer needs and shape corporate strategy (*sourcing, satisfying* and *strategy*).

- *Following the big boys.* Being seen to be doing something that trailblazing global businesses are doing is often an attractive proposition. Category management is now a core philosophy and approach and regarded as essential across many of today's most successful global businesses. Today, and especially post-global recession, it is the one thing no self-respecting CEO would want to do without.

- *Departments need to work together more.* By working together we break out of functional silos, and the process of engaging and sharing ideas and knowledge begins to unlock benefits and potential benefits. This is of course a fundamental pillar of category management.

- *Show me the money.* Of course category management can do this, but it can get beyond price and deliver dramatic benefits in terms of reduced cost, risk, increased value and also innovation, then there are the many soft benefits also. Many of these could be converted into an equivalent dollar benefit value.

- *What if it doesn't work?* Category management will only be successful if all the right conditions are created to enable success. It is the role of the executive team to ensure this is the case, but they will need help to identify what needs to be put in place.

Securing executive support requires a champion at executive level who can make the case and engage with peers to get them on board with the proposal before any formal decision-making forum is convened. Without such a champion it would be hard for a non-executive member to secure the necessary support, although not impossible.

There is one final dimension here, and that is to secure agreement that senior executives take on the role of sponsor for key projects. Those involved must therefore have a full appreciation of what is involved and what will be expected of them.

# INTRODUCING 5P GOVERNANCE

It seems the word 'governance' does not have universal recognition; indeed in the United States the word is not commonplace, yet it is the perfect world to help describe the arrangements needed for SRM. Bevir (2013) describes governance as 'all processes of governing, whether undertaken by a government, market or network, whether over a family, tribe, formal or informal organization or territory and whether through laws, norms, power or language'. That seems to pretty much cover everything. Within an organization, governance sits at the centre of the universe that is category management. It relates to how the philosophy is realized within the organization; what gets done, the processes that support it, decisions that are taken, how roles and responsibilities are agreed, and arrangements to verify performance and demonstrate success.

There are five components within governance defined in the 5P governance framework (Figure 9.1). These are *people, proficiency, promote, payoff* and *programme* and I will explore each over the next five sections. Governance is not necessarily unique to category management, but rather

**FIGURE 9.1**  The 5P governance framework

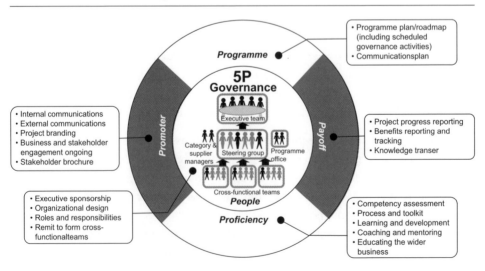

a well-founded governance approach could support, coordinate and enable multiple strategic initiatives and projects within a purchasing function or indeed across the entire organization. It is governance that plays a key role in realizing corporate strategy by providing the means to integrate various strategic initiatives including category management but also including other cross-functional initiatives such as SRM, Lean or Six Sigma, CSR projects or any other project that helps realize corporate goals. Therefore governance should be constructed as the enabler for the function, not just category management.

## 5P GOVERNANCE: *PEOPLE*

The first component of governance is *people* and is concerned with structure and organizational design. We need the right people, with the right capability doing the right things. Category management, and indeed other strategic purchasing initiatives, may not naturally overlay a traditional hierarchical organizational structure but rather requires a more matrix-based way of working that fosters cross-functional teams and groups. This does not necessarily mean a complete organizational redesign, but rather a refocusing of roles or even parts of roles of individuals.

## Creating the right structure

For category management any structure needs to provide for individuals to have assigned roles and responsibilities to lead and manage or participate in category projects. Remember category management is not the only strategic game in town, and so good governance will also provide for individuals to have assigned roles and responsibilities for SRM and managing supplier and supply chain interventions together with any other initiatives in play. These could be different individuals or the same professional who will champion different special projects that could be either category- or supplier-focused projects.

Cross-functional engagement becomes core to any strategic project, requiring a cross-functional team to be formed, meet regularly and work towards delivering a specific outcome such as a new breakthrough sourcing strategy or collaborative strategic relationship. In fact, and as we saw in Chapter 2, cross-functional working lies at the heart of category management and indeed every other strategic purchasing and business improvement project. Governance must therefore create the structure and conditions, and agree roles and responsibilities to enable this.

# A 'virtual structure' to foster cross-functional working

As you read this, you may be thinking that your organization already works cross-functionally, and what's the big deal? Or, the concept could be alien to what happens currently. Cross-functional working isn't something all organizations naturally do; for some it comes easy, for others such a concept would threaten power bases – it all depends upon the established culture and ways of working. In any case, it would be impractical to structure many organizations around cross-functional working but it is possible to create a new 'virtual structure' specifically for a category project where a series of individuals can come together in a team for a set period of time, meet and work together to deliver a goal (Figure 9.2). These teams would typically be led by someone from purchasing, perhaps the category manager (described below) but could equally be led from elsewhere in the business. Each team requires a sponsor to support the team, ensure resources are available and remove obstacles, and may also demand facilitation support for key meetings. Team members may be core members but could also be extended team members or stakeholders who are involved, consulted or kept informed.

Cross-functional team working sounds an attractive and obvious pursuit for any organization, but embracing it requires commitment from the executive team and then the wider organization to make it happen. If someone from a technical function is to join a category team for a specific project, then it is likely they will need to step back from their day job and instead be seconded onto the team for a few half days each month until the project is completed. This is quite a commitment and one the business must provide for from the top down, with individual objectives and even incentives supporting this; after all if people are to contribute to a team they need to want to be there and believe there is something in it for them. Incentives could be money, but could equally be personal or career development or just the interest of something different.

At any one time a number of cross-functional teams might be needed, each working on key initiatives. How many and what they work on is a product of availability of resources and organizational priorities. Here good governance is founded on the principle that there is only so much resource and

**FIGURE 9.2** A typical cross-functional team

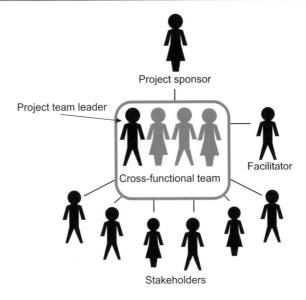

potentially many competing projects and so determines an overarching programme of priority projects and assigns these to cross-functional teams; some may work on strategic category projects, whilst others work to drive in new collaborative supplier relationships or CSR projects. This assignment of resources against opportunities is the backbone that connects corporate strategy to action and intervention and it requires a small steering group and programme manager to do this, informed by good opportunity analysis.

## The steering group

The steering group sits at the heart of governance (Figure 9.3) and is the small group of typically senior individuals responsible for coordinating all the components of governance and therefore determining how strategic corporate objectives are met. The role of the steering group is ultimately to ensure that all strategic purchasing projects are aligned to corporate strategy and are adequately contributing to corporate goals and objectives. This is effected by the steering group meeting regularly and being responsible to:

- assume overall responsibility and accountability for all category, supplier or strategic procurement programmes;
- determine and prioritize the category or supplier opportunities;
- define the overall programme objectives, benefit targets and timing;

- ensure a planned approach to individual category or supplier projects to support achievement of overall programme objectives, benefits and timing;
- monitor the programme, receive and review reports from project teams and report on overall progress against the plan to the executive team and wider business;
- ensure the right capability and resources are in place to deliver the programme;
- initiate positive communication concerning the programme, on-going progress and successes to the wider business;
- resolve any issues or remove obstacles.

There are a number of practical components to this including programme management, benefits tracking and reporting which I shall cover shortly, but this suggests the need for some analytical or administrative support as well as a good programme manager to support the steering group. This is shown in Figure 9.3 as 'programme office', as a resource separate but connected to and supporting the steering group. Dedicated resources here may be a luxury, but if governance is to be effective it is essential that these roles are provided for, even if part time.

**FIGURE 9.3**    A typical governance structure

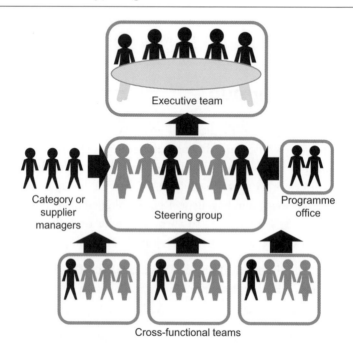

Executive team

Category or supplier managers

Steering group

Programme office

Cross-functional teams

# The category manager role

The category manager is the individual who has a specific responsibility to establish and implement a category-based sourcing strategy within the organization, and to monitor and maintain the category ongoing. The role of category manager may by a dedicated role for an individual, but is more likely to be one of many roles an individual has. Category managers need to hold a high proficiency in category management, but also need to be able to lead and manage the cross-functional category project teams. The job description and list of responsibilities for a senior category manager might therefore include:

- To lead and manage category management projects, supported by cross-functional teams as appropriate.

- To research and maintain a current deep-level understanding of the category, the current and potential supply base, the current and potential supply market, and internally to understand the current and future needs and wants of the organization and its stakeholders.

- To research and maintain an understanding of what the end customer needs and might want from our organization with respect to a specific category of spend.

- To research and maintain a current understanding of all supplier and supply base risk, ensuring ongoing contingency and mitigation actions as appropriate and watching for any changes that might require intervention.

- To deploy a managed approach to engage with and communicate to the wider business, especially focusing on relevant stakeholders, to secure and maintain buy-in and support for category projects.

- To identify and implement the most effective, impactful and demonstrable strategic sourcing strategy for those categories assigned to the category manager.

- To identify and put in place appropriate SRM interventions including supplier management activities around supplier reviews and ensuring the contract continues to be robust.

- To keep a watchful eye on the market, environment and the changing needs of the business and identify when action is needed in response to any change.

- To report progress ongoing against project milestones and benefits delivery.

The category manager role demands certain skills and capabilities in order to be effective. In the perfect world a company implementing category management would go and recruit a team of individuals perfectly matched to this role. In practice we are more likely to be working with the team we have and developing capability as needed. Category management, and indeed all strategic purchasing initiatives, requires a skill set that is quite a leap on from that of the traditional purchasing buyer, especially for those soft skills that support leading and motivating a team. These skills are given in Table 9.1.

**TABLE 9.1**   Category manager competencies

| Competency area | Competency | What is required | Level required |
|---|---|---|---|
| Category management practitioner skills | Technical and process skills | Understanding of the category management methodology, can work through the process and determine what to use/leave out, understands and can apply the individual tools and approaches with good standard of process rigour | Advanced, able to coach others |
| | Research skills | Able to gather and synthesize deep market, supplier, category and internal data | Advanced (or access to advanced) |
| | Business requirements definition | Able to develop, based upon business wide, a synthesized set of business requirements with an agreed, consolidated definition of what the business needs and wants for a category | Advanced |
| | Sourcing strategy creation | Able to develop robust sourcing strategies based upon the insights and outputs of the team-based project. | Advanced |

**TABLE 9.1**     *continued*

| Competency area | Competency | What is required | Level required |
|---|---|---|---|
| Implementing sourcing strategies | Project management | Able to use basic tools and techniques to plan and project manage implementation of sourcing strategies | Moderate |
| | Change management | Understands the principles of change management and can develop implementation plans based upon these | Strong |
| | Negotiation | Moderate to advanced ability to negotiate internally and with suppliers. Able to apply a process to structure the negotiation from category management outputs | Advanced |
| | Contracting | Moderate level of understanding of law of contracts, strong understanding of contracting approaches | Moderate to strong |
| | SRM and supplier skills | Understanding of different methodologies for SRM intervention and ability to identify and implement the most appropriate approach and intervention | Moderate |

**TABLE 9.1** *continued*

| Competency area | Competency | What is required | Level required |
|---|---|---|---|
| Leading a team | Leadership and motivation | Able to lead and inspire cross-functional teams to work on procurement-led initiatives for the good of the business. | Developing |
| | Facilitation skills | Able to work with a group and lead meetings to achieve an outcome. Able to use facilitation techniques and process tools to solve problems within a group environment. | Developing |
| | Coaching skills | Can coach members of the team in the application of key tools. | Developing |
| Soft skills | Communication skills | To present complex messages to many and varied stakeholders and secure buy in. | Developing |
| | Action planning and prioritization skills | Able to combine with project management skills to ensure timely delivery. | Strong |
| | Listening skills | Essential for good stakeholder engagement. | Strong |
| | Analytical skills | Able to use techniques and approaches to analyse, make sense of and share insights from complex data and information | Strong |
| | Conflict management | To deal with difficult stakeholders and manage through conflict and challenge. | Developing |
| | Engaging with the business and suppliers | Ability to build rapport and cultivate a good working relationships | Developing |

## 5P GOVERNANCE: *PROFICIENCY*

# Ensuring the right capability

The second component of governance is *proficiency* and includes ensuring the right capability and supporting resources are in place to deliver category management and any other strategic purchasing initiative. This involves selecting the right individuals to lead or participate and ensuring those selected are adequately trained and equipped for the job they are required to do. Specific actions led by the steering group might include:

- competency assessment of core team individuals;
- a rolling programme of learning and development to equip those who will lead and participate in the skills defined previously;
- coaching and mentoring before support along the way from an experienced practitioner;
- education of the wider business and those who will provide a support role to key initiatives.

Companies that make a significant investment in category management will attend to this aspect thoroughly, using specialist outside providers to establish and deliver an appropriate programme for developing members of the team and others in the business. Investing in this aspect can make the difference between success and failure. If the category manager does not know the category management process inside out to a degree that enables them to train the rest of the cross-functional team in how the team applies certain tools, then the power of the process from these key tools will be diluted. Equally, if the same individual is not able to lead, motivate and facilitate the cross-functional team, then the power of collaboration may not be realized. An alternative to external support is to use internal champions to support the people development aspect of process roll-out and I'll cover this when we explore category management 'black belts' in the next chapter. This can be very powerful, providing the champions are sufficiently freed from other commitments to afford the category teams adequate support.

Developing capability requires a blended learning approach (Remesal and Friesen, 2014). Education and training are essential, especially for those who are to become category management practitioners, but other learning methods are needed. Kolb and Fry (1975) describe experiential learning where individuals learn by making sense of concrete experience, observation and reflection; in other words, the learning comes from reflecting on practice. This means that within category management individuals need the opportunity to turn theory into practice as part of the development programme, in order to achieve the required capability.

When I teach category management to organizations, there are always several noticeable 'light bulb' moments within any course, usually when people consider how the various analytical and insight tools illuminate what is happening within the categories they know. These are the moments when individuals suddenly make sense of the theory and understand how it relates to what they do and more importantly begin to make the leap from tactical to strategic thinking.

Learning and development should therefore be geared as much as possible to learning by doing, otherwise the power of the process will not be grasped, and some aspects of category management cannot be taught by classroom training alone. They require learning by doing – by working on real category management projects.

So what does this look like in practice? Traditionally organizations have opted for classroom training, ideally coupled with ongoing workplace coaching and individual mentoring. This combination has a proven track record. Yet is this still the most effective approach given the online information age we now live in? The short answer is 'yes'. Good e-learning solutions are out there and can help augment category management training by providing refresher or top-up training for specific tools; however, the extent and complexities of the category management methodology mean e-learning as it exists today is less effective as the sole primary learning vehicle.

Lombardo and Eichinger (1996) present a model for adult learning that suggests that to be effective 70 per cent of development should come from challenging jobs and assignments, 20 per cent from learning from others (both good and bad examples) and 10 per cent from course work and readings. This 70:20:10 model has since been popularized by Charles Jennings, who has applied the concept as a change agent for developing thinking around capability development beyond the classroom environment (Jennings and Wargnier, 2011). Yet this model was first developed at the pioneering stages of the internet and before we had the social media and networking we have today. Furthermore, for category management, if 70 per cent of learning should come from challenging jobs and assignments ie actually running a category, then those practitioners first need to learn how to apply the process and that requires some initial training or at least coaching.

For the 20 per cent, learning from others is very different today, and arguably this is happening more online than anywhere else. The modern purchasing practitioner is securing new learning through sharing via social media or other forms of online interaction whether managed or just happening.

Today, and for category management, the 70:20:10 model has its merits, but possibly does not go far enough. It makes sense as an aim, a point to aspire to, but the key to success is supporting novice learners whilst unleashing expert learners into a self-directed environment. It is a model that rightly places learning as a continual process that can take a variety of forms ranging from classroom training, coaching, on-the-job experience, online learning and interaction (online and face-to-face). Modern-day strategic purchasing and category management require that we rethink the model. This requires a disruption to the conservative position. It demands blended learning (Remesal and Friesen, 2014).

The steering group should determine the mix of assessment, training and development activity. This should be designed as an ongoing journey, not a once-only activity. The overall level of effort required for people development should not be underestimated. As a rule of thumb, think of the number of days of training or development that each category manager or team leader should receive, and double it.

Classroom training still remains the most effective means to initiate a new programme or kick off a new team, or where there is no prior capability. If training can be combined with the kick-off of actual category projects then it is even more impactful as is combining this training with real on-the-job experience. Generally I allow three to four days just to teach the process. Additional days are needed to focus on specific, more complex tools. Beyond that learning and development should transition away from directed learning into a more self-directed learning. Classroom training should give way to coaching and mentoring from internal or external expert practitioners and the ongoing use of online learning and interaction. Of course, as practitioners begin to work on their categories the value and learning from on-the-job experience cannot be underestimated. In order for 70:20:10 model to be relevant for category management today and be effective we must begin with a complete inverse. Novice teams demand a 10:20:70 model that transitions to the 70:20:10 mix using a range of learning approaches. This is given in Figure 9.4. This mix and the speed of transition will vary depending upon whether the organization is blessed with an army of ready-made category management practitioners who have learnt their trade in big

**FIGURE 9.4** Progress of learning and development approaches

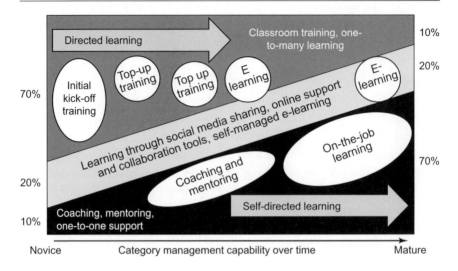

corporations or are only just starting out with the methodology. However, my experience is that in many organizations the concept is new for most people or only just beginning to be understood. Quite simply, the development of people requires effort, energy and investment and it is important to plan for this journey and that is the role of the steering group.

The learning journey is also different according to who is involved and their individual needs as follows:

- *Category manager.* The first time category management is deployed, the category manager or team leader might first require initial training in category management followed by support and coaching to help get initial projects rolling with good process rigour. The support should not only attend to application of the tools, but should also help provide understanding of the overall path through the process, and develop leadership and facilitation skills.

- *Team members* need to have a basic understanding of category management at the outset of the project, but ongoing just-in-time and on-the-spot training from the team leader as the project is worked through should gradually increase capability.

- *Project sponsors* also need a basic understanding of the approach at the outset and their role to support it.

# Establishing common language and ways of working

Ensuring an effective process and toolkit is also part of *proficiency* and relates to establishing a single, effective methodology for applying category management and any other strategic initiative. This includes process, supporting tools, techniques, approaches and templates for category management or indeed any initiative. The process and toolkit for category management are laid out in this book. They exist as part of the third component of governance as clearly practitioners and the organization need something to work to, but it is even more essential for the organization to establish a common language and common ways of working. I've worked with many organizations who have been moderately successful at purchasing for many years without any unified process, yet they still have some method to define the requirements for what they buy or how they run a supplier selection activity or put a contract in place. The core components of any buying process are pretty universal, but they exist in many different forms with a variety of different labels. I've observed that where an organization has not established a single agreed, company-wide sourcing methodology, what gets used are the various tools and approaches individual buyers bring to the organization. This seems to drive individualistic buyer behaviour; buyers do their jobs by operating in their own individual world defined by their unique and individual understanding and experience. Yet this approach limits potential and prevents cross-functional working because people name and interpret the core components in different ways – one person's *business requirements* are another person's *specification* and so on. It can be as if everyone is talking a different language. 'Common language and common ways of working' is one of those much-flaunted phrases that define corporate aspirations, yet it is possibly one of the single most powerful enablers for business success. It seems that the companies who establish a common language, defined in a common process and toolkit, available to and used by all as standard and underpinned by a common language, are generally more successful at category management. When staff can chat about *day one analysis* or *price model* at the water cooler, or share a source plan to help someone in another country build theirs, then knowledge is being shared and capability is increasing organically, from the ground up. Therefore establishing a single process and toolkit and driving its complete, business-wide adoption, are one of the most crucial enablers of category management and a core component of *proficiency* within governance.

# 5P GOVERNANCE: *PROMOTE*

The third component of governance is *promote* and is concerned with internal and external communication and engagement.

# Driving business engagement

Categories and suppliers are managed on behalf of the entire business, therefore our efforts to manage category or supplier must be in concert with all the relevant stakeholders in the organization. Business-wide engagement and participation is unlikely to happen by itself but instead needs to be won. Whilst those out in the business, outside the purchasing function, might see themselves as owning a particular dimension of an area of spend, category or supplier relationship, it is perhaps unlikely these stakeholders would believe they have any role to coordinate what they do with the efforts of the purchasing team. Yet, with an appreciation of the benefits of working more closely with an effective strategic purchasing function, such stakeholders would most likely embrace and support a coordinated approach.

Governance involves purchasing establishing and actively maintaining deep penetration into the business with ongoing engagement of key stakeholders. It is for purchasing to drive this engagement and to open channels of communication internally. Business engagement is not a once-only activity, and to be effective purchasing need to have a regular and ongoing dialogue with those in the business who have an interest in a category or supplier. The purpose of purchasing-led business engagement ongoing is to:

- establish the needs and wants of users and build and maintain business requirements;

- secure cross-functional involvement to support category and supplier projects;

- recruit team members to actively participate in cross-functional category management projects with the purpose of securing some new significant benefit;

- share what purchasing are doing contribute to achieving business goals as well as what purchasing want from the business to support this;

- ensure that those who have a relationship with a supplier of a category being worked on are 'on message': in other words they are communicating agreed messages designed to condition the supplier and show complete alignment within our business;
- educate the business on the headline principles of category management, why it is important and what is needed to support it.

# Managing internal communications

Internal communications are frequently forgotten but if done well can make the difference between success and failure of a business initiative. Internal communications enable business engagement, particularly for category management if the business is to be aligned towards a single cause and will adopt and embrace single agreed category sourcing strategies for each area of spend. They also help to ensure that the resultant category strategies reflect the entire needs and wants of the business and ultimately corporate strategy. Communication does this by informing, inviting participation and diffusing potential resistance to change. It therefore is essential for category management and any business initiative.

Within category management, internal communication is part of Stage 1, *initiation*. Here as the cross-functional team is formed we develop a *stakeholder map* and then a *communication plan* to engage with the business. These two tools allow us to identify *who* we need to engage with and to plan *how* we will do this. It also helps us to then assign specific communication actions and ownership for their delivery. This internal communications activity is core to establishing our *business requirements*. Within governance, however, the approach is identical, except here we are attempting to communicate with the business, and to solicit their involvement and support at a high level for all of the initiatives and the overall goals of the purchasing function. Our stakeholder map must consider the entire organization and the communications plan should feature approaches that are likely to have impact at an organization-wide level. Approaches that can help here include:

- establishing a 'mini-brand' for the purchasing function and/or key initiatives (subject to overall corporate communication rules);
- a section on the purchasing intranet or internal website;
- direct internal marketing to those in business units;

- articles in internal magazines promoting success stories from key initiatives;
- internal roadshows;
- presentations at key managers meetings and briefings;
- getting out there and selling the message.

A useful key tool to support all of these is the *stakeholder brochure.*

# The stakeholder brochure

A stakeholder brochure is an internal publication to all key stakeholders designed to help educate the business about the role of purchasing, key objectives and initiatives and what is expected of the business.

Ideally stakeholder brochures should be short, simple, professionally produced, appealing to read and typically might include:

- how purchasing adds value today and how it will need to add value in support of corporate goals in future;
- the key initiatives that support this;
- the role the wider business plays to support this;
- an introduction to the category management methodology, why we have adopted it, how it works and the value it will bring;
- what to do and not to do when engaging with suppliers;
- how to get support for a significant sourcing opportunity or issue, or report a supplier-related problem;
- how to get involved or get help;
- introduction to purchasing: who, where, how to contact.

As with any form of internal communication 'just sending it out' will only have so much impact; instead stakeholder brochures have most impact when handed out following a face-to-face engagement or presentation. My experience of working with companies that have introduced a stakeholder brochure is that this simple step puts purchasing on the organizational map and sets the stage for new ways of engagement. It is however not the brochure that does this, but the fact that to hand it out purchasing people need to go and talk to people out in the business and explain it.

# Getting the wider organization on page

One key aim within internal communications as part of governance must be to get the wider organization aligned. If we have developed a breakthrough strategy and we are about to go out to the marketplace and invite suppliers to make formal proposals, then our potential power can easily be diluted if stakeholders have close relationships with suppliers and say the wrong things. Suppliers will of course make it their mission to establish relationships far and wide, and they will also 'divide and conquer' if given the opportunity. When I used to be in a front-line buying role and I ran RFPs leading into some sort of supplier selection process, I would frequently encounter stakeholders who would say something like, 'Oh yes, the supplier called me yesterday about another matter and also asked my view on the RFP.' My immediate question would of course be, 'So what did you tell them?' Sometimes the reply was OK, sometimes it would cause that familiar sinking feeling that meant we would need to work harder to recover this. At that time I was too polite to comment on this, largely because the stakeholder genuinely had no idea that he or she had done anything wrong, and as I had worked so hard to build my internal relationships I didn't want to damage them. However, I soon learnt that a key step at the outset was to agree with stakeholders what they would and would not say if they had contact with the supplier. Doing this meant that I needed to explain how suppliers seek information and the risks involved, and I found that in most cases, once the stakeholders understood my concerns they would then decide for themselves, and agree on a standard aligned message. From that point RFPs got a lot easier.

Getting the organization aligned means ensuring that everyone in the organization presents the same unified set of messages to the supplier and any prospective suppliers that prevents a position we are laying out with a supplier from being undermined. Remember that more often than not, those outside purchasing in any organization have never had any instruction on how to engage with suppliers, so that means it is our job to do this.

Alignment is achieved through our ongoing engagement with the business and, if we have a stakeholder brochure where we have defined dos and don'ts for supplier engagement, promoting this. For specific categories, where we are implementing a new category strategy and looking to run RFPs, select suppliers, negotiate and agree a new contract, then we need to agree a central aligned message with our key stakeholders and secure their commitment to stick to it.

Some companies have strict rules for supplier engagement and enforce policies such as 'no communications with a supplier in a tender or pre-tender scenario'. Such rules make things very clear, but for the rest of us alignment is something we need to actively manage.

# External communications

Governance extends to the overall management of all supplier and supply base communications. That doesn't mean every external discussion must be routed via the steering group, but rather that there is a planned and systematic approach for all high-level communications. This might include:

- Releasing high-level supplier briefing statements, specifically designed to communicate certain messages or changes, made available to those who interface with suppliers and, of course, containing embedded conditioning messages as appropriate.

- Publishing some form of *supplier code of conduct* to all suppliers – a simple document that describes what is required from all suppliers at a high level and might include compliance with core legal obligations or CSR policies, and might set out expected behaviours and rules of engagement. Organizations rarely set out what is expected of their suppliers beyond the immediate area of supply and that leaves the door open for the suppliers to determine how to engage. A supplier code of conduct, that the supplier is required to accept, changes this.

## 5P GOVERNANCE: *PAYOFF*

The forth component of governance is *payoff* and is concerned with the arrangements to measure, monitor, report and publish the benefits secured from specific purchasing projects. It could be specific to category management or form part of a wider purchasing benefits tracking system.

# Developing a benefits tracking approach

Category management, and indeed any strategic purchasing initiative, requires significant investment so there must be a return on that investment and we need to be able to quantify the degree to which our work is adding value to the organization overall.

The problem here is around the definition of value. If we drive in a new category strategy and achieve a reduction in price then the benefit is clear and measurable. Similarly, if we can reduce our costs we should be able to quantify this. At the outset of our project we can identify these projected via an opportunity analysis, and as we move through the process, anticipated benefits turn into actual benefits which hopefully are then realized. However, category management delivers other value, and increasingly it is the value of risk reduction, increased effectiveness and innovation that is more attractive than price or cost reduction. Not only do we need to be able to quantify this value in order to measure the payoff, but we also need to satisfy the wider organization and perhaps a finance team that there is a bottom-line impact, particularly if not everyone understands and agrees what other incremental value has been secured.

*Payoff* within governance means putting in place a benefits tracking system that allows us to measure, monitor and report both hard benefits and value-add benefits in a way that keeps the interest of the executive team to which we are accountable and shows progression against all strategic aims and objectives.

Key to establishing any benefits tracking system is to agree the approach with the finance team, and ideally have them manage it. In practice this might mean either converting less tangible benefits into a tangible number or instead having a means to tell the story in a compelling and unforgettable way that links intervention and effort to a particular outcome. We classify category management benefits under three main headings, which are price reduction, cost avoidance and efficiency improvement. However, effective strategic *sourcing*, linked to how an organization *satisfies* its end customers and has a *strategy* that connects these two can secure wider benefits for the organization that include other value benefits such as those that can be realized through a collaborative relationship with a strategic supplier and brand development where a supply arrangement and relationship can help drive competitive advantage. Therefore it is appropriate to consider benefits under five headings, and these, together with supporting explanation and examples, are given in Table 9.2.

Once the arrangements for benefit determination have been agreed, then benefits tracking is simply a case of putting in place a regular reporting regime for each category project, either requiring individual category manager to report benefits secured from time to time or a cross-functional team working on a specific initiative to report progress, for example against the milestones set in the programme plan aligned to 5i stage reviews and benefits at each stage.

**TABLE 9.2**    Benefit types and qualifying factors

| Benefit type | Qualifying factors/acceptable benefits |
| --- | --- |
| **Price reduction** | The new price paid is less than that previously paid for a similar product/service. Price reduction can include:<br><br>● A new lower price.<br><br>● Rebates based on volumes.<br><br>● Kickbacks or signing bonuses.<br><br>● Securing additional added value at no or lower additional cost, thus lowering the overall price for the new, enhanced value-added specification. Note that this type of saving is valid only if the added-value component was actually required and identified within the business requirements.<br><br>● A price lower than the normal market price (and which is demonstrable). This saving type is relevant where the product or service has not been purchased before.<br><br>● A price that is lower than the original price provided (for example, within a quotation), and where the internal customer agrees that a valid price reduction has been achieved. |
| **Cost avoidance** | Avoiding costs that would otherwise have to be paid. Examples might include:<br><br>● Dispensing with the area of expenditure as a result of the sourcing strategy.<br><br>● Reducing spend that is contractually obligated with a supplier.<br><br>● Reducing penalty payments.<br><br>● In the case where budget pricing is being used, perhaps on a complex construction project, coming in under budget can count as cost avoidance.<br><br>● Savings from using exchange rate fluctuations to an advantage. |
| **Efficiency improvements** | Improving the overall effectiveness and efficiency within a product, process or area. Efficiency savings must be quantified in terms of tangible benefits and where possible translated into financial savings through lower cost, cost avoidance or some form of increased value that is required. Efficiency savings include both those that are within the business and those within the supplier that are passed on and might include:<br><br>● Improvements to a process.<br><br>● Reduction in inventory. |

**TABLE 9.2**  *continued*

| Benefit type | Qualifying factors/acceptable benefits |
|---|---|
| **Value improvements** | Improvements that deliver some form of value to the business. Where possible, value improvements should be quantified in terms of tangible benefits over a given time frame. However, value improvements can be harder to quantify, so where this is not easily possible, value improvements should be recognized by maintaining a 'value register'; a record listing the different forms of non-financial benefit and the way each has added value, agreed and signed off by key stakeholders in the same way as direct financial benefits. Value improvement benefits include:<br>● Reduced cost of production, supply or acquisition.<br>● Synergy benefits from resource sharing.<br>● Benefits from collaboration or joint working.<br>● Economy of scale benefits.<br>● Benefits from outsourcing.<br>● Reduction of risk. |
| **Brand development** | Specific supplier contributions that directly create business growth or build and develop a brand. Such benefits are typically difficult to quantify, and so need to be measured in terms of linking specific initiatives to increased market share, brand awareness or brand penetration. Where benefits cannot be quantified a 'value register' approach with benefits agreed and signed off by key stakeholders should be maintained. Brand development benefits include:<br>● Supplier innovations or ideas that create new products and or allow new markets to be reached.<br>● Supplier-driven enhancements or improvements to current products.<br>● Business growth linked to supplier initiatives.<br>● Competitive advantage or differentiation from supplier initiatives.<br>● Benefits from association with supplier's brand.<br>● Benefits from exclusive access to supplier capability or product. |

# Accuracy in benefits tracking

So there will always be 'value-add' benefits that we can only describe by telling the story of what value we are gaining and why this helps. However, most organizations will still need and seek the hard numbers, and it is most likely it is these numbers that will form the most important measure of success, and perhaps the one that is used as part of any personal incentive and reward mechanism. Yet a benefit is only real when it has been realized and is clearly visible on the bottom line. At the outset of the project, benefits are only *projected benefits:* little more than an estimate based on the opportunity analysis work and some other factors. However, as the category management project progresses, and as more robust analysis leads to the generation of a sourcing strategy, these projected benefits can be refined into a more realistic *anticipated benefit* figure. Following negotiations with the supplier the *actual benefit* possible will become known, but this is still subject to successful implementation. A benefit can only be deemed to be *realized* when implementation is complete, the cash is in the bank, the savings are visible on the bottom line or a tangible value improvement has been achieved.

These four distinct stages of benefit realization must be considered when tracking benefits and it is important to recognize them (Figure 9.5). A category management programme will soon be deemed a failure if the purchasing team is declaring great savings but the finance community cannot see the bottom-line impact. These stages of benefit realization should therefore

**FIGURE 9.5**   The four stages of 'hard benefits' realization

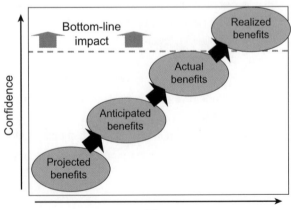

form the backbone of any reporting system used to monitor overall category management programme progress. By using this staged approach, the actual benefit progressively comes into focus and the confidence in the benefit number becomes stronger as the project progresses.

In addition to the definition of benefit types, the timeframe over which savings may be considered as realized must be defined. Companies adopt different rules here to determine what an allowable saving is. Rules should therefore be defined around both one-off and annual savings. In the case of the latter there is the option of allowing only the first year of benefit to count towards the overall benefit target; alternatively, the year-on-year benefits may be considered or there could even be a mix of the two. Whatever the rule, it should be consistent and well understood.

# Project reporting

Project reporting is concerned with the arrangements for individual project teams, working on category or other strategic purchasing projects, to report progress towards benefits realization and against stated project milestones. The steering group needs visibility of what is happening in each of the project teams in order to understand the status of the overall programme and this is established through a system of regular reporting from each of the project teams. The discipline of submitting regular reports regarding progress in terms of time and benefits helps category teams to focus on what is expected. Furthermore, if the process is two-way and there is challenge or feedback from the steering group regarding progress or delays, then the category team has little scope for allowing the project to drift.

Finally, executive teams will seek to be kept informed regarding overall progress. This is a role of the steering group. A simple system is for each category team to report its progress to the programme manager, who then combines the reports and provides the summary findings to the steering group. This allows the steering group to act on the information as required. Figure 9.6 shows the reporting structure.

For category management projects, the report format from the category teams should be kept as simple as possible. The four stage review points within category management provide natural milestones against which progress can be measured (Chapter 3, Figure 3.12). Combining the timing information from the original programme with the delivery timing of the projected benefits from the opportunity analysis allows the project milestones to be

**FIGURE 9.6**    Progress and benefits reporting for individual category management (or other) projects

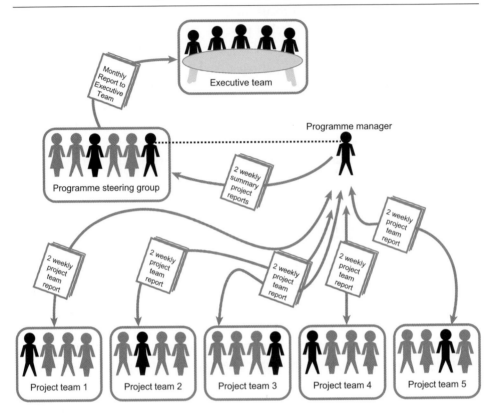

identified and defined in a reporting tool. Category teams can then report progress in terms of the timing of hitting targets and the degree of benefits realization at each stage.

Figure 9.7 shows a simple category team report. Each line represents a different milestone with defined deliverables and set timing (derived from the programme plan). At each stage, all four states of benefits realization are defined so that as the project progresses the original 'projected benefits' cascade through to 'realized benefits'. Additional, less quantifiable value benefits are noted and if these are 'realized' or not. A red/amber/green (RAG) analysis, with comments, is used to give an instant indication of overall status, thus showing areas where steering group intervention is required. This format can be adapted as needed and is readily created using an excel format or similar.

The reporting system is fundamental to a governance system, and it must be implemented and driven without reserve. In the midst of a busy project,

**FIGURE 9.7** A typical category project report

| Project milestone | Deliverables | Planned completion date | Expected completion date | Benefits realization at each stage | Additional value identified | Value realized? | Overall RAG Status and | Comments |
|---|---|---|---|---|---|---|---|---|
| Stage 1 – (Initiation) stage review complete | • Projected scoped and planned<br>• STP<br>• Team formed<br>• Stakeholder Map<br>• Comms plan<br>• First insights<br>• Complete<br>• Business requirements<br>• Value levers | 23 Nov | 30 Nov | £300k Projected<br>£312k Anticipated<br>£0k Actual<br>£0k Realized | 1. Reduced transactions and processing time with common ways of working across business units possible | N | GREEN | Projected benefits from OA. New quick wins benefits identified and underway. All Stage 1 deliverable met |
| Stage 2 – (Insight) stage review complete | • Data gathering<br>• Price/cost analysis<br>• External environment mapped<br>• Portfolio<br>• Preferencing | 21 Feb | 20 Mar | £300k Projected<br>£362k Anticipated<br>£0k Actual<br>**£12k Realized** | 1. Reduced transactions and processing time with common ways of working across business units possible<br>2. Use of new supplier technology to bring competitive advantage | N<br><br>N | AMBER | Additional £12k quick wins underway, additional changes to project scope following stakeholder engagement has delayed data collection activity, anticipated benefits increased |
| Stage 3 – (Innovation) stage review complete | • Options generation<br>• Options evaluation<br>• Risk analysis<br>• Source plan<br>• Approval to proceed | 21 Mar | 21 Apr | £300k Projected<br>£370k Anticipated<br>£0k Actual<br>**£20k Realized** | 1. As previous | N | AMBER | Additional quick wins realized, project delays not recovered |
| Stage 4 – (Implementation) stage review | • Implementation plan<br>• Supplier selection<br>• Negotiation<br>• Contract | 1 Oct | 1 Dec | £300k Projected<br>£370k Anticipated<br>£390k Actual<br>**£40k Realized** | 1. Transaction time reduced by 30%, common ways of working in place<br>2. New technology being evaluated | Y<br><br>N | RED | Negotiation successful, additional £20k signing bonus. Planning difficulties due to stakeholder concerns causing delays |
| Stage 4 – Implementation complete | • Implementation fully in place | 31 Mar | 30 Apr | £300k Projected<br>£370k Anticipated<br>£390k Actual<br>**£385k Realized** | 1. Transaction time reduced by 30%, common ways of working in place<br>2. New technology will increase value proposition to end customer from next year | Y<br><br>Y | GREEN | Variation in volumes impact realized benefits slightly. Implementation completed ahead of time |
| Stage 5 – Project completed and steady state – improvement underway | • Ongoing management approach | 31 May | 31 May | £300k Projected<br>£370k Anticipated<br>£390k Actual<br>**£385k Realized** | 1. Transaction time reduced by 30%, common ways of working in place<br>2. New technology will increase value proposition to end customer from next year | Y<br><br>Y | GREEN | Category manager in place and monitoring regime agreed |

if there is scope to delay submitting a progress report, it will be delayed. If there is no scope for delay without incurring the wrath of a senior manager, then the discipline will be upheld. This is part of good project management. One individual needs to work to make sure that all category teams report progress, without fail and in the correct format, so that the steering group can deal with any non-compliance.

Once the status of all category teams has been analysed and combined into a format suitable for the steering group, the group must act on the findings. If a category project is drifting behind schedule or does not appear to be poised to deliver the required benefits, then the underlying reasons must be understood and the appropriate interventions initiated with the team. This is an integral part of the steering group meetings.

# 5P GOVERNANCE: *PROGRAMME*

*Programme* is the fifth component of governance and is the means by which all initiatives, interventions and projects are planned and managed for category management or indeed all strategic purchasing initiatives.

## Defining the programme plan

*Programme* is about identifying priorities and planning how these will be acted upon based upon available resource. This part of governance is managed using a dynamic programme plan identifying the key projects and activities over the short to medium term (Figure 9.8). For each project, milestones correlate to the completion of each stage and the stage reviews. The plan shows category management projects, but also some SRM projects to recognize the fact that governance and programme planning is an approach for all strategic purchasing projects. Each project is arranged in 'waves' so as to balance the demand on the finite resources of purchasing and the wider business; category management projects naturally demand greater resource at the early stages. It is the role of the programme manager to establish and maintain the programme plan and the associated reporting regime.

In addition the programme plan is most effective when used as the single planning tool for all governance activities and so should include key time-bound activities such as steering group reviews, key communications and any key events.

**FIGURE 9.8** An example programme plan for category management projects and other strategic initiatives

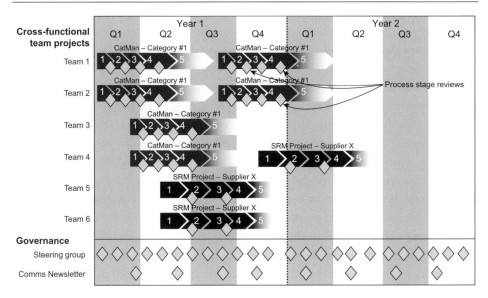

The programme plan is determined, reviewed and updated by the steering group, informed by corporate strategy, aims and objectives, the outputs from opportunity analysis, and prioritization.

# Agenda for steering group reviews

The role of the steering group is to develop and maintain a current programme, meeting regularly to review progress and update the programme as appropriate. These reviews should cover:

- overall progress against delivering headline benefits;
- review of progress against benefits for individual initiatives;
- review of progress to milestones for individual initiatives;
- review of communication plan;
- ensuring availability of the required capabilities and resources;
- review and update of the programme plan.

# SETTING UP 5P GOVERNANCE

If well implemented, 5P governance provides the all-encompassing framework that will ensure category management success, and indeed success for a purchasing function using several forms of strategic intervention. It is challenging to drive in governance 'bottom up' as the support and commitment of the organization is essential, especially at executive level. This reinforces the simple fact that if category management is to make any sizeable positive impact on the organization it must become an organization-wide approach, embraced and actively supported top down. It is at this point where enthusiastic heads of purchasing can easily despair at the scale of what is involved to secure buy-in; sometimes the mountain of internal politics, other priorities and outdated views of purchasing can seem just too hard to climb. However, 5P governance not only demands support and commitment, it helps find it and the process of driving in governance creates forums for discussion, education and can create a burning platform that compels senior executives to jump one way or another, but at least to jump. The various components of governance need to be put in place in a structured sequence, and this is given in the checklist in Figure 9.9.

**FIGURE 9.9**    The checklist for setting up 5P governance

## Governance set-up checklist

| Step | Action | Chcek |
|------|--------|-------|
| 1 | Programme name, scope and purpose defined | ☐ |
| 2 | Executive sponsor appointed | ☐ |
| 3 | Steering group recruited | ☐ |
| 4 | Steering group terms of reference and team charter agreed by all members | ☐ |
| 5 | Programme manager in place | ☐ |
| 6 | Communications Manager in place | ☐ |
| 7 | Steering group meetings set up short term | ☐ |
| 8 | Opportunity analysis completed | ☐ |
| 9 | Programme plan developed | ☐ |
| 10 | Benefits definitions agreed | ☐ |
| 11 | Benefits and progress reporting in place | ☐ |
| 12 | Assessment of competency for team leads | ☐ |
| 13 | Training and development program for team leads in place | ☐ |
| 14 | Programme stakeholder map developed | ☐ |
| 15 | Programme communications plan developed | ☐ |
| 16 | Programme 'mini-brand' agreed | ☐ |
| 17 | Central message agreed | ☐ |
| 18 | Programme communications implemented to plan | ☐ |

### Chapter 9 summary

Recap on the key points from this chapter:

1 There are many things that need to be put in place and planned for in order for category management to be successful within an organization. This involves creating the right conditions within the organization for category management with robust and visible executive support.

2 'Governance' is the arrangements we put in place to make category management happen. The *5P governance* methodology provides the framework to do this by considering the *people* who will make category management happen, their *proficiency*, the *programme* plan, how we will measure *payoff* and how we will *promote* the programme. A governance approach spans all strategic purchasing projects including category management.

3 *People* is concerned with enabling cross-functional working in a 'virtual structure', putting in place a steering group to oversee the entire programme, ideally supported by someone with programme management responsibilities.

4 *Proficiency* is concerned with ensuring the right capability for those practising category management through a managed programme of learning and development, and working to establish a common process, toolkit, language and ways of working.

5 *Promote* is concerned with securing the right level of business engagement far and wide so the value of the programme is understood and there is a shared 'felt need' to get involved.

6 *Payoff* is concerned with establishing and managing a system to track benefits realization. Whilst hard savings are easy to measure, category management delivers value in many forms so it is essential we can identify and quantify these and measure overall project progress against organizational targets.

7 *Programme* is concerned with establishing and managing ongoing a programme plan of all the individual strategic purchasing projects, including category management projects, and managing progress of the plan.

# Guaranteeing success – now and for the future

In this final chapter we will review two case studies of best-practice implementation and highlight some potential pitfalls; we will examine what makes category management successful, how category management can be applied in different ways to organizations big and small and how the approach can respond to the challenges that organizations will potentially face for the future. Finally, we will consider the developing role of category management in response to future changes in the global market and landscape.

Pathway questions addressed in this chapter:

**14** How does the company need to structure and organize itself to deploy category management effectively?

**15** Is category management an approach that will still be relevant in the future?

## TWO INSPIRATIONAL SUCCESS STORIES

## How Cardiff Council used category management to drive procurement transformation

In the UK, Cardiff Council is the unitary authority for the city and county of Cardiff, home to around 300,000 people. The authority spends £350 million each year. Turn back the clock and this spend was highly fragmented, procurement was highly tactical and there was precious little cooperation with the important players in the supply base. As part of an overarching commercial strategy Cardiff launched a procurement transformation programme to kick-start a wholesale change, setting a hard target to deliver £18 million in savings over five years. The target and indeed the entire programme were born out of an extensive spend analysis and review of supplier performance. Category management was selected as the vehicle to achieve this target and so Cardiff set about implementing the approach and a five-year programme was born.

The starting point was a restructuring of the tactical procurement function. A new category-centric organization structure designed around the 44 market-facing categories was put in place. These were aligned under three umbrella categories of social care, construction and buildings maintenance, and corporate, transport and ICT. A new category management process and toolkit was created and Cardiff then attempted to build capability through training and the recruitment of experienced practitioners. Initially process application was kept as simple as possible, empowering teams to figure out the most effective route through the methodology but building more structure later on. Category teams worked up programme plans and project management approaches were initiated to look after the all projects. As teams began to apply the new tools and techniques cross-functional working emerged. Governance built steadily and the leadership team worked to drive in a new culture built around good practice, challenge and compliance with the process. Category teams started to report quarterly to the executive team on performance to targets.

So far this might read like any other good category management implementation where you put certain things in place and results emerge. However, it was not quite that straightforward. Once the programme was up and running savings delivery was initially lacking. This was due in part to difficulties recruiting individuals of the right calibre; however, there was one other key factor and that was that outside procurement the wider business had not yet begun to own the initiative. In fact, the transformation programme only really got going once the different authority directorates put some 'skin in the game' by giving commitment to supporting the achievement of savings targets by removing the savings from their forward budgets, creating the compelling need to ensure they were delivered.

Five years on and Cardiff has exceeded the savings targets it set out to achieve, but a much deeper transformation has been achieved. Procurement has transitioned into a strategic function with the buy-in and support from across the business and they are now looking to the next wave of projects. A recent fitness check conducted by KPMG rated Cardiff procurement as 'developing to advanced', with leadership and strategy scoring highly.

The work at Cardiff featured a number of steps and activities that contributed to overall category management programme success. These were:

- use of detailed analysis and hard data to determine programme targets;
- creation of a branded transformation programme built around category management;
- restructuring procurement around categories;
- developing capability in category management;
- installing strong programme management;
- driving in cross-functional working;
- embedding strong governance;
- building ownership by the business for programme outcomes;
- building senior management buy-in.

In reviewing lessons learned from the programme, the executive team at Cardiff were clear that category management is about driving a wholesale change in procurement, but this was only successful when the wider organization could change together with it. Senior management buy-in was crucial and a lot of success depended upon education and training as well as striking the right balance between tactical and strategic work; after all, while the big procurement project is rolling along there is still the day job. Finally Cardiff identified that the most important success factor was getting people to trust and have faith that the programme would work and was worthwhile.

# Learning from GSK – one of the all-time great examples of a quality category management implementation

Looking back in time, there is one category management implementation that stands out from most others and could be regarded as a benchmark for excellence in how to establish and use category management to drive dramatic value from the supply chain.

GlaxoSmithKline (GSK) is one of the world's leading research-based pharmaceutical and healthcare companies. Its stated mission is to *help people do more, feel better, live longer* (**www.gsk.com**, 2015). GSK remains possibly one of the best examples of leading-edge category management deployment. Back in 2001, the programme was born out of regulatory pressure to increase competition within the industry, as well as shareholder demands for greater efficiencies and synergy benefits from the amalgamation of Glaxo Wellcome and SmithKline Beecham. GSK recognized both the need and the opportunity to significantly increase effectiveness and efficiency across the organization. Such improvements came from a number of areas, initially by business consolidation (ie removing duplicate facilities) and headcount reduction, but a significant contribution came from the supply chain as a direct result of the global category management programme.

With a then-global spend of approximately £8.5 billion and a supplier base where complacency and comfortable relationships had gained footholds, the opportunity for purchasing within GSK to make a sizeable contribution to shareholder equity through the bottom line was obvious and compelling. GSK embarked on the category management journey across its global business (internally calling it 'sourcing group management' to avoid confusion with marketing category management). Within just two years the programme was a visible success, having delivered real savings to the business of around £800 million (10 per cent of turnover). This was the most obvious tangible benefit, but the programme also delivered other less obvious and in some cases unexpected benefits.

As the momentum of the programme increased, so did the profile of the initiative, both across the wider business and with suppliers. HR, R&D, marketing and production all finally had to take notice. It didn't take long for any hopes that the programme might fizzle out and disappear to be dismissed. Category management workshops became the way in which cross-functional teams engaged and worked together through the process, often incorporating elements of training to help stakeholders fully engage. Cross-functional teams held workshops around the world, of course at major centres such as London and Philadelphia, but also in remote facilities as far flung as Kuala Lumpur and Costa Rica. Line managers received requests from staff to join category teams in order to be part of the success story. Together people began to think the unthinkable and challenge the way things had been done. Energy to drive hard changes emerged.

A dramatic shift in supplier behaviour occurred. Comfortable relationships that could be maintained by discounting a few per cent here and there were replaced by the prospect of having to fight to retain business. Suppliers contemplated the risk of losing a major prestigious brand account, and an urgent imperative to find ways of providing more for less was born.

Those involved in the category management programme found a new source of motivation. People found themselves part of a success story that not only presented new, exciting challenges but also gave them more opportunity than ever before to learn from, and interact with, other parts of the business.

Initial conflict emerged as teams formed and developed, quickly to be replaced by performance and integration. Groups became highly dedicated. They pushed for success; they even achieved breakthrough in some cases, despite many team members believing at the outset that this was against the odds. For many, this was the first time in their careers that they had been associated with such a success story. People felt they were achieving something dramatic and worthwhile, and a wave of excitement over certain breakthroughs ran through the organization. Amongst the breakthroughs were fundamental changes in materials used, specification reviews which eliminated need, and radical changes to the way parts were sourced. All of this was, of course, only possible through cross-functional engagement and hard work. The value in being part of the programme to boost future career progression was clearly understood by all.

These benefits did not simply happen once GSK had taken the initial step. The tangible signs of a successful programme resulted directly from a properly structured, planned, executed and resourced programme with visible support from the top down. The GSK programme is potentially one of the best examples of category management deployment because, simply, it contained all the right ingredients in the right proportions, a fact that won the company a series of industry awards for purchasing excellence. Among the critical success factors that made the programme so successful were:

- *Establishing 'the way GSK buys'*. At the outset, GSK established a category management process and toolkit aligned with GSK language and ways of working and translated into four languages. The GSK category management process provided an anchor for the entire programme. Communication experts found ways to promote and publicize the programme that encapsulated the purpose and benefits. Soon it was almost impossible for anyone within central functions not to have heard of the programme. This company-wide awareness proved very powerful in the battle for people's attention, encouraging them to make the time to get involved and support the projects.

- *Capability development.* GSK appointed a head of education and development within the purchasing function, with a global remit to increase the capability of purchasing teams to become expert practitioners. A large-scale global education and training programme followed, with coverage at all levels and depth to match respective roles. A total of 1,200 people received training during 85 workshops in 11 countries, conducted in four languages, the majority being four-day events. Additional on-the-spot training formed part of the subsequent workplace coaching programme and cross-functional workshops.

  GSK didn't rely solely on training and coaching to provide the capability development framework. Individuals were encouraged to take responsibility for self-development. All practitioners were required to take simple tests of understanding before they could be considered as having achieved base-level competence. But the true learning came from applying the process for real. GSK recognized this and introduced a certification programme. Category managers could, if they met the tough criteria, attain category management 'champion' status. To become champions, they had to have managed a category through one cycle of the category management process to the point of completion at which the strategy had been implemented. Practitioners were required to present their category and the journey they had undergone to an assembled panel of senior staff and experts who would award champion status to only a select few. The programme created a healthy competitive tension within purchasing staff. Line managers competed to have the purchasing team with the first champion, or to be first to have their whole team qualified, while staff jostled for position in the limited schedule of candidates to go through the panel. Overall, GSK managed to create a desire for progression, development and recognition that led to a distinct uplift in overall capability.

- *Inspirational executive support.* The company's CEO at the time, J P Garnier, demonstrated his full support for the programme to both the organization and suppliers. He made sure his executive team was also behind the initiative, and attention was paid to ensuring that the signs of this support were highly visible. Every category management training event began with a professionally produced video featuring the CEO and executive staff talking with a united voice about the GSK category management programme, its importance to the future of GSK, and what was expected of the business in supporting it. Feedback from delegates who watched the video demonstrated that the strategic imperative to this was well understood; and, moreover, the video disarmed any delegates who may have had it in their mind to question the priority of engaging in the programme.

- *Large-scale workplace coaching, facilitation and development programme.* GSK recognized that training and education alone were not enough to change the way people worked. Using support from experienced category management practitioners GSK launched a programme of coaching and development for their category managers. Coaching staff were made available to support small groups of category managers, intensively at first for the early stages of each practitioner's first category projects and then easing off and moving on to work with new practitioners. The approach varied from individual to individual according to need, but typically, at the outset of a project, the coach's support would be more 'doing' than 'guiding', including facilitation of workshops, developing templates and point-of-need training in tools, approaches and the process.
  Over time, this balance would shift to guiding and to providing the practitioners with individual feedback and development to help make them self-sufficient. Finally, the support was withdrawn completely. This coaching support was hugely powerful. It not only helped to embed the learning from training sessions, but also provided the required momentum and energy for the programme. It also set the standard for how the process should be deployed, leaving the organization truly self-sustaining when the external support was removed.

- *Cross-functional imperative.* Outside purchasing, the business was given the clear objective to make time for and get involved in category management projects. Indeed, key staff had this added to their personal objectives and therefore the basis on which any bonus would be paid. An internal stakeholder brochure was published, describing the category management programme and what was expected of the business in participating in and actively contributing to cross-functional teams. Meeting rooms and locations became in short supply as category management workshops began around the business, and busy people made time not only to attend meetings but also to attend to the supporting activities required in order to progress through the process.

- *Sharing best practice.* 'Lighthouse' examples of best practice and success stories were published. Best-practice sourcing strategies were shared with other practitioners online, being available as a global point of reference. Similar intranet-based systems were made commonplace for supplier contracts and market intelligence gathered by category teams.

- *Governance.* The purchasing leadership team set up and maintained an effective governance system. It conducted regular reviews of the capability development programme and overall progress of category projects. Stage reviews formed the backbone of governance and ensured that appropriate process rigour was applied. Before moving from one key stage of the process to another, category managers were required to present their work so far to an assembled panel including senior purchasing individuals and relevant senior stakeholders for the business area concerned. The governance approach played a vital role in ensuring overall programme success by setting the standard for how the process should be used in practice, as well as securing active support and participation at all levels.

- *Getting it moving.* GSK recognized that category management programmes can become long haul, delivering significant benefits, but only at the end of a long journey. The company overcame this by putting energy into securing early benefits. Practitioners, together with their cross-functional teams, were pushed hard to identify and pursue quick-win opportunities; this helped to develop momentum and report initial results early, which established programme success.

There was, however, one other factor that played a significant role in launching the programme and catapulting it into the fast lane in the space of just one day. A supplier forum, convened by the senior vice-president of purchasing, was attended by suppliers of key or strategic importance to GSK as well as those with whom the company spent most. The suppliers' senior staff listened intently as they were told that things needed to change and why, where GSK needed to be in the market, and the role of the supply base in supporting this. They were told about the category management programme and what they could expect to happen over coming months. Then everyone in the room was provided with an opportunity to join what was at the time termed the '777' initiative. Suppliers were told they needed to play a part in GSK's journey. This could be done by making an immediate reduction of 7 per cent in the cost of their goods or services. It didn't stop there. They were also invited to commit to an additional 7 per cent in the next year and a further 7 per cent the year after that. They were left in no doubt that in order to secure a possible future with GSK, they could not ignore this request. Some reached for their chequebooks, some sat back to see how things would play out, and some dismissed this as a crude tactic, believing the strength of their position was too great. Subsequent work over coming months, using category management, quickly identified and addressed any unbalanced relationships. The savings started to roll in, the process had begun, the breakthroughs appeared, the depth of opportunities increased; and the supply base became very attentive.

Today, category management continues to be the solid process that is 'the way GSK buys'. The process has of course been updated, modernized and optimized from lessons learnt and developments in best practice. However, once the big ripe early opportunities were largely realized, it was SRM that then helped to secure the next wave of benefits for the new critical or strategic supplier relationships that emerged from category management.

Overall, this leading-light programme enabled GSK to reach a level of sourcing maturity beyond many of its peers and competitors at that time.

# FACTORS AND CONSIDERATIONS FOR SUCCESSFUL CATEGORY MANAGEMENT

## The key success factors

In our journey through this book we have explored what category management is, how it can add value and how it can be deployed and used. At the start of this book I described the importance of a quality implementation if real breakthrough is to be realized, and now it is appropriate to pause and look back at what this actually means. If you have hung in there until this point in the book then by now you will have a pretty good grasp of category management. So it is at this point that we draw on everything we have learned and we can review the success factors to make category management really work well in the form of the 10 primary success factors for category management.

The 10 primary success factors for a quality category management implementation:

1  *Enabling active participation* – A business structure that enables, encourages and embeds cross-functional working to underpin category management.

2  *Top-down remit* – Robust executive support and active endorsement – making category management 'the way we buy' from the top down.

3  *Sourcing, satisfying and strategy* – Business mindset that seeks to connect sourcing with satisfying end customers, informing and shaping corporate strategy accordingly.

4  *Robust governance* – Driving and underpinning the entire programme supported by good programme management.

5  *Sufficient resources* – Any busy business attempting to make the leap from transactional to strategic purchasing is unlikely to succeed simply by 'bolting on' category management. Something needs to change, which either means new suitably competent resource or stopping doing something in order to create headroom.

6  *High profile and 'felt need'* – Making the programme high profile across the business so all are aware of and share the 'felt need' for it.

7  *Common process, toolkit and ways of working* – Available to and used by all, driven in without exception and actively working to ensure good process rigour by all.

8  *Game-changing mindset* – Drive in a shared mindset top down to seek and secure breakthroughs and active review and challenge along the way to make this a reality.

9  *The right capability* – Highly capable practitioners, with the required competencies to apply the methodology and with the supporting soft skills to run category projects effectively, enabled and supported by an ongoing managed programme of blended learning and development, initially directed but transitioning to a self-directed learning environment.

10  *Celebrate success, create and maintain momentum* – Category management programmes are long term, so if it is to remain one of the central areas of focus for a business it is essential that success stories are shared far and wide, that those involved celebrate success so as to create and maintain a positive momentum for the programme ongoing.

# Developing category management 'black belts'

The critical success factors for category management described earlier not only demand 'the right capability' but an organizational mindset of challenge and seeking breakthrough underpinned by good process rigour.

This means practitioners not only need to be advanced in the application of the toolset and overall deployment of the process, but also the organization needs to know this is effectual. Training alone may not deliver this as what we need here is not just a learned set of skills, but something that comes from experience of having done this. Experienced practitioners know how to drive category management projects and when and how to challenge; those further back on the development curve may have no sight of what *good* looks like. Without a reference point it is all too easy for project outcomes to be underwhelming or to merely be a fancy name for the tendering and contracting approach that existed previously. I know from my own experience that I didn't truly understand category management until I had done it for real in an environment where those around me were delivering game-changing results and I was expected to do likewise.

Ongoing learning and development are therefore essential and these need to be planned and resourced, which is why they are part of the 5P governance methodology. Coaching can help here and a programme of external coaching support for category teams can have enormous impact. It can also have a big price tag. Focused external coaching support is perhaps more in reach for some organizations – bursts of support from time to time just when needed. Yet even with external coaching the results can be mixed, especially if left to practitioners to decide what they need or if the knowledge transfer is suboptimal (a common outcome if external coaching overly *does* rather than *guides*).

Good coaching, and the associated learning and development ongoing, needs to be both stage managed and available on demand. It needs to exist with the sole purpose of accelerating capability at a practical level and making it sustainable in the long term. This is possible with external support if well managed, but it is also possible to do internally, or with a mix of the two. Core to this is the identification of the experienced practitioners within the organization who could support this.

The concept of a *black belt* of course denotes the highest level of proficiency within martial arts. The term was adopted by the world of Lean and

a level of proficiency in these methodologies where
onstrated not only an advanced understanding of
but is sufficiently experienced at applying them
.tuations and can coach others in doing so. Sound
..igma and category management have a lot in common.
, management is founded on the business improvement ap-
...nd in Lean Six Sigma. So the concept of a 'category manager
oelt' fits nicely into our world.

Category manager black belt is a status and position that an organization
can create internally. It allows individuals to have a designated role to coach,
support and develop other practitioners. It also creates a new level for other
practitioners in the organization to aspire to, especially if there is some sort
of incentive to do so. Setting up a black belt system is straightforward; it
is simply a matter of defining what 'black belt' means in the organization,
creating a system to award and reward this status, perhaps based upon
completing certain steps or achieving defined outcomes, and then creating
the environment for the black belts to operate. This might involve a plan of
coaching engagement with category teams, with black belts conducting
stage reviews and generally being available to and getting involved with
category teams as needed. Therefore it is imperative that these individuals
are afforded sufficient time to perform their role. Typical attributes which
could form a basis for qualification to black belt status might include:

- Has demonstrated master practitioner ability with the category
  management process and all supporting tools – can teach, coach
  and apply the tools at a master or advanced level.

- Can lead and facilitate cross-functional workshops and demonstrate
  team leadership and motivational skills. Is able to deal with difficult
  stakeholders and resolve conflict easily.

- Has completed at least two complete category management cycles
  with categories moving into Stage 5, *improvement*.

- Has published at least two source plans detailing compelling
  sourcing strategies and demonstrating effective process rigour.

- Can demonstrate a breakthrough mentality and point to active
  pursuit of game-changing outcomes within the work done so far.

- Is able to coach and guide internal practitioners, ideally holding
  a coaching qualification.

- Can lead and manage category management stage reviews.

# Avoiding 'tick box' category management

One of the most common reasons why category management implementations fail to deliver is 'tick box' category management. This is when the organization successfully introduces a credible process and toolkit, and invests in training practitioners as well as creating the right conditions for the approach to operate, yet practitioners work through the process at a superficial level as if 'ticking boxes' as they progress. I've seen entire category teams present outputs from a process stage or an entire source plan that contain all the expected worked tools, and even include lots of graphics that appear to suggest on the face of it a good output, yet examination soon reveals precious little substance or insight, little that is new or different to current arrangements, and unclear strategy. This is a common problem and is primarily due to an absence of effective review and challenge. When people undergo training in category management, they usually get it by the end of the workshop, yet when they begin to apply the tools for real the leap from theory to practical situations can be daunting, often creating more questions and challenges. As we have seen, it is a common mistake to view training in category management as a single event, rather than an ongoing learning and development approach. If practitioners, and perhaps peers are operating in a vacuum post training they will do their best in the absence of any reference point around what good looks like. If this remains unchallenged then 'tick box' category management is established and the organization ends up investing heavily in deploying a complex process that perpetuates current sourcing arrangements. Once again we find that the interventions that prevent 'tick box' category management are part of good governance, specifically:

- ongoing coaching and support;
- knowledge sharing of what 'good looks like' and so setting the bar high;
- active culture of challenge with a breakthrough mindset with managers 'dropping in' and asking to see new insights or questioning if more can be done to find a breakthrough;
- robust stage reviews ongoing as 'stage gates' that have to be satisfied before further progression.

# SMAC and category management

Significant aspects of our personal and business worlds now happen online, and purchasing and category management are no exception. Many aspects of category management are already 'e-enabled' in some way with new solutions emerging using a range of Social, Mobile, Analytics and Cloud (SMAC) technologies. Traditionally category management has been executed using Excel, Word and PowerPoint and even paper, storage shelves and filing cabinets. As the old methods evaporate before our eyes a range of SMAC applications, networks, B2B systems and tools for greater effectiveness now drives what we do and how we do it. The scale of change when compared with how we worked 10 years ago is enormous, but also unstoppable. SMAC technologies will underpin and enable the way we will work in the future; it's just a matter of the rate of adoption. The world of category management will benefit from SMAC, but the way in which this will happen, whilst preserving good process rigour and the overall effectiveness of the approach, is only beginning to be understood. In the short term caution is needed by any organizations seeking to be at the forefront of technology not to trade quality category management for an e-enabled alternative without fully considering how it will operate and deliver the required outcomes.

There is a plethora of B2B solution and platform suppliers in this space offering analytics and cloud-based applications and systems, and some claim to have that much sought-after all-encompassing 'electronic purchasing' solution that does everything. However, the reality is that there is a range of providers offering a good e-solution for a specific area of purchasing need, yet the all-encompassing solution still remains illusory, despite what the marketing material might say. Outside transactional systems, there are some great eSourcing suites, contract management software, supplier collaboration tools, performance measurement tools, market data portals, toolkits and a world of e-learning with different degrees of usefulness. A 'combined' solution is clearly attractive, hence the big players' attempts to offer one, yet it seems there is no shortage of organizations who have invested in large corporate systems that do some things really well, but fall short in other areas. A category management 'bolt on' module might appear to provide a dashboard of management information regarding category team progress, but this will be worthless if the category teams are just ticking boxes online to satisfy the system. When buying or specifying any online solution in this space it is essential to keep the success factors for category management (above) front and centre in our thinking. Category management is successful because people collaborate across organizations and apply their combined deep thinking to doing something differently, with the outputs being a record of that thinking. If the e-solution automates this too much then practitioners will take the path of least resistance and thinking can get diluted. If it is possible to simply enter some data and work through some online forms in order to complete an entire stage of the process then this is exactly what some will do; the management dashboard will look great but process rigour will be lacking, business engagement will suffer and breakthroughs will become fewer. That said, the internet opens up a world of possibilities for category teams to collaborate and work on their projects online. The key to adopting any sort of B2B online solution for category management is to be really clear about the functionality needed, so a good set of business requirements is essential. Furthermore, online tools also need to be intuitive and user friendly if people are to want to adopt them. I know some very extensive and comprehensive sourcing tools that do incredible things, but require users to undergo vast training before they can find their way around, resulting in poor adoption. It is still early days for solutions in this space. The different components of category management that can be provided for online in one way or another, with different solution providers offering one or more of these, are:

- access to process, tools and templates;
- e-learning;
- workflow management (monitoring progress and benefits realization);
- online source plans;
- online collaboration;
- market research and information;
- eSourcing tools (eAuction and eRFX);
- contract management tools;
- supplier performance measurement tools;
- supplier management tools;
- supplier relationship and collaborative management tools;
- knowledge management and document-sharing platforms.

For now, companies that are enjoying success from online enablement are the ones that are buying a selection of platforms rather than a single integrated solution; taking the best provider for each need. Clearly the risk here is creating a series of 'islands' with little integration or data sharing; however, as we move forward these islands will become more and more integrated.

A further consideration here is data security, a growing risk as we increasingly move online and become cloud based, and one that is slow to be taken seriously. For a B2B category management or purchasing solution it is important to understand what happens to your data – data about categories, markets, suppliers, perhaps commercially sensitive information or information that reveals future strategies and so on. Clearly anything 'cloud' has risk of being hacked into, but that risk can be understood and provided for. More pertinent is how any solution provider might use your data for other purposes. B2B providers in this space are beginning to accumulate huge data from multiple companies about buying patterns, market pricing, market trends and so on. This, in theory, affords the provider with scope to realize the value of the insights from this data so it is important to determine what data that flows and is stored outside the traditional bounds of an organization needs to be protected and how this will be provided for.

We can't leave this section without considering the increasing role of social media and forms of online networking for category management. The modern purchasing practitioner is connected in real time to an array of information feeds and sources. Finding a solution to a purchasing challenge is just a tweet away and getting access to examples of best practice just needs a post in the right place. The entire world of purchasing is now able to benefit from the shared collective wisdom and knowledge of those who are leading the charge. There is huge value in being a part of, and contributor to, this modern phenomenon. Increasingly category management projects are benefiting from practitioners being able to gain confidence in what they are doing, access market, supplier and category insight, and learn from those who have gone before for a given category. Yet despite this many organizations still discourage or prevent the use of social media tools professionally. Sometimes there are good safety and security reasons behind this, but not always. Some organizations have been slow to consider the role of social media to support purchasing and with this comes uncertainty or a lack of clarity regarding what is appropriate. If there are no clear guidelines then there is a risk staff unwittingly share information that should not be shared. The reality here is that the world of online social media and networking is unstoppable. It's unlikely to go away, will just get more refined and useful, and can increasingly contribute to supporting category management projects, but it is important for organizations and functions to define what is and is not appropriate.

# Scalability for small businesses

The power and benefit potential of category management for large global businesses with huge spends are clear, but what about small or medium-sized businesses where the aggregate spend in a certain area may not yield much leverage in a marketplace? Well, the approach can still be beneficial but with some limits. As a concept category management requires a degree of leverage by size, spend, volumes, brand attractiveness and so on. For a small business these factors would most likely be limited. However, there are many aspects to the category management approach that can still drive a highly effective and strategic purchasing approach. Furthermore, many of the tools can help to ensure that every dollar or euro is spent well. There is no substitute for understanding the marketplace you are buying from. If you can understand whether the price you pay is fair or otherwise, then you can make good buying decisions.

Thinking in terms of categories of spend and then identifying the respective opportunities using an analysis of spend and the opportunity analysis tool can help an organization identify the areas where it is worth expending the effort. For example, a medium-sized construction company with a turnover of £5 million identified the biggest spend area was with builders' merchants. Buying was project based and teams would source what was needed from whichever merchant was nearby, believing it was better to minimize the time spent on the road getting supplies. However, this turned out to be false economy and a review led to identifying the top-spend common products (such as blocks and plasterboard) and sourcing direct from a main distributor with delivery to site as needed. The review also led to putting preferential agreements in place with just two merchants and employing a dedicated driver to go and source materials for all jobs. The net result was a significant reduction in cost and better utilization of expensive skilled tradesmen. Initiatives similar to this, using elements from category management, can make a dramatic difference to a small business. The process, whilst not fully scalable, can still be beneficial and entirely relevant, and many of the tools will help bring great insight and inform business decisions.

# WHAT THE FUTURE HOLDS

## The challenges facing organizations over the next 20 years

We began this book by considering the relevance of category management today and how it sits within an ever-changing landscape. Change is set to define the future and two things are almost certain: the rate of change we have come to see is unlikely to abate, and the challenges facing organizations are set to get harder. The global economic crisis of recent years has deeply impacted countries, markets, organizations, societies and individuals, shown us that there is little certainty and brought the issue of security of supply into the spotlight as entire marketplaces suddenly shrank.

Perhaps the age of affordable fossil fuel-based energy is over or perhaps fracking will unlock new, previously unobtainable, reserves and revive the age once more. Have we reached or have we passed the peak in terms of available oil that can be pumped, or is there still plenty? And if so will we continue to be at the mercy of OPEC, or will increased supply from the non-OPEC producers create a new competitive tension that results in a steady decline in oil prices bringing us lower prices for the foreseeable future? This will open up new opportunities throughout the supply base as oil-based commodity prices realign and make previously unfavourable sourcing strategies in some areas suddenly become attractive where the cost of logistics is a key determinant.

Advances in technology at an ever-increasing pace will keep changing the game. Cars will drive themselves, powered using technology not yet perfected which may even be created where we least expect it. The current quest for a new generation of low- or near zero-emission cars will bear fruit, perhaps just awaiting that breakthrough in battery capacity and charging time. Perhaps the next global car brand will be Chinese or perhaps the slow-down of China's economy will halt this. The same revolution will transform logistics even more than any reduced oil price.

Medicine is set for a revolution too when smart nano particles will be available to enter our bodies, like tiny microscopic submarines travelling through the human body on the hunt for specific cells or damaged tissues, ready to change state or release chemicals when they find them – precisely where needed to deliver highly precise healing. It won't just be advancements made in laboratories of global corporations that drive progress, but brilliant minds, somewhere in the world, somehow connected together to achieve common goals. In the same way that a talented teenage musician can now write, record and release a song to the global market from his bedroom and become an overnight success. Small companies with the hunger and a unique and desirable offering will be better placed to become successful without the need for any significant overheads; somewhere out there may lie a brilliant contributor. The ability to find and nurture innovation externally to a business will become an important part of purchasing's role, engaging individuals and companies more as collaborators than traditional suppliers, with a relationship and commercial model to suit.

As the world's population continues to grow and people live longer, future food security will demand new approaches. In the next 20 years, world cereal demand is likely to increase by 50 per cent, driven by both increased consumption and growing animal-feed use. Our attitudes to food production are also predicted to change and the food supply chains of the future will look very different, with commodities originating from new places as our global climate shifts and we need to find new land to grow crops. This land may well exist in developing countries, but owned by the wealthier countries who will have long since bought up available agricultural real estate to preserve future food security. This, coupled with more crop failures around the world as drought and floods become an everyday news story, could mean rising costs for all and potentially less for consumers to spend elsewhere. It could also drive new attitudes to and methods of food production; genetically modified may become the food of choice for consumers.

Despite the population expansion, the world will continue to shrink. Developing countries have the eager labour pool ready to satisfy the demand for people to fill jobs and are learning how to trade with the rest of the world. People are on the move and it's not just employment that is driving migration; increased wealth, climate change and social changes are tempting more people than ever before to consider relocating or retiring to another country. Whilst migration to help fill the jobs that would otherwise remain vacant is set to continue, the demand for talented people is set to become much fiercer at a global level. Organizations will have to work harder to attract and retain the key staff that can make a difference. Providing for lifestyle balance and people working less and less at organizational centres will change the way business is done and increase our reliance upon IT solutions to enable new ways of working.

Globalization, yes, but localization and personalization too, as 'better, faster and just for you' defines our future demands and preferences. Our suppliers could exist anywhere in the world but interact with us as if they are just next door, and they may not ever need to ship anything, but rather transmit a design for us to print using 3D printing technology. 3D printing will also transform the assembly line, creating parts with fully integrated electronics, and will equip niche providers with a never-before-seen tool to realize whatever they dream up whenever they want. Innovation from the supply base may not be about making or shipping things but connecting ideas with where they will be turned into reality.

Water will cease to be taken for granted, as is already the case in Middle East countries. Waste will become big business and in some industries will shift from being simply a facilities management activity to being a strategic function actively minimizing bottom-line impact.

The impact of climate change on business and our everyday lives is set to continue to be significant enough to warrant wholesale action. Climate change is now a global concern and one that is being taken seriously, driving new social norms and legislation, and in turn the way people, organizations and entire economies act.

Our future modern lives will demand innovation across technological boundaries which will connect industries and practices that sit separately today. Companies with a core competency in one area will find themselves needing to acquire and connect with new core competencies in another and will turn to the supply base to help. The minute, electronic, wireless revolution means medicine bottles will become intelligent and message our phones to remind us to take a tablet. Intelligent refrigerators will update our shopping list as things run out. 'Things' will become the biggest users of the internet (Valéry, 2013). Today we can have a watch with the computing power of the space shuttle; tomorrow that computer will be many times more powerful, perhaps worn as spectacles or something else, but something we will interact with effortlessly. It will be more connected to the rest of the world, will be intelligent and will interact on our behalf with the world around us in ways we have not yet considered. Our cars, pets, clothing, medical implants, toys and tools will all have their own digital intelligence and interact with us and sources of information via the internet. A successor to silicon-based devices is a real possibility and our children might only find the keyboard and mouse in a museum. Data will become a highly valued commodity causing our every interaction with the real and virtual world to be monitored, measured and analysed. At some point the deep implication of governmental and corporate bodies amassing data about who we are and our preferences will become fully appreciated, by which time it will be too late to reverse things. Perhaps this will be a good thing that will improve our lives; perhaps it will have other consequences and drive a revolution in future data protection and security.

All this is set against the backdrop of heavy politics and new tensions that concern us all. Not long ago Russia was thought to be the next emerging market, now it is flexing its muscles and asserting its position on the global stage. The relentless expansion of other developing economies continues, each claiming the right to growth without the obligation of environmental regulation. Yet for other 'recent boom' economies things are changing. In the wake of China's credit boom, things are now slowing up along with others such as Japan, Brazil and South America (GEP, 2015). Uncertainty and difficulty within the eurozone are also likely to continue worry financial markets in the near term.

# Future implications for purchasing

There is no doubt there are some exciting things that will shape our future lives, but no matter which area of human progression we consider there is one common theme emerging and that is that we can't leave all this to chance. The future role of purchasing will be one to help organizations navigate through this increasingly changing landscape and it is the strategic approaches of category management together with SRM that will help do this.

Purchasing will need to be the architects of a new generation of sourcing strategies that balance capitalizing on the new opportunities available from an ever more global and innovative supply base whilst managing in an ever more volatile and unpredictable environment.

The way purchasing functions exist and are structured will need to change. Purchasing will need to make a direct contribution to helping organizations face the challenges ahead, and it is well placed to do so. Tactical buying alone will simply not be sufficient for any business that wishes to keep up. Purchasing must be a strategic contributor to overall business success. Pick up any good purchasing textbook and it will offer commentary on centralized versus decentralized purchasing versus a mixed approach and the various attributes of each approach as if this is merely an organizational choice. The reality here is that our future landscape will eliminate the option of a fully decentralized purchasing function that is anything other than purely tactical. Purchasing will need to make an even more strategic contribution to the business that will demand either centralization or central coordination of the firm's entire purchasing effort.

Dramatic cost reductions may, in some sectors and for some categories, become the subject of purchasing history books, with the focus shifting towards value enhancement, managing risk and assurance of supply. Innovation, creativity and breakthrough ideas will all be required, and to an ever greater extent. Finding ways to *satisfy* customer demand, but also reduce the cost, be green, sustainable, use no or little energy, and not produce waste, will be the new challenges. The role of purchasing will be essential to connect the innovators in the supply chain with the needs of the organization. Smart organizations will recognize the opportunity for a greater contribution from purchasing to determine overall organization strategy based on watching supply chain developments and changes closely.

In the short term, strong strategic purchasing talent for this new world will be in short supply, but as organizations develop their teams and the function naturally becomes a more strategic enabler of overall business capability, and thus a more attractive place to be, this is likely to soften and rebalance over the next 20 years.

Purchasing functions may also find themselves returning to a 'policeman' role in some areas. In the 1980s many large purchasing functions incorporated a supplier quality assurance team with remit to manage risk exposure through the qualification and auditing of the supply base. Such approaches are still relevant in certain critical supply areas but generally are not so mainstream, largely due to a widespread increase in organizational capability and accreditations such as ISO9001. However, the corporate social responsibility (CSR) agenda may once again revive the need for purchasing functions to actively assess supply chains and original factories/plantations ahead of any global certification and accreditation system in this area.

# The role of category management for the future

The philosophy of category management will, if well deployed, equip and enable organizations for the future. Category management together with SRM provides the complete strategic purchasing intervention necessary to safeguard an organization and help bring competitive advantage as the world around us changes. This can only happen with quality implementation of the methodologies within a business. *Sourcing* must connect with *satisfying* and both must inform and be informed by corporate *strategy*.

As this book draws to a close, it is worth reflecting on the fact that in this third edition I have added many updates, enhancements and new insights to help practitioners better understand and apply the concept, but the fundamental category management approach remains largely unchanged. Recently I was asked why the process hadn't changed and was still almost the same as it was more than 10 years ago. This question came with a hint of criticism together with an expectation that for things to move on they have to keep being redefined. The reality here is that the underlying category management methodology is an absolute, just the same as any good business improvement methodology. It hasn't changed and is unlikely to change. Individual tools and labels may change, and different practitioners will put their own flavour on it. Perhaps we may even call it by a different name in the future. What is certain to change is the way it is applied and our ever-changing landscape will demand that we use and deploy specific tools in new ways or to achieve new outcomes.

Business requirements will need to include robust CSR needs and wants. They will also be shaped and defined by the future needs and aspirations of the end customer, not just those within the firm who have a view. Break-throughs will, in part, come through new, more far-reaching research and data gathering about current and potential suppliers and marketplaces. Looking to immediate suppliers will no longer be sufficient and, for some categories, purchasing and supply chain management will need to converge, bringing supply chain mapping and supply chain management to the fore. What do we need for the future? The brilliance that will carry an organization forward may not necessarily reside within that organization; some of it might, and some of it may be unobtainable in the traditionally employed resource model but might exist somewhere on the planet. It may need to be sourced using a new type of strategy that connects different sorts of con-tributors and producers, from all over the world, using the latest technology whilst protecting security of data and supply. Risk management will become core business for purchasing and integral to category management for supplier, supply base and strategy implementation risk.

How we manage categories of spend and how we manage suppliers and the supply base can no longer be separate concerns, and it is the integration of both approaches that will prove the most impactful for organizations. An arm's-length supply base may continue to be good commercial practice for many, but not all. If we view our suppliers passively as just 'suppliers' responding to demand we determine then we could be left behind, sat on the sidelines watching as the world around us changes. Many suppliers now need to be regarded as 'enablers' or 'innovators', 'connectors' or 'assurers', operating within a new type relationship and commercial framework that encourages them to be share brilliance with us. We need new skills, new mindsets, new outlooks; to shift focus to what is important; to link supply base intervention to corporate objectives; to understand where in our supply base we need to focus our effort, all according to the current and future needs of the business and the environment it sits in. It is the providers who are agile and flexible enough to respond quickly who can most help us in future and purchasing will help create this agility with thorough effective and integrated category management and SRM.

The category management philosophy provides all the components for the future and can help enable organizations to face the challenges ahead but only with a quality implementation. It can help retain and even build market share whilst protecting the organization against the new risks of our changing world.

This brings me to my last point. Earlier I outlined the 10 key success factors for a quality category management implementation – the 10 things that make category management work well. It is no coincidence that *enabling active participation* through cross-functional working is number one. It is cross-functional working that will help organizations pull together to solve difficult challenges, using the supply base to find solutions. This is undoubtedly the most important point of all. With organizations set to face incredible challenges in the next 20 years, purchasing's role to support this at a strategic level, using proven strategic approaches and including category management, is crucial. It is the ability of organizations to work collaboratively in our changing world to find ways through complex problems that will unleash the true power of human brilliance. With that, organizations can achieve anything.

---

## Chapter 10 summary

Recap on the key points from this chapter

1  A quality category management implementation depends upon a number of success factors. These include having a top-down remit, a means to connect *sourcing* with *satisfying* and so informing and shaping *strategy*. Robust governance and sufficient resources are essential and the programme should be high profile, creating a 'felt need' across the business for it. Common process, toolkit and ways of working need to be mainstream, and the organization must work to enable active participation whilst creating a 'game-changing mindset'. The right capability needs to be provided for and finally the organization should celebrate success whilst creating and maintaining programme momentum.

2  Category management black belts are a concept of creating an internal advanced level of practitioner capability and designating individuals to help with ongoing learning and development as well as driving in process rigour in the capacity of internal coaches.

3  A common mistake to be avoided is that organizations create 'tick box' category management where practitioners work through the tools, producing much output but with shallow insight and little breakthrough.

4  There are many online systems out there e-enabling some aspect of what purchasing does, but there is as yet no single system that does all of these things well in one place despite many attempting to put category management online. There is risk of 'tick box' category management and a good set of business requirements should be developed for anyone considering specifying an online system.

5  Category management is not necessarily scalable to small businesses as the leverage required to make it work may not be present. However, many of the tools and approaches are relevant and can help drive in good buying practices.

6  Our future landscape will be an ever-changing one and presents many and varied opportunities, risks and challenges for organizations in the future. Purchasing's role will need to change to respond to these new challenges and category management, together with SRM, will provide the essential strategic methodologies to help do this.

# APPENDIX
## Tools and templates

## The complete set of tools and templates to begin practising category management

New to this third edition, this appendix provides a collection of the essential tools and templates for practitioners to apply category management. If you have purchased this book then you may copy and reproduce the tools within this appendix for your own personal use as you practise category management. They may not be copied and distributed to others or used for commercial gain. They may not be modified and the copyright designation must remain in place.

For more information on corporate licensing of category management processes and toolsets please contact: jonathan.obrien@positivepurchasing.com.

# STAGE 1 TEMPLATES

**FIGURE A1** Opportunity analysis

## Opportunity Analysis

| Category | Date |
|---|---|

Use for categories or sub-categories. Determine spend, assess organizational and market difficult (HML). Assess price flexibility and category maturity (HML) and determine like savings % (from figure 3.5). Calculate projected savings. Identify other value. Determine priorities.

| Category | Spend | Organiz't'nal Difficulty | Market Difficulty | Price flexibility | Category maturity | Savings% | Projected savings | Value Opportunity | Priority |
|---|---|---|---|---|---|---|---|---|---|
| | | | | | | | | | |
| | | | | | | | | | |
| | | | | | | | | | |
| | | | | | | | | | |
| | | | | | | | | | |
| | | | | | | | | | |
| | | | | | | | | | |
| | | | | | | | | | |

Total potential savings

**FIGURE A2**  STP template

| Category | | | Date |
|---|---|---|---|
| **STP** *(Situation, Target, Proposal)* | | | |
| Problem statement | | | |
| Situation | | | |
| S | | | |
| Target | | | |
| T | | | |
| Proposal | | | |
| P | | | |

© Jonathan O'Brien, 2015

**FIGURE A3** Team charter

**Team Charter**

| Category | Date |
| --- | --- |

Category name and boundaries

Category team purpose

Targets for this category

1
2
3
4
5

Key project deliverables | Due date

*Stage 1 planned completion date*

*Stage 2 planned completion date*

*Stage 3 source plan ready*

*Stage 4 implementation begins*

*Stage 4 implementation complete*

**Team members, roles and responsibilities**

Sponsor name

Sponsor responsibilities

Team leader name

Team leader responsibilities

Team members (names) | Roles

1
2
3
4
5

Team member responsibilities

© Jonathan O'Brien, 2015

**FIGURE A4**   Stakeholder map

## Stakeholder Map

| | Category | | Date | |
|---|---|---|---|---|

| | Name | Role | RACI | | | | Support level | | | | Comments | Action |
|---|---|---|---|---|---|---|---|---|---|---|---|---|
| | | | R | A | C | I | AIH | LIH | HIH | MIH | | |
| 1 | | | | | | | | | | | | |
| 2 | | | | | | | | | | | | |
| 3 | | | | | | | | | | | | |
| 4 | | | | | | | | | | | | |
| 5 | | | | | | | | | | | | |
| 6 | | | | | | | | | | | | |
| 7 | | | | | | | | | | | | |
| 8 | | | | | | | | | | | | |
| 9 | | | | | | | | | | | | |
| 10 | | | | | | | | | | | | |
| 11 | | | | | | | | | | | | |
| 12 | | | | | | | | | | | | |
| 13 | | | | | | | | | | | | |
| 14 | | | | | | | | | | | | |
| 15 | | | | | | | | | | | | |

**FIGURE A5** Communications plan

| Communications Plan | Category | Date | | |
|---|---|---|---|---|
| To **Whom** (name or group) | **What** – key messages | **How** – channel or media | Frequency or timing | Owner |
| 1 | | | | |
| 2 | | | | |
| 3 | | | | |
| 4 | | | | |
| 5 | | | | |
| 6 | | | | |
| 7 | | | | |
| 8 | | | | |
| 9 | | | | |
| 10 | | | | |
| 11 | | | | |
| 12 | | | | |
| 13 | | | | |
| 14 | | | | |
| 15 | | | | |

**FIGURE A6**    Project plan

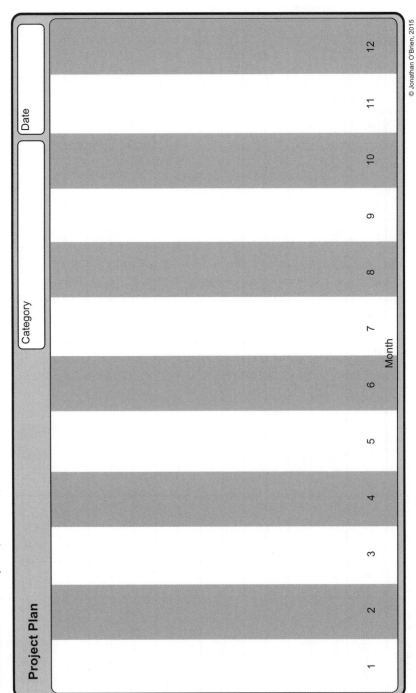

**FIGURE A7** Quick wins

## Quick Wins

Brainstorm potential quick-wins ideas as a group then classify them using the matrix below. Finally, for the quick wins that are the most worthwhile, determine and assign actions to pursue them.

*Quick-win classification and prioritization*

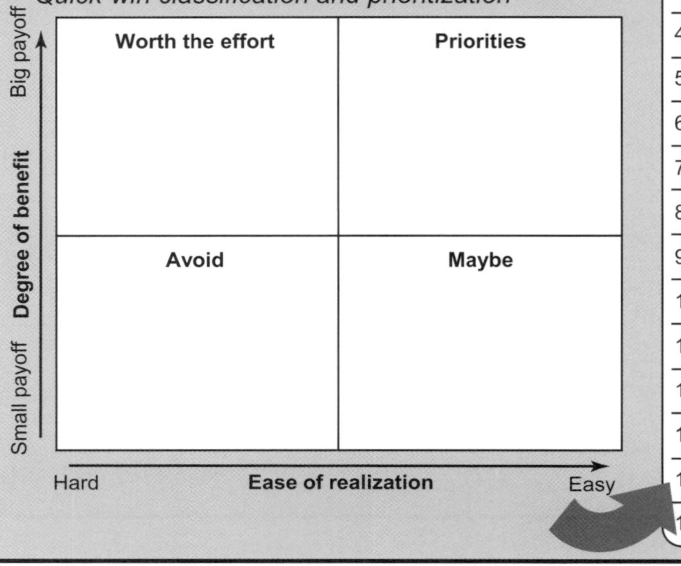

| Worth the effort | Priorities |
|---|---|
| **Avoid** | **Maybe** |

**Degree of benefit** (Big payoff ← → Small payoff)

**Ease of realization** (Hard → Easy)

| Category | | Date | |
|---|---|---|---|
| | What | Who | When |
| 1 | | | |
| 2 | | | |
| 3 | | | |
| 4 | | | |
| 5 | | | |
| 6 | | | |
| 7 | | | |
| 8 | | | |
| 9 | | | |
| 10 | | | |
| 11 | | | |
| 12 | | | |
| 13 | | | |
| 14 | | | |
| 15 | | | |

© Jonathan O'Brien, 2015

**FIGURE A8** Day one analysis

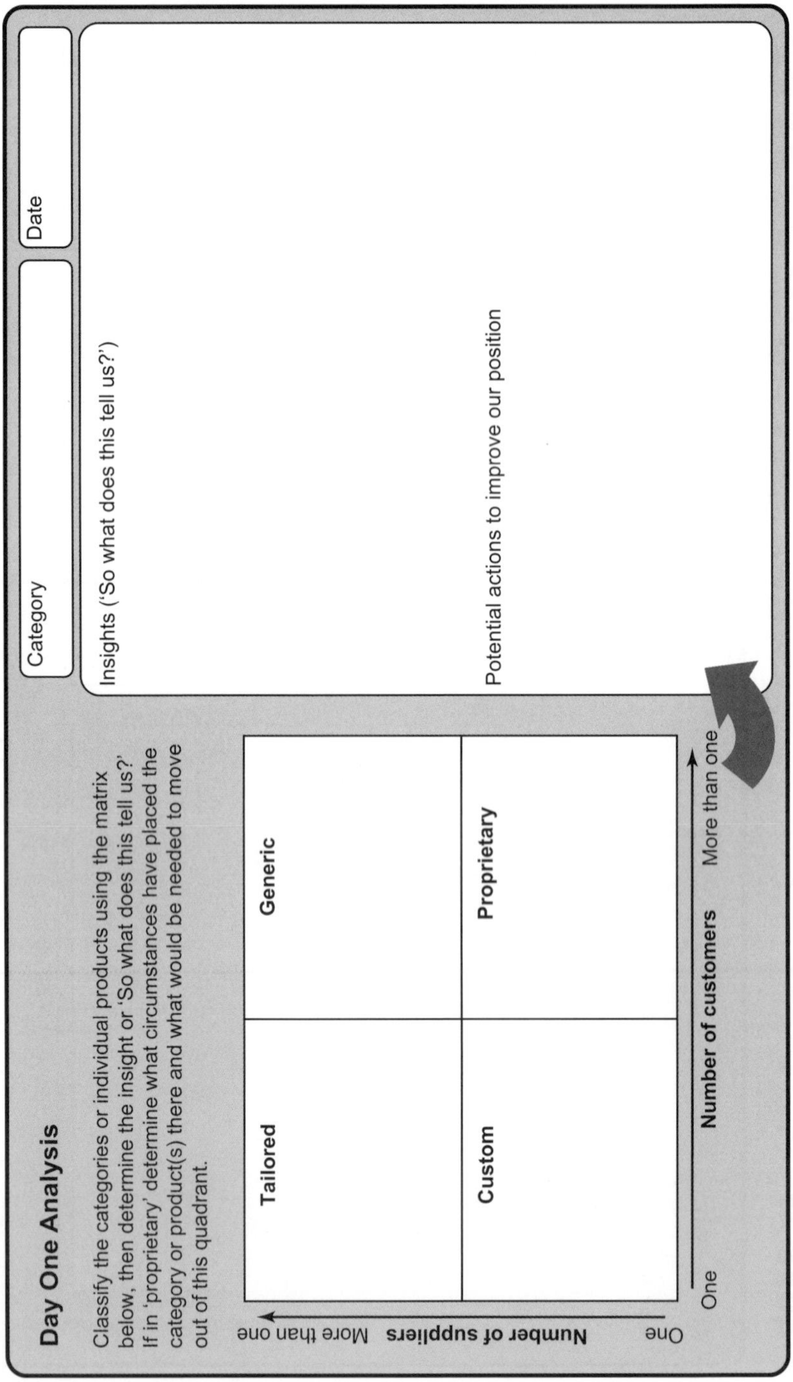

**Day One Analysis**

Classify the categories or individual products using the matrix below, then determine the insight or 'So what does this tell us?'. If in 'proprietary' determine what circumstances have placed the category or product(s) there and what would be needed to move out of this quadrant.

| Category | | Date |

Insights ('So what does this tell us?')

Potential actions to improve our position

**Tailored**

**Generic**

**Custom**

**Proprietary**

**Number of suppliers** — One / More than one

**Number of customers** — One / More than one

© Jonathan O'Brien, 2015

**FIGURE A9** Value levers

| Value Levers | | |
|---|---|---|
| Identify all the potential levers that could unlock value for the category. | Category | Date |

| Category | | |
|---|---|---|
| *Supply & value chain* | Change specification | Change design | Aggregate spend |
| *Supply market* | Improve process efficiency | Analyse and remove cost | Improve logistics |
| *Supplier relationship* | Increase competition | Find new markets | Restructure supply base |
| *Supplier incentivization* | Improve relationship | Performance development | Seek innovation |
| *Demand management* | Offer commitment | Improve payment terms | Support route to market |
| | Buy less or eliminate | Policy and compliance | Increase asset utilization |

© Jonathan O'Brien, 2015

**FIGURE A10**   Business requirements

| Business Requirements | | Category | | Date | |
|---|---|---|---|---|---|
| | | | | | |

| | Requirements | Now | | Future | |
|---|---|---|---|---|---|
| | | Need? | Want? | Need? | Want? |
| **R** Regulatory | 1 | | | | |
| | 2 | | | | |
| | 3 | | | | |
| **A** Assurance of supply | 1 | | | | |
| | 2 | | | | |
| | 3 | | | | |
| **Q** Quality | 1 | | | | |
| | 2 | | | | |
| | 3 | | | | |
| **S** Service | 1 | | | | |
| | 2 | | | | |
| | 3 | | | | |
| **C** Cost/commercial | 1 | | | | |
| | 2 | | | | |
| | 3 | | | | |
| **I** Innovation | 1 | | | | |
| | 2 | | | | |
| | 3 | | | | |

# STAGE 2 TEMPLATES

**FIGURE A11** Data-gathering plan

| Data-Gathering Plan | Plan Type: Category/Internal ☐ Supplier ☐ Market ☐ | Category | Date |
|---|---|---|---|

| Data to collect | RFI | RFP | Desktop research | F2F with Stakeh'dr | Other (specify) | Who | By when |
|---|---|---|---|---|---|---|---|
| 1 | ☐ | ☐ | ☐ | ☐ | | | |
| 2 | ☐ | ☐ | ☐ | ☐ | | | |
| 3 | ☐ | ☐ | ☐ | ☐ | | | |
| 4 | ☐ | ☐ | ☐ | ☐ | | | |
| 5 | ☐ | ☐ | ☐ | ☐ | | | |
| 6 | ☐ | ☐ | ☐ | ☐ | | | |
| 7 | ☐ | ☐ | ☐ | ☐ | | | |
| 8 | ☐ | ☐ | ☐ | ☐ | | | |
| 9 | ☐ | ☐ | ☐ | ☐ | | | |
| 10 | ☐ | ☐ | ☐ | ☐ | | | |
| 11 | ☐ | ☐ | ☐ | ☐ | | | |
| 12 | ☐ | ☐ | ☐ | ☐ | | | |
| 13 | ☐ | ☐ | ☐ | ☐ | | | |
| 14 | ☐ | ☐ | ☐ | ☐ | | | |
| 15 | ☐ | ☐ | ☐ | ☐ | | | |

*How data will be collected*

**FIGURE A12**   Data-gathering summary

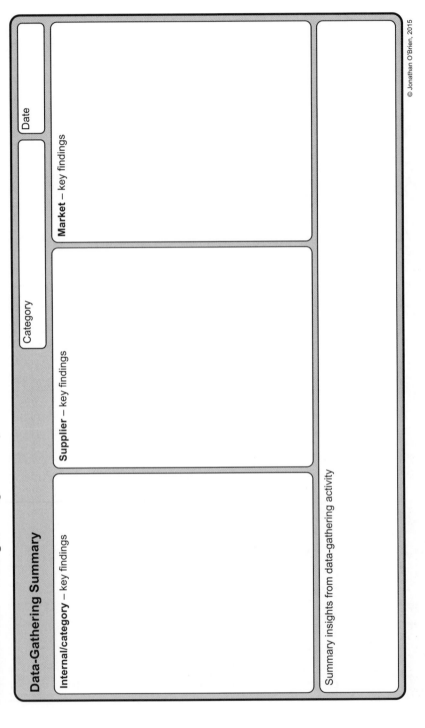

| Data-Gathering Summary | | Category | Date |
| --- | --- | --- | --- |
| **Internal/category** – key findings | **Supplier** – key findings | **Market** – key findings | |
| Summary insights from data-gathering activity | | | |

© Jonathan O'Brien, 2015

**FIGURE A13** Price model

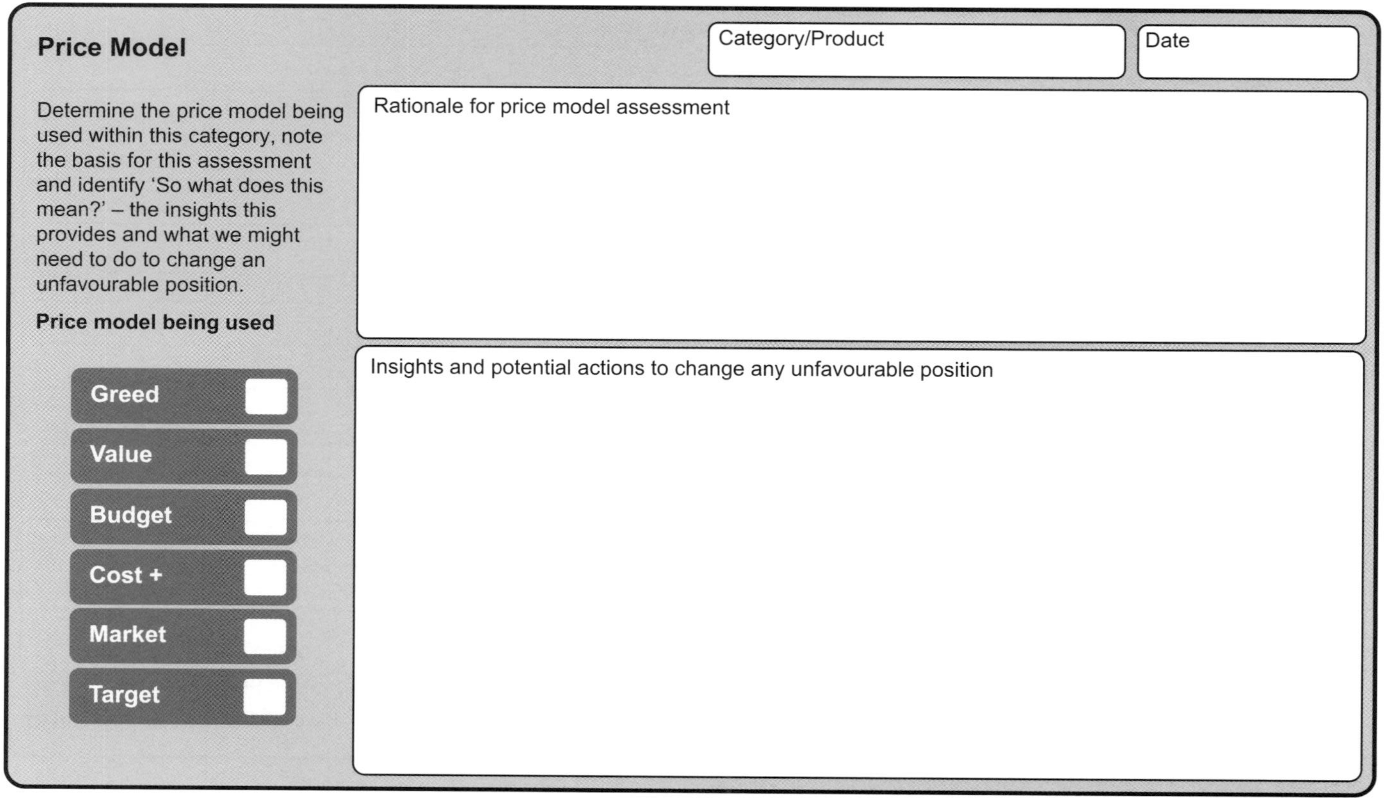

## Price Model

Category/Product

Date

Determine the price model being used within this category, note the basis for this assessment and identify 'So what does this mean?' – the insights this provides and what we might need to do to change an unfavourable position.

**Price model being used**

- Greed
- Value
- Budget
- Cost +
- Market
- Target

Rationale for price model assessment

Insights and potential actions to change any unfavourable position

© Jonathan O'Brien, 2015

**FIGURE A14** Purchase price cost analysis

## Purchase Price Cost Analysis

| Item | Price paid |
| --- | --- |

### Direct cost components

| | Cost component | Calculations | Total |
| --- | --- | --- | --- |
| 1 | | | |
| 2 | | | |
| 3 | | | |
| 4 | | | |
| 5 | | | |
| 6 | | | |
| 7 | | | |
| 8 | | | |

### Indirect cost components

| | | | |
| --- | --- | --- | --- |
| 1 | | | |
| 2 | | | |
| 3 | | | |
| 4 | | | |
| 5 | | | |

Difference between price paid and PPCA 'should cost' analysis

Total 'should cost'

© Jonathan O'Brien, 2015

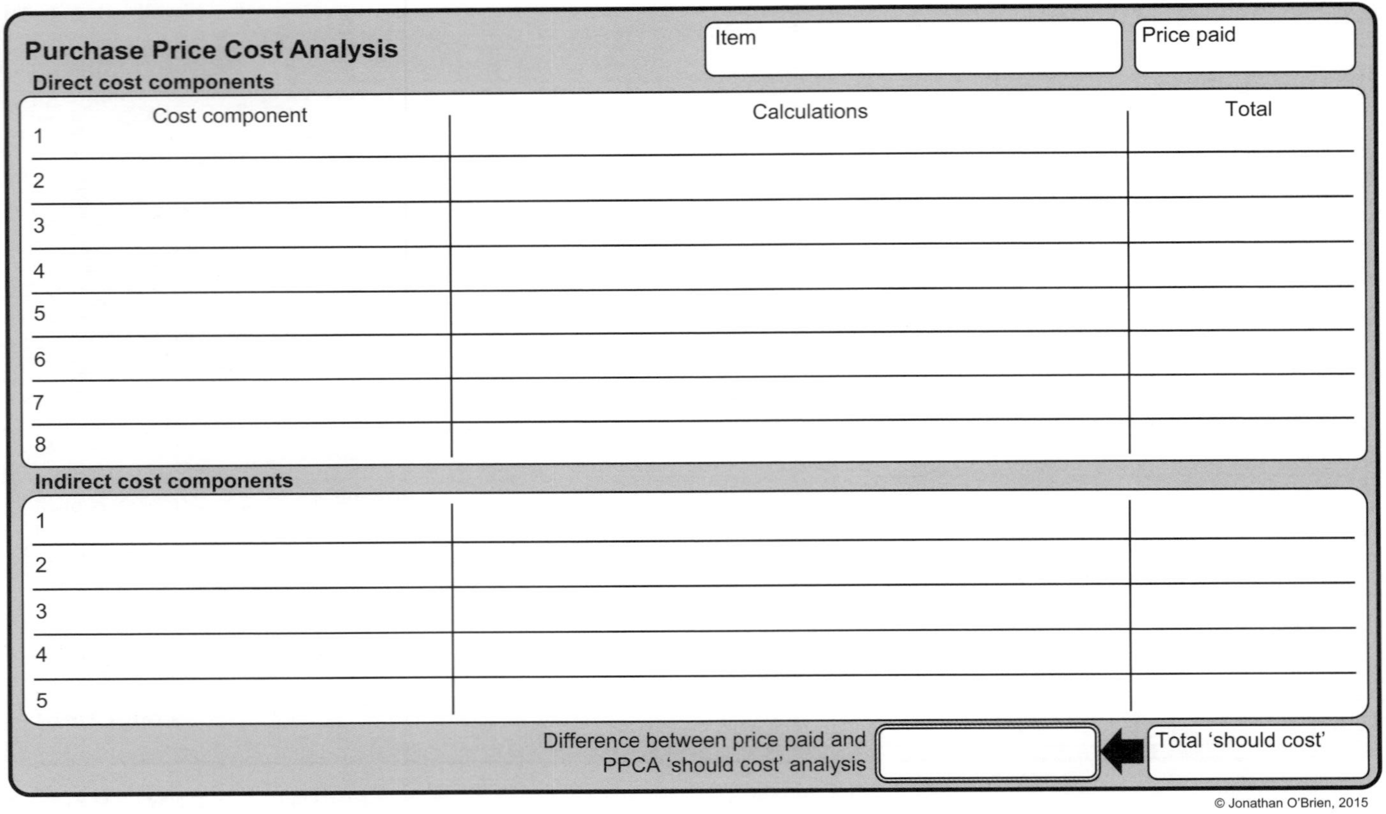

**FIGURE A15** Technology road map

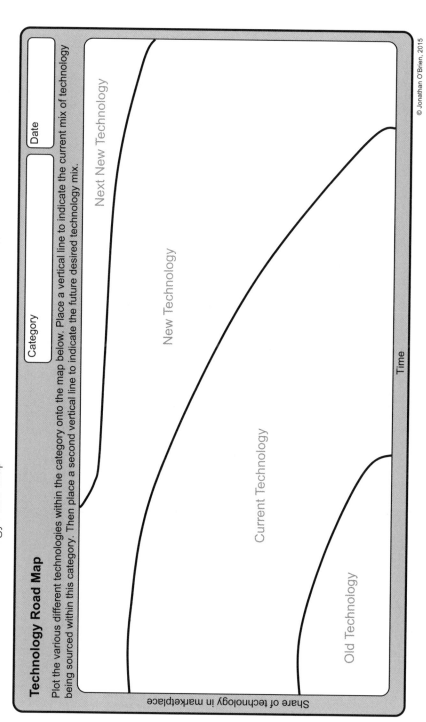

## Technology Road Map

| Category | | Date |
|---|---|---|

Plot the various different technologies within the category onto the map below. Place a vertical line to indicate the current mix of technology being sourced within this category. Then place a second vertical line to indicate the future desired technology mix.

Next New Technology

New Technology

Current Technology

Old Technology

Share of technology in marketplace

Time

© Jonathan O'Brien, 2015

**FIGURE A16**   PESTLE analysis

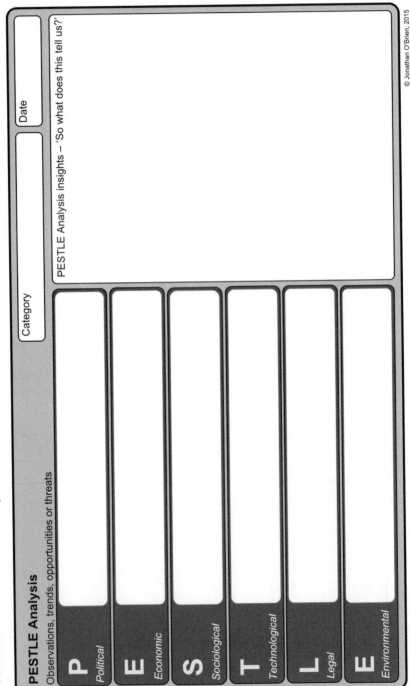

**PESTLE Analysis**

Observations, trends, opportunities or threats

| Category | Date |
| --- | --- |

PESTLE Analysis insights – 'So what does this tell us?'

**P** *Political*

**E** *Economic*

**S** *Sociological*

**T** *Technological*

**L** *Legal*

**E** *Environmental*

© Jonathan O'Brien, 2015

**FIGURE A17** Porter's five forces

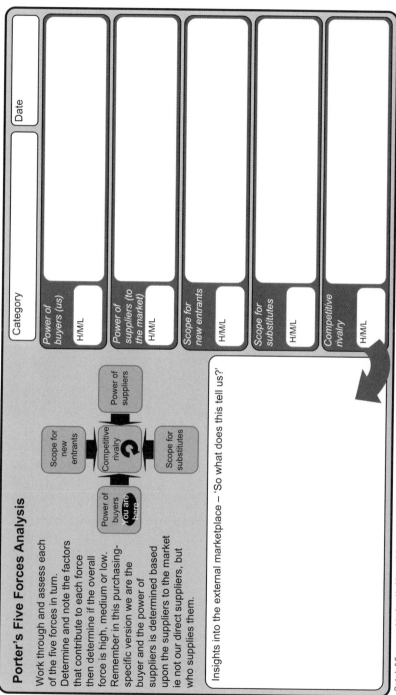

## Porter's Five Forces Analysis

Work through and assess each of the five forces in turn. Determine and note the factors that contribute to each force then determine if the overall force is high, medium or low. Remember in this purchasing-specific version we are the buyer and the power of suppliers is determined based upon the suppliers to the market ie not our direct suppliers, but who supplies them.

Scope for new entrants

Power of buyers — You are here

Competitive rivalry

Power of suppliers

Scope for substitutes

Insights into the external marketplace – 'So what does this tell us?'

| Category | Date |

Power of buyers (us) — H/M/L

Power of suppliers (to the market) — H/M/L

Scope for new entrants — H/M/L

Scope for substitutes — H/M/L

Competitive rivalry — H/M/L

Porter's 5 Forces was introduced by Michael E Porter in the 1980s and has proved a useful tool for understanding market or industry dynamics. This version is adapted from Michael Porter's original work.  © Jonathan O'Brien, 2015

**FIGURE A18**   Portfolio analysis

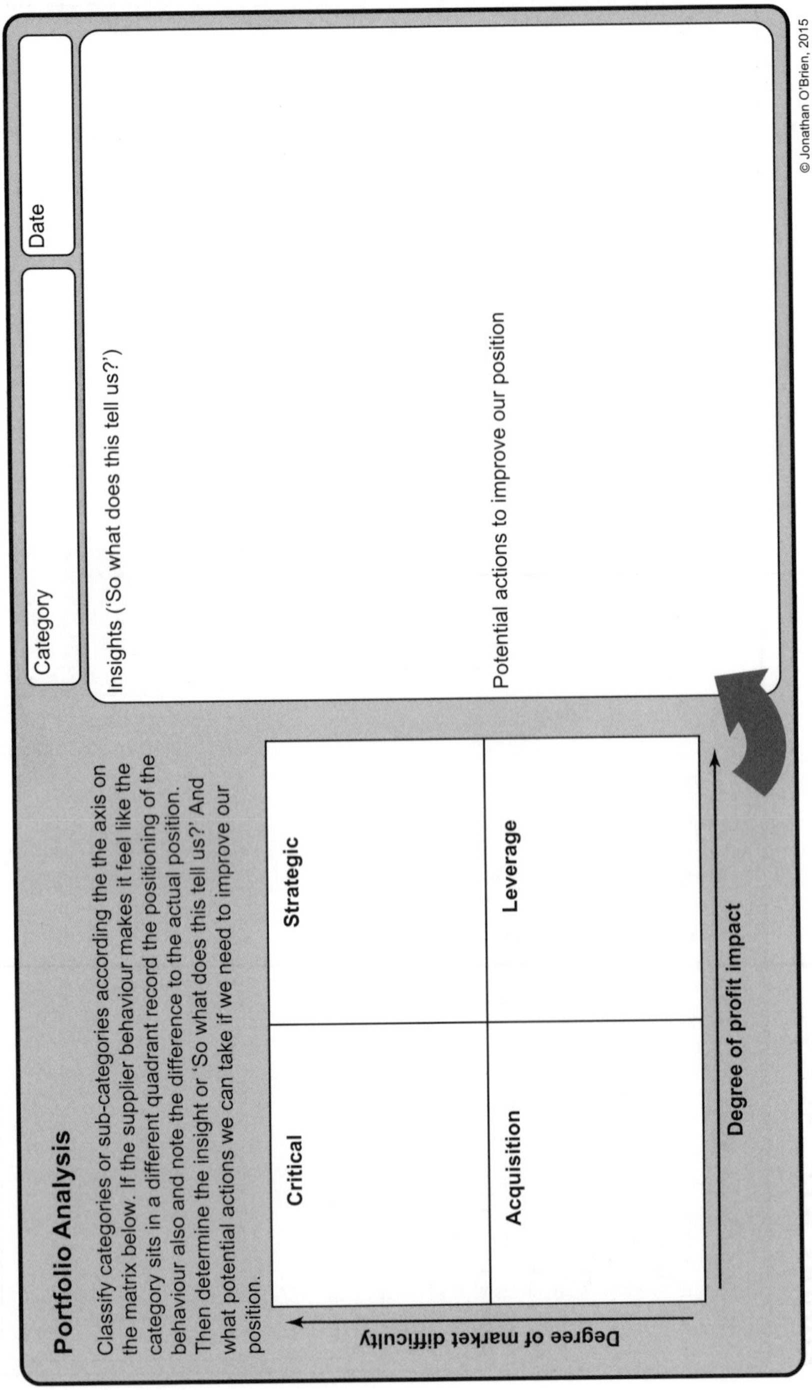

| Category | | Date |
|---|---|---|

**Portfolio Analysis**

Classify categories or sub-categories according the the axis on the matrix below. If the supplier behaviour makes it feel like the category sits in a different quadrant record the positioning of the behaviour also and note the difference to the actual position. Then determine the insight or 'So what does this tell us?' And what potential actions we can take if we need to improve our position.

| Critical | Strategic |
|---|---|
| Acquisition | Leverage |

Degree of profit impact

Degree of market difficulty

Insights ('So what does this tell us?')

Potential actions to improve our position

© Jonathan O'Brien, 2015

**FIGURE A19** Supplier preferencing

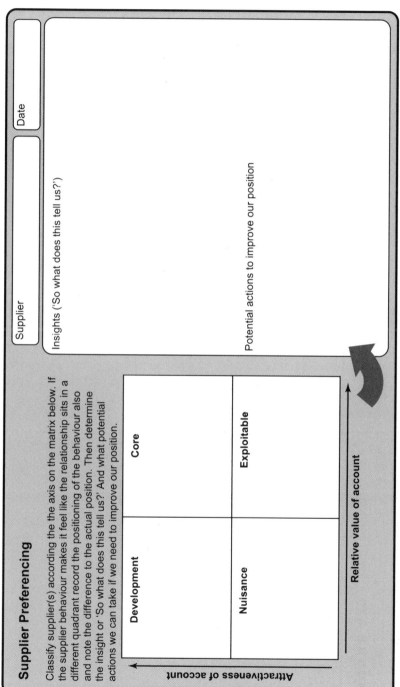

**Supplier Preferencing**

Classify supplier(s) according the the axis on the matrix below. If the supplier behaviour makes it feel like the relationship sits in a different quadrant record the positioning of the behaviour also and note the difference to the actual position. Then determine the insight or 'So what does this tell us?' And what potential actions we can take if we need to improve our position.

Development | Core

Nuisance | Exploitable

Attractiveness of account

Relative value of account

Supplier

Date

Insights ('So what does this tell us?')

Potential actions to improve our position

© Jonathan O'Brien, 2015

# STAGE 3 TEMPLATES

**FIGURE A20**   SWOT analysis

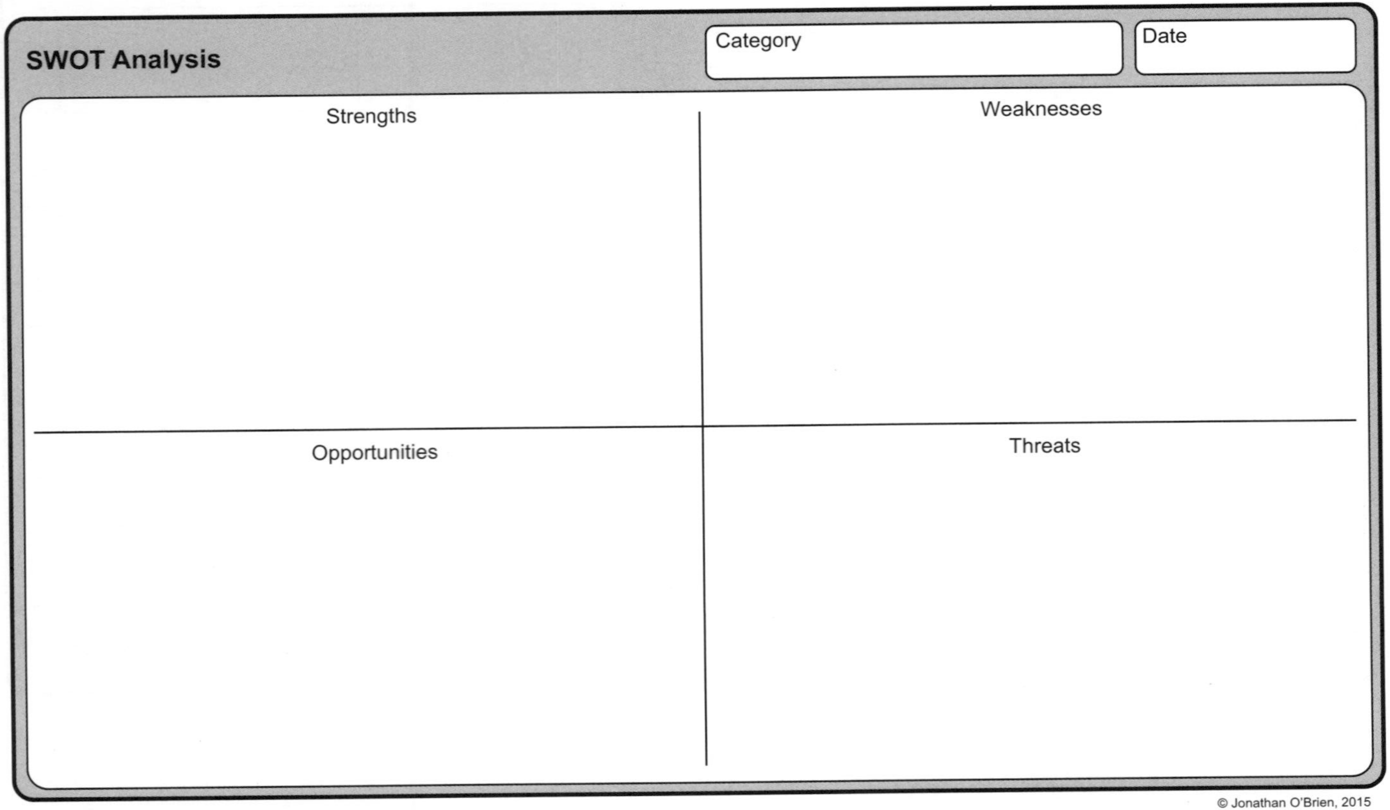

| SWOT Analysis | | |
|---|---|---|
| Category | | Date |

Strengths

Weaknesses

Opportunities

Threats

© Jonathan O'Brien, 2015

**FIGURE A21** Options evaluation

## Strategic Options Evaluation

**Business requirements evaluation**

| Category | | Date | | | | |
|---|---|---|---|---|---|---|

| Evaluation criteria | Weighting | Max score | Option 1 | Option 2 | Option 3 | Option 4 | Option 5 |
|---|---|---|---|---|---|---|---|
| 1 | | | | | | | |
| 2 | | | | | | | |
| 3 | | | | | | | |
| 4 | | | | | | | |
| 5 | | | | | | | |
| 6 | | | | | | | |
| 7 | | | | | | | |
| **Business requirements totals** | | | | | | | |

**Implementation evaluation**

| | | | | | | |
|---|---|---|---|---|---|---|
| 1 | | | | | | |
| 2 | | | | | | |
| 3 | | | | | | |
| 4 | | | | | | |
| 5 | | | | | | |
| **Implementation totals** | | | | | | |

© Jonathan O'Brien, 2015

**FIGURE A22** Strategy definition

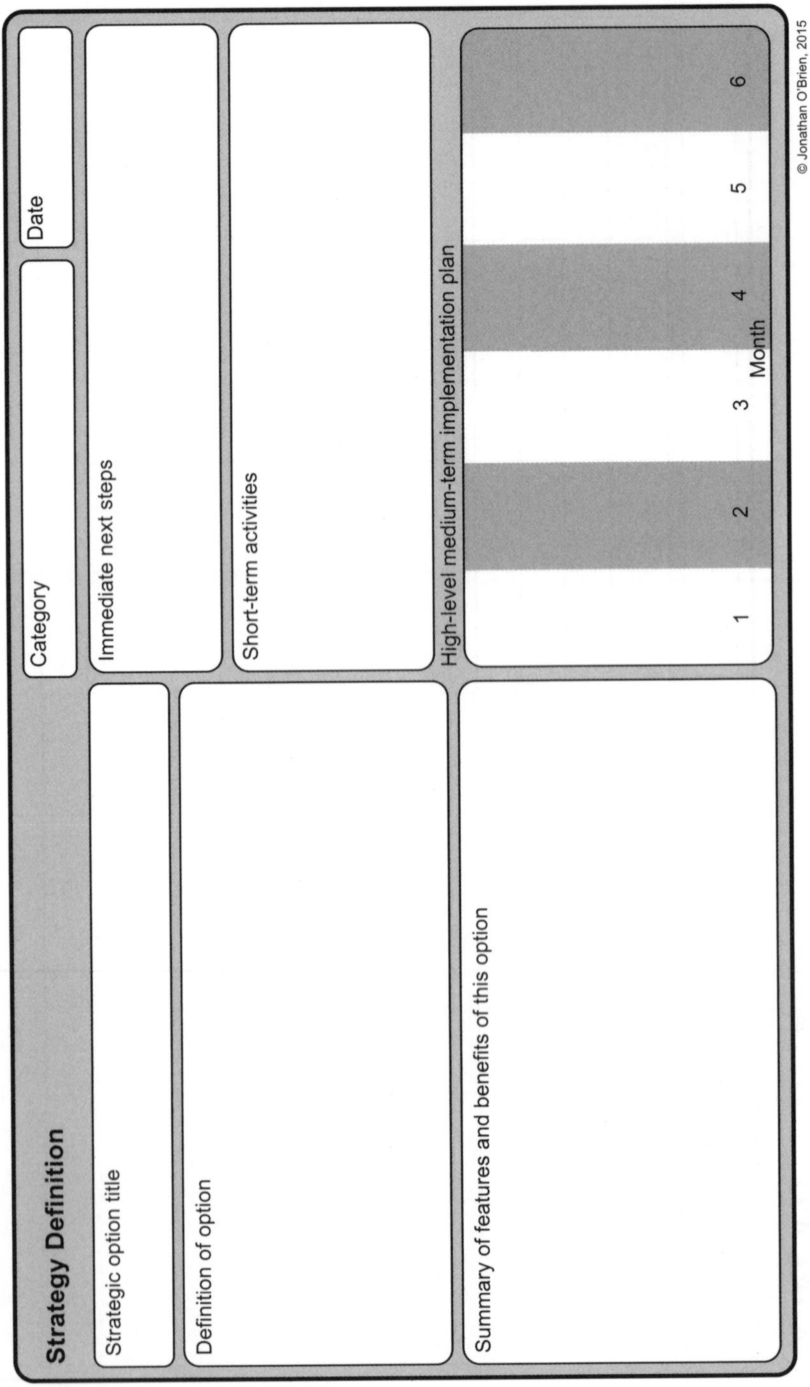

| Strategy Definition | | | Category | | | | Date |
|---|---|---|---|---|---|---|---|

Strategic option title

Definition of option

Immediate next steps

Short-term activities

Summary of features and benefits of this option

High-level medium-term implementation plan

| 1 | 2 | 3 | 4 | 5 | 6 |
|---|---|---|---|---|---|

Month

© Jonathan O'Brien, 2015

**FIGURE A23** Risk and contingency planning

## Risk and Contingency Planning

| | Category | | Date | | |
|---|---|---|---|---|---|
| Risk | Likelihood (H/M/L) | Severity (H/M/L) | Action | Owner | By When |
| 1 | | | | | |
| 2 | | | | | |
| 3 | | | | | |
| 4 | | | | | |
| 5 | | | | | |
| 6 | | | | | |
| 7 | | | | | |
| 8 | | | | | |
| 9 | | | | | |
| 10 | | | | | |
| 11 | | | | | |
| 12 | | | | | |
| 13 | | | | | |
| 14 | | | | | |
| 15 | | | | | |

**FIGURE A24**  Cost–benefit analysis

## Cost–Benefit Analysis

| Category | | | | | | Date |
|---|---|---|---|---|---|---|

Summary of category strategy

| Costs | Immediate | Year 1 | Year 2 | Year 3 | Year 4 | Year 5 |
|---|---|---|---|---|---|---|
| | | | | | | |
| | | | | | | |
| | | | | | | |
| | | | | | | |
| | | | | | | |
| **Totals** | | | | | | |

Total quantifiable cost over term [                    ]

| Benefits | Immediate | Year 1 | Year 2 | Year 3 | Year 4 | Year 5 |
|---|---|---|---|---|---|---|
| | | | | | | |
| | | | | | | |
| | | | | | | |
| | | | | | | |
| | | | | | | |
| | | | | | | |
| **Totals** | | | | | | |

Total quantifiable benefit over term [                    ]

# STAGE 4 TEMPLATE

## FIGURE A25 Supplier selection evaluation

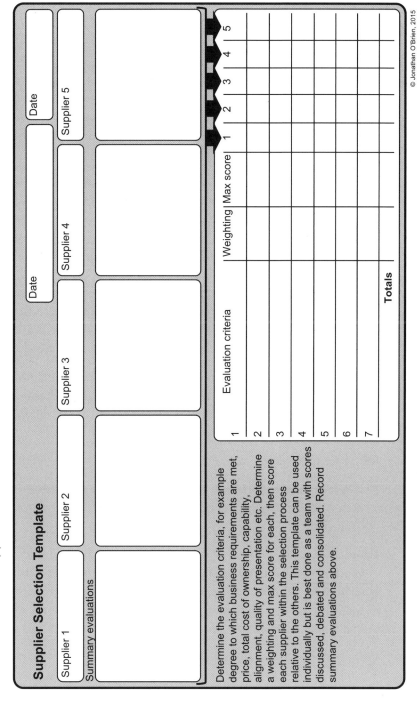

**Supplier Selection Template**

| Supplier 1 | Supplier 2 | Supplier 3 | Supplier 4 Date | Supplier 5 Date |
|---|---|---|---|---|

Summary evaluations

| Evaluation criteria | Weighting | Max score | 1 | 2 | 3 | 4 | 5 |
|---|---|---|---|---|---|---|---|
| 1 | | | | | | | |
| 2 | | | | | | | |
| 3 | | | | | | | |
| 4 | | | | | | | |
| 5 | | | | | | | |
| 6 | | | | | | | |
| 7 | | | | | | | |
| **Totals** | | | | | | | |

Determine the evaluation criteria, for example degree to which business requirements are met, price, total cost of ownership, capability, alignment, quality of presentation etc. Determine a weighting and max score for each, then score each supplier within the selection process relative to the others. This template can be used individually but is best done as a team with scores discussed, debated and consolidated. Record summary evaluations above.

© Jonathan O'Brien, 2015

# GLOSSARY

**attribute analysis**  A deep data-gathering approach to examine the individual attributes or features of a product (or service) and to identify measures that allow direct comparison of attributes and entire products (or services) to another. The purpose of attribute analysis is to identify opportunities for improvement by direct comparison

**commodities**  A raw material or primary agricultural product that can be bought or sold, such as copper, coffee, grain, energy etc

**Corporate Social Responsibility (CSR)**  This is about organizations understanding the impact they have on people, society, the environment and the world at large, and taking steps to reduce or eliminate detrimental impacts

**critical path analysis**  A mathematically based algorithm for scheduling a set of project activities as part of project management. Developed in the 1950s in a joint venture between DuPont Corporation and Remington Rand Corporation for managing plant maintenance projects

**EBITDA**  Earnings Before Interest, Taxation, Depreciation and Amortization – a financial measure used to measure the earnings of a business without any of the cancelling effects of accruals, taxation and different capital structures

**F2F**  Face to Face

**First World**  The countries of the world that have very advanced economies and high human development indices, typically democratic and capitalistic

**Gantt chart**  A type of bar chart that illustrates a project schedule. Gantt charts show the start and finish dates of each event in a project

**globalization**  The increasing unification of the world's economy through reduction of such barriers to international trade as tariffs, export fees, and import quotas

**Lean**  Often referred to as Lean Manufacturing or Lean Production, or simply Lean, it represents the optimal way of producing goods through the removal of waste and implementing flow, as opposed to batch and queue. Lean manufacturing is a generic process management philosophy derived mostly from the Toyota production system (TPS)

**Lean Sigma**  A business improvement methodology which combines both Lean and Six Sigma

**metaplanning**  A collaborative team process tool that allows a group to make contributions regarding a particular topic or question, without the need to state them aloud to the team. Metaplanning typically involves teams writing ideas on Post-it notes and placing them on a flip chart or poster. It is particularly suitable for teams in which people are not naturally forthcoming

**NHS**  National Health Service – UK tax-funded public sector organization responsible for providing healthcare for all UK citizens based upon their need for healthcare rather than their ability to pay for it

**NPD**  New Product Development

**OPEC**  The Organization of Petroleum Exporting Countries

**original equipment manufacturer (OEM)**  Refers to when spare parts are sourced from the manufacturer who provided the original product or equipment

**plan**  In the context of this book a plan is a sequence of activities organized in a defined and structured way using techniques such as milestone planning or Gantt charts to form a programme of work

**product evaluation and review technique (PERT)**  This is a model for programme management, designed to analyse and represent the tasks involved in completing a given project

**product life cycle**  A product life cycle describes the degree of customer adoption at different points in the life of the product, commencing when the product is first launched onto the market and ending when the product is no longer required, purchased or sought out by consumers. Marketing organizations adopt different strategies to manage the product, depending on the stage it is at within the product life cycle

**R&D**  Research and Development – a team within an organization tasked with researching what consumers or customers want and new product development

**red/amber/green (RAG) analysis**  Based on traffic lights, this is a system to add a colourful, visual status check to a progress report, indicating whether status is good or progress is going to plan (green), or there is some cause for concern but overall status is still on track (amber), or activities are behind plan (red)

**RFI**  Request for Information – an information-gathering approach used with suppliers and internally

**RFP**   Request for Proposal – a solicitation approach for gathering proposals from suppliers

**RFQ**   Request for Quotation – a solicitation approach for gathering firm quotations from suppliers

**RFx**   Request for? – a generic term for RFI, RFP and RFQ

**root-cause analysis**   A means of problem solving that seeks to identify the root causes for problems or issues. A root cause is the original reason for the problem, perhaps one or many times removed from the apparent problem

**SEO**   Search engine optimization – the process of optimizing websites so search engines will find them and rank them as highly as possible in listings

**Six Sigma**   A business management approach, originally developed by Motorola, that is used in many industry sectors. Six Sigma seeks to identify and remove the causes of defects and errors in manufacturing and business processes. It uses a set of quality management methods, including statistical methods, and creates a special infrastructure of people (eg black belts) within the organization who are experts in these methods

**SKU**   Stock-keeping unit – a unique identifier for each distinct product or service that can be purchased by a business

**Supplier Relationship Management (SRM)**   The arrangements to identify the required management and relationship approach for each supplier or supplier type and, for the critical few, to put in place relationships and supplier improvement programmes that will help build overall value

**value chain**   The concept of all the steps within an organization that add value starting with the input products or services and ending with the finished goods. See Porter (1985)

**value system**   A phrase used by Porter (1985) to describe the concept of multiple value chains across multiple companies to illustrate the flow of raw materials into end products

# REFERENCES AND FURTHER READING

Adair, J (1987) *Effective Teambuilding*, Pan Books, London

ADR (2011) Advanced Category Management, CIPS South Africa Conference 2011, *CIPS* [online] https://cips.org/Documents/Wed%20track%203%20 John%20McClelland%20ADR.PDF [accessed Oct 2014]

Atrill, P and McLaney, E (1996) *Accounting and Finance for Non-Finance Specialists*, Prentice Hall, Hemel Hempstead

Baily, P, Farmer, D, Jessop, D and Jones, D (1998) *Purchasing Principles and Management*, Financial Times, London

Bennet, A and Bennet, D (2004) *Organizational Survival in the New World: The intelligent complex adaptive system*, Elsevier, Boston, MA

Bevir (2013) *A Theory of Governance* (Studies in Governance) University of California Press

Borlaug, N E (2008) Challenges facing crop scientists in the 21st century, *American Society of Agronomy* [Online] www.acsmeetings.org/shared/files/borlaug-2007.pdf [accessed 31 December 2008]

Brock, D (2011) Implementing Category Management, Future Purchasing, *CIPS* [online] https://www.cips.org/Documents/Membership/Category%20 Management%20-%20CIPS%20Manchester%2021%20June.pdf [accessed Oct 2014]

Brookfield, S D (1983) *Adult Learners, Adult Education and the Community*, Open University Press, Milton Keynes

Burnes, B (1996) *Managing Change*, Pitman Publishing, London

Caniëls, M C J and Gelderman, C J (2005) Power and interdependence in Kraljic's purchasing portfolio matrix, Open University of the Netherlands, competitive paper presented at IPSERA conference 20–24 March 2005, Archamps, France [Online] http://www.ou.nl/Docs/Faculteiten/MW/Congres%20 Papers/2005/20-23%20maart%202005.pdf [accessed 31 December 2008]

Cardiff Council [online] https://www.cardiff.gov.uk/ENG/Business/Tenders-commissioning-and-procurement/pages/default.aspx [accessed June 2015]

Carter, J R (1993) *Purchasing: Continued improvement through integration*, Business One, Irwin, IL

Cottrell, R (2007) The future of futurology, *Economist: The world in 2008*, 15 November, pp 110–11

Cousins, P, Lamming, R, Lawson, B and Squire, B (2008) *Strategic Supply Management*, Prentice Hall, Harlow

Christopher, M (2011) *Logistics and Supply Chain Management*, 4th edition, FT Prentice Hall, Harlow

Cunningham, J E and Fiume, O J (2003) *Real Numbers*, Managing Times Press, Durham, NC

Defense.gov (2002) DoD News Briefing – Secretary Rumsfeld and Gen. Myers [online] http://www.defense.gov/transcripts/transcript.aspx?transcriptid=2636 [accessed June 2015]

Deming, W E (1982) *Out of the Crisis*, Massachusetts Institute of Technology

Flores (M) for The Hackett Group, (2011) *Procurement Excellence: How world-class procurement manages growth and uncertainty*, The Hackett Group Inc

Future Purchasing (2014) Category Management, *Future Purchasing* [online] www.futurepurchasing.com/category_management [accessed June 2015]

Gelderman, C J (2000) *Rethinking Kraljic: Towards a purchasing portfolio model, based on mutual buyer–supplier dependence*, Open University of the Netherlands

Gelderman, C J and Weele, A J V (2005) *Purchasing Portfolio Usage and Purchasing Sophistication*, Open University of the Netherlands

George, M L (2002) *Lean Six Sigma*, McGraw Hill, New York

GEP, 2015, GEP Trend Report, Strategic Sourcing and Procurement Outlook 2015, *GEP* [online] www.gep.com [accessed June 2015]

Girard, J and Girard, J A (2009) *A Leader's Guide to Knowledge Management: Drawing on the past to enhance future performance*, Business Expert Press

GlaxoSmithKline [online] www.gsk.com [accessed June 2015]

Hughes, J, Ralf, M and Michels, B (2000) *Transform Your Supply Chain*, Thomson, London

Huse, E F (1980) *Organization Development and Change*, West Publishing, St Paul, MN

*Information Literacy Toolkit* (2009) Techniques for Advanced Internet Searching, *Open University* [online] www2.open.ac.uk/students/iltoolkit [accessed January 2015]

Jacka, M and Keller, P (2009) *Business Process Mapping: Improving customer satisfaction*, John Wiley and Sons Inc, New York

Jennings, C and Wargnier, J (2011) Effective learning with 70-20-10, White Paper, *CrossKnowledge* [online] http://www.crossknowledge.com/en_US/elearning/media-center/news/702010.html [accessed June 2015]

Johnson, G and Scholes, K (1993) *Exploring Corporate Strategy*, Prentice Hall, Hemel Hempstead

Kaplan, R S and Norton, D P (1996) *The Balanced Scorecard*, HBS Press, US

Kolb, D A and Fry, R (1975) Toward an applied theory of experiential learning, in *Theory of Group Processes*, ed C Cooper, John Wiley and Sons Inc, New York

KPMG (2012) *The Power of Procurement*, KPMG

Kraljic, P (1977) Neue Wege im Beschaffungsmarketing, *Beschaffung Aktuell*, December, pp 20–26

Kraljic, P (1983) Purchasing must become supply management, *Harvard Business Review*, **61** (5), pp 109–17

Kübler-Ross, E (1969, 1989 and 2003) *On Death and Dying*, Scribner, New York, and Routledge, London

Lanning, M J (1980) *Delivering Profitable Value*, Basic Books, 1998

Lewin, K (1958) *Group Discussions and Social Change: Readings in social psychology*, Holt, Rhinehart and Winston, San Diego, CA

Local Government Association (2013) *Procurement Category Management Projects: The story so far*, Local Government Association

Lombardo, M M and Eichinger, R W (1996) *The Career Architect Development Planner*, 1st Edition, Lominger. Minneapolis

Lysons, K (1996) *Purchasing*, Financial Times Management, London

Lysons, K and Farrington, B (2006) *Purchasing and Supply Chain Management*, Prentice Hall, Harlow

Markillie, P (2013) Manufacturing in the future, *Economist: The world in 2013*

Mentzer, J T, De-Witt, W, Keebler, J S, Soonhong, M, Nix, N W, Smith, C D and A'charia, Z G (2001) Defining Supply Chain Management, *Journal of Business Logistics*, **22** (2)

Mintzberg, H and Waters, J A (1982) Tracking strategy in an entrepreneurial firm, *Academy of Management Journal*, **25** (3), pp 465–99

National Geographic Channel (2009) *Ultimate Factories: IKEA*, Produced by Hoff Productions, producers Michael Hoff and Ashley Adams

O'Brien, J (2013) *Negotiation for Purchasing Professionals*, Kogan Page, London

O'Brien, J (2014) *Supplier Relationship Management: Unlocking the value in the supply base*, Kogan Page, London

*OJEU (Official Journal of the European Union)* [online] www.ojec.com [accessed June 2015]

Pelsmacker, P De, Driesen, L and Rayp, G (2005) Do consumers care about ethics? Willingness to pay for fair-trade coffee, *Journal of Consumer Affairs*, **39** (2)

Penn Schoen Berland (2010) Corporate Social Responsibility Branding Survey, *Brandchannel* [online] http://brandchannel.com/2010/03/30/consumers-want-socially-responsible-brands/ [accessed April 2013]

Porter, M E (1979) How competitive forces shape strategy, *Harvard Business Review*, March/April, pp 137–45

Porter, M E (1985) *Competitive Advantage*, Free Press, New York

Porter, M E (2008) The five competitive forces that shape strategy, *Harvard Business Review*, January, pp 79–93

Rachman, G (2007) The paradoxical politics of energy, *The World in 2008*, *Economist*, pp 101–2

Remesal, A and Friesen, N (2014) Inquiry Into 'Communities of Inquiry': Knowledge, communication, presence, community, *E-Learning and Digital Media*, **11** (1) pp 1–4

Roberts, A (2007) A world in flux, *Economist: The world in 2008*, p 104

Sheth, J N and Sharma, A (2007) Relationship Management, in *Global Supply Chain Management*, eds J T Mentzer, M Meyers and T Stank, , Sage, CA, pp 361–71

Sony Pictures Home Entertainment (2006) *Who Killed the Electric Car?* Director Chris Paine [DVD]

Sun Tzu (1981) *Art of War*, Hodder & Stoughton, London

Thomas, D (2007) *Deluxe*, Penguin, London

Tuckman, B (1965) Development sequence in small groups, *Psychological Bulletin*, **63** (6), pp 384–99

US General Accounting Office (1994), Partnerships: Customer-supplier relationships can be improved through partnering, Report No 94–173 [online] http://www.gao.gov/assets/230/220148.pdf [accessed March 2015]

Valéry, N (2013) Welcome to the thingternet, *Economist: The World in 2013*

Wheat, B, Mills, C and Carnell, M (2003) *Leaning into Six Sigma*, McGraw Hill, New York

Womack, J P and Jones, D T (2003) *Lean Thinking*, Free Press, London

# INDEX

Page numbers in *italic* denote figures or tables.